IN THE VICINITY OF THE RIGHTEOUS

ISLAMIC HISTORY AND CIVILIZATION

STUDIES AND TEXTS

EDITED BY

ULRICH HAARMANN

AND

WADAD KADI

VOLUME 22

IN THE VICINITY OF THE RIGHTEOUS

Ziyāra *and the Veneration of Muslim Saints in Late Medieval Egypt*

BY

CHRISTOPHER S. TAYLOR

BRILL
LEIDEN · BOSTON · KÖLN
1999

This book is printed on acid-free paper.

Library of Congress Cataloging-in-Publication Data

Taylor, Christopher Schurman.
In the vicinity of the righteous : ziyāra and the veneration of Muslim saints in late medieval Egypt / by Christopher S. Taylor.
p. cm. — (Islamic history and civilization. Studies and texts, ISSN 0929-2403 ; v. 22)
Includes bibliographical references (p.) and index.
ISBN 9004110461 (cloth : alk. paper)
1. Muslim saints—Egypt—History. 2. Saints—Cult—Egypt—History. 3. Sufism—Egypt—History. 4. Egypt—History—640-1882. I. Title. II. Series.
BP188.8.E3T39 1998
297.6'1—dc21 98-30091
CIP

Die Deutsche Bibliothek – CIP-Einheitsaufnahme

Taylor, Christopher S.:
In the vicinity of the righteous : Ziyāra and the veneration of Muslim saints in late medieval Egypt / by Christopher S. Taylor.
Leiden ; New York ; Köln : Brill, 1998
(Islamic history and civilization ; Vol. 22)
ISBN 90-04-11046-1

ISSN 0929-2403
ISBN 90 04 11046 1

PRINTED IN THE NETHERLAND

for Maggy

CONTENTS

Acknowledgments ix
Note on Transliterations xiii
Abbreviations xv

Introduction 1
Chapter I: Al-Qarāfa: "A Great Medium of Divine Blessing" 15
Chapter II: The Ziyāra 62
Chapter III: Images of Righteousness and Piety 80
Chapter IV: Baraka, Miracle, and Mediation 127
Chapter V: "Idolatry and Innovation": The Legal Attack on Ziyārat al-Qubūr 168
Chapter VI: "To Remember, Perform Good Deeds, and Receive Blessing": The Legal Defense of Ziyāra 195

Conclusion 219
Appendix 227
Note on Sources 229
Glossary 235
Bibliography 239
Index 251

ACKNOWLEDGMENTS

The writing of every book, it is said, is a journey. Although some journeys are short and direct, others are long and circuitous. This one has certainly been the latter. Since writing the original dissertation upon which this book is based, the process of expansion, revision, and reorganization has been interrupted many times for reasons that most young scholars will readily recognize and probably empathize with: emotionally draining job searches, the considerable shifting of mental gears that inevitably accompanies the transition from graduate school to the demanding first years of teaching and professional responsibility, and the simple unfolding of the life cycle (the birth of a son, the death of a father). Despite the sense of frustration which frequently accompanied delay, I hope that greater intellectual maturity and more profound insight are reflected in the final product. Whether or not this is true, others must judge.

No book is solely the product of one person, and my debts to others are indeed great. Orest Ranum, Frank Knight, George Krotkoff, Richard Kagan, and especially Philip Curtin first excited me about the study of history as an undergraduate at Johns Hopkins and they set me on the path to what has since become both my profession and an abiding passion. Later, as a graduate student at Princeton, I accumulated many more debts. First, I would like to thank Avrom Udovitch, who was so much more than my adviser. He was a wonderful and inspiring guide in the important intellectual journey that led me, like so many of my peers, to explore new approaches in medieval Islamic social and cultural history. A fortuitous encounter with Peter Brown first convinced me that an inquiry into the veneration of medieval Muslim saints was an important and needed project. His continuing interest, support, and encouragement over the years have been both generous and profoundly important in shaping my historical imagination. In addition, I wish to thank my other mentors at Princeton for all their kindness and support, particularly: L. Carl Brown, Mark Cohen, Michael Cook, Charles Issawi, Norman Itzkowitz, Bernard Lewis, and Hossein Modarressi. My colleagues in graduate school, Jonathan Berkey, Remie Constable, Jonathan Katz, and Amy Singer, each offered valuable criticism in the early stages of my research. Jonathan Berkey has continued to share with me the benefit of his perceptive insights into medieval Egyptian history and has consistently been the best and most reliable of friends.

Many colleagues at the American University in Cairo and at Cairo University offered invaluable advice and help while I was conducting research in Egypt. At AUC I would particularly like to mention John Swanson, George Scanlon, Bernard O'Kane, Tarek Swelim, and Laila Ali Ibrahim. Muḥammad Muḥammad Amīn and Muḥammad Hassanein Rabie of Cairo University were both wonderful teachers and later reliable advisers.

While writing this book many people have offered me the benefit of their wisdom, advise, and criticism. Yūsuf Rāghib became a good friend, and I am enormously indebted to him for both his many references and thoughtful criticism. No scholar knows this source material better than Yūsuf, and I have clearly benefited greatly from his many detailed topographic studies of al-Qarāfa. Bernard O'Kane, Lucette Valensi, and Carl Petry offered many important suggestions right up to the point where the final manuscript went to press. Emil Homerin and Donald Little carefully read and commented extensively on the penultimate version of the book. Thanks to their sharp and critical eyes a number of errors were avoided and some important additions were made. The editors of this series, Professors Ulrich Haarmann and Wadad Kadi were invaluable. Not only did they have faith in this project but they also identified several key structural changes which have immeasurably strengthened the final work. I would also like to express my thanks to the staff at E.J. Brill, particularly Peri Bearman, who was very kind before her departure from Brill. Jan Fehrmann, Trudy Kamperveen, and Julie Plokker have been most patient and reassuring throughout the final production process. At a critical moment Margaret Case came to my rescue and made time in her busy schedule to edit the final manuscript. Without her keen insight, venerable editorial skill, and sharp pen, this book would not be what it is.

To my colleagues in the Religious Studies Department at Drew University, Bill Stroker, Don Jones, Peter Ochs (now at the University of Virginia), and Karen Prentiss I am also indebted. It is impossible for me to imagine more supportive colleagues. I am truly honored and blessed by their collegiality as well as by their friendship. The administration at Drew, especially Deans Paolo Cucchi and Barbara Salmore, could not have been more helpful or encouraging. My students in Religion 36 and 46 have made this book richer through the many insights prompted by their thoughtful questions.

I would also like to acknowledge the generous financial support of the Princeton University Graduate School. The Dean's Council at Drew also provided financial assistance in the final writing of this book. U.S. Government funding was essential both in supporting my graduate studies and through a USIA-funded research grant administered by the American Research Center in Egypt. I deeply regret that such federal support seems increasingly limited.

To my family, of course, I owe the greatest debts of all. I thank my parents and my brothers for all of their emotional support and love. I would especially like to acknowledge my mother, Lydia Schurman, who made many more sacrifices in her own professional and scholarly life through the years than she should have to ensure that I received the best education possible. Her love, emotional support, and encouragement have been both unfailing and inspiring. My parents-in-law, William Shafik Ghaly and Hannā' Fahmy, have been the most gracious and loving hosts during my many visits to Cairo. Finally, my wife Magda and my son Silas have been ceaseless in their support and devotion; even in those frequent moments when, like most writers, I was not the most lovable of people. Silas has sometimes had to muster more patience for a preoccupied father than a four-year old should have to. Maggy has been unfailing in her advice, devotion, and reassurance. She has repeatedly read this manuscript and has made countless corrections and suggestions for improvement. To her this book is lovingly dedicated as the smallest token of my lasting appreciation and deepest affection.

NOTE ON TRANSLITERATIONS

Arabic words are transliterated here according to the system employed by the *International Journal of Middle East Studies* (*IJMES*). Conjunctions such as *wa* and *fa*, and prepositions such as *li* and *bi* are joined to the words which follow them by a hyphen.

Consonants

ء	=	ʾ	ط	=	ṭ
ب	=	b	ظ	=	ẓ
ت	=	t	ع	=	ʿ
ث	=	th	غ	=	gh
ج	=	j	ف	=	f
ح	=	ḥ	ق	=	q
خ	=	kh	ك	=	k
د	=	d	ل	=	l
ذ	=	dh	م	=	m
ر	=	r	ن	=	n
ز	=	z	ه	=	h
س	=	s	و	=	w
ش	=	sh	ي	=	y
ص	=	ṣ	ة	=	a ("at" in the construct)
ض	=	ḍ			

The article *al-* is not elided.

Vowels

short	*long*
a	ā
u	ū
i	ī

Dipthongs

aw
ay
iyy
uww

ABBREVIATIONS

AI – *Annales islamologiques*
BEO – *Bulletin d'études orientales*
BIE – *Bulletin de l'Institut d'Egypte*
BIFAO – *Bulletin de l'Institut française d'archéologie orientale du Caire*
EI[1] – *Encyclopaedia of Islam*, first edition
EI[2] – *Encyclopaedia of Islam*, second edition
BSOAS – *Bulletin of the School of Oriental and African Studies*
EMA – *Early Muslim Architecture* (by K.A.C. Creswell)
IC – *Islamic Culture*
IJMES – *International Journal of Middle East Studies*
IQ – *Islamic Quarterly*
IS – *Islamic Studies*
JA – *Journal asiatique*
JNES – *Journal of Near Eastern Studies*
JRAS – *Journal of the Royal Asiatic Society*
MAE – *Muslim Architecture of Egypt* (by K.A.C. Creswell)
MW – *Muslim World*
RA – *Revue africaine*
RCEA – *Répertoire chronologique d'épigraphie arabe* (E. Combe *et al.*)
RSO – *Rivista degli studi orientali*
SI – *Studia Islamica*

INTRODUCTION

In the month of Rajab of the year 764 A.H. (April/May, 1363 A.D.), Shaykh Ibn Abī Ḥajala buried his beloved son Muḥammad, a victim of the plague then ravaging Cairo, in the vast cemetery of al-Qarāfa al-Kubrā near al-Fusṭāṭ. The spot he chose was the tomb of the saint ʿUqba b. ʿĀmir al-Juhanī (d. 677/678), "the companion of the Prophet of God." After performing this most painful of parental duties, Ibn Abī Ḥajala composed a book entitled *Jiwār al-akhyār fī dār al-qarār* (The Vicinity of the Righteous in the Abode of the Hereafter). Most of this book recounts and extols the life and accomplishments of Sīdī ʿUqba, including a careful compilation of all ḥadīth related on his authority.

Why was it important to Ibn Abī Ḥajala to bury his son near the tomb of the Prophet's companion, and what prompted him to write his book? This study is, in large part, an attempt to answer these questions by entering into the thought-world of Ibn Abī Ḥajala and his contemporaries. On one level he plainly sought personal solace, but his actions bespeak more than one anguished father's quest for relief and consolation. Despite the intervening centuries, Ibn Abī Ḥajala's book still provides great insight into the nature of his religious faith and the meaning that it held for his life. In particular, he illuminates a vital dimension of Islamic piety—the veneration of Muslim saints, specifically dead saints.

In the Islamic tradition saints need not be dead before they become the objects of veneration. This book, however, does not consider living saints or their roles in Islamic society. It is an inquiry into the cult of Muslim saints that centered around their tombs, specifically in Egypt between roughly 1200 and 1500 A.D. It provides the first full descriptive overview and analysis of the veneration of Muslim saints in the great cemeteries surrounding medieval Cairo, and is motivated by an interest in what the veneration of dead saints reveals about the living expression of Muslim faith and piety in the later Middle Ages, as opposed to textual idealizations of normative practice.[1]

---

[1] For two diachronic studies of individual Egyptian saints see Hallenberg, "Ibrāhīm

In contrast with the impressive scholarly work on saints in the Western Christian experience, research of similar phenomena in the Islamic cultural tradition lags far behind.[2] The most comprehensive synthetic treatment of the subject today remains an insightful work published more than a century ago by the great Hungarian Orientalist Ignaz Goldziher.[3] Although there have been some excellent studies about the veneration of saints in various Muslim societies over the past century, these would not yet support a comprehensive new synthesis.[4]

In view of the pervasive presence of saints throughout the Islamic world, regardless of period, as well as the large quantity and diverse nature of primary source material available, it is puzzling that so little work on them has been undertaken. In part this oversight may be explained by certain strains of thought within the Islamic tradition itself, particularly pronounced in the nineteenth and twentieth centuries. Many Muslims have either resisted acknowledging the existence of Muslim saints altogether or have viewed their presence and veneration as unacceptable deviations from normative practice. While conducting research for this book in Egypt, for example, I was frequently informed by devout believers, who were interested but sincerely puzzled by my research, that there are no saints in Islam. When I responded by noting some of the numerous and most obvious manifestations of saint veneration around us, my interlocutors

---

al-Dasūqī (1255–96)," and Homerin, *From Arab Poet to Muslim Saint.* For an excellent study of a certain category of living saints and their roles in a specific premodern Muslim community, see Eaton, *Sufis of Bijapur.*

[2] For an extensive and useful annotated bibliography of the literature in this field see Wilson, *Saints and Their Cults*, 309–419. Of the more than 1,300 entries in Wilson's bibliography a mere 30 deal directly with the cult of the saints in Islam.

[3] Goldziher, "Veneration of Saints in Islam."

[4] Much of the research that has been conducted on Muslim saints and their cults to date has been devoted to the geographic peripheries of the Islamic world. Scholars interested in comparative analysis who are working outside the field of Islamic studies have thus had to rely primarily on literature dealing with North Africa and the Indian subcontinent. Significant works dealing with aspects of the cult of Muslim saints in Egypt include: De Jong, "Cairene Ziyara-days," and his *Ṭuruq and Ṭuruq-Linked Institutions*; Garcin, "Deux saints populaires," and his "Histoire et hagiographie de l'Égypte;" Gilsenan *Saint and Sufi in Modern Egypt*; Hallenberg, "Ibrāhim al-Dasūqī;" Hoffman, *Sufism, Mystics, and Saints*; Homerin, *From Arab Poet to Muslim Saint*; Massignon, "La cité des morts au Caire;" McPherson, *The Moulids of Egypt*; Olesen, *Culte des saints*; Ohtoshi, "The Manners, Customs, and Mentality of Pilgrims;" Rāghib, "Sur un groupe de mausolés du cimetière du Caire" and numerous other articles; Shoshan, *Popular Culture*; and Williams, "The Cult of ʿAlid Saints."

were usually quick to dismiss these as insignificant aspects of "popular" or "folk" religion that are not part of "true Islam."

Explaining this resistance is not complicated, but understanding the lack of interest on the part of modern scholarship is more problematic. In part, the dearth of attention reflects the bias of the textual sources on which scholars usually rely. It also derives from a now outdated two-tier model of cultural discourse borrowed from the study of Western European history.[5] This view, echoing the perception of devout Muslim scholars, counterpoises "elite" and "popular" expressions of religious experience as a useful distinction, and focuses on "high" cultural traditions to the exclusion of what have been dismissively, even derisively, identified as corrupted versions of "popular religion."[6] In any event, there is still much research to be done on Muslim saints and their veneration, and it is hoped that this study will encourage work in this promising field of the social history of religion.

This study is not an attempt to inquire into the origins of the cult of Muslim saints in Egypt. Egyptian history, from the beginning of the dynastic period to the Arab conquest in 642 A.D., spans nearly 4,000 years. Although it is likely that there were some influences from earlier periods on later Muslim practice, as has recently been suggested, it is still too early to theorize about the nature and extent of continuities.[7] Even within the Islamic period, as I have demonstrated elsewhere, there has sometimes been a tendency among scholars to reach premature conclusions about the origins of the cult of the saints, and attribute them to exclusively Shīʿite sources.[8]

Egypt in the later Middle Ages was a thoroughly multi-confessional society. In fact, historians believe that it was not until this period that Egypt finally became decisively and irrevocably a predominantly

---

[5] For a critical challenge to this tendency within scholarship on Western history, see Brown, *The Cult of the Saints*; Bourdieu, *La Distinction*; and Chartier, "Culture as Appropriation," and his "La culture populaire en question." For an alternative view and defense of the distinction between "high" and "popular" culture, see Le Goff, "The Learned and Popular Dimensions of Journeys," his *L'imaginaire médiéval*, and his earlier *Pour un autre Moyen Age*.

[6] For an example of the challenge to the two-tier paradigm of culture in the medieval Islamic world, see Chodkiewicz, *Seal of the Saints*, 11–12. For the opposite view, see Shoshan, *Popular Culture*, 6–7, 10, 67, and his "High Culture and Popular Culture."

[7] See Wickett, "For Our Destinies."

[8] Taylor, "Reevaluating the Shiʿi Role."

Muslim society.[9] Even after a significant majority of Egyptians were converted to Islam, there remained sizable communities of Christians and Jews in the country. It is, therefore, important to stress that this is a study about *Muslim* saints and their veneration, although Egyptian Jews and Christians have historically been deeply engaged in and committed to the veneration of their own saints. Their practices are beyond the purview of this study, but there was clearly a certain amount of syncretism as Muslims, Christians, and Jews crossed religious boundaries to participate in the veneration of each other's saints.

Moreover, this book focuses on the Cairene experience and does not offer examples from rural Egypt. In large part this is due to the bias of the surviving sources, which almost exclusively reflect urban settings. There is little evidence to suggest that in this instance what holds for Cairo did not hold also for the rest of Egypt. Upper Egypt and the Delta are dotted with local saints' tombs, as are virtually all the major and minor towns and cities along the Nile. Both in their veneration of these local tombs and in their frequent treks into the major cities of Egypt, peasants seem to have been familiar with the ways of their city cousins in relation to the veneration of the holy dead.[10] Frequently saints' festivals in rural areas follow the Coptic solar calendar, rather than the Islamic lunar one, a reflection of the inflexible demands of the agricultural cycle. But these are minor variations of little significance in terms of either the manifestations of the cult or its meaning in people's lives.

Furthermore, here, as in so many other respects, Islamic civilization in the medieval period was primarily shaped in an urban context. Cities were central to the formation of Muslim society far more than was true in medieval Europe. And yet Islamic cities were not as distinct from their rural hinterland as was typical of the ancient Greek polis or the commune in the medieval West. In fact, there was nothing that we might recognize as an exclusively urban corporate identity in the medieval Islamic world. There were rarely any formal lines or boundaries between rural and urban populations, as

[9] See for example Lapidus, "The Conversion of Egypt to Islam."

[10] The late-twelfth century pilgrimage guide of al-Harawī, *Kitāb al-ishārāt ilā maʿrifat al-ziyārāt* makes it clear that there were organized ziyāras, to the tombs of Muslim saints throughout Egypt. See also the translation, *Guides des lieux de pèlerinage*, 78–120.

the groups which constituted medieval Muslim society transcended rural-urban distinctions.[11]

Therefore, although this study of the veneration of Muslim saints focuses on the great cemeteries around Cairo, it would be wrong to view this phenomenon as exclusively, or even distinctively, urban. Surely rural manifestations of the cult of the saints differed in certain ways from those in urban settings, but these were more distinctions of scale and local expression than they were of fundamental meaning and content.

In conducting research for this book I have sought to cast a wide net. In addition to the variety of textual sources described below, I also found epigraphic and architectural evidence to be particularly helpful in shaping my ideas and understanding of the practice of visiting the tombs of the saints (ziyāra) and the veneration of Muslim saints in medieval Egypt. I was greatly aided by the fact that substantial portions of the cemeteries of medieval Cairo still exist, and the many modern pilgrims I encountered in my walks through the cemeteries helped to bring the textual sources alive for me.

The most important, though least familiar, textual sources are a series of contemporary pilgrimage guides to the cemeteries of medieval Cairo. Although pilgrimage guides are a venerable genre of pious literature in the Islamic world, they have not received much scholarly attention. The first reference to such a guide dates to al-Ḥasan b. ʿAlī b. Faḍḍal al-Taymī al-Kūfī, who died in 838/839. The oldest guides about which we possess more than passing references, however, can be traced to the end of the tenth century. The research of Yūsuf Rāghib reveals that the earliest guide of Cairo's cemeteries about which we have much knowledge is *Maḥajjat al-nūr fī ziyārat*

[11] Ira Lapidus has identified four seminal groupings, or communities, basic to the organization of medieval Islamic society: neighborhoods; fraternities, such as youth gangs and Ṣūfī orders; religious communities, such as Muslim law schools and dhimmī or protected non-Muslim communities; and states and empires. None of these groups, he explains: "was a city community, except insofar as cities were naturally the headquarters of all groups"; Lapidus, "Muslim Cities and Islamic Societies," in his *Middle Eastern Cities*, 59–60. Lapidus cogently dismisses the usefulness of a notion of rural/urban divide as a tool of analyzing the social organization of medieval Muslim populations, 73–74. See also his *Muslim Cities in the Later Middle Ages* for the best general description of urban life and organization in Egypt and Syria. A good summary of the literature on Islamic cities may be found in Humphreys, *Islamic History*, especially chapter 8.

al-qubūr (The Path of Light in Visiting Tombs) of Abū ʿAbd Allāh Muḥammad b. Ḥāmid b. al-Mutawwaj al-Mārīnī (or al-Māridīnī), which dates to the middle of the twelfth century.[12] Between the death of this author in April 1166 and the first quarter of the seventeenth century, Rāghib has identified twenty additional pilgrimage guides devoted to Cairo's cemeteries. Only four of the guides written during the three centuries between 1200 and 1500 A.D., however, have survived.[13] Three have now been published and the other remains in manuscript. They are described in some detail in the Note on Sources at the end of this book. A fifth guide, written by Taqī al-Dīn ʿAlī b. Abū Bakr al-Harawī (d. 1215) has also been edited and translated into French by Janine Sourdel-Thomine, but rather than dealing exclusively with Cairo, it provides brief descriptions of tombs and cemeteries throughout the Islamic Middle East.

Although each guide makes corrections and additions to its predecessors, they are structurally alike, and duplicate a significant amount of information. Except in those cases where the guide was written soon after the death of the particular saint discussed, we cannot be sure of the historical origin or source of the information provided. The material contained in the guides is heterogeneous both in regard to the type of sources employed, whether oral or written, and the historical provenance of the information. For example, when considering an individual who may have died three centuries or more before the guide was written, it is virtually impossible to determine whether either the date or the origin of the material is roughly contemporary to the individual or more recent. And if the material is older in origin, it is hard to tell how it changed prior to its incorporation in the pilgrimage guide. By their very nature, then, the pilgrimage guides consist of ideas and understandings—a sort of cultural style of belief—that were created over and shaped by many centuries of unrecorded intergenerational transmission of knowledge and practice. We are not dealing here with the fleeting moments of "l'histoire événementielle." Rather, we are deep in the rich and timeless soil of Braudel's "longue durée," the realm of "mentalité," where

---

[12] Yūsuf Rāghib, "Essai d'inventaire chronologique," 259–60.

[13] The fragment of another guide, apparently written in the sixteenth century by an unknown author, is preserved in the Bibliothèque de l'Institut des Langues et Civilisations Orientales in Paris, manuscript no. 404. This short manuscript consists of a simple list of tombs with little further explanation. Although I have read it, I have not included it here.

change occurred too slowly to be noted, except from the perspective of great historical distance.

The local knowledge and practices connected with the cult of the saints did not change quickly, and one might argue whether many elements of them have changed even to this day. It is through this very valuable and previously unexplored material that we must listen carefully for the voices of everyday people. For although the authors of the pilgrimage guides drew on scholarly texts, as discussed in the Note on Sources, they also relied on oral tradition and customary practice. The incorporation of oral—and therefore popular—tradition and some description of local custom is what sets the pilgrimage guides apart as a unique resource in examining the social history of religion in medieval Egypt.

In a number of instances the source of information cited in the guides is simply identified as "al-ʿawāmm" or "al-ʿāmma" (the populace). It is through such accounts that the pilgrimage guides have preserved for us an invaluable body of otherwise inaccessible information about the beliefs, practices, and traditions that helped to give shape and meaning to the everyday understanding of Islamic faith in the later Middle Ages. And, if we listen carefully and closely enough to those voices, we can use the guides, almost as an anthropologist would probe his or her informants, to explore the articulation of Islamic piety in an age now very distant from our own. The understanding of Islam that the guides reveal is not always a faith with which we are familiar.

Historical setting

In the period covered by this study Egypt, the western Arabian Peninsula, Palestine, and Syria were ruled by two powerful empires: the Ayyūbids (1171–1250) and the Mamlūks (1250–1517). The Ayyūbid dynasty officially came to power in 1171 when the great Kurdish military leader Saladin (1138–1193), Ṣalāḥ al-Dīn in Arabic, quietly terminated the already largely fictitious Fāṭimid regime upon the death of its last caliph, al-ʿĀḍid (r. 1160–1171).

The Fāṭimids, a remarkable dynasty of Ismāʿīlī Shīʿites, had ruled Egypt for the previous two centuries. Although the Fāṭimid period was, as a whole, prosperous and illustrious, by the late twelfth century the regime was faced with internal divisions and external challenges it was unable to overcome. Weakened by long and bitter internecine struggles, and with the Crusader king of Jerusalem, Amalric (r. 1163–1174), leading his army's siege of Cairo, the Fāṭimids were finally prompted in 1168 to call on the assistance of a neighboring rival Muslim Sunnī ruler, Nūr al-Dīn (r. 1146–1174), the Zangid sultan of Aleppo. It was this alliance that first brought Saladin to Egypt as an assistant to his uncle, Shīrkūh, the commander of the Zangid relief expedition. When Shīrkūh died unexpectedly of natural causes in March 1169, Saladin was quickly named to replace his uncle as vizier. Over the course of the next two and a half years, Saladin consolidated his political and military position in Egypt while skillfully negotiating contradictory and tense relationships with both the last Fāṭimid caliph in Cairo and the Zangid sultan in Aleppo. With the mysterious death of Caliph al-ʿĀḍid at age 21, however, Saladin swiftly and decisively terminated the Shīʿite dynasty. The khuṭba, or Friday sermon, was now offered throughout Egypt in the names of the Sunnī ʿAbbāsid caliph, al-Mustaḍīʿ (r. 1170–1180), and the Zangid sultan, Nūr al-Dīn. But although Saladin made some honorific gestures and symbolic payments to the Zangid sultan, the latter's demands for significant sums of money were consistently ignored, and Saladin retained most of Egypt's wealth for himself, using it to strengthen his own position in Cairo. As the independent ruler of a powerful new empire, Saladin presented a dramatic challenge to the Crusader states in Syria and Palestine.

The Ayyūbids were, like their original Zangid employers, ardent Sunnīs. They promoted themselves as zealous restorers and committed defenders of Sunnī "orthodoxy" following a two century interlude of "heretical" Shīʿite control over much of the Islamic Middle East. Following the death of Saladin in 1193, the divided Ayyūbid house managed to rule the empire through a loose and contentious family federation for little more than five decades. The dynasty was brought to an end in 1250 when Tūrānshāh, the presumptuous and overbearing son of the last effective Ayyūbid sultan, was assassinated by his own corps of slave soldiers, known as mamlūks. A tumultuous decade of jockeying for power ensued before the mamlūk amir al-Ẓāhir Rukn al-Dīn Baybars was finally able to establish his own firm control between 1260 and 1277. The Mamlūk empire would last more than two and a half centuries after this, until the Ottoman conquest in 1517.

Mamlūks, a word literally meaning "owned" in Arabic, were primarily Circassians and Kipchak Turks who were purchased as young boys and brought into the Islamic world as slaves. After their purchase by the sultan or by other leading amirs, these mamlūks were converted to Islam, taught some basic Arabic, and trained extensively in the arts of war. They were military as opposed to domestic slaves, specially selected for their physical prowess and potential as warriors. Enormous resources were expended on their care and training. On completion of their years of specialized military education, mamlūks were manumitted and incorporated into the military retinues and households of their former masters.[14]

Under the Ayyūbids the Sunnī ʿulamāʾ, or religious scholars, of Egypt enjoyed renewed prestige after their long sojourn out of official favor under the Fāṭimid Shīʿite establishment. In part, this newfound power came from the fact that they conferred religious legitimacy on the ruling establishment in an age when central caliphal authority had virtually ceased to exist. The Sunnī ʿulamāʾ, who transcended class distinctions, also became important intermediaries between the military regimes and the general populace.[15] The Ayyūbids actively cemented their bond with the ʿulamāʾ in two ways: by aggressively restoring Sunnī Islam to official prominence in public life, and by extensive patronage of religious institutions and projects important to the ʿulamāʾ. The most obvious expression of this financial nexus between the political and religious elites was the establishment of endowed trusts known as waqfs.[16] These pious endowments were used to undertake and maintain large building projects such as madrasas (teaching mosques), zāwiyas and khanqāhs (Ṣūfī retreats and hostels), public water fountains, and hospitals. Many of these buildings were enormous, such as the Madrasa of Sultan Ḥassan constructed between 1356 and 1361.[17]

The Mamlūks maintained this pattern of close association with the ʿulamāʾ for several reasons including personal glory and the desire to circumvent the Islamic law of inheritance and ensure the inter-

---

[14] For an excellent study of the Mamlūk military system see Ayalon, *Gunpowder and Firearms in the Mamlūk Kingdom.*

[15] For thoughtful discussions of the role of the ʿulamāʾ and their role as intermediaries between the ruling Mamlūk establishment and the general populace of Egypt, see Lapidus, *Muslim Cities* and Petry, *The Civilian Elite.*

[16] On the expansion and role of waqfs under the Mamlūks, see Amīn, *Al-Awqāf.*

[17] Two excellent studies of Islamic education in the Mamlūk period are Berkey, *The Transmission of Knowledge in Medieval Cairo* and Chamberlain, *Knowledge and Social Practice in Medieval Damascus.*

generational transfer of wealth by sheltering it from the frequent and unpredictable expropriations that characterized their own regime. But some Mamlūks contributed generously to various religious institutions out of genuine personal piety, and many of them located their own tombs in or near important religious structures they had built. As in the case of Shaykh Ibn Abī Ḥajala with which we began this book, Mamlūks also tried to arrange burials for themselves and their families in the vicinity of the righteous, thereby benefiting from the reflected baraka (divine blessing) associated with saints.[18]

Ethnically, linguistically, culturally, and religiously alien at birth to the society over which they ruled, the Mamlūks were careful to maintain strong links to the indigenous religious establishment. They also benefited from extensive kinship ties between the ʿulamāʾ and other segments of the civilian elite who staffed the administrative bureaucracy of the Mamlūk state. On occasion the Mamlūks were tied directly to the ʿulamāʾ by marriage. The sons of Mamlūks, largely precluded from military service themselves, sometimes joined the ranks of the ʿulamāʾ.[19]

Frequently arbitrary and rapacious in its fiscal demands, the Mamlūk regime, which encouraged the survival and promotion of the fittest and most capable military talent, was well suited to the challenges of the age. Not only were the Mamlūks able to drive the last Crusaders from Palestine in 1291 but they also turned back an advanced force of Mongols at the Battle of ʿAyn Jalūt in 1260. Egypt therefore escaped the terror of the Mongol invasions, which wreaked such tremendous devastation in the eastern Islamic world. In fact, the Mamlūk empire benefited from the talents and expertise of refugees fleeing west before the advance of Mongol armies.[20]

In addition to the Crusades and Mongol invasions, Mamlūk society faced the demographic disaster posed by the worldwide pandemic of bubonic and pneumonic plague known as the Black Death,

---

[18] Berkey, *Transmission of Knowledge*, 132–42. Berkey may go too far in discounting the importance of political legitimization as a significant objective in Mamlūk patronage. However, he is clearly right to question the tendency among earlier scholars to view political legitimization as the only, or at least central, explanation for Mamlūk patronage of religious buildings and the ʿulamāʾ. See his chapter 3 for a thoughtful evaluation of the various reasons motivating Mamlūk patronage.

[19] Lapidus, *Muslim Cities*, 109–10, 117, 185. Carl Petry also reminds me that al-Sakhāwī, *al-Ḍawʾ al-lāmiʿ* contains in volume 12 a number of examples of Mamlūk intermarriage with ʿulamāʾ families.

[20] Ayalon, "The Wafidiyya in the Mamluk Kingdom."

which struck Egypt and Syria in 1348. Cairo was one of the greatest urban centers anywhere in the world throughout this period, and the plague bacillus decimated the city's population. As Michael Dols has demonstrated, the demographic disaster of the Black Death was seriously compounded for the Mamlūk empire by the endemic pattern of plague recurrence that struck the region.[21] Beyond the initial loss of as much as a quarter of Cairo's residents, the population of the city, and indeed the empire as a whole, remained suppressed for centuries due to the repeated occurrence of plague. It was one such outbreak that claimed the life of Shaykh Ibn Abī Ḥajala's son Muḥammad in 1362, and the shaykh himself died in yet another outbreak of plague in 1375.

Despite the combination of a frequently chaotic, capricious, and avaricious political order, the challenges posed by formidable external enemies, and demographic disaster of catastrophic proportions, the Mamlūk period was one of remarkable cultural and artistic achievement. Most of what remains of the great monumental architecture of medieval Cairo dates from this period, and those impressive remnants bear eloquent testimony to both Mamlūk wealth and their financial largess as great patrons of the religious establishment. Cairo was a stunning city. By the best available and most conservative estimate, the population of the city prior to the onset of the Black Death was 250,000. The city of Paris, by contrast, was home to 80,000 in 1328.[22] Although the core of medieval Cairo is today gravely threatened by modern urban encroachment, one may still wander among the alleys of the old city and appreciate the awe that struck the great North African historian Ibn Khaldūn (d. 1406) upon his arrival in Cairo in 1382:

> I beheld in Cairo the garden of the Universe, the orchard of the world, the assemblage of the nations, the myriad flow of humanity, the portico of Islam, the seat of power. Palaces and arcades glimmer in her air. Monasteries and colleges blossom along her horizon. I beheld orbs and stars shining among her scholars. The shores of the Nile resembled the river of Paradise, the waters of Heaven. Its flow quenches the thirst of the Egyptians without cease, collecting for them fruits and riches. I walked through the streets of the city crowded with the masses of passers-by, their markets filled with luxuries. We continuously talked

---

[21] Dols, *The Black Death.*

[22] Raymond, "Cairo's Area and Population," 30. Raymond adds that in 1377 London was a city of 60,000.

> about this city, marveling at the extent of its buildings, the magnitude of its stature.[23]

This was a dynamic and vibrant era of remarkable accomplishment in many spheres. It was, for instance, in this period that the famous stories of the *Thousand and One Nights* took their final shape, and it is this society more than any other which is reflected in those stories. Despite their frequent complaints about the corruption and other abuses by the Mamlūk political establishment, this was also a golden age for the ʿulamāʾ. The literary and scholarly output of the period was prodigious; there is no other premodern Islamic society for which such a substantial collective body of literary, textual, and documentary evidence remains.

It was also in this period that Ṣūfism, the mystical tradition in Islam, underwent profound transformations, both intellectually and institutionally.[24] Earliest Islamic mysticism of the eighth and ninth centuries was usually characterized by individual ascetics and wandering mystics, who were sometimes surrounded by informal groups of followers. Although many central Ṣūfī ideas and concepts were articulated earlier, Ṣūfism itself—as a clearly identifiable tradition with its own systematic body of doctrine and discipline—does not emerge fully into the historical record until the early tenth century.[25] Intellectually, Ṣūfism found in Ibn ʿArabī (1165–1240) its greatest doctrinal systematizer and an imaginative and creative genius of the first order. Building upon a brilliant synthesis of classical Ṣūfī thought, neo-Platonic philosophy, and Islamic theology, Ibn ʿArabī articulated a complex, rigorous, and comprehensive body of mystical thought that laid the foundations of subsequent Ṣūfī speculation and continues to exercise lasting and profound effect upon it.[26] Organizationally, Ṣūfism was increasingly characterized by an expanding series of brotherhoods known as ṭarīqas from the beginning of the thirteenth century onward. These brotherhoods were usually distinguished by

---

[23] Translated in Petry, *The Civilian Elite*, xxi.

[24] Although there is still debate among scholars about dating significant developments in the emergence and elaboration of Ṣūfism, I have adopted here the dating and framework proposed by Chodkiewicz in *Seal of the Saints* and Baldick in *Mystical Islam*, among others.

[25] Baldick, *Mystical Islam*, 50.

[26] See Chodkiewicz, *Seal of the Saints*, 10; Baldick, *Mystical Islam*, 82–85. For the most comprehensive presentation and translation of Ibn ʿArabī's thought, see Chittick's three volumes: *The Sufi Path of Knowledge, The Self-Disclosure of God*, and *The Breath of the All-Merciful.*

a founding master, from whom the fraternity frequently took its name; a chain of designated successors; and a body of doctrine concerning both daily life and the spiritual exercises designed to enhance and guide the adept's mystical encounter with the divine. The originally informal groups of followers surrounding early mystical masters were now replaced by more clearly defined and hierarchically structured master-disciple relationships. New initiates to the brotherhoods gained admission through careful spiritual examination of prospective candidates by the fraternity's shaykh, to whom the initiates usually took an oath of allegiance as the living heir of the ṭarīqa's founder.

Following the demise of the central ʿAbbāsid caliphate, the pervasive political fragmentation of the Islamic world, eclipse of Shīʿite alternatives, and the challenge of external invasions from both the Crusaders and the Mongols, the emergence of ṭarīqa-based Ṣūfism in the early thirteenth century played a critical role in the reconstitution of Sunnī authority throughout the Islamic Middle East in the later Middle Ages. And Ṣūfism itself now achieved heretofore unprecedented levels of respect and acceptance among the Sunnī ʿulamāʾ at large. Previously hostile to the ecstatic outbursts of individual mystics, who frequently expressed their mystical experiences in powerfully expressive but doctrinally suspect terms, the larger Sunnī religious establishment as a whole reached an accommodation with mysticism by the mid-thirteenth century. The establishment of coherent mystical brotherhoods with their designated masters, carefully chosen disciples, internal discipline, and established bodies of theory and practice assured many among the ʿulamāʾ that a measure of doctrinal control over Ṣūfism had finally been achieved. Along with greater acceptance and tolerance of Ṣūfism generally among the Sunnī ʿulamāʾ came increasing integration between the two, as active participation in the ṭarīqas by respected religious scholars and functionaries became widespread.

An important parallel development in Ṣūfism during the thirteenth and fourteenth centuries was the rapid growth of mass followings around the proliferating ṭarīqas. The brotherhoods increasingly attracted a broad cross-section of the general population who were eager to share in the sacred charisma associated with the Ṣūfīs. The weekly gatherings of Ṣūfī ṭarīqas, with their distinctive, colorful, ecstatic, frequently fantastic, and highly entertaining ritual exercises known as dhikr (remembrance) or samāʿ (listening) drew large, mixed, and enthusiastic crowds of uninitiated observers from among all strata of the society. These regular weekly gatherings, like the great annual commemoration of the order's founding master, were usually held at the grave of the order's founder or at the tombs of other great shaykhs venerated by the ṭarīqa.

Ziyāra—the visiting of the tombs of the holy dead—seems to have served as an essential agency in the process whereby Ṣūfī ṭarīqas became a broad-based popular phenomenon in Egypt, and indeed much of the Islamic world, during the later Middle Ages. And it was this rapid expansion in the popularity of ṭarīqa-based Ṣūfism among all social classes which, in turn, greatly enhanced and confirmed the pivotal new role of the Sunnī ʿulamāʾ as prime intermediaries between the ruling political establishment and the general population. It is to the locus of the ziyāra, and to the activities that defined it that we now turn our attention.

CHAPTER ONE

AL-QARĀFA: "A GREAT MEDIUM OF DIVINE BLESSING"

On the rocky, dusty, and barren plateau just to the east of al-Fusṭāṭ, the original Arab capital of Egypt, lies the oldest and most extensive graveyard of Islamic Egypt.[1] This area, referred to today simply as al-Qarāfa, was historically divided into two sections that were known, respectively, as the "lesser" Qarāfa (al-Qarāfa al-Ṣughrā) to the north, and the "greater" Qarāfa (al-Qarāfa al-Kubrā) further south (see Maps 1 and 2). Hemmed in by al-Fusṭāṭ and the successive settlements of al-ʿAskar and al-Qaṭāʾiʿ on the west, and the Muqaṭṭam hills to the east, the two Qarāfas stretch from just below the Cairo Citadel southward in a gradually expanding arc toward the town of Ḥulwān. The southern boundary of the cemetery is formed by the lake known as Birkat al-Ḥabash and the adjoining depression upon which the village of Basātīn was eventually built. The low plateau on which al-Qarāfa is situated rises in places to a height of approximately thirty meters above the floor of the Nile valley. The drop in height between the plateau, known as the ʿAmal

[1] It is important to note that there were several other significant graveyards nearby. With the establishment of the Fāṭimid capital at Cairo in 969, the focus of life in the region shifted north of al-Fusṭāṭ, and new cemeteries were also established. The first of these lay in the area south and east of Bāb Zuwayla. Al-Maqrīzī relates that the number of tombs in this area multiplied during the civil disturbances that brought Badr al-Jamālī to power in 1075; (see al-Maqrīzī, *Kitāb al-mawāʿiẓ wa-al-iʿtibār bi-dhikr al-khiṭaṭ wa-al-āthār* (hereafter *Khiṭaṭ*), 2:443. This Armenian general himself established yet another major cemetery north of Cairo, outside of Bāb al-Naṣr, when he built his own tomb there around 1087. Thereafter the surrounding area also became a major graveyard, especially for the residents of al-Ḥusayniyya quarter, located just north of Cairo. With the decline of al-Ḥusayniyya, following the Black Death in 1348, this graveyard seems to have extended west and north of Bāb al-Futūḥ (see al-Maqrīzī, *Khiṭaṭ*, 1:360–61 and 2:464). The extensive area today known as the Northern Cemetery emerged as a burial site only after 1320 (al-Maqrīzī, *Khiṭaṭ*, 2:463–64). Lying east of Cairo and stretching north of the Citadel to the Jabal al-Aḥmar, this area was once used as a racetrack that was abandoned during the reign of al-Nāṣir Muḥammad b. Qalāwūn. Soon thereafter, amīrs began erecting their own mausolea here. Although most burials occurred outside of Cairo, the Fāṭimids buried their caliphs within the city walls in Turbat al-Zaʿfarān (al-Maqrīzī, *Khiṭaṭ*, 1:362), and there were other special mausolea within the city such as Mashhad al-Ḥusayn.

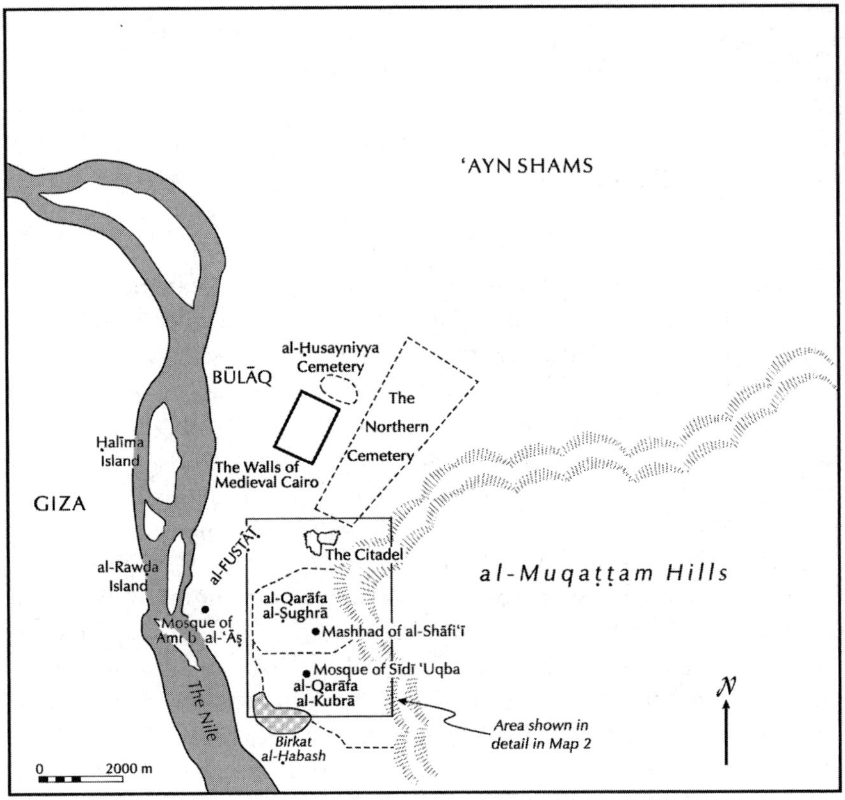

Map 1 – Medieval Cairo and Environs

Fawq, and the narrow river lowland, known as the ʿAmal Asfal, is quite sharp. To the east the plain slopes more gradually toward the Muqaṭṭam hills.[2]

Al-Fusṭāṭ was originally a makeshift garrison town and, as with other Arab garrison towns of the conquest period, it initially consisted of a series of quarters or sections, known in Arabic as khiṭaṭ (s. khiṭṭa). These khiṭaṭ were traditionally assigned to and accordingly known by the names of the more significant tribal and subtribal groups that first settled there. The early Arab geographers tell us that the name al-Qarāfa comes from an Arab clan known as the Banū Qarāfa, which settled in this area at the time of the original

[2] Kubiak, *Al Fusṭāṭ*, 40–41 and chapter 2. See also the dated but still valuable work of Clerget, *Le Caire*, especially the first chapter of volume 1.

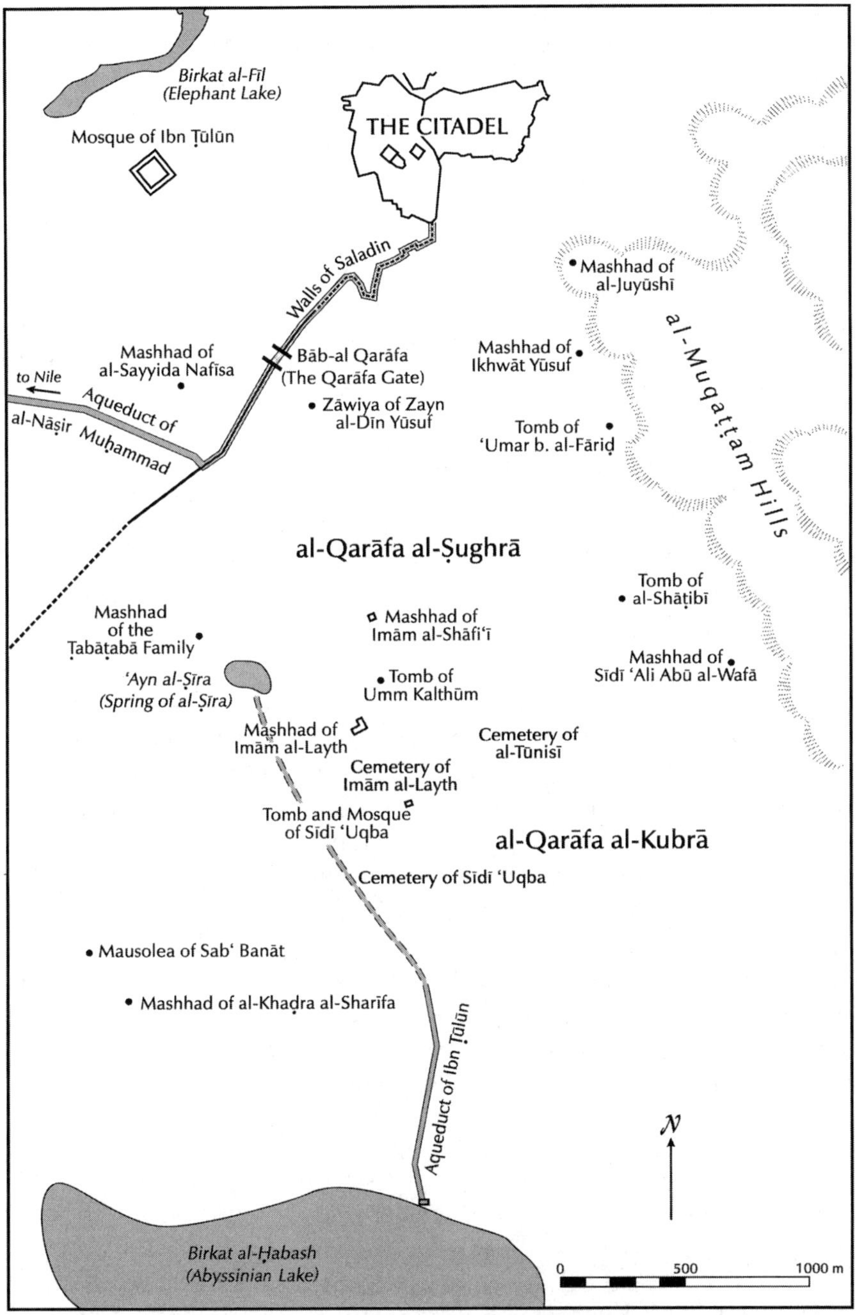

Map 2 – al-Qarāfa

Islamic conquest of Egypt in 642 A.D.[3] This explanation indicates that parts of the expansive area which ultimately took the name "al-Qarāfa" may have been settled as early as the initial Islamic conquest, and it is likely that significant portions of it were always inhabited. Modern visitors to Cairo are often struck by the sight of hundreds of thousands of living people making their homes among the tombs of the city's vast cemeteries. The famous "City of the Dead" (Figure 1) in Cairo's Northern Cemetery, for example, is thought to be the home today of more than a million living people. Extreme population pressures plaguing the modern city are blamed for this phenomenon, but from a historical perspective the idea of the living residing among the dead is not alien.

The growth and expansion of al-Qarāfa followed the general settlement pattern of the neighboring city of al-Fusṭāṭ; the primary axis ran from southwest to northeast. According to the famous medieval Egyptian historian al-Maqrīzī (d. 1442), the original burial ground stretched from the Mosque of al-Fatḥ on the northeastern shore of Birkat al-Ḥabash to the base of the Muqaṭṭam hills.[4] For two centuries after the Muslim conquest of Egypt, most building in al-Qarāfa was confined to the southernmost portion of the plateau. In the late ninth century Aḥmad ibn Ṭūlūn (r. 868–884), the independent governor of Egypt, built an enormous aqueduct that ran from the Birkat al-Ḥabash through the heart of al-Qarāfa al-Kubrā to ʿAyn al-Ṣīra, approximately 700 meters southwest of the site where the great mausoleum of Imām al-Shāfiʿī would eventually loom. This aqueduct provided water for a much larger portion of al-Qarāfa al-Kubrā, thereby facilitating both the expansion of population and further construction in the area.[5]

The Fāṭimids (969–1171) built extensively in al-Qarāfa al-Kubrā, adding numerous mosques, palaces, mausolea, and additional water works. In November 1168, however, al-Fusṭāṭ and much of al-Qarāfa al-Kubrā along with it were deliberately burned to the ground by

---

[3] Al-Maqrīzī, *Khiṭaṭ*, 2:444–45. Although there is disagreement about the correct lineage of this clan, most writers concur that they were part of the larger subtribe of al-Maʿāfir, part of the Yemeni tribal confederation of Ḥimyar; see ibid. See also Ibn al-Zayyāt, *al-Kawākib*, 179; and Yāqūt, *Muʿjam al-buldān*, 4:317.

[4] Al-Maqrīzī, *Khiṭaṭ*, 2:444.

[5] For the history of this aqueduct see ibid., 2:457–58 and al-Sakhāwī, *Tuḥfat al-aḥbāb*, 180. See also Creswell's description of the aqueduct and interesting plates from the early part of this century in *Early Muslim Architecture* (hereafter *EMA*), 2:329–32 and plates 94a–d and 95a–c.

Figure 1 – The Northern Cemetery of Cairo as viewed today from Shāriʿ Ṣalāḥ Sālim looking toward the Citadel

the Fāṭimids in an unsuccessful effort to forestall the siege of Cairo by the advancing forces of Amalric, the Crusader king of Jerusalem. Although Amalric never took Cairo, the destruction of al-Fusṭāṭ decisively shifted the focus of urban life in the area toward Cairo to the northeast.

In the Ayyūbid period there was a corresponding northward shift in the development of al-Qarāfa. In 1180 Saladin completed the construction of a large madrasa near the tomb of the great Sunnī jurist al-Shāfiʿī (d. 820). Three decades later Sultan al-Malik al-Kāmil (r. 1218–38) built an enormous mausoleum over al-Shāfiʿī's grave itself. Thus the active focus of construction and settlement in al-Qarāfa shifted to this area, which became known as al-Qarāfa al-Ṣughrā. As rapidly as this new quarter developed, the older al-Qarāfa al-Kubrā declined.[6]

The final stage in the development of al-Qarāfa occurred early in the Mamlūk period, during the third reign of al-Nāṣir Muḥammad ibn Qalāwūn (1309–1340). A large maydān, or hippodrome, which had previously occupied the area between the tomb of Imām al-Shāfiʿī and Bāb al-Qarāfa, just below the Citadel of Cairo, was converted from a race track to a burial ground. As the historian al-Maqrīzī relates:

> Thus the Amīr Yalbughā al-Turkumānī, the Amīr Taqtumar al-Dimashkī, and the Amīr Qūṣūn, as well as others, built in this area. The soldiers and the rest of the populace followed their lead, building tombs, khānqāhs [Ṣūfī hostels], markets, mills and public baths, until the entire area from Birkat al-Ḥabash to the Gate [of al-Qarāfa], and from the residences of al-Fusṭāṭ to the mountain [Jabal al-Muqaṭṭam] were built up. Thoroughfares were portioned off and streets multiplied in al-Qarāfa. Many wished to live there because of the magnificence of the palaces built there as tombs, and also because of the many khānqāhs made by the builders of the tombs and their repeated distribution of ṣadaqa [alms] and charity to the inhabitants of al-Qarāfa.[7]

Thus, in the eight centuries between the original establishment of al-Fusṭāṭ and the fifteenth century when al-Maqrīzī was writing, the Qarāfa cemetery came to encompass a vast area. The sources make clear that by the Mamlūk period generations of intensive building in al-Qarāfa had left virtually no significant open spaces. It had

---

[6] Al-Maqrīzī, *Khiṭaṭ*, 2:444–45.
[7] Ibid., 445.

become a composite of many historical layers of architectural expression, a crowded agglomeration of structures large and small, and without question the most famous cemetery in the Islamic world. Al-Maqrīzī wrote: "It is the consensus that nowhere in the world is there a more wondrous graveyard."[8] The great carved stone domes and striking monumental funerary architecture, combined with the many famous and venerated figures buried there, impressed Muslims visiting Cairo from all over the Islamic world in the later Middle Ages. Writing in the late twelfth century, the Arab traveler Ibn Jubayr (d. 1217), for example, called al-Qarāfa "one of the wonders of the world."[9] In the fourteenth century another famous Arab traveler, Ibn Baṭṭūṭa (d. 1377), marveled at the great domes that defined the horizon of the Qarāfa, and he referred to the site as "a great medium of divine blessing."[10] Arab travelers were not the only ones struck by al-Qarāfa. A number of European visitors to medieval Egypt were equally, or perhaps even more, impressed. In 1335 Jacques de Vérone visited Cairo and left the following description of the city's cemeteries: "There are large cemeteries where the tombs of the Moslems are found and where magnificent monuments have been erected of marble, porphyry, alabaster, and other fine stones, admirably constructed and gilded. I have not seen any of comparable magnificence in all of Christendom. These are tombs of old sultans, emirs, and noble Saracens."[11] Nearly a century later the Venetian merchant Emmanuel Piloti commented on the vast size of al-Qarāfa: "One mile away from Cairo is a city which is not walled, is as large as Venice, and has tall structures and short ones; in this city are buried all those who die in Cairo. Every Saracen and townsman has a building in this city."[12] It was the great size of the Qarāfa that most impressed Europeans. In calculating the size of the city of Cairo in 1483, Félix Fabri specifically excluded the cemetery from his estimation, saying that by European standards al-Qarāfa would by itself be an enormous city.[13]

---

[8] Ibid., 444.

[9] Ibn Jubayr, *Riḥlat Ibn Jubayr*, 20.

[10] Ibn Baṭṭūṭa, *Travels*, 51. See also *Riḥlat Ibn Baṭṭūṭa*, 39.

[11] Dopp, "Le Caire," 128; quoted without attribution in Wiet, *Cairo*, 135.

[12] Piloti, *L'Egypte au commencement du quinzième siècle*, 34–35. See the translation in Wiet, *Cairo*, 135.

[13] Fabri, *Voyage en Egypte*, 2:527. At 3:927 Fabri states that the cemetery is larger than the city of Augsburg.

It would be wrong to imagine al-Qarāfa as merely a "city of the dead," however. It was also an integral and very active part of what might be termed medieval "greater Cairo." Apparently always inhabited, it was increasingly filled with its own markets, streets, public baths, and bakeries, all mingling with the tomb complexes, mosques, and graveyards. It was, too, a place that generated its own special lore, not unlike other quarters of the city. There is, for example, the famous story of the Quṭriba, a ghoulish figure who sometimes assumed the likeness of a wizened old woman. Al-Maqrīzī relates that in about 1042 this fantastic and horrifying creature was said to have descended from the Jabal al-Muqaṭṭam, and shortly thereafter the children of al-Qarāfa began to disappear. As a result, many inhabitants of the area fled in fear. One day a certain Ḥamīd, a leading citizen of Cairo, rode out on his donkey. On his way to the town of Ḥulwān, some thirty kilometers south of Cairo, he encountered an old woman sitting by the side of the road. She complained to Ḥamīd of the weakness of her advanced age, so he allowed her to ride behind him on his donkey. After some distance the donkey suddenly collapsed under Ḥamīd who, collecting himself, looked around in amazement to discover the old woman had torn open the belly and disemboweled his mount with her long nails. He fled in panic to al-Fusṭāṭ, where he recounted this ordeal. A group of men returned with Ḥamīd to the site where these strange events had occurred. They discovered only the carcass of his donkey with its innards eaten away. The Quṭriba subsequently began to exhume the dead of the Qarāfa, devour their entrails, and scatter the discarded cadavers throughout the graveyard. According to al-Maqrīzī, people abstained from burying their dead in the cemetery until these strange events came to an end as suddenly and inexplicably as they had begun.[14]

Medieval population estimates are as hard to come by as they are notoriously unreliable. However, we can gain some sense of the relative proportion of Cairo's inhabitants living in the Qarāfa from the figures provided by Leo Africanus for the year 1526. He set the population of al-Qarāfa at 2,000 families which, following Michael Dols's method of multiplying the numbers in Leo Africanus by an average family size of five or six, yields a total figure of between 10,000 and 12,000 people living in al-Qarāfa.[15] This equals almost

[14] Al-Maqrīzī, *Khiṭaṭ*, 2:445.
[15] Cited in Dols, *The Black Death*, 196.

half the number living in al-Fusṭāṭ at the time, and a full quarter of those residing within the walled city of Cairo. If we accept Dols's calculation of a total contemporary population for all areas of Cairo at between 177,500 and 213,000, this means that nearly 6 per cent of Cairo's inhabitants lived in the Qarāfa cemetery by the early sixteenth century.

At certain points in the Mamlūk period, al-Qarāfa seems to have functioned as a distinct administrative section of Cairo. For example, the fifteenth-century Egyptian historian Ibn Taghrī Birdī (d. 1470) tells us that in February 1385 Sultan al-Malik al-Ẓāhir Barqūq (r. 1382–1389 and 1390–1399) made the amir Sulaymān al-Kurdī the governor (wālī) of al-Qarāfa—a new position, as supervision of the cemetery was previously the responsibility of the governor of al-Fusṭāṭ.[16] In his biographical dictionary *al-Ḍawʾ al-lāmiʿ*, Shams al-Dīn al-Sakhāwī briefly mentions that Abū Bakr al-Shāṭir served as controller (nāẓir) of al-Qarāfa in the second quarter of the fifteenth century.[17] This position apparently involved supervision of the many endowed institutions located there. Although we do not know much about either of these posts, the fact that they were created probably indicates increasing complexity in the administration of an expanding al-Qarāfa by the late fourteenth and fifteenth centuries.

Al-Maqrīzī, in his great topographical work on medieval Cairo, the *Khiṭaṭ*, begins his description of al-Qarāfa with a discussion of its mosques. Although he selects only several dozen of the most notable examples to describe in detail, al-Maqrīzī cites an estimate that twelve thousand mosques stood in al-Qarāfa al-Kubrā at one time or another. The figure is doubtless greatly exaggerated, and many of these buildings were in ruins or had disappeared altogether by the later Middle Ages, but al-Maqrīzī's estimate conveys an accurate impression of al-Qarāfa's size.[18]

In his catalogue of the 130 great communal mosques used for Friday prayer in the Cairo area by the Mamlūk period, al-Maqrīzī lists 11 located in the Qarāfa. There was, for example, the Jāmiʿ al-Qarāfa,

---

[16] Ibn Taghrī Birdī, *al-Nujūm al-zāhira*, 2:241, and Popper, trans., 13:13.

[17] Al-Sakhāwī, *al-Ḍawʾ al-lāmiʿ*, 5:163. I am grateful to Jonathan Berkey for bringing this reference to my attention. On the position of nāẓir see Petry, *Civilian Elite*, 213.

[18] Al-Maqrīzī, *Khiṭaṭ*, 2:445–52. Ibn al-Zayyāt, *al-Kawākib*, 183, 185.

which was built in 976 on the site of the earlier Masjid al-Qubba (Mosque of the Dome) by Durzān, mother of the Fāṭimid caliph al-ʿAzīz (r. 975–996). Although we do not know its exact dimensions or plan, al-Maqrīzī's comparison with the still surviving Jāmiʿ al-Azhar suggests that the mosque was indeed enormous.[19]

The Jāmiʿ al-Qarāfa was apparently a favorite gathering place for the Egyptian elite during the Fāṭimid period. On Friday evenings throughout the summer they would congregate in its courtyard, where they would talk, eat, celebrate, and sleep by the light of the moon. During cooler winter months these leading members of the Fāṭimid establishment would gather instead around the minbar (a raised seat from which the Friday homily, or khuṭba, was offered) in the larger and covered qibla portion of the mosque.[20] Such assemblages of society's elite invariably included numerous protégés and assorted clients. The very prominence of these gatherings, along with the considerable quantities of food, drink, and other provisions they required also attracted much of the general populace. This pattern of mixed social gatherings seems to have been typical for the larger communal mosques spread throughout al-Qarāfa.

The Fāṭimids celebrated four "nights of light," referred to in the sources as layālī al-wuqūd al-arbaʿa. Although little is known about these uniquely Ismāʿīlī celebrations, they occurred on the eve of the sighting of the new moons marking the start of the Islamic months of Rajab and Shaʿbān, as well as on the full moons during each of these two months.[21] Layālī al-wuqūd al-arbaʿa were apparently joyous

---

[19] Al-Maqrīzī, *Khiṭaṭ*, 2:245. Jonathan Bloom has proposed a hypothetical reconstruction of the plan of the Jāmiʿ al-Qarāfa: Bloom, "The Mosque of the Qarafa," Yūsuf Rāghib, however, has raised serious objections to Bloom's plan; see his note "La mosquée d'al-Qarāfa."

[20] Al-Maqrīzī, *Khiṭaṭ*, 2:318–20, 444.

[21] Ibid., 1:465–67. See also 2:444 and al-Qalqashandī, *Ṣubḥ al-aʿshā*, 3:497–98; and Magued, *Nuẓum al-fāṭimīyīn*, 2:120–22. See also *EI*[1], s.v. Shaʿbān, Here Wensinck notes "the middle of Shaʿbān, a day which, up to the present time, has preserved features of a New Year's day. According to popular belief, in the night preceding the 15th the tree of life on whose leaves are written the names of the living is shaken. The names written on the leaves which fall down, indicate those who are to die in the coming year. In *hadīth* it is said that in this night Allāh descends to the lowest heaven; from there he calls the mortals in order to grant them forgiveness of sins." This belief may explain the significance of the cemetery, like al-Qarāfa, in this celebration. Professor ʿAbbās al-Ḥamdānī informs me (personal communication) that the middle of Shaʿbān is also the traditional date of the marriage of ʿAlī and Fāṭima, which would make this day significant for the Fāṭimids.

occasions filled with much festivity and amusement, as the night sky was aglow with great bonfires and thousands of candles and lanterns. Jāmiʿ al-Qarāfa was among one of six great congregational mosques in and around the Fāṭimid capital where the celebrations took place.

Ibn al-Zayyāt tells us also that Jāmiʿ al-Qarāfa was a particularly holy mosque where Egyptians traditionally sought refuge in times of calamity, and begged God for assistance and refuge.[22] The mosque was totally destroyed, except for its famous green miḥrāb, in the great fire that consumed most of al-Fusṭāṭ in 1168. It was later rebuilt, and in al-Maqrīzī's time the mosque, which was then known as Jāmiʿ al-Awliyyā', was surrounded by the dwellings of West African immigrants who apparently inhabited this area in large numbers in the late fourteenth century. A new crisis in 1403, however, resulted in further depopulation of al-Qarāfa al-Kubrā. After this date the mosque's doors were generally locked except on certain Fridays.[23]

There were a number of other large communal mosques in al-Qarāfa, but most worshipers performed their daily cycle of prayers alongside friends, family, fellow pilgrims, and neighbors in one of the scores of smaller mosques and oratories located throughout the cemetery. Although the sources rarely provide us with a description of these smaller mosques, in their many brief and scattered references to them we do hear the distant echo of local traditions and beliefs probably known only to a small circle of regular worshipers and neighbors. For example, we hear that Masjid Zinkāda was named for its builder who built this mosque in 1140 after repenting for having been a homosexual (mukhannath).[24] Near the Mosque al-Aqdām was the Mosque of Abū Ṣādiq, which was named for a revered local

---

[22] Ibn al-Zayyāt, *al-Kawākib*, 174–75. One must be circumspect in accepting Ibn al-Zayyāt's information concerning this mosque as he incorrectly states it was built in 947. He also confuses it with the Jāmiʿ al-ʿĀtīq in that he states this is where the treasury of Egypt was located.

[23] Al-Maqrīzī, *Khiṭaṭ*, 2:320; al-Sakhāwī, *Tuḥfat*, 184 and 289–90. Al-Sakhāwī offers a much more colorful version of the decline of this mosque. He relates that the devil once played a trick by allowing vipers to escape from a magician one night while a crowd of people was sleeping in the mosque. They awoke to the shouts of the magician, and when everyone discovered what was wrong they all clung to the columns, minbar, and lanterns of the mosque in fear. At dawn, when the morning call to prayer was heard, everyone fled the mosque. This event marked the decline of the mosque, according to al-Sakhāwī.

[24] Al-Maqrīzī, *Khiṭaṭ*, 2:451. The word *mukhannath* literally means "effeminate," but Lane indicates that the term is also used to describe homosexuals, which certainly seems to be the implication here. See Lane, *Lexicon*, 815.

Qur'ān reciter who loved and cared for stray dogs and cats.[25] In the Mosque of Banū ʿAwf, according to tradition, there was a famous water jar that belonged to one of the Prophet's companions. If a passersby offered tainted or illicit money in exchange for water from this jar they would always find it empty. On the other hand, if the money offered was lawfully obtained the jug was inevitably full. According to Ibn al-Zayyāt this magical water jar remained in the mosque until the early Mamlūk period, when it disappeared during disturbances in 1261–62.[26] The mosque known as Sakan Ibn Mirra al-Ruʿaynī was revered for a special well, famous for its curative powers. This mosque was destroyed during earlier civil strife in 1200–1201.[27] In times of trouble people traditionally made their way to the mosque known as al-Raḥma, where they prayed, placed their backs against the mosque's central column, and begged for God's assistance.[28] There were also mosques with perhaps more dubious claims, such as the small mosque where Moses reportedly prayed.[29] The sources also contain many notices of other minor mosques that served as gathering points during the great Islamic feasts.[30]

Mausolea, mashāhid (s. mashhad), defined much of the architectural character of al-Qarāfa. They commemorated both the celebrated dead and those of whom history has left little or no record. Although al-Qarāfa was filled with thousands of mausolea, large and small, most of the descriptive information and surviving architectural evidence relates to the monumental structures for which this Egyptian necropolis was internationally famous.

There were two basic types of monumental mausolea in medieval Egyptian funerary architecture. The first, often referred to in the sources as a qubba or turba, consisted of a cubical chamber surmounted by a dome. Although a mausoleum might house only one tomb, more often it contained a number of individual graves. Frequently one finds under the dome a large solitary and ornate marble cenotaph indicating not a single grave but rather a burial vault

[25] Al-Maqrīzī, 2:449–50.

[26] Ibn al-Zayyāt, *al-Kawākib*, 183–84.

[27] Ibid., 184. Al-Sakhāwī, *Tuḥfat*, 297–98.

[28] Al-Sakhāwī, *Tuḥfat*, 294.

[29] Ibid., 141. See also Ibn ʿUthmān, *Murshid al-zuwwār* fol. 208r°. There is no mention of this mosque in the printed text, although it should appear on page 425.

[30] For example, see Ibn al-Zayyāt, *al-Kawākib*, on Masjid al-Nabbāsh, 180; and al-Maqrīzī on Masjid Tāj al-Mulūk, *Khiṭaṭ*, 2:450, and also on Maṣallat Khūlān, 2:454–55.

lying below floor level, containing numerous remains placed on shelves lining the vault. The basic form of the cubical domed mausolem is clearly visible in the remains of a series of tombs known as Sabʿ Banāt, "the seven virgins," located at the southern end of al-Qarāfa al-Kubrā (Figure 2). These were built in 1012 after the Fāṭimid Caliph al-Ḥākim bi-Amr-illāh (r. 996–1021) executed six members of the al-Maghribī family in 1010 following an extended struggle between the vizier ʿAlī b. al-Ḥusayn al-Maghribī and his Christian successor Abū Naṣr Manṣūr b. ʿAbdūn. The Caliph later built these tombs over their remains in an effort to appease the poet Abū al-Qāsim al-Maghribī, a member of the victims' family, who sought refuge and rose to a powerful position in the rival Ḥamdānid Empire in Syria.[31] These tombs, along with several others in the vicinity of Cairo, subsequently became pilgrimage sites, as they were collectively identified in legend either as the tombs of seven virgins who fought at the side of the Prophet Muḥammad or, alternatively, as the tombs of seven virgins with whom the famous Fāṭimid vizier and military commander-in-chief Badr al-Jamālī (d. 1094) reputedly fell in love.[32] These structures are open on all sides, with arched doorways or windows piercing each face and level of the mausoleum. Domes originally sat atop the octagonal drums that form the third level. A walled enclosure known as a ḥawsh originally surrounded each of these mashhads. The majority of mausolea surviving from the Middle Ages are similar in basic plan to these buildings, although not all are free-standing.

The most famous mashhad based on this cubical domed plan is that of the great Sunnī jurist Imām al-Shāfiʿī. This immense structure (Figure 3), which still towers over al-Qarāfa al-Ṣughrā, was built in 1211 on the orders of the Ayyūbid prince al-Malik al-Kāmil before he was elevated to the sultanate. The mausoleum stands nearly seventeen meters in height, and its walls are approximately three meters thick.[33] Unlike the Sabʿ Banāt, its four sides are largely enclosed,

---

[31] Creswell, *MAE*, 1:108–10. For corrections and additions see Rāghib, "Sur un groupe." As Rāghib points out (191), there were never seven tombs, but the site later took on the name Sabʿ Banāt because the nearby tomb of an ascetic was mistakenly linked in popular imagination to the six tombs originally built by al-Hākim. Ironically, Manṣūr b. ʿAbdūn's triumph proved short-lived as he too was executed by al-Ḥākim later in 1010.

[32] Rāghib, "Sur un groupe." 189.

[33] Creswell, *MAE*, 2:65–76.

Figure 2 – The Mausolea of Sabʿ Banāt

Figure 3 – The Tomb of Imām al-Shāfiʿī in al-Qarāfa al-Ṣughrā

with the exception of the entrance and a few large windows. Inside we find several tombs, including those of Imām al-Shāfiʿī, Sultan al-Malik al-Kāmil, and his mother. This magnificent stone structure has extensive interior decoration, and the qibla wall contains three miḥrābs. But despite its massive size and other differences, the mausoleum of Imām al-Shāfiʿī is essentially an extension of the basic cubical domed mashhad.

The second principal type of monumental mausoleum, usually referred to in the sources simply as a mashhad, was less prevalent than the first.[34] Mashhad al-Khaḍra al-Sharīfa, located near the remains of the Sabʿ Banāt at the southern extremity of al-Qarāfa al-Kubrā, is the best surviving example of this second type.[35] As is evident from Creswell's plan (Plan 1), the structure consists of a covered vestibule connected to a series of anterior rooms, the central one of which leads to a large open courtyard. At the far end of the courtyard lie three more connecting chambers, each with its own miḥrāb. A dome once covered the central burial chamber. This enormous structure, measuring nearly 20 by 30 meters, has been dated to the period between 1013 and 1021, although the identity of the original builder remains a mystery.[36]

---

[34] It would be incorrect to refer to all domed mausolea as *qubba* and all other mausolea as *mashhad*. Whereas the latter refers in the late medieval Egyptian context to virtually any large mausoleum, the term *qubba* seems to refers only to a type of mashhad which consisted of a square base surmounted by a dome. Therefore, we find numerous qubba-type mausolea referred to as mashhad, but not all mashāhid were characterized by a qubba. See also the Glossary.

[35] Creswell identified this structure as the "Mosque of Khaḍrā Sharīfa" and dated it to 1107/08 (Creswell, *MAE*, 1:224–25). Yūsuf Rāghib convincingly challenged both this date and the function Creswell originally assigned to this building (Rāghib, "Sur deux monuments funéraires"). Rāghib dated the structure to nearly a century earlier (between 1013 and 1021), and demonstrated that it was primarily a mausoleum rather than a mosque. The different interpretations of al-Khaḍra al-Sharīfa highlight the fact that the medieval sources often employ the words *mashhad* (mausoleum) and *masjid* (mosque) interchangeably, suggesting an underlying elasticity in their understanding of a structure's function which modern scholarship has yet to appreciate fully (see Grabar, "The Earliest Islamic Commemorative Structures," especially 9–10). Johannes Pedersen long ago correctly identified the mixture of functions that mosques have historically served (*EI*[1], s.v. Masdjid, especially 322–24). He pointed out that mosques combining a commemorative funerary function with a sanctuary emerged early and became common in the Islamic world despite persistent legal arguments against such practice. Modern concern with drawing clear distinctions between mashhads and masjids is misplaced and obscures understanding of the dynamic interplay between the architectural environment and contemporary modes of pious expression.

[36] Rāghib, "Sur deux monuments funéraires," 72–83.

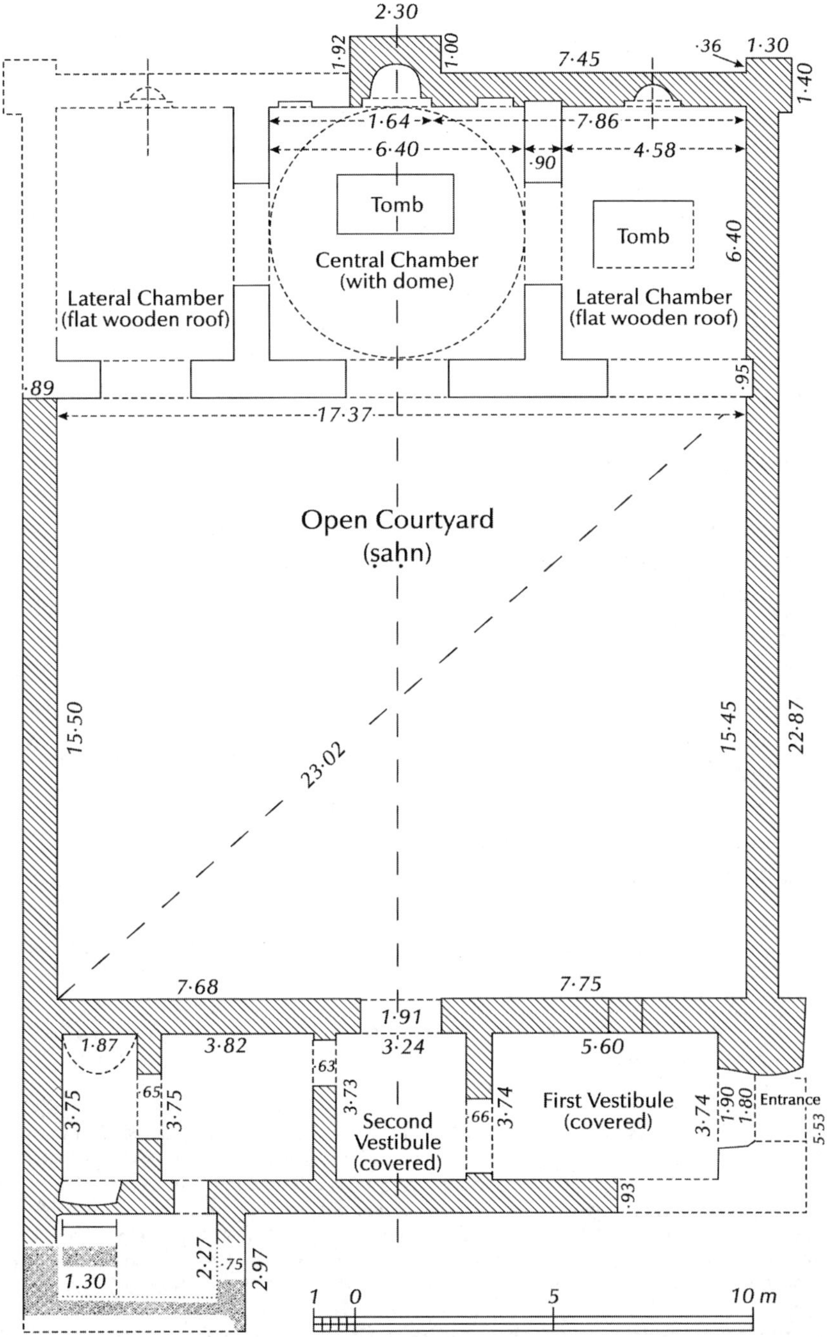

Plan 1 – The Mashhad of al-Khaḍra al-Sharīfa
After K.A.C. Creswell, *The Muslim Architecture of Egypt*. 2 vols. (Oxford, 1952–1960), I:224, fig. 127.

Not all mausolea, of course, were of such monumental scale as these two. Mashhads commemorated a wide variety of individuals; most were figures of largely local prominence, although a few would have been widely recognizable in the medieval Islamic world. Some of these mashhads seem to have replaced earlier, probably more modest monuments. Others, however, were built solely in response to the dreams of either a pious benefactor or someone revered by the patron.[37] Known in the sources as "vision mausolea" (mashāhid al-ru'yā), these often large and impressive buildings were erected on the instructions of the holy dead through dreams, usually without any corroborating evidence to authenticate the original site of the burial. In fact, in numerous cases there was little evidence to suggest the person commemorated had actually ever even been to Egypt. Although pilgrims clearly trusted and relied on the authenticity of these vision mausolea, most contemporary scholars did not. Even among those who rejected these sites as apocryphal, however, there were differences of opinion as to the permissibility of visiting them. Some scholars believed that the falsification of Islamic tradition should never be tolerated, regardless how well intended or how unintentional, especially when fantastic or patently fictitious claims were made.[38] Other writers, however, although acknowledging that a tomb was incorrectly identified, stressed that visits to such sites were allowed because they were generally made with "good intention."

Pious and wealthy believers were similarly commanded through the medium of dreams to build vision mosques. For example, a foundation inscription dated 1102–1103 A.D. informs us: "Our lord al-Ṣādiq Jaʿfar, son of Muḥammad, the son of ʿAlī, the son of al-Ḥusayn, the son of ʿAlī b. Abī Ṭālib, may the blessings of God be upon

[37] Rāghib, "Al-Sayyida Nafīsa," 61–64. Rāghib has constructed a useful typology which, although specifically designed for application to ʿAlid monuments, can be applied to the tombs of saints in Egypt in general.

[38] Ibn al-Nāsikh rebukes the author of another pilgrimage guide, Ibn ʿUthmān, on a number of occasions for reporting the apocryphal burial sites of famous people. For example, he chides his predecessor for noting the grave of ʿAbd Allāh b. al-Zubayr (d. 692), a major contender for the caliphate after the death of the first ʿUmayyad caliph Muʿāwiyya (d. 680), was located in al-Qarāfa (*Miṣbāḥ*, fols. 48r°–48v°). Ibn al-Nāsikh clearly had little patience for such a conspicuous error when the facts of Ibn al-Zubayr's death and burial in Arabia were presented at great length in standard medieval histories (see al-Ṭabarī, *Ta'rīkh*, 2:852). Ibn al-Nāsikh is himself taken to task for the same kind of error by Ibn al-Zayyāt for incorrectly identifying a tomb of unknown ashrāf (descendants of the Prophet Muḥammad) as a mashhad al-ru'yā built for the grandson of ʿAlī b. Abī Ṭālib (*al-Kawākib*, 37).

them all, ordered his servant, the Amīr Zaʿīm al-Dawla Jawāmard al-Afḍalī, to construct this mosque in a dream."[39] Similarly, the Prophet himself requested Fakhr al-Dīn al-Fārisī to construct a mosque near the tomb of Shaykh Abū al-Khayr al-Tīnnātī, as we will discuss in Chapter 4.

Besides large communal mosques, countless smaller oratories, and mausolea, there were many other structures, large and small, that filled the Qarāfa cemetery. Unfortunately, few examples of these buildings exist today, and we must rely on surviving examples from other parts of Cairo or on descriptions provided in the textual sources. In considering each of these institutions we must also bear in mind that, as in the case of mosques and mausolea, there was often considerable versatility in the functions of individual structures. The general features outlined here should be understood to allow for considerable variation between actual structures.

Al-Maqrīzī states that among the many houses in al-Qarāfa there were a number of ribāṭs. In late medieval Egypt the word ribāṭ seems to have designated primarily hospices for men or women who sought quiet refuge where they might withdraw from the distractions of the everyday world and pursue religious knowledge and contemplation.[40] Regarding the ribāṭs located in the Qarāfa, as in much of Cairo, al-Maqrīzī's *Khiṭaṭ* suggests that they were mainly hospices for devout older women and widows. Al-Maqrīzī lists six ribāṭs located in al-Qarāfa and he describes them as being "like the homes of the wives of the Prophet."[41]

In al-Qarāfa, as elsewhere, the establishments called khanqāhs were essentially hostels providing lodging, meals, and frequently stipends for resident Ṣūfīs.[42] The khanqāh usually contained a number of cells for individual Ṣūfīs to perform their daily rituals of spiritual exercise, as well as larger facilities for group performances of the dhikr. The term *zāwiya* was also frequently applied to places where Ṣūfīs gathered, but this word in particular seems to have encompased a wide range of functional meanings. The earliest surviving Mamlūk

---

[39] Combe, Sauvaget and Wiet et al., *Répertoire chronologique d'épigraphie arabe* (hereafter *RCEA*), 8: 53–54, no. 2887. The source of the instructions here is the great sixth Shīʿite imām, Jaʿfar al-Ṣādiq (d. 765).

[40] See *EI*², s.v. Ribāṭ for an excellent overview; J. Chabbi makes it clear that the meaning of this term varied greatly according to both time and place.

[41] Al-Maqrīzī, *Khiṭaṭ*, 2:454.

[42] See *EI*², s.v. Kh̲ānḳāh.

structure with a foundation inscription specifically identifying it as a zāwiya is that of Shaykh Zayn al-Dīn Yūsuf (d. 1325). Located in al-Qarāfa al-Ṣughrā not far from the Mausoleum of Imām al-Shāfiʿī, this zāwiya was first constructed in 1298 by a descendant of the Umayyad dynasty who founded the ʿAdawiyya Ṣūfī brotherhood. The structure consists of a vestibule that leads to the left into an interior court with four irregular arched and barrel-vaulted estrades (iwāns) laid out in a cruciform pattern. A domed mausoleum housing the tomb of Shaykh Zayn al-Dīn Yūsuf fills the space between the southern (qibla) and western estrades. Although no Ṣūfī cells survive, there once were some cells on the building's upper level.[43]

Another type of establishment, madrasas were essentially teaching-mosques where scholars offered lessons in law and the various other Islamic sciences.[44] Many madrasas also offered lodging for professors and students, and frequently these institutions possessed well-endowed waqfs that generated stipends for both students and teachers. Madrasas emerged and proliferated in the high and later Middle Ages throughout the Islamic world. The sources speak of only one built within the traditional boundaries of al-Qarāfa. This was the famous Madrasat al-Ṣāliḥiyya, built near the tomb of Imām al-Shāfiʿī by Saladin between 1176 and 1180.[45] The monumental domed mausoleum of Imām al-Shāfiʿī, the madrasa, and all the tombs and graveyards surrounding these buildings eventually formed a large integrated complex, which was the core around which al-Qarāfa al-Ṣughrā grew.[46]

Al-Maqrīzī mentions eight jawsaqs in al-Qarāfa. These were apparently large pavilions that clearly belonged to the earlier Islamic

---

[43] Behrens-Abouseif, *Islamic Architecture in Cairo*, 111–12.

[44] There is some debate among scholars concerning the role of madrasas in Islamic higher learning. The traditional view is that madrasas were specialized and formal institutions of higher learning, which became central to the transmission of knowledge in the later Middle Ages (see Makdisi, *Rise of Colleges*). More recent scholars have cast doubt this view (see Berkey, *Transmission of Knowledge*, and Chamberlain, *Knowledge and Social Practice*).

[45] Al-Maqrīzī, *Khiṭaṭ*, 2:400–1.

[46] Ibid., 394 and 399–400. This site also combined functions, serving as both a madrasa and turba. Several other major madrasas were located on the fringes of the Qarāfa and should also be noted. These included the Madrasa of Turbat Umm al-Ṣāliḥ, near the Mashhad of al-Sayyida Nafīsa, the Madrasa of Aljāy, and the Madrasa of Umm al-Sulṭān near the base of the Citadel of Cairo. These madrasas all seem to have incorporated the tombs of their founders, or those in whose honor they were built, as was frequently true of other madrasas in and around Cairo.

period. He states that he had seen two of them himself, and that only one, the Jawsaq al-Mādhrā'ī, survived by the time that the *Khiṭaṭ* was written. According to al-Maqrīzī's description, it was an enormous fortresslike building that resembled the Kaʿba in Mecca. The structure was built by Abū Bakr Muḥammad b. ʿAlī al-Mādhrā'ī among the tombs of his family, apparently to serve as a sort of rest house for prominent and wealthy families to stay in while visiting the Qarāfa.[47] Both Ibn al-Zayyāt and al-Maqrīzī provide extensive descriptions of Jawsaq al-Mādhrā'ī.[48] They tell us, for example, that in the Fāṭimid period, especially during the evening before the middle of the month of Shaʿbān and during the great Islamic festivals the leaders of society would gather with candles and light great bonfires, around which they would sit and recite the Qur'ān. Frankincense, benzoin, aloes, and aromatic incense were burned, and alms were liberally distributed among the populace attracted by such gatherings.

Some of these jawsaqs must have been impressive indeed, with fountains, watering holes for horses, gardens, and even large balconies from which to view the proceedings below. For example, the jawsaq known as Qaṣr al-Qarāfa was renovated by the Fāṭimid Caliph al-Āmir bi-Aḥkām Allāh in 1126; he also built a bench next to its entrance for Ṣūfīs to sit on. Al-Maqrīzī describes how the caliph would watch from the balcony as dervishes danced before him on the grounds below.[49]

But the jawsaqs that had served as focal points of social gathering during the Fāṭimid era were by the later Mamlūk period only objects of curiosity and looting. The Jawsaq of Ḥubb al-Waraqa, which al-Maqrīzī saw before its destruction, fell victim to the pillaging of tombs and palaces which seems to have occurred widely in al-Qarāfa al-Kubrā, especially after 1403. The active focus of the great cemetery had by this time already shifted far to the northeast, to the area around the tomb of Imām al-Shāfiʿī in al-Qarāfa al-Ṣughrā.

As might be gathered from this discussion, the Qarāfa was not a single cemetery, but an interconnected series of graveyards (maqbara)

---

[47] Ibid., 452–53.

[48] Ibn al-Zayyāt, *al-Kawākib*, 74 and 155; al-Maqrīzī, *Khiṭaṭ*, 2:453; see also al-Sakhāwī, *Tuḥfat*, 274; Ibn al-Nāsikh, *Miṣbāḥ*, fols. 32r°–32v°; and Ibn ʿUthmān, Murshid, 269–70.

[49] Al-Maqrīzī, *Khiṭaṭ*, 2:453.

and burial complexes. It would appear that a maqbara consisted of a collection of individual graves, many of which were related to each other through any of a number of possible connections.[50] For example, family members might be buried near each other, just as the students of a great religious scholar or the followers of a famous Ṣūfī shaykh might likewise be buried around the tomb of their master. Whether these smaller graveyards were usually defined by actual physical boundaries, such as an enclosure wall, is not clear. An inscription recorded in the *Répertoire* refers to the "gate" of a graveyard.[51] More often, however, the pilgrimage guides simply indicate that a maqbara was defined by certain informal landmarks, usually other tombs.

Another term often used in the sources, which seems to refer generally either to a graveyard or to a collection of tombs, is ḥawma.[52] Thus, Ibn al-Zayyāt speaks of the ḥawma of Ibn al-Fāriḍ which is located in the Maqbarat al-Ḥanafiyya.[53] Clearly in this case the ḥawma is smaller than, and is actually a part of a maqbara. However, when describing the burial complex around the grave of great early ḥadīth specialist and jurist al-Layth b. Saʿd (d. 791), the same author uses the words *ḥawma* and *maqbara* interchangeably.[54]

A ḥawsh, on the other hand, was almost certainly an enclosed area (as noted above in our description of the Sabʿ Banāt). The term usually refers to a corral for livestock, such as the famous ḥawsh constructed by Sultan al-Nāṣir Muḥammad b. Qalawūn near the Cairo Citadel in 1337/38.[55] In its most basic form the ḥawsh was simply a walled enclosure within which many tombs were located. A reference in Ibn al-Zayyāt to a ḥawsh without a roof indicates that these structures may sometimes have been at least partially covered.[56]

---

[50] The sources do not employ consistent vocabulary in describing the smaller assemblages into which most tombs were grouped. The term maqbara is used often in the general sense of a graveyard. See Grabar, "The Earliest Islamic Commemorative Structures," 7 and 9–10.

[51] Combe, *RCEA*, 4:147, no. 1495. See also Ibn al-Zayyāt, *al-Kawākib*, 297.

[52] According to Lane, *Lexicon*, 678, the word usually means "The *main part* or *portion*" usually of the sea or of water, or alternately "the *most vehement part* [or the *thickest*] of a fight."

[53] Ibn al-Zayyāt, *al-Kawākib*, 297.

[54] Ibid., 102. Layth b. Saʿd was a pupil of Mālik, the eponymous founder of one of the four surviving schools of Sunnī jurisprudence. See *EI*[2], s.v. "Layth b. Saʿd".

[55] Al-Maqrīzī, *Khiṭaṭ*, 2:229.

[56] Ibn al-Zayyāt, *al-Kawākib*, 121.

The ḥawsh was probably not very different in design from the thousands of structures seen in Figure 1, which now fill the City of the Dead between the ring road and Shāriʿ Ṣalāḥ Sālim on the eastern fringe of Cairo. One enters these modern walled complexes through a locking entrance gate that opens onto a small courtyard housing a number of tombs. The rear portion is frequently covered and divided into two or more chambers that may house additional tombs. Here family and friends of the dead stay or rest in the shade during their regular visits to the cemetery. A host of "custodians" and their families, along with thousands of outright squatters, also make their homes in these often substantial structures.

The great carved domes, the monumental mausolea, madrasas, ribāṭs, and jawsaqs were obvious and important architectural features of the Qarāfa, as were the maqbaras and ḥawshes that subdivided this vast cemetery. Many of these impressive stone structures serve as powerful reminders of extensive and continuous participation in the veneration of the holy dead by the elite of medieval Egyptian society. But what of the thousands upon thousands of smaller mausolea and individual graves that crowded this vast plateau like so many "bright stars in a sky whose light not even the full moon can conceal?"[57] These more pedestrian markers are usually glossed over in modern topographical descriptions of Cairo's graveyards. And yet it was primarily in this chaotic jumble of dusty and broken tombstones and smaller mausolea that the cult of Muslim saints thrived in late medieval Egypt. For it was among these more pedestrian markers that participants in the ziyāra carefully picked their way in search of the awliyāʾ Allāh—the special friends of God.

The most common word in the sources for a simple individual grave is qabr. Many individual graves were designated by an inscribed flat marble, limestone, or granite marker (lawḥ) or, less frequently, by an elaborately carved marble column (ʿamūd). The largest number of surviving gravestones from the medieval Islamic world come from Egypt, and through the thousands of tombstone inscriptions recorded in the *Répertoire chronologique d'épigraphie arabe* one can figuratively "stroll" through a composite medieval Egyptian graveyard. And as we "wander" among these epitaphs the texture of the faith, the hope, and the pain that inspired them suddenly becomes more palpable.

---

[57] Ibn ʿUthmān, *Murshid*, 3; and Ibn al-Zayyāt, *al-Kawākib*, 277.

We find, for example, among the earlier tombstones of the late eighth and the ninth centuries strong and emphatic professions of Islamic faith. The gravestone of ʿAbd Rabbihi b. Amīn b. ʿAbd Allāh al-Ghāfiqī, who died on August 21, 803 tells us:

> This is what he professed: there is no god but God Himself. He has no partner. And Muḥammad is His servant and His apostle. The departed bore witness that death is real, that Paradise is real, that Hell is real, and that the Resurrection is real. Upon this he lived, upon it he died and upon it, God willing, he will be resurrected again. O Lord, forgive him, be tolerant of him, illuminate his grave for him. Teach him how to plead his case and widen his path to heaven. Judge him by the best of his deeds and lead him to your Paradise. Join him with your Prophet Muḥammad, may the Peace and blessings of God be upon him, in your enduring good will. . . .[58]

In the ninth century, Egypt was still a heavily Christian country, and it is not surprising that we encounter expressly anti-Trinitarian formulations. For instance, ʿAbd al-Raḥmān b. Yaḥyā al-Maʿāfirī, who died in January 806, testified on his grave marker that "there is no god but God Himself, and He has no partner. And Muḥammad is His servant and His apostle. God is one, everlasting and single. He took no female companion and has no son. It is God who permits the living to die and who raises the dead to life. The Resurrection is His. Upon this the departed lived, upon it he died, and, God willing, upon it he will be resurrected to life."[59] By the later Middle Ages, however, many epitaphs seem to have become shorter and more utilitarian in content. For example, a tombstone from December, 1125 simply reads, "*Bismillah.* This is the grave of ʿAbd Allāh b. ʿAbd al-Majīd al-Maghrāwī. He died on ʿĪd al-Adḥā [in] the year five hundred and nineteen. May God have mercy upon whoever asks for God's mercy on his behalf."[60] An equally austere fourteenth-century stone states, "This is the grave of Fāṭima, daughter of Manṣūr. She died in the month of Rabīʿ al-Ākhar, seven hundred and twenty-seven [March, 1327]."[61]

---

[58] Combe, *RCEA*, 1:55–56, no. 71.

[59] Ibid., 57–58, no. 74. A number of tenth- and eleventh-century Muslim gravestones employ the Coptic month and the Islamic year in noting dates. See also nos. 1,466, 1,521, 1,559, 1,825, 2,317 and 2,318.

[60] *Bismillah* is a conventional contraction of *Bi-ism allāh al-raḥmān al-raḥīm* (In the Name of God, the Merciful, the Compassionate). Combe, *RCEA*, 8:145–46, no. 3,010.

[61] Ibid., 14:230–231, no. 5,540.

Not all late medieval markers were as basic as these two, as is demonstrated by an elaborate late fourteenth-century marble column from Alexandria reading:

> In the name of God the Merciful, the Compassionate. May the blessings of God be upon Muḥammad. "Every soul will taste of death. And ye will be paid on the Day of Resurrection only that which ye have fairly earned. Whosoever is removed from the Fire and is made to enter Paradise, he indeed is triumphant. The life of this world is but a comfort of illusion." Muḥammad, who is called with honor, Ibn ʿAbd al-ʿAzīz b. ʿAbd . . . died on Sunday, the seventh of the exalted month of Shaʿbān, seven hundred and seventy-eight [December 20, 1376].[62]

We find among these stones the epitaphs of many people, some great but most now long forgotten. Some speak to us eloquently across more than a millennium like these two, which vividly preserve in stone the pathos of anguished parents confronting the deaths of their infants:

> *Bismillah.* O Lord, ʿAmr ibn al-Ḥārith died as an infant with a natural predisposition for Islām, the word of salvation, the rightfulness of the faith, the community of Abraham and the religion of Muḥammad, may peace be upon him. O Lord, make him a reward, a beacon, an honor and a treasure, prepared in advance for his parents.[63] Fortify their hearts with patience and make greater their reward and their recompense. Join them together in your Paradise, O generous Lord! He died in Rabīʿ al-Ākhar, two hundred and forty-eight [June 862].[64]
>
> *Bismillah.* Accepting the Will of God, believing in His power and submitting to His command, this is the garden of the beautiful, graceful and handsome infant Abū ʿUmar b. Isḥāq b. Ibrāhīm . . . who drowned a blissful martyr. His Lord gave him to his parents as a young boy, and took him away from them chaste and pure. He was without sin or error when his Lord submerged him. He bore witness that there is no god but God Himself and He has no partner. And Muḥammad is His servant, His apostle and His prophet, may the blessings of God be upon him. Indeed his Lord has a greater claim on him than his parents. They consider him now to be with God. They say in his death: "You died small, but our grief is not small. You were once my

---

[62] Ibid., 17:267, no. 778,007. The verse is Qur'ānic, see 3:185.

[63] *Allāhum ijʿalahi li-wālidayhi faraṭan wa nūran wa karāmatan wa dhukhran.* For the translation of this expression see Lane, *Lexicon*, 2,377: "You say, of an infant that has died (Ṣ, Mṣb,) *O God, make him to be a [cause of] reward, or recompense, prepared in advance, or beforehand, for us.*"

[64] Combe, *RCEA*, 2:58, no. 480.

> scion, and you have become a sweet myrtle among the tombs."[65] Oh what marvelous and beautiful branches illuminate this plant in the garden of everlasting fortune! He died in Shawwāl, two hundred and fifty-nine [August 873].[66]

Scattered among the thousands of grave markers we find a few commemorating individuals mentioned in the medieval pilgrimage guides. For example: "This is the grave of the honest judge Ṣafī al-Dīn Abū Muḥammad ʿAbd al-Wahhāb Ibn al-Ṭāhir Ismāʿīl b. Muẓaffar b. al-Furāt. His death was proclaimed in the month of Rabīʿ al-Ākhar of the year five hundred and eighty-six [May 1190]."[67] The epitaphs speak to us, too, of the virtue of those buried as demonstrated through specific acts of piety.

> *Bismillah.* This is the grave of the humble servant, the virtuous woman who has performed the ḥajj, Khadīja, daughter of Shaykh Hārūn al-Maghrabiyya al-Dukāliyya. She performed the ḥajj fifteen times, thirteen times walking and twice riding. She recited the glorious Qur'ān in the seven ways of recitation, and she memorized the *Shāṭibiyya.* She was born in six hundred and forty and . . . [several words are missing]. O Lord, have mercy on whosoever asks for mercy on her behalf [November 14, 1295].[68]

The last line of this epitaph is particularly relevant here, as is the one of ʿAbd Allāh b. ʿAbd al-Majīd al-Maghrāwī cited above, because they both address future visitors to the grave and encourage specific action—pleading for God's mercy (taraḥḥum) on behalf of the dead. As one reads through the hundreds of gravestone inscriptions from Egypt, the regularity with which this and similar expressions appear is striking and attests to both the antiquity and the continuity of the ziyāra.[69]

As is typical with Western Christian funerary formulae, one can trace subtle shifts of expression in medieval Egyptian Islamic stelae. What is remarkable in this instance, however, is the continuity with which this particular formula is repeated, regardless of broader shifts

---

[65] *Kunta rīḥānatī fa qad aṣbaḥta rīḥānat al-qubūr.* There appears to be a play on the word *riḥān* here. It can mean bounty or offspring, or it can mean a myrtle tree. For the first sense see Lane *Lexicon,* 1,181–82.

[66] Combe, *RCEA,* 2:162–63, no. 631. See also corrections in 3:216.

[67] Ibid., 9:170, no. 3,442. See also nos. 3,225, 3,621 and 5,005, and Ibn al-Zayyāt, *al-Kawākib,* 246.

[68] Combe, *RCEA,* 13:140–41, no. 5,000.

[69] Ibid.; see, for example, 1:161–62, no. 204 (from the year 831); 4:91–92, no. 1,388 (from 945); 12:255–56, no. 4,785 (from 1280); and 15:79–80, no. 5,719 (from 1337).

in funerary idiom. From the late eighth and early ninth century, when we first begin to find sizable numbers of grave markers from Egypt, it is clear that visiting the tombs of the dead was already an accepted and well-established practice. Further, it is evident from these inscriptions that the dead and their visitors were engaged in a sort of mutually beneficial process of requesting God's mercy on behalf of each other. The reciprocal character of this intercession points to an important aspect of the ziyāra to which we shall return in Chapters 2 and 6.

In terms of the physical appearance of individual tombs, there seems to have been a limited range of styles.[70] Some graves were marked by an inscribed stone, whereas others were designated more elaborately by rectangular stone or wooden cenotaphs (tābūt) placed over them. A number of times the sources also refer to tombs in the shape of a "mastaba."[71] These citations apparently refer to cenotaphs, still prevalent today, which consist of a larger rectangular base upon which smaller rectangular levels are arranged like steps. The pilgrimage guides also mention two seemingly unusual tombs "built in the shape of a pyramid."[72] For the vast majority of less privileged Egyptians, however, death—like life—seems to have offered humbler accommodations. Unfortunately, these simpler graves have not withstood the test of time, but one suspects that, as is the case in modern Egyptian cemeteries, the graves of the poor were not fundamentally different from those of the wealthy, only cruder and less durable examples of widely accepted cultural prototypes. Instead of a well-cut and inscribed gravestone of marble, for example, a simple tomb may have been designated only by a large rock or a crudely shaped and uninscribed stone marker.

By the later Middle Ages, al-Qarāfa was a confusing place. The passage of time, the accretion of many centuries of burial, habitation, and construction, the destructive scavenging of ancient or abandoned sites for building materials, expansions and restorations of earlier structures, as well as the wear and tear of heavy traffic through the cemetery had all taken their toll. This was not, as we have said, a

[70] See Ory, *Cimetières et inscriptions*, for a good discussion of tomb typology, especially pages 11–14 and plates 2–9.

[71] Ibn al-Zayyāt, *al-Kawākib*, 123; and Ibn al-Nāsikh, *Miṣbāḥ*, fols. 35r° and 71r°.

[72] Ibn Uthmān, *Murshid*, 277; and al-Sakhāwī, *Tuḥfat*, 186.

"city of the dead," frozen in time; it was also a place of the living. Transformations, decline, expansion, and shifts in the active focus of the cemetery were as much a part of the development of al-Qarāfa as they were for other parts of the city. All of these factors combined to make the Qarāfa a maze for the uninitiated.

The pilgrimage guides frequently mention the deterioration of specific tombs as well as the decline of larger expanses of the cemetery. For example, while referring to tombs near the grave of the Mālikī jurist Ibn Thaʿlab, al-Sakhāwī reports: "among these tombs now not one is distinguishable from another."[73] Ibn al-Nāsikh tells us that all the graves between the tomb of Abū al-Ḥusayn al-Jallād and the Mosque of al-ʿAṣāfīrī were destroyed.[74] Ibn al-Zayyāt notes, among other casualties, "a large stone mausoleum of which nothing remains except the qibla wall."[75] Al-Sakhāwī mentions a turba in which "most of the graves have been destroyed and no longer have tombstones."[76] The authors of the guides themselves were clearly aware of the process of deterioration, and remark on the transformation of certain sites since the descriptions of previous writers. For instance, while noting Ibn al-Nāsikh's report of the large tomb of the merchant Faḍl b. Baḥr, with its impressive marble tombstone, Ibn al-Zayyāt, writing about a century later, concludes, "it is now a pile of dust."[77] In still another instance, while describing the cemetery of al-Jārūdī, Ibn al-Zayyāt acknowledges that according to al-Qurashī's earlier account there were numerous tombs and mausolea between Jawsaq al-Mādhrāʾī and the Qubba of Fāṭima al-Sughrā and Fāṭima al-Kubrā, which "have since been destroyed and have become part of one graveyard now known as Maqbarat al-Jārūdī."[78]

The passage of more than five centuries of active use is enough to account for a good portion of the ruin noted in the sources. But there were other forces at work, as well. Take, for example, the transfer of graves to create space for new building projects. One of

[73] Al-Sakhāwī, *Tuḥfat*, 355.

[74] Ibn al-Nāsikh, *Miṣbāḥ*, fol. 50r°. For similar observations, see fols. 16r° and 54v°.

[75] Ibn al-Zayyāt, *al-Kawākib*, 122.

[76] Al-Sakhāwī, *Tuḥfat*, 237.

[77] Ibid., 42–43. Ibn al-Zayyāt, *al-Kawākib*, 43. He also relates that Ibn al-Nāsikh described the tomb of Zaynab, daughter of al-ʿAbājilī, as "a beautifully built qubba." The observation "*kān qabruhā*" clearly indicates that her tomb could no longer be so characterized by Ibn al-Zayyāt's time.

[78] Ibn al-Zayyāt, *al-Kawākib*, 156.

the most notable accounts of this sort of relocation was the construction of the Mausoleum of Imām al-Shāfiʿī in the midst of the Banū Zahra cemetery. To provide the necessary room for this huge structure, a number of graves, many containing the remains of descendants of the famous historian Ibn ʿAbd al-Ḥakam, were moved to Maqbarat al-ʿAynāʾ.[79] Theft was yet another problem. The grave of Shaykh ʿAbd al-Nūr was left as only a pile of earth after the carved wooden cenotaph that once marked it was stolen.[80] More significant was the appropriation of elements of existing structures by the builders of new monuments. The Mamlūk sultan al-Muʾayyad Shaykh (r. 1412–1421) was notorious for this sort of plunder when he built his great communal mosque just inside Bāb Zuwayla, but he was certainly not alone in this practice.[81]

The restoration of various sites in al-Qarāfa also altered the landscape of the cemetery. There were many occasions on which wealthy patrons sought to repair or "rebuild" neglected or damaged structures. The Fāṭimid caliph al-Ḥākim built the Luʾluʾa Mosque in 1015/16 on the site of an earlier mosque. And we have already noted that Jāmiʿ al-Qarāfa was built in 976 on the site of an earlier mosque. In addition to the reconstruction and repair, there were frequent additions and modifications to earlier structures. Sites viewed as particularly sacred were likely to undergo significant alterations as wealthy and powerful patrons sought to express their own reverence, affection, or gratitude by expanding existing monuments. Likewise, existing mausolea were often expanded to accommodate those wishing to be buried in close proximity to a saint. This seems to have been the process at work in the mausolea of both Sayyida Nafīsa and her brother Yaḥyā.[82]

Although these rebuilding and expansion efforts guaranteed the renewed or continued importance of such sites, they obviously also contributed to the constantly changing face of the Qarāfa. There were undoubtedly many other random well-intended and informal efforts by individuals to counter the continual effects of deterioration

[79] Ibid., 209. There is another mention of the transfer of a number of "kings, amirs, and viziers" on 278.

[80] Ibn al-Zayyāt, *al-Kawākib*, 321; and al-Sakhāwī, *Tuḥfat*, 402.

[81] Al-Maqrīzī, *Khiṭaṭ*, 2:329.

[82] Creswell, *MAE*, 1:264–69. Rāghib, "Les sanctuaires des gens de la famille," especially 61–71. He demonstrates conclusively that Creswell misunderstood the history and organization of this structure.

in the cemetery, which would explain why we encounter so many incorrectly reset gravestones. For instance, al-Sakhāwī remarks that although the ancient marble stele at a certain grave states that it marks the tomb of Shaykh ʿUmar b. Ḥafs, this is actually the tomb of the jurist Jamāl al-Dīn ʿAbd Allāh b. Abū Jaʿfar al-Laythī.[83]

Heavy pilgrimage traffic through the Qarāfa was yet another cause of much destruction in parts of the graveyard. In early May 1442, for example, the Mamlūk sultan al-Ẓāhir Jaqmaq (r. 1438–1453) descended from the Citadel and visited the area surrounding Bāb al-Qarāfa. He was appalled by the deterioration of the area and the debasement of tombs caused in large part by the comings and goings of pilgrims performing the ziyāra. The sultan therefore ordered Bāb al-Khūlī closed permanently except for one day during the month of Rajab for the annual pre-pilgrimage procession of the maḥmal, in order to protect the tombs in this area.[84]

The continuous physical transformation of al-Qarāfa was not the only factor that made al-Qarāfa a confusing place. The cemetery was filled with incorrectly identified graves. In many cases mistakes were caused by an innocent confusion caused by a similarity in names. In other instances, however, the claims were too fantastic to be explained by casual error. For example, we find near the Luʾluʾa Mosque, just below the Jabal al-Muqaṭṭam, a mausoleum still known today as Ikhwāt Yūsuf. During the later Middle Ages this tomb was widely believed to contain the remains of Yasaʿ and Rūbayl, children of the Prophet Jacob. While denying the authenticity of this site, al-Sakhāwī describes the process by which this belief gained wide circulation. He explains that many years earlier a man spent the night near this site and during his stay recited the twelfth Sūra of the Qurʾān, "Joseph." Later, while sleeping, the man experienced a vision in which he was asked: "This is our story, who told it to

---

[83] Al-Sakhāwī, *Tuḥfat*, 204.

[84] Ibid., 159. The maḥmal was a richly decorated camel-borne palanquin, usually containing only a copy or two of the Qurʾān. The maḥmal was carried at the front or in the middle of the great pilgrimage caravans to Mecca. This practice, which began in 1266 under the Mamlūk sultan Baybars (r. 1260–1277), was intended to signify the political independence of Muslim rulers. A complete history of this practice can be found in the excellent study by Jacques Jomier, *Le maḥmal*; see also also *EI*^{2}, s.v. Maḥmal. Dawrat al-maḥmal was a procession in which the palanquin was marched through various parts of Cairo before the pilgrimage. For an early nineteenth-century account of this procession, see Lane, *Manners and Customs*, 475–82.

you?" The man responded that his source was the Qur'ān and then he queried the person in his dream as to their identity. The dream visitor responded: "Rūbayl, brother of Joseph." When the man awoke from his sleep he informed everyone of what he had experienced. People believed in his dream, and the mausoleum was subsequently constructed.[85] As we have noted above, such mashāhid al-ru'yā were fairly common in al-Qarāfa.

We also find a host of graves dubiously identified as those of associates, friends, and servants of the Prophet Muḥammad. There was, for instance, the tomb of Bilāl b. Rabāḥ (d. 641), the first person designated by the Prophet Muḥammad to announce the Islamic call to prayer.[86] When the tomb of "the holder of the Prophet's cloak" was doubted, al-Sakhāwī informs us, the grave was unearthed and a corpse was found still wrapped in the robe.[87] This exhumation supposedly confirmed the identity of the tomb because the corpse had not deteriorated despite its long interment. Notwithstanding an inscribed tombstone to the contrary, we also come across a grave popularly believed to be that of 'Antar, "the neighbor of the Prophet Muḥammad."[88] Even the tomb of "the Prophet's jeweler" was identified, as was that of his standard bearer.[89] Finally, we find a grave that is identified as belonging to "the suckling brother of the Prophet."[90]

As any tour of al-Qarāfa would quickly reveal, the Prophet Muḥammad was not the only major figure in early Islamic history whose associates, however obscure, found their way into this most famous of Egyptian cemeteries. An inscription designating the tomb of "Asmā' daughter of Abū Bakr," for instance, was attributed to the daughter of the first caliph, Abū Bakr al-Ṣiddīq (d. 634).[91] From the 'Umayyad

---

[85] Al-Sakhāwī, *Tuḥfat*, 373–74.

[86] Ibn al-Nāsikh, *Miṣbāḥ*, fol. 11r°; and al-Sakhāwī, *Tuḥfat*, 149.

[87] Al-Sakhāwī, *Tuḥfat*, 266. See also Ibn al-Nāsikh, *Miṣbāḥ*, fol. 49v°; and Ibn 'Uthmān, *Murshid*, 294.

[88] Ibn al-Nāsikh, *Miṣbāḥ*, fol. 16r°. The identity of this individual is unclear. Perhaps there was a confusion in the popular imagination, and the great pre-Islamic poet 'Antar b. 'Amr b. Shaddād, who figures in the famous romance *Sīrat 'Antar*, was cast as a neighbor and companion of the Prophet Muḥammad.

[89] Ibn al-Zayyāt, *al-Kawākib*, 117, 303; and Ibn al-Nāsikh, *Miṣbāḥ*, fols. 43r°–43v°, 69v°.

[90] Al-Sakhāwī, *Tuḥfat*, 267; Ibn 'Uthmān, *Murshid*, 294; and Ibn al-Nāsikh, *Miṣbāḥ*, fol. 49v°. This would have been 'Abd Allāh b. Ḥārith, the son of Ḥalīma d. Abū Dhu'ayb, who was the Prophet's wet-nurse. See Ibn Hishām, 1:160–61; Guillaume, trans. as *Life of Muhammad*, 70.

[91] Ibn 'Uthmān, *Murshid*, 419.

period we find a grave variously identified as belonging to Muʿāwiyya, the first ʿUmayyad caliph (r. 661–680), or to his son and successor Yazīd (r. 680–683).[92] Challengers to the authority of the Banū ʿUmayya are also represented, as in the case of the erroneously identified grave of ʿAbd Allāh b. Zubayr noted above.[93] Nor were the ʿAbbāsids neglected in this creative process of historical recovery; we find what is supposed to be the tomb of al-Sabtī, a son of the famous caliph Harūn al-Rashīd (r. 786–809); who was actually buried in Iraq.[94] The Qarāfa was also rich in tombs, many of them spurious, of major figures in the ʿAlid drama. For instance, Ibn al-Nāsikh is incredulous that Fāṭima the daughter of a certain Isḥāq has been identified as Fāṭima b. al-Ḥusayn, the granddaughter of ʿAlī b. Abī Ṭālib, even though an original inscription in marble is present at the grave and correctly identifies the woman actually buried there.[95] Likewise, a certain ʿAnbasa is identified as the commander of ʿAlī's army, even though there is no such person cited as occupying this post in the traditional sources.[96] The graves of two unknown sons of Jaʿfar al-Ṣādiq, the sixth Shīʿite Imām, are also mentioned.[97]

Whether the result of a simple confusion between names, or any of a host of other causes, al-Qarāfa was full of incorrectly and even absurdly identified tombs. Ibn al-Nāsikh tells us, "In Cairo there are tombs which are not correct. There are written on them names which are wrong."[98] Ibn al-Zayyāt was even more emphatic, he stated, "there is disagreement about most of the tombs of the Egyptians."[99] The constant physical changes in the graveyard, the vastness of al-Qarāfa, and the complicating factor of incorrectly attributed graves all combined to make this a place of considerable confusion. But there was a solution. There were, as we shall explore in the next chapter, a host of experts and guides ever ready to assist pilgrims unfamiliar with the cemetery in navigating this "great medium of divine blessing" in search of the special friends of God.

---

92 Al-Sakhāwī, *Tuḥfat*, 162.

93 Ibn al-Zayyāt, *al-Kawākib*, 141.

94 Al-Sakhāwī, *Tuḥfat*, 270; Ibn al-Nāsikh, *Miṣbāḥ*, fol. 51r°; and Ibn ʿUthmān, *Murshid*, 292.

95 Ibn al-Nāsikh, *Miṣbāḥ*, fol. 23v°.

96 Ibn al-Zayyāt, *al-Kawākib*, 46; Ibn al-Nāsikh, *Miṣbāḥ*, fols. 23v°–24r°. Both sources identify Abū Mūsa al-Ashʿarī as the leader of ʿAlī's forces.

97 Ibn al-Nāsikh, *Miṣbāḥ*, fols. 5v° and 28v°.

98 Ibid., fol. 4v°.

99 Ibn al-Zayyāt, *al-Kawākib*, 103.

Baraka

Let us return for a moment to Ibn Abī Ḥajala's painful task of selecting a place to bury his dead son, because in making this critical choice he goes to the heart of the nexus between place and understandings of the holy in the thought-world of his contemporaries. Although most of his book is devoted to recounting the life and accomplishments of Sīdī ʿUqba, and providing a compilation of all ḥadīth related on ʿUqba's authority, Ibn Abī Ḥajala also provides a thoughtful explanation of why it was so important to bury his son Muḥammad near this saint's tomb. In the fifth chapter of *Jiwār al-akhyār* he explains that it is essential to bury the dead close to persons whose righteousness and grace is assured and as far from the graves of the sinful as possible.[100] He begins this discussion with a famous and still common Arabic proverb: "choose the neighbor before the house, and the companion before the journey" (al-jār qabl al-dār wa-al-rafīq qabl al-ṭarīq). His point is that one's associates and neighbors in death, just as in life, bring either benefit or harm. This position is reinforced with a Qurʾānic citation and a series of ḥadīth.

The verse Ibn Abī Ḥajala selects from the Qur'ān relates to the story of Āsiya, "the wife of Pharaoh" who was martyred by her husband for her monotheistic beliefs. The doomed woman's plea for God to deliver her from the company of wrongdoers is offered by Ibn Abī Ḥajala as proof reflecting the general desire of the righteous to be free from the company of evildoers: "And Allah citeth an example for those who believe: the wife of Pharaoh when she said: My Lord! Build for me a home with thee in the Garden, and deliver me from Pharaoh and his work, and deliver me from evil-doing folk" (66:11). The author of the *Jiwār* then provides several ḥadīths in which the Prophet specifically instructs Muslims to bury their dead among the righteous because the dead are offended by bad neighbors, just as the living are. Good neighbors, by comparison, are a benefit for both the living and the dead. The ʿulamā, according to Ibn Abī Ḥajala, also report that we bury the dead near the righteous, thereby seeking God's blessing for them.[101]

Just as being close to the graves of saints can benefit the dead, proximity to the graves of the sinful can be harmful. For example,

[100] Ibn Abī Ḥajala, *Jiwār al-akhyār*, fols. 37v°–41v°.
[101] Ibid., fol. 38r°–38v°.

a dead woman once came to members of her family in their dreams to ask why they had buried her near a kiln. Upon awaking, her family went to the location of the grave but were unable to find a kiln anywhere nearby. Upon inquiring who was buried near her, they discovered that an executioner was. Since the heat emanating from the evil man's tomb was causing the dead woman such great discomfort, her body was exhumed and buried elsewhere.[102]

When a certain Aʿrābī's dead son visited him in a dream, Aʿrābī asked his son what had become of him. The son reassured his father that he was fine except for the fact that he was buried near the grave of a sinner, and the agonizing sounds of the dead man enduring his punishment in the grave were frightful and disturbing.[103] Zubayda also visited ʿAbd Allāh b. al-Mubārak after her death in one of his dreams. He asked what judgment God rendered on her, and she assured him that God had forgiven her. Then ʿAbd Allāh asked why her face had become yellow, and ʿAbd Allāh began to shudder as Zubayda explained this was caused by having to listen to the groans of an evil man buried nearby.[104]

Ṭāwūs b. Dhukrān al-Yamānī once saw the candle of an approaching funeral procession while praying in a cemetery near a freshly dug grave. The person buried near the open grave suddenly begged Ṭāwūs to protect him from the fate of an evil neighbor. After completing his prayers, Ṭāwūs went to meet the funeral procession to ask if they would consider burying the body in another place. They refused, pointing out that the new grave had already been prepared. Ṭāwūs then asked to speak to the leader of the procession, who was the son of the dead man. He pleaded with the son not to bury his father there, in exchange for which Ṭāwūs offered his own fine robe, purchased in Yemen for seventy dīnārs. Even after being assured that Ṭāwūs's fine robe would bring at least ninety dīnārs, the son refused, doubting the value of the offer. Ṭāwūs then asked if those in the funeral procession knew the reputation of Ṭāwūs al-Yamānī. When they responded they did, Ṭāwūs revealed his identity and assured them he was telling the truth about the robe's value. Ṭāwūs and the son of the dead man then exchanged robes and the funeral procession departed, taking the corpse with them. Ṭāwūs went to

---

102 Ibid., fol. 38vº.
103 Ibid.
104 Ibid., fols. 39vº–40rº.

the grave from which the plea for assistance emanated and he offered his assurance that he would never let a offensive neighbor be placed nearby as long as it could be prevented.[105]

On the basis of such testimony, there could be little doubt in Ibn Abī Ḥajala's mind that choosing the right neighborhood for his son's body was a matter of great consequence. In the preface to *Jiwār al-akhyār*, Ibn Abī Ḥajala expressed his own fervent hope that one day he too would be laid to rest near the grave of Sīdī ʿUqba. In this way the shaykh also hoped to be encompassed by God's mercy, which he believed was spread through the blessing (baraka) of the saint to those buried around him in the cemetery.[106]

When the jurist Fakhr al-Dīn ʿAlī b. al-Qafṣī was near death he requested that he be buried in the turba of Shaykh Abū al-Faḍl b. al-Jawharī, so as to obtain some of the saint's baraka. And the judge Abū Muḥammad al-Zahrī asked on his deathbed to be buried near the tomb of Shaykh al-Mufaḍḍal b. Faḍāla, also in order to receive some of the saint's baraka.[107] Al-Muzanī stated near his death that he wished to be laid to rest near the tomb of Shaybān al-Rāʿī because the saint "was a gnostic of God" (fa-innahu kān ʿārifan bi-llāh).[108] Shaykh Ḥusayn al-Shādhilī asked to be buried near the tomb of his teacher. The aged Shaykh Hibat al-ʿAttāl, who died while performing the ziyāra, even picked out his own grave site and announced he would die that very day—which he did.[109]

The pilgrimage guides make clear that there were many important tombs in the Qarāfa that functioned like great magnets to attract those wishing to pass the barzakh, that interval between death and resurrection, near the baraka of a saint.[110] For example, the tomb of Imām al-Layth stood in the midst of the Maqbarat al-Ṣadafiyīn, surrounded by four hundred tombs.[111] The great mausoleum of Imām

---

105 Ibid., fols. 38v°–39r°.

106 Ibid., fol. 2r°.

107 Ibn al-Zayyāt, *al-Kawākib*, 125, 140; al-Sakhāwī, *Tuḥfat*, 254, 263; and Ibn al-Nāsikh, *Miṣbāḥ*, fols. 42r°, 48r°.

108 Al-Sakhāwī, *Tuḥfat*, 305. This is a difficult concept to translate into English, but it essentially implies an inner mystical knowledge of God. Gnosis is the closest equivalent. See Nasr, *Sufi Essays*, 160.

109 Ibn al-Zayyāt, *al-Kawākib*, 157, 320; al-Sakhāwī, *Tuḥfat*, 276; Ibn al-Nāsikh, *Miṣbāḥ*, fol. 33r°; and Ibn ʿUthmān, *Murshid*, 270.

110 For a discussion of barzakh, see Smith and Haddad, *The Islamic Understanding of Death*, 7–8.

111 Ibn al-Zayyāt, *al-Kawākib*, 105, and al-Sakhāwī, *Tuḥfat*, 231–33.

al-Shāfiʿī, as we have noted, became an especially desirable place to bury the dead in the later Middle Ages. But the Ayyūbid sultan al-Malik al-Kāmil was not the only major political figure to build a massive tomb in al-Qarāfa. Powerful patrons sometimes went to great lengths to establish impressive burial complexes for themselves and their families. The inclusion of a saint's tomb and even Ṣūfī khānqāhs were often essential features of these massive funerary complexes. For example, the Amir Ṭughā Tumr al-Najmī built a turba-khānqāh complex that included a bath and shops around it. He populated the structure with Ṣūfīs and Qur'ān reciters so that those buried there would benefit from the baraka of the mystics and from constant recitation of the Qur'ān.[112]

During the last half of the period covered by this study the trend toward the construction of enormous royal burial complexes accelerated. Al-Qarāfa was already too crowded to support ambitious new building initiatives, so the Northern Cemetery began to emerge as a major new necropolis in the early fourteenth century. The area was soon dominated by the imposing Mamlūk imperial funerary architecture that still impresses visitors to Cairo. Al-Maqrīzī, for instance, tells us how Sultan Nāṣir al-Dīn Faraj (r. 1399–1405 and 1405–1412) built the large structure housing the grave of his father, Sultan Barqūq (r. 1382–1389 and 1390–1399) in the Northern Cemetery.[113] This impressive complex, which still stands, also included cells and a burial place for Ṣūfīs, almost certainly to guarantee that the dead sultan would be close to a perpetual source of baraka. In addition, Sultan Nāṣir al-Dīn Faraj built near the tomb a mill, a public bath, and an oven. He also transferred the camel and donkey markets here from below the Citadel, and al-Maqrīzī reports that he intended to build a large caravansary near the tomb to house traveling merchants. After Faraj's death in 1412, however, the camel and donkey markets were returned to their traditional locations, and the whole complex was soon abandoned. By combining so many functions in the mausoleum dedicated to the memory of his father, Faraj may have sought to replicate in the Northern Cemetery al-Qarāfa's character as an urban space for the living as well as a burial place for the dead. To counteract the effects of the considerable distance and relative isolation of the new site from the traditional centers of daily

---

112 Al-Maqrīzī, *Khiṭaṭ*, 2:464.
113 Ibid.

life in and around Cairo, the sultan was inspired to redirect forcibly at least part of the city's commercial activity to the huge monument he was building in the desolate expanse northeast of Cairo.

The saints themselves, however, were not always cooperative with the building plans of powerful patrons. When Sultan al-Malik al-Kāmil sought the permission of the famous mystic Ibn al-Fāriḍ (d. 1235) to prepare a tomb for him near the grave of the sultan's mother in the mausoleum of Imām al-Shāfiʿī, Ibn al-Fāriḍ flatly refused. He also subsequently turned down the sultan's offer to establish a suitable tomb in a place that would attract pious visitors, (zuwwār). Nevertheless, when Ibn al-Fāriḍ was finally laid to rest in 1235 at the base of the Jabal al-Muqaṭṭam, his tomb did become an important destination of the ziyāra. The site also attracted other saints and prominent Ḥanafī jurists wishing to be buried near him.[114]

The demand for burial space near saints was so great that abuses occasionally arose in the allocation of burial plots. For instance, al-Sakhāwī relates how a famous mausoleum, known as Turbat al-Ṣūfiyya, was debased into a gathering place for women and a general site of revelry when the guardian of the complex began accepting payments in exchange for allowing a large number of corrupt people to be buried in this holy place.[115] Abū al-Ṭayyib Kharūf may have been concerned about such corruption near his own grave because he specifically asked God to allow him to be buried alone. When a group of people subsequently tried to bury someone near this saint's tomb, blithely dismissing warnings against such action, they were unpleasantly surprised the next day to find the newly buried corpse disinterred. Thereafter greater care was taken not to bury the dead near the grave of Abū al-Ṭayyib Kharūf.[116]

The general sanctity associated with the graves of saints and the powerful force of the baraka connected to them were widely acknowledged in medieval Egypt. Even a great opponent of the cult of the saints such as Aḥmad b. Taymiyya freely admitted: "the fact that these places are avoided by evil spirits and animals, the immunity from fire of these places and their visitors, the intercession of some saints for those buried near them, the commendability of being buried

---

[114] Ibn al-Zayyāt, *al-Kawākib*, 297–98. See also Homerin, *From Arab Poet*, 34–35.
[115] Al-Sakhāwī, *Tuḥfat*, 32.
[116] Ibn al-Zayyāt, *al-Kawākib*, 245; al-Sakhāwī, *Tuḥfat*, 348; and Ibn ʿUthmān, *Murshid*, 355.

near such saints, attainment of grace in their neighborhood and visitation of chastisement upon those who make light of them—these things are all true."[117] In a moment of profound grief, as he buried his son Muḥammad near the tomb of Sīdī ʿUqba, Ibn Abī Ḥajala was clearly acting on a deeply and widely held conviction about the importance of saints as repositories of divine blessing.

As known repositories of baraka, the tombs of the awliyāʾ also indicated special places where prayers of supplication might be offered with particular effectiveness. Such supplicatory prayers, known in Arabic as duʿāʾ, are distinct from the ritual prayers (ṣalāt) that Muslims perform five times each day. Duʿāʾ might be offered on behalf of the dead as well as the living, and these personal petitions were an important aspect of the ziyāra.

As the pilgrimage guides and other contemporary sources make clear, the tombs of the saints were widely viewed as particularly efficacious places from which to offer duʿāʾ. The phrase consistently repeated in the sources is makān maʿrūf bi-ijābat al-duʿāʾ, (a place known for the fulfillment of prayer). Because the baraka associated with saints remained present even after their deaths, the graves of the saints attracted an endless stream of visitors hoping that their duʿāʾ might be accepted by God through the agency of the saints. Thus, visitors to the grave of Muʿīn al-Dīn Abū al-Ḥasan were told "the fulfillment of duʿāʾ in this place is known." Likewise, the tomb of Fāṭima the daughter of al-Ashʿath was "tested for the fulfillment of duʿāʾ." Abū Aḥmad b. ʿAbd Allāh b. al-Ḥasan al-Muthannā b. al-Ḥasan al-Ṣibt b. ʿAlī b. Abī Ṭālib was buried in "a small mashhad in which duʿāʾ is fulfilled." Supplication offered near the tombs of Aḥmad b. Ibrāhīm b. Sunān al-Baṣrī and his brother Muḥammad would be "answered." The miḥrāb in the tomb of Yaʿīsh al-Gharābilī was also thought to be a particularly efficacious place to supplicate. Likewise, whoever stood between the tombs of al-Anbārī and al-Muḥāmilī and performed the duʿāʾ would surely be answered. Those who stood with their backs to the partially collapsed qubba of Fāṭima al-Ṣughrā and Fāṭima al-Kubrā, faced in the direction of the tomb of al-Idfūwī, spread their hands and performed the duʿāʾ, were also likely to be answered.[118] A sick man on the verge of death was in-

---

[117] Memon, *Ibn Taimīya's Struggle*, 294. For the Arabic text see Ibn Taymiyya, *Iqtiḍāʾ al-ṣirāṭ*, 374–75.

[118] Ibn al-Zayyāt, *al-Kawākib*, 55, 79, 89, 147–48, 156; Ibn al-Nāsikh, *Miṣbāḥ*, fol. 20r°, 41v°.

structed in a dream to go to the tomb of Shaykh Abū Muḥammad ʿAbd al-ʿAzīz b. Aḥmad b. Jaʿfar al-Khwārizmī and beseech God for assistance. He went and was cured.[119] These are only a handful of the countless examples that occur repeatedly in the sources. They testify both to the importance of the duʿāʾ as a seminal activity of the cult of the saints and to the significance of the tombs of the saints as reservoirs of baraka, famous for their efficacy as places in which to supplicate God.

Duʿāʾ might be offered by groups of supplicants as well as by individuals. A famous example of a mass collective offering of duʿāʾ occurred during a recurrence of the plague in the spring of 1419. On May 11, Sultan al-Muʾayyad Shaykh, dressed only in the simple robe of a Ṣūfī mystic, rode out to the barren expanse of the Northern Cemetery in a great procession that included the caliph, the chief qāḍīs, leading members of the ʿulamāʾ, a number of Ṣūfī brotherhoods, and much of the general populace. Upon his arrival the sultan spread his hands and led the assembled crowd in the performance of duʿāʾ, seeking deliverance from the plague.[120] Early in 1349, during the cataclysmic visitation of the Black Death on Cairo, thirty thousand people are said to have attended the funeral of Shaykh ʿAbd Allāh al-Munūfī because his death occurred on the same day people went to the cemetery to perform duʿāʾ seeking deliverance from the plague.[121] Beyond these dramatic examples arising from moments of particular crisis, however, the duʿāʾ was also offered collectively on more routine occasions, such as the weekly ziyārāt through the Qarāfa.

The baraka enveloping the tombs of dead saints was also frequently associated with amazing miracles and great medicinal powers. A recurrent theme is the healing effect of the dust from certain graves. For example, some mashāyikh al-ziyāra contended that dust from the grave of al-ʿAqīlī was efficacious in curing unspecified afflictions.[122] Dust from the tomb of Abū al-Ḥasan al-Ṣāyigh was said to cure back pain, and might be rubbed on various parts of the body to relieve other complaints, as well.[123] Those suffering from eye disease were urged to rub dust from the tomb of Shaykh Abū al-Ḥasan ʿAlī

[119] Ibn ʿUthmān, *Murshid*, 327; and Ibn al-Nāsikh, *Miṣbāḥ*, fol. 41vº.
[120] Ibn Tagrī Birdī, *al-Nujūm al-zāhira*, 14:77–79 translated in Popper, *History of Egypt*, 64–65. Also cited in Dols, *Black Death*, 248–49.
[121] Al-Sakhāwī, *Tuḥfat*, 52.
[122] Ibn al-Zayyāt, *al-Kawākib*, 197, and al-Sakhāwī, *Tuḥfat*, 308.
[123] Ibn ʿUthmān, *Murshid*, 337–38.

b. Ṣāliḥ al-Andalusī in their eyes.[124] Pilgrims also used to wallow in the dust of the tombs of Sanā and Thanāʾ, even though this practice was discouraged. Similarly, water used to wash the corpses of dead saints in preparation for burial was also valued for medicinal uses. For example, the water used to bathe the body of Shaykh Abū al-Qāsim al-Aqṭaʿ was carefully collected as it rolled off the saint's body and was put into kohl bottles for use in curing eye diseases. Much the same story is told about Shaykh ʿAbd Allāh al-Asmar.[125]

These examples illustrate yet another way in which the saints, in their capacity as great repositories of divine blessing, attracted zuwwār. But not everyone who came to the tombs of the saints was seeking immediate assistance for specific problems. Many zuwwār sought only to be in the presence of the baraka associated with saints. Rubbing, kissing, touching, or applying the dust of holy tombs were all manifestations of this intensely physical dimension of the cult of the saints, which we consider further in Chapter 4.

Peter Brown, in his study of the cult of Christian saints in late antiquity, discusses the concept of praesentia, which bears comparison with the notion of baraka as it was understood in the medieval Islamic world. Brown defines praesentia as "the physical presence of the holy," and he stresses that the cult of Christian saints "gloried in particularity." The most significant difference between praesentia and baraka seems to have been the portability of the former. In the Christian experience the blessing attached to the person of the saint came to apply equally to every fragment of the physical remains, regardless of how infinitesimal those remnants might be. This attitude opened the way to an endless division and transfer of the earthly remains of saints throughout Christendom in late antiquity and the early medieval period. Brown stresses that it was the translation of relics, with their elaborate ceremonials of adventus, or arrival, that characterized the cult of Christian saints in this period, rather than the pilgrimage of people to the remains of the saints.[126] This dismemberment of the physical remains of saints would have been deeply offensive to Muslim sensibilities as a violation of the sanctity

[124] Ibid.; Ibn al-Zayyāt, *al-Kawākib*, 119; al-Sakhāwī, *Tuḥfat*, 248–49; and Ibn al-Nāsikh, *Miṣbāḥ*, fol. 44v°.

[125] Ibn al-Zayyāt, *al-Kawākib*, 201, 207, 244–45; al-Sakhāwī, *Tuḥfat*, 314, 348; and Ibn ʿUthmān, *Murshid*, 357–58.

[126] Brown, *Cult of the Saints*, 88–89.

of the grave and an appalling lack of respect for the dead. The simple act of moving or disturbing graves was enough to generate substantial anxiety in the Muslim community. Death, in the Muslim understanding, was only a sequel to life, and burial marked no fundamental boundary between the two. The dead were due the same courtesy and respect they received in life. This attitude explains why the cult of relics never became well established in the Islamic world, and the baraka of Muslim saints was not made portable through the translation of their relics. Even minor exceptions such as the water collected in small kohl bottles from the freshly washed bodies of the saints, or the application of dust from certain tombs for medicinal purposes, seem to have remained closely linked to the actual site of the grave.

In the crowded and confusing environment of al-Qarāfa it must have been reassuring that there were frequently unmistakable, and even fantastic, physical signs pinpointing the exact location of saints' tombs, especially those which could no longer be otherwise identified. One of the most common signs was the mysterious appearance of light over tombs. For instance, the lost tomb of al-Sayyida al-Sharīfa Maryam, the daughter of ʿAbd Allāh b. Aḥmad b. Ismāʿīl b. al-Qāsim al-Rassī b. Ṭabāṭabā, was rediscovered when the people of Gīza saw a column of light over it. Light also marked the grave of Abū Bakr al-Iṣṭablī.[127] An unknown saint near the tomb of Ibn al-Fāriḍ was referred to as the "possessor of the candle" because a candle usually appeared at his grave on dark nights.[128] Another unknown saint was referred to simply as ṣāḥib al-nūr, "possessor of the light" because a shaft of light was commonly seen over his tomb on Friday nights. Still another unidentified saint was noted by the authors of all four pilgrimage guides as the "possessor of the lamp" because a lamp also frequently marked his grave on dark nights.[129]

The miraculous appearance of light was the most common indicator of the location of baraka, but there were other signs as well. For instance, visitors to the tomb of ʿAbd al-Jabbār Ibn al-Farrāsh

---

[127] Ibn al-Zayyāt, *al-Kawākib*, 184, and al-Sakhāwī, *Tuḥfat*, 298, 379.

[128] Al-Sakhāwī, *Tuḥfat*, 380, and Ibn al-Zayyāt, *al-Kawākib*, 297. An identical story is told of another saint also known as ṣāḥib al-shamʿ. See Ibn al-Zayyāt, *al-Kawākib*, 189; and al-Sakhāwī, *Tuḥfat*, 301.

[129] Ibn al-Zayyāt, *al-Kawākib*, 127, 220; al-Sakhāwī, *Tuḥfat*, 255–56, 329; and Ibn al-Nāsikh, *Miṣbāḥ*, fols. 24r°, 44v°; and ʿUthmān, *Murshid*, 327.

often detected a pleasant smell there.[130] Saints were also believed to be immune from the physical corruption of the grave.[131] Thus, the graves of saints were sometimes discovered accidentally when their tomb was mistakenly opened, revealing a pristine corpse inside.

Al-Qarāfa in sacred geography and urban space

Al-Qarāfa was more than the sum of its parts. It was above all a place of ancient sanctity, characterized by a sacred quality established long before the Arab conquest of Egypt—established long before even the birth of the Prophet Muḥammad. It was here, in the shadows of the Jabal al-Muqaṭṭam, that descendants of Noah were said to have settled before establishing Memphis, the first city in Egypt.[132] Here too Jacob once lived, and Joseph was initially buried.[133] Jesus, standing on the Muqaṭṭam hills, was said to have predicted to his mother Mary that one day members of Muḥammad's community (umma) would bury their dead on the plateau below.[134] It was this same barren and seemingly useless tract of land that Cyrus, the last Byzantine governor of Egypt, attempted to secure for the country's Christian population by offering the newly arrived Arab conqueror of Egypt, ʿAmr ibn al-ʿĀṣ (d. ca. 663), the enormous sum of 70,000 dīnārs in exchange for perpetual title to it. The Caliph ʿUmar (r. 634–644), however, bewildered by this suspiciously generous offer, instructed ʿAmr to inquire why Cyrus, who was also the Chalcedonian patriarch of Alexandria, valued this seemingly desolate real estate so highly. Cyrus finally revealed that Christian texts promised that buried in this ground lay the "seedlings of heaven." The Caliph then instructed ʿAmr not to sell the land at any price, and instead to make it a Muslim burial ground, as ʿUmar knew of

[130] Ibn al-Zayyāt, *al-Kawākib*, 295–96; see also al-Sakhāwī, *Tuḥfat*, 379, and Ibn ʿUthmān, *Murshid*, 602–3.
[131] See in this regard Ibn ʿUthmān, *Murshid*, 129.
[132] Ibn al-Zayyāt, *al-Kawākib*, 7.
[133] Ibn ʿUthmān, *Murshid*, 14. According to this account Joseph was first buried in al-Qarāfa. However, when vegetation grew only on the southern side of his grave, his body was moved to Giza. There plants only grew on the northern side of his grave. As a result he was finally buried in a marble coffin on the island of Rawḍa in the Nile. He remained there approximately three hundred years until Moses took him out of Egypt during the Exodus.
[134] Ibn al-Zayyāt, *al-Kawākib*, 13, and Ibn ʿUthmān, *Murshid*, 8.

no "seedlings of heaven" aside from those who believed in God and Muḥammad, the seal of His prophets. It was therefore on this dusty plateau that ʿAmr himself and four other close companions of the Prophet, including ʿUqba b. ʿĀmir al-Juhanī, were later laid to rest.[135]

These ancient connections with the prophets of Islam, however, only confirmed the sacred quality that God Himself had previously bestowed on the Qarāfa. Ibn al-Zayyāt recounts how al-Qarāfa achieved its sacral quality as a recompense from God to the Jabal al-Muqaṭṭam for the gift offered Him by the mountain itself. When God announced that He would speak with Moses on a mountain, each mountain save one proudly sought the honor. Only Mount Sinai was humble before God. When God asked why, the mountain explained, "In honor of you, my Lord." God therefore commanded every other mountain to sacrifice to Him one thing of great value, and each mountain yielded to the Almighty in its turn one precious quality. The Jabal al-Muqaṭṭam, however, offered up every stream, tree, and plant that adorned it, so that the mountain became as completely barren as it was in the Middle Ages. In recognition of this great sacrifice God revealed that the "seedlings of heaven" would one day lie in the Qarāfa at the foot of this mountain.[136]

Al-Qarāfa long played an extraordinary role in the social and moral economy of medieval Cairene urban space. In a traditional society bound by complicated social boundaries between genders and among classes, occupations, residential quarters, ethnic groups, and religious communities, the Qarāfa was a rare place that afforded opportunities for social mixing not generally possible in the confines of the city itself.[137] The closest equivalent within the city proper was probably the public market (sūq). But even there the market inspectors were in large part responsible for maintaining a modicum of "moral order."[138] Al-Qarāfa had the quality of being a marginal zone,

[135] The earliest known account of this tradition is provided by the ninth-century Egyptian traditionalist and historian Ibn ʿAbd al-Ḥakam, *The History of the Conquest of Egypt*, 156–57. Ibn ʿAbd al-Ḥakam also provides an alternative version of this event, in which the phrase employed by Cyrus is shajar al-janna (trees of heaven). In this second account ʿUmar also confirms the accuracy of Cyrus's claim. For a later medieval version of the same story, see al-Maqrīzī, *Khiṭaṭ*, 2:443.

[136] Ibn al-Zayyāt, *al-Kawākib*, 12–13.

[137] For the best general discussion of the nature of urban life in Mamlūk Cairo, see Lapidus, *Muslim Cities*, especially chapter 3.

[138] Ibid., 98.

enticingly beyond the reach of the ʿulamāʾ, the traditional guardians of routine social conformity.

Contemporary medieval observers were certainly not unaware of the special character of the Qarāfa. The ʿulamāʾ were cognizant of and clearly disturbed by the opportunities for dangerous social mixing that a place such as al-Qarāfa offered. Nowhere is this more evident than in the concern expressed by the fourteenth-century Mālikī jurist Ibn al-Ḥājj (d. 1336) about women visiting tombs in al-Qarāfa. Although Ibn al-Ḥājj raises a number of general objections to women visiting graveyards based on ḥadīth, his central concern lies with the opportunities this activity presented for improper and unseemly contact between the sexes. Beginning with the ride to and from the cemetery, he asserts, mule and horse drivers were known to exploit the situation by physically embracing their female customers while assisting them in mounting and dismounting from the animals. During the trip to and from the cemetery, guides often unnecessarily placed their hands on women's thighs. Women, in turn, he says put their uncovered hands on the shoulders of their guides. Furthermore, female riders and their male guides often engaged in casual banter as if they were husband and wife. According to Ibn al-Ḥājj, the ziyāra itself resulted in even more disgraceful and dangerous occasions on which men and women mixed on a regular basis: "And among numerous scandalous acts, women walk at night with men during the ziyāra of the tombs, among all the secluded places there and the many easily accessible buildings. And they expose their faces, and other parts of their bodies, as if they are with their husbands in the privacy of their own homes. And added to this, they have conversations with strange men, and women jest and play around, and there is much laughter and singing in this place of humility." Even when Ibn al-Ḥājj digresses into a brief criticism of the poor quality of the preachers and Qurʾān reciters whom women visitors hear during their trips to the cemetery, he never strays far from his central concern with the dangerous "mixed gathering of men and women."[139] Such observations bring into sharp relief the apprehension and fear that an unsupervised or poorly supervised space like the Qarāfa, where jealously guarded rules of normative social order were clearly broken on a routine basis, generated among the ʿulamāʾ.

---

[139] Ibn al-Ḥājj, *al-Madkhal*, 1:267–68.

Victor Turner's concept of "liminal" space in his work on ritual and pilgrimage is useful for our understanding of al-Qarāfa's role in the social and moral economy of medieval Cairo. Turner posits two dialectically opposed concepts, "social structure" and "social anti-structure," also referred to as "communitas."[140] Social structure Turner defined as "the patterned arrangements of role sets, status sets, and status sequences consciously recognized and regularly operative in a given society and closely bound up with legal and political norms and sanctions." Communitas, in contrast, he described as a spontaneous and unmediated sense of community, or a shared sense of belonging, which arises between distinct identities among groups of people. Although individual identities do not become confused in the experience of communitas, they are freed from the normally prevailing bonds of conformity. Turner saw communitas as an "immediate, concrete, not abstract" experience of undiferentiated egalitarianism—a sense of homogeneous comradeship.[141] He further distinguished between three types of social antistructure, or communitas, which he identified as spontaneous, normative, and ideological. Spontaneous communitas is the exact anthithesis of social structure. It consists of an unfettered and nonrational expression of existential solidarity transcending all other normative distinctions. Unlike the existential nature of spontaneous communitas, normative and ideological communitas are artificial attempts to prolong, secure, and harness the powerful force of group solidarity generated by spontaneous communitas so as to mold it in the service of social structure.[142]

Al-Qarāfa seems to have provided precisely the sort of liminal or marginal space where communitas—social antistructure—was developed on a regular basis. The extensive legal debate over the permissibility of the ziyāra, as well as consistent efforts to codify the proper conduct of visitors that we will discuss in the next chapter, suggest efforts to tap the unmediated solidarity of spontaneous communitas while seeking to render it more normative in character.

The Qarāfa was thus a unique kind of liminal urban space located on the fringes of this greatest of Islamic metropolises. The cemetery

[140] Turner's approach is described in several of his major works, including: *Forest of Symbols, Ritual Process, Dramas, Fields and Metaphors, Image and Pilgrimage in Christian Culture* (Edith Turner), and *Process, Performance and Pilgrimage.*

[141] Turner and Turner, *Image and Pilgrimage,* 250–52.

[142] Ibid., 188–93. Turner identified the *ḥajj* to Mecca as a classic example of normative *communitas.*

had its own living residents, its own elaborate system of thoroughfares, water works, and markets. And yet al-Qarāfa was also an integral part of a greater urban complex. It was mainly the space in which the city buried its dead, and it is this function which primarily brought the citizens of Cairo to al-Qarāfa in such large numbers, both to bury their dead and to visit the dead through the ziyāra. But the cemetery was a place not only where the living mixed with the dead; it was also well known for the mixing of men and women. Not only jurists such as Ibn al-Ḥajj but the pilgrimage guides too suggest that many who came to the cemetery did so with this purpose in mind. And beyond the mixing of the living and the dead, and the dangerous mixing of male and female that made al-Qarāfa such a complex and problematic space, this was also a place where rich mixed with poor and the powerful mixed with the weak. We can find in the words of a fifteenth-century European observer, Emmanuel Piloti, an echo of the great festive gatherings that brought together society's rich and poor at Jāmiʿ al-Qarāfa many centuries earlier: "all the lords who own them [the mausolea of al-Qarāfa] give alms to the poor every Friday. It is on this day that they have their holiday, say their prayers, and prepare large meals of meat. And it is on this day that all the poor of Cairo go there to eat and to receive the money which is given them."[143]

There were, of course, panic-filled gatherings of communal supplication as well, in moments of great collective crisis when the Qarāfa served as an important place for public assembly. In addition, al-Qarāfa was a place where the sacred mixed with the profane more broadly, as a host of itinerant merchants, self-appointed guides, popular entertainers, and others competed with each other to service the various needs of those living in or visiting the cemetery. Finally, al-Qarāfa was probably a place where Muslims mixed with non-Muslims. All these sorts of morally charged interactions seem to have

[143] Quoted without citation in Wiet, *Cairo*, 135. Piloti was a Venetian merchant who lived in Cairo for more than forty years (1398–1441); see Dopp, "Le Caire vu par les voyageurs occidentaux." Dopp also published extensive passages from Piloti's work; see *L'Egypte au commencement du quinzième siècle d'après traité d'Emmanuel Piloti de Crète*, (Cairo, 1950). In addition to the impressionistic evidence of contemporary observers such as Piloti and al-Maqrīzī concerning the distribution of food and charity to the poor at important tombs, Adam Sabra informs me that Mamlūk period waqfiyyas document endowments that include provisions for the distribution of food to the poor at certain major tombs in Cairo. See Sabra, "Poverty and Charity in Mamluk Cairo," especially chapter 4.

been an enduring feature of the cemetery throughout the Middle Ages, and they collectively made it a perilous place from the perspective of many members of the ʿulamāʾ. For the Qarāfa remained, by and large, a place physically and spiritually beyond the control of these watchful guardians of the holy Law of Islam.

In the Qarāfa other experts were in charge, experts who led pilgrims on carefully defined and ancient circuits of the ziyāra. Here guides who could navigate the confusing and ever-changing landscape of the vast cemetery delivered their charges to the tombs of the awliyāʾ. It is the ziyāra itself that we now consider more fully.

CHAPTER TWO

THE ZIYĀRA

Visiting graves, ziyārat (pl. ziyārāt) al-qubūr, the central activity defining the cult of Muslim saints in the later Middle Ages, in fact, comprised a wider series of customary devotional practices centered around visiting graves in general, regardless of whether these were the tombs of relatives, friends, associates, or teachers. The ziyāra, therefore, was undertaken both by individuals visiting the graves of their relatives as well as large organized groups being guided through appointed circuits of saints' tombs. It also came to designate, however, a particular expression of Muslim piety specifically involving visits to the tombs of the holy dead. Ziyāra thus designated not a specific action so much as a mode or style of pious expression. It was an activity that transcended all social boundaries and appealed to the vast majority of Egyptian Muslims in the later Middle Ages.

As we have seen, the ziyāra was clearly an ancient practice. Extensive discussions of the propriety and admissibility of the ziyāra were found in early works of Islamic jurisprudence (fiqh) and in the great collections of ḥadīth.[1] That there were sometimes contradictions in ḥadīth and fiqh concerning the ziyāra suggests that the practice was not only very old but that the dispute over its propriety was also long-standing.

As an organized group institution ziyāra was led by individuals called mashāyikh al-ziyāra (s. shaykh al-ziyāra). Although we know relatively little about these individuals, the mashāyikh al-ziyāra appear to have been minor scholars and mystics familiar with both the biographies of the saints and the location of their tombs. These shaykhs led pious visitors (zuwwār) through the cemetery on appointed routes, and at designated tombs would relate stories and information about individual saints. These accounts usually stressed the special

---

[1] For example, see "Kitāb al-janā'iz" in Muslim, *Ṣaḥīḥ* 2:635–39; or "Bāb al-ziyāra" of the "Kitāb al-manāsik" in Abū Dāwūd, *Sunan*, 2:218–19. In translating ziyāra as "pious visit" rather than "pilgrimage," I hope to avoid confusion with the ḥajj, the great pilgrimage to Mecca.

quality of the saint's piety, as well as any miracles associated with them. There were doubtless different levels of ability and knowledge among the mashāyikh al-ziyāra—many were probably self-appointed residents of the Qarāfa—and this informal aspect of the office was probably a factor that contributed to the prevailing confusion over the location and identity of many tombs in the cemetery. The mashāyikh al-ziyāra apparently received some compensation for their services, but it is not clear how much, or whether this remuneration represented primary or supplemental income; it may well have varied from one individual shaykh to another.

Although the practice of ziyāra is clearly an ancient one in the Islamic tradition, the late medieval historian al-Maqrīzī states that the organization of the ziyāra, as a group activity occurring on specified days, emerged during the first half of the thirteenth century. If this dating is accurate, it would correspond exactly with the link between ṭarīqa Sūfism and the mass followings the brotherhoods began attracting in the same period.[2] In describing the group ziyāra, al-Maqrīzī tells us, "They go out Friday evenings, early every Saturday morning and each Wednesday afternoon. They invoke God's name and visit [the cemetery]. They gather together innumerable men and women, and among them are those who make the appointed sermons. The leader of each group is called the pilgrimage shaykh, and during the ziyāra some good things happen as well as others which are regrettable."[3] Al-Maqrīzī and the authors of the pilgrimage guides go to some length to trace the origin of the ziyāra on the various nights when it was conducted. For instance, the first person to lead groups of zuwwār on Wednesdays, starting from the Mashhad of al-Sayyida Nafīsa, was supposedly Shaykh Abū Muḥammad ʿAbd Allāh b. Rāfiʿ b. Yuzḥam b. Rāfiʿ al-Sāriʿī al-Shāfiʿī al-Maʿāfirī, also known as ʿĀbid b. ʿAbd Allāh (d. 1241).[4] According to al-Maqrīzī, the first shaykh to lead zuwwār on the Friday evening ziyāra was Shaykh Abū al-Ḥasan ʿAlī b. Aḥmad,

[2] Some caution must be exercised in accepting al-Maqrīzī's dates for the origins of the organized group ziyāra since he was already removed from these events by two centuries. However, Ibn al-Nāsikh, who died in 1297, in a brief notice identifies a certain "ʿĀbid," who is surely Shaykh Abū Muḥammad ʿAbd Allāh b. Rāfiʿ b. Yuzḥam b. Rāfiʿ al-Sāriʿī al-Shāfiʿī al-Maghāfirī, known as ʿĀbid b. ʿAbd Allāh (see below at n. 4), as the first person to lead the ziyāra during the day.

[3] Al-Maqrīzī, *Khiṭaṭ*, 2:461.

[4] Ibid. See also Ibn al-Nāsikh, *Miṣbāḥ*, fol. 85r°; Ibn al-Zayyāt, *al-Kawākib*, 220 and 302; and al-Sakhāwī, *Tuḥfat*, 330.

known as Ibn al-Jabbās (1161–1241), the famous author of a now lost pilgrimage guide.[5] About this shaykh al-Maqrīzī states, "The people gathered and he led them in the ziyāra every week on Friday evening. And on some nights the Sulṭān, al-Malik al-Kāmil Nāṣir al-Dīn . . . and the leading ʿulamāʾ visited with him." As for the group ziyāra on Saturdays, al-Maqrīzī tells us there was a dispute about its origin. Some argued it was a recent innovation, whereas others contended that it was much older.[6]

The sources make some distinction between shaykhs who led the ziyāra at night and those who led it during the day. For example, while mentioning the tombs of the descendants of Ibn al-Jalāl, Ibn al-Zayyāt notes: "and they were mashāyikh al-ziyāra at night." Ibn al-Nāsikh tells us that Shaykh Abū al-Ḥasan ʿAlī b. Muḥammad was the first one to lead the ziyāra at night, during the reign of the Ayyūbid sultan al-Malik al-Kāmil. Al-Sakhāwī contradicts this by stating that Shaykh ʿAlī al-Ghamrī was the first one to lead the ziyāra at night "with a group (ṭāʾifa)." Shaykh ʿUmar b. al-Zurayqa, however, is mentioned as having led the ziyāra both at night and during the day.[7]

What is clear from these discussions about the origins of the group ziyāra is that at least as early as the Ayyūbid period large groups of organized zuwwār were making their way through the great cemeteries of Cairo on a regular basis under the guidance of special shaykhs, esteemed for their knowledge of the deeds and attributes of the saints. Furthermore, these group ziyārāt seem to have been conducted on several different days of the week. The exasperation of the fourteenth-century Mālikī jurist Ibn al-Ḥājj is quite clear as he describes how women eventually began visiting the tombs of al-Qarāfa virtually every day of the week.[8]

In addition to the weekly ziyāra there were special days on which important saints were commemorated in large informal public gatherings. These "saints' days," known in Arabic as mawālid (s. mawlid), are popular and festive observances, held around the saint's tomb; they sometimes span several days and nights each year.[9] Mawālid

---

[5] Rāghib, "Essai d'inventaire," 270–71, and al-Maqrīzī, *Khiṭaṭ*, 2:461.
[6] Al-Maqrīzī, *Khiṭaṭ*, 2:461.
[7] Ibn al-Zayyāt, *al-Kawākib*, 96, 311.
[8] Ibn al-Ḥājj, *al-Madkhal*, 1:269.
[9] Although the word means "birthday," the *mawlid* frequently marks the saint's death—or "birth into Paradise"—rather than the date of earthly birth. Although

were usually organized by Ṣūfī orders (ṭuruq), and they involved rhythmic dancing, processions of various sorts, the dhikr, recitation of the Qur'ān, recounting stories of the saint's life, as well as a variety of ancillary public attractions and entertainment. The mawālid frequently drew large crowds of people to the site of the saint's tomb, some of them from great distances.

Most mawālid essentially function even today as large regional fairs, attracting numerous vendors who sell traditional festive sweets and cakes as well as a wide variety of services, crafts, and commercial wares. At the mawlid of Aḥmad al-Badawī (d. 1276), Egypt's greatest saint, in the large Delta city of Tanta, for example, families frequently bring their infant sons to one of the many booths specializing in circumcision, as this mawlid is closely associated with the celebration of fertility. Magicians, poets, fortune tellers, and other street entertainers also commonly participate in these great gatherings. Many of the itinerant merchants and entertainers found at mawālid today, in fact, make a living traveling around Egypt from one mawlid to the next. In the 1970s, Knappert indicates, the Egyptian Ministry of Awqāf registered nearly 300 mawālid throughout the country.[10]

Medieval observers dated the first appearance of the mawlid in Egypt to the early thirteenth century. Modern scholars have generally tended to accept this date, like that of the weekly group ziyāra, and have seen the mawlid as yet another aspect of the Sunnī restoration in Egypt after the demise of the Fāṭimids in 1171.[11]

There was no single itinerary for zuwwār to follow as they navigated their way through the Qarāfa. Presumably mashāyikh al-ziyāra specialized in one or more routes that wound through various parts of the cemetery, many of which probably overlapped at major tombs. Although it is doubtful that we can ever fully reconstruct any of these individual circuits, one discrete ziyāra involved a group of seven

---

there is no complete description of the *mawlid* in the medieval period see Gilsenan, *Saint and Sufi*, especially chapter 2. See also *EI*², s.v. Mawlid. Two useful documentary films on modern Egyptian mawālids include: *For Those Who Sail to Heaven*, produced and directed by [Eleanor] Elizabeth Wickett (New York, First Run Icarus Films, 1990), which deals with the mawlid of Sīdī Abū al-Ḥajāj in Luxor; and *El-Moulid*, produced and directed by Fadwa El Guindi (Los Angeles, El Nil Research, 1990) which treats the mawlid of Aḥmad al-Badawī in the Egyptian Delta city of Tanta.

[10] See *EI*², s.v. Mawlid.

[11] See *EI*¹, s.v. Mawlid.

tombs that are mentioned in all of the pilgrimage guides, as well as in al-Maqrīzī's *Khiṭaṭ*. These tombs are referred to as al-sabʿ al-abdāl, "the seven substitutes" (one of several ranks in traditional Ṣūfī classifications of Muslim saints). Although the sources agree on the number seven, they indicate that precisely which tombs were included in the ziyārat al-sabʿ varied. The historian Muḥammad b. Salāma al-Quḍāʿī (d. 1062) seems to be the original source for the history of this particular ziyāra.[12] Al-Maqrīzī, however, provides two alternate lists of seven tombs that some claimed should be included in this circuit.[13] Zuwwār traditionally visited these seven tombs on foot after morning prayers on Friday, according to al-Maqrīzī, until the time of Shaykh Muḥammad al-ʿAjamī al-Saʿūdī (d. 1407), who led this ziyāra of the seven tombs from horseback because his crippled feet made it impossible for him to walk. Thus, although the ziyārat al-sabʿ is the closest thing we have to an actual itinerary, even in this case there was no agreement on exactly which seven tombs should be included.

The pilgrimage guides are of little help in reconstructing the itineraries of specific ziyārāt because they were primarily intended to present the location and relevant information associated with *all* significant tombs in the vast and confusing expanse of al-Qarāfa. Although the guides are similar to each other in this respect, their approaches to the project vary.

Ibn ʿUthmān, the author of *Murshid al-zuwwār*, began with a description of the huge Mosque of Aḥmad b. Ṭūlūn. He felt this mosque would serve as an easily identifiable landmark because it stands in

---

[12] His list contained the following tombs: Shaykh Abū al-Ḥasan ʿAlī b. Muḥammad b. Sahl b. al-Ṣāʾigh al-Dīnawarī (d. 943), ʿAbd al-Ṣamad b. Muḥammad b. Aḥmad b. Isḥāq b. Muslim b. Ibrahīm al-Baghdādī (d. 946/947), Ismāʿīl b. Yaḥyā b. Ismāʿīl b. ʿUmar b. Isḥāq b. Bahdala b. ʿAbd Allāh al-Muzanī (d. 877/878), Bakkār b. Qutayba (d. 883/884), al-Mufaḍḍal b. Faḍāla (d. 866), Abū Bakr ʿAbd al-Malik b. al-Ḥasan al-Qumanī (d. 1041), and Abū al-Fayḍ Dhu ʾl-Nūn Thawbān b. Ibrahīm al-Miṣrī (d. 859/860). Al-Maqrīzī, *Khiṭaṭ*, 2:461. See also Ibn al-Zayyāt, *al-Kawākib*, 321; al-Sakhāwī, *Tuḥfat*, 402; and Ibn ʿUthmān, *Murshid*, 332.

[13] Al-Maqrīzī, *Khiṭaṭ*, 2:461. The two most prominent names to appear on this list are ʿUqba b. ʿĀmir al-Juhanī and Imām al-Shāfiʿī. There were also four other places that al-Maqrīzī tells us Egyptians went to pray, particularly during times of crisis and poverty. He does not, however, indicate that they were visited in conjunction with each other, and only one of the four sites, the Mashhad of al-Sayyida Nafīsa, was actually a tomb. The other three were the reported location of the prison of the Prophet Joseph, the Mosque of Moses, and a small chamber located in the qibla side of Masjid al-Aqdām.

the most direct path of the cemetery from the southern gate of Cairo. He begins his tour of al-Qarāfa at Bāb al-Ṣafā, about 1,500 meters west of the Mashhad of al-Sayyida Nafīsa.[14] The rest of his guide consists of a tour of the saints buried in the Qarāfa. Each tomb typically receives a few lines or a paragraph, in which Ibn ʿUthmān identifies the person buried and offers an account of the qualities which distinguished the deceased or the miracles worked through his or her association with God. These brief descriptions typically read something like this: "after a few steps you come to the grave of the jurist so and so. It is a place known for the efficacy of prayer. Next to this tomb is the grave of. . . ." Although the accounts of many saints are obviously more extensive than this, much of the guide is characterized by this sort of basic formula. This particular guide is difficult to follow today because Ibn ʿUthmān did not provide a clear overview of his plan for organizing the cemetery.

Starting within the walls of Fāṭimid Cairo itself, Ibn al-Nāsikh, the author of *Miṣbāḥ al-dayājī*, begins with Mashhad of al-Ḥusayn, which he strenuously denies actually contains the head of the Prophet's grandson. He also briefly mentions the tombs of the Fāṭimid caliphs in the famous Turbat al-Zaʿfarān nearby. Ibn al-Nāsikh then proceeds outside the city gates to the Mashhad of Zayn al-ʿĀbidīn, east of the Mosque of Aḥmad b. Ṭūlūn. He turns his attention to the Qarāfa after briefly touching on the Mosque of ʿAmr, the Island of Rawḍa, and Gīza. After criticizing Ibn ʿUthmān for beginning with Bāb al-Ṣafā, Ibn al-Nāsikh argues that the best place to begin a description of the cemetery is Bāb al-Qarāfa, just below the Citadel. From there his guide moves through the graveyard in three vertical sections. From Bāb al-Qarāfa, according to Ibn al-Nāsikh, one should move south, grave by grave, until reaching the tomb of al-Ḥarār, the southernmost tomb of his first section. One then returns north through the second vertical zone, starting from the tomb of Ibn ʿAbd al-Salām and concluding with the Mashhad of Imām al-Shāfiʿī. To complete the third section, one exits again through Bāb al-Qarāfa, passes below the Citadel, and then visits the tombs located against the side of the Jabal al-Muqaṭṭam to the east of al-Qarāfa al-Ṣughrā.[15]

---

[14] Ibn ʿUthmān, *Murshid*, 205. For the exact location of this gate see Casanova, *Essai de reconstitution topographique*, 1:56–57, and Plan 1, no. 34.

[15] Ibn al-Nāsikh, *Miṣbāḥ*, fol. 13v°.

Ibn al-Zayyāt, the author of *al-Kawākib al-sayyāra*, begins slightly southwest of Bāb al-Qarāfa at the Mashhad of al-Sayyida Nafīsa. He then turns his attention to al-Qarāfa itself, and his guide offers what is for modern readers the most comprehensible description of the cemetery.[16] Although it is not possible to reestablish all the divisions of his guide today, as most of the tombs he uses as landmarks no longer exist, we can reconstruct the broad outlines of his plan of the cemetery. Like his predecessor Ibn al-Nāsikh, Ibn al-Zayyāt began with Bāb al-Qarāfa and divided the cemetery into three unequal north-to-south vertical sections, called jiha (pl. jihāt). He then established a grid by further dividing each vertical section into ten subsections called shuqaq (s. shuqqa), or, alternately furūʿ (s. farʿ), arranged into horizontal bands of three shuqaq each, with a final shuqqa completing the jiha. Within each individual section of this grid the bands of three shuqaq are also arranged vertically, like the jihāt, from north to south. Again, like the three jihāt, Ibn al-Zayyāt usually describes the individual sets of shuqaq in order moving from west to east. His guide is particularly useful for modern scholars because using it we can still locate ourselves at least generally in modern al-Qarāfa, even though most of what he describes no longer survives. Ibn al-Zayyāt starts each jiha from the same point, Bāb al-Qarāfa, which fortunately does still exist. The jihāt can perhaps best be thought of as imaginary rays, originating from the same point and trisecting the cemetery into unequal vertical sections.[17]

Al-Sakhāwī, the author of *Tuḥfat al-aḥbāb*, is distinguished from his three predecessors in that he devotes a substantial portion of his guide, well over 150 pages, to various graves outside al-Qarāfa. He begins far to the north of Cairo in al-Maṭariyya, and gradually works his way south through the cemeteries outside of Bāb al-Futūḥ. After describing tombs within Cairo itself, as well as those south of the city, he finally reaches Bāb al-Qarāfa. The fact that al-Sakhāwī

[16] Louis Massignon relied heavily on this guide, with varying degrees of success in his efforts to reconstruct the topography of al-Qarāfa; see his "La cité des morts au Caire," especially 38–45. Although Massignon's work was pioneering at the time of its publication, he made a number of mistakes. His topographical catalog (54–68) is useful for organizing the major tombs cited in the pilgrimage guides geographically, but here too there are some errors. For example, Massignon accepted Creswell's assumption that the remains of the Khaḍra al-Sharīfa were actually those of Jāmiʿ al-Awliyāʾ.

[17] For a discussion of the horizontal relation of the three *shuqaq* to each other see Ibn al-Zayyāt, *al-Kawākib*, 189, and the Appendix below.

spends so much time on sites located outside al-Qarāfa may point to an expansion of the cult of the saints, and possibly a shift in the focus of the ziyārāt, by the late fifteenth century to areas far beyond the traditional boundaries of al-Qarāfa, where the cult was traditionally centered. When he does describe the Qarāfa, al-Sakhāwī essentially follows the same system of dividing the cemetery as followed by Ibn al-Nāsikh and Ibn al-Zayyāt before him, although al-Sakhāwī's discussion of the jihāt, which at one point he numbers as four, and of the shuqaq is extremely confusing and hard to follow.[18]

It is unclear from *Tuḥfat al-aḥbāb*, as it is from the other three guides, exactly what portion of the cemetery zuwwār might reasonably cover during a single ziyāra. Did the jiha, or even the shuqqa, represent meaningful units or itineraries for a single visit? This seems unlikely. The main objective of the authors of the pilgrimage guides was to furnish a clear and systematic list that zuwwār could refer to, as "if they were to take it in hand and visit each [tomb] successively, one after the other."[19] Thus, the guides were never meant to reproduce an established itinerary of the ziyāra, and should be viewed instead as inventories of the important sites in al-Qarāfa as a whole.

The various activities associated with the ziyāra in the later Middle Ages may be partially established from a number of contemporary sources. Jurists critical of the institution, for example, have left numerous reports about the conduct, or perhaps one should say misconduct, of the ziyāra. We will consider the accusations of hostile jurists in Chapter 5, but the problem with this sort of evidence from the law books, aside from the fact that it is dispersed and repetitive—often to the point of being formulaic—is that it tends to dwell on fantastic and sensational accounts of abuse.

The pilgrimage guides yield the most useful information about the nature of the ziyāra, and we focus here on the material they provide. This information falls into two main categories. First, the guides offer descriptive anecdotal evidence about the activities of zuwwār at specific tombs. For example, Ibn al-Zayyāt tells us that at the tomb of al-Baghdādī zuwwār used to grasp or shake each other's

[18] Al-Sakhāwī, *Tuḥfat*, 186.
[19] Ibn al-Nāsikh, *Miṣbāḥ*; fol. 2r°.

hands because the saint once told someone in a dream that God would forgive those who did this at his tomb. And there were apparently other tombs in the Qarāfa where zuwwār routinely did this.[20] Al-Sakhāwī tells us that people wishing to perform the ḥajj used to circumambulate the tomb of Fāṭima al-ʿĀbida al-Mūṣiliyya seven times, believing that as a result they would be able to perform the ḥajj within the year.[21] In some cases the authors of the pilgrimage guides report activities occurring at specific tombs without further comment. In other cases they offer critical assessments.

In addition to this sort of anecdotal evidence, two of the pilgrimage guides shed light on what was considered normative conduct of the ziyāra through guidelines they suggest for its proper performance (adab al-ziyāra). Since these guidelines were intended to be prescriptive as well as proscriptive, they are useful because they systematically contrast what the authors, and many of their peers among the ʿulamāʾ, considered permissible behavior in the conduct of the ziyāra. At the same time, the guidelines afford us a more balanced view of the total range of activities associated with the ziyāra than is normally provided by those jurists hostile to the institution altogether. Many of these activities were clearly not objectionable, which explains why antagonistic jurists ignored them in their attacks on the ziyāra. Thus although we should not ignore the legal evidence about what happened in the course of the ziyāra, we should place that information within a balanced perspective of the institution as a whole.

Ibn ʿUthmān offers the most systematic presentation of guidelines governing the correct performance of the ziyāra.[22] He prefaces his remarks with a short chapter stressing that zuwwār should never wear shoes while walking among tombs.[23] This observation then leads him to a long consideration of adab al-ziyāra consisting of twenty rules, or waẓāʾif (s. waẓīfa). In the outline below I have reorganized the order of Ibn ʿUthmān's twenty rules somewhat so as to group similar and connected themes.

---

[20] Ibn al-Zayyāt, *al-Kawākib*, 77.

[21] Al-Sakhāwī, *Tuḥfat*, 251.

[22] Ibn ʿUthmān, *Murshid*, 32–81. Ibn al-Zayyāt, *al-Kawākib*, also deals with the matter of adab al-ziyāra (see 14–18), but his presentation is less well organized and relies heavily on the earlier work of Ibn ʿUthmān.

[23] Ibn ʿUthmān, *Murshid*, 28. He cites a *ḥadīth* to support the prohibition.

First, the zāʾir must have pure intentions in wishing to perform the ziyāra. Sincerity is evidenced by a desire to carry out the ziyāra strictly for the sake of God and for the elimination of corruption in the zāʾir's heart. It is not acceptable for the zāʾir to visit the dead merely to impress relatives of the deceased, and thereby secure a reciprocal obligation from them to visit the dead relatives of the zāʾir. Ibn ʿUthmān decries this attitude, which he says "preoccupies people today, and is so widely acknowledged that people do it openly." He compares such hypocrites to those identified in Qurʾān 37:105: "Those whose effort goeth astray in the life of the world, and yet they reckon that they do good work."[24]

The second waẓīfa is that it is best if the zāʾir visits the cemetery on Friday, the day on which it is reported the Prophet Muḥammad performed the ziyāra and on which some believe the souls of the dead return to their bodies. When asked if the ziyāra could be postponed to Monday, the Prophet responded that the dead were aware of their visitors on Friday as well as on Thursday and Saturday. Ibn al-Zayyāt reports, however, that many people preferred to make the ziyāra on Wednesday. The reasons for this include the fact that the cemetery is less crowded on Wednesday, and Wednesday is also the day on which God created light. Ibn ʿUthmān explains, "visiting tombs is light, and praying is light, so this is light upon light."[25] In Islamic eschatology there is no general agreement concerning the fate of the soul between the moment of death and the Day of Judgment.[26] The space and time between death and resurrection are jointly referred to in medieval Islamic sources as barzakh. One belief, certainly widely accepted by the authors of the pilgrimage guides, is that the souls of the dead remain with the body or at least near the grave, and the dead are fully conscious of the actions and deeds of their visitors, at least on certain days.

The fourth waẓīfa is that the zāʾir should especially visit the tombs of prophets as well as relatives of the Prophet Muḥammad and his

---

[24] Ibn ʿUthmān, *Murshid*, 32.

[25] Ibid., 32, 34. This question as to which days the souls of the dead return to their bodies is raised again under the ninth waẓīfa, when Ibn ʿUthmān quotes Shaykh Abū al-Qāsim b. al-Jabbās, who reports that the souls of the dead return to their bodies on Friday afternoon and remain there through Monday. Others, however, say that they return Thursdays and remain until sunrise on Saturday, see also 53.

[26] For a general discussion of the different theories see Smith and Haddad, *The Islamic Understanding of Death*, especially chapter 2.

companions. Ibn ʿUthmān notes that countless zuwwār have visited these tombs and witnessed the wonders with which God has favored His servants, just as the zuwwār have experienced God's mercy through the baraka of the ziyāra itself. The twelfth waẓīfa calls on visitors to bear in mind the best deeds and qualities of the dead. This practice multiplies their merits and inspires zuwwār with a desire to enter into the company of the righteous.[27]

Proper deportment during the ziyāra was necessary, not only to ensure the correct attitude and state of mind of the zāʾir but also out of respect for the dead. This concern reflects very deep and basic cultural sensibilities and attitudes about issues of propriety and courtesy. The zāʾir should see himself or herself as a visitor in precisely the same way as when visiting the homes of living friends and relatives. Thus, the third waẓīfa is that the zāʾir should avoid walking or sitting on graves. Here Ibn ʿUthmān cites a tradition from Abū Hurayra to the effect that it is better to sit on a live ember, even if it should burn clear through one's clothing to the skin, than to sit on a grave.[28] The dead themselves sometimes took matters into their own hands. Ibn al-Zayyāt mentions a thoughtless visitor who once sat on the grave of the Shāfiʿī jurist Ibn Khalīfa al-Makhzūmī only to be rebuked by the dead saint: "Do not sit on the grave of a man who loves and is loved by God!"[29] A menstruating woman who sat on the tomb of Shaykh Abū Bakr al-Iṣṭablī likewise received a warning from the dead shaykh for being so thoughtless as to sit on his tomb, especially while in a state of ritual impurity.[30]

The proper attitude in approaching and greeting the dead was also important. The fifth waẓīfa states that visitors should always approach and face the grave from the front, with their back to the qibla, or direction of prayer, just as they would converse with a living person face to face. The sixth waẓīfa urges the zāʾir to greet the dead exactly as he would the living.[31] Here Ibn ʿUthmān relates an extended formula of greeting and blessing that zuwwār reportedly

---

[27] Ibn ʿUthmān, *Murshid*, 36, 60.
[28] Ibn ʿUthmān, *Murshid*, 35.
[29] Ibn al-Zayyāt, *al-Kawākib*, 305.
[30] This story first appears in Ibn ʿUthmān, *Murshid*, 603. We encounter the same story in Ibn al-Zayyāt, *al-Kawākib*, 296, but in this version the offending woman trampled on the grave, rather than sat on it. Also in this version, the voice the woman heard did not originate from within the grave itself.
[31] Ibn ʿUthmān, *Murshid*, 36.

recited when visiting the tomb of al-Sayyida Nafīsa.[32] He also notes a similar greeting to the descendants of the Prophet buried at the Mashhad of Ṭabāṭabā.[33]

As an example of a proscriptive guideline, Ibn ʿUthmān points out in his seventh waẓīfa that the zuwwār should not kiss tombs or rub dust from tombs on themselves, nor should they roll in the dust of a tomb, either to obtain baraka or to cure an illness. He notes that these are Christian practices which no Muslim theologian has sanctioned.[34] Yet it is clear from repeated examples in the guides themselves that this type of physical contact with the tombs was a pervasive and consistent feature of the ziyāra.

The most common and obvious activity of the ziyāra was duʿāʾ, prayer or supplication. It is important to stress that duʿāʾ, specifically asking God for some favor or assistance, is distinct from ṣalāt, the ritual of worshipful prayer that Muslims are required to perform five times each day.[35] Although duʿāʾ was encouraged in cemeteries, performing the ṣalāt there was not. According to Ibn ʿUthmān's nineteenth waẓīfa, the ṣalāt should not be performed next to tombs. He notes in support of this view a ḥadīth, related through the caliph ʿUmar, which lists cemeteries among seven places where the ṣalāt was expressly not to be performed.[36] The many mosques in al-Qarāfa testify to the fact that this injunction was not, however, generally observed in Egypt during the Middle Ages.

The eleventh waẓīfa in Ibn ʿUthmān's list of twenty permits zuwwār to offer duʿāʾ on behalf of themselves among the tombs. Such petitions are encouraged particularly at the graves of the prophets and other virtuous people because, Ibn ʿUthmān points out, people are commanded to pray when the heart is pure, and in these places the heart is generally pure. He even suggests certain prayers which the zāʾir might wish offer on their own behalf. The first of these is:

> Oh Lord, I ask what the Prophet Muḥammad, may the blessings and peace of God be upon him, asked of you. I take refuge in you from that which the Prophet Muḥammad, may the blessings and peace of God be upon him, took refuge from in you. I seek from you forgiveness

[32] Cited in Ibn al-Zayyāt, *al-Kawākib*, 34.
[33] Ibn ʿUthmān, *Murshid*, 252–55.
[34] Ibid., 37. For examples of these practices see Ibn al-Zayyāt, *al-Kawākib*, 119, 197, and 201; Ibn ʿUthmān, *Murshid*, 333; and al-Sakhāwī, *Tuḥfat*, 248–49.
[35] See Gaborieau, "The Cult of Saints in Nepal," 298. See also pp. 169–70 below.
[36] Ibn ʿUthmān, *Murshid*, 63–65.

> and well-being. So make me well and forgive me. Oh Lord, you are forgiving, forgiveness pleases you, so forgive me![37]

The zuwwār are frequently reported in the guides as standing near certain tombs, or between particularly important tombs, and spreading out their open hands to beseech God with such supplications.[38]

The ninth waẓīfa encourages prayers of supplication on behalf of the dead. Here Ibn ʿUthmān notes a ḥadīth from the Prophet comparing a dead person to someone who is drowning and appealing desperately for help. Thus the dead are anxiously waiting in their graves for the prayers of a father, brother, or friend to reach them. He points out that the ʿulamāʾ confirm that "the gift of the living to the dead is praying and asking forgiveness on their behalf."[39] Thus visiting the graves of relatives and praying for their salvation was also encouraged.

Ibn ʿUthmān's thirteenth waẓīfa urges the zuwwār to visit their dead relatives frequently. He relates the story of a man who was forgiven his disobedience to his parents because he visited their tombs and prayed for them often. The fourteenth waẓīfa counsels the zuwwār to have patience and control their anguish when visiting the graves of their relatives. In a similar vein the fifteenth waẓīfa prohibits the zuwwār from wailing, striking their cheeks, or rending their clothes during the ziyāra. These sorts of guidelines were also primarily proscriptive in their intent. The Prophet is cited as denouncing wailing as a practice of the jāhiliyya (the pre-Islamic "Age of Ignorance"). Weeping, as opposed to wailing, is permitted, and the Prophet is reported to have wept when visiting the grave of his mother. The seventeenth waẓīfa deals with the matter of how zuwwār should conduct themselves in the presence of their dead enemies. They are especially instructed to restrain malicious joy on such occasions.[40]

The tenth waẓīfa urges zuwwār to pray for the Prophet Muḥammad while walking among graves. To demonstrate the efficacy of such petitions, Ibn ʿUthmān relates the story of a woman whose daughter had died. The mother wished to see her daughter, so she asked a certain Shaykh al-Ḥasan to teach her a prayer that might enable

---

[37] Ibid., 59.

[38] See for example the discussion of the Qubba of Fāṭima al-Kubrā and Fāṭima al-Ṣughrā and the tomb of al-Idfūwī, Ibn al-Zayyāt, *al-Kawākib*, 156.

[39] Ibn ʿUthmān, *Murshid*, 46.

[40] Ibid., 60–62.

her to see her dead child. The shaykh taught the woman a prayer, and after reciting it the woman did see her daughter in a dream. The mother, however, was greatly alarmed because her child was covered in tar and was wearing an iron collar around her neck. The distraught mother related her experience to Shaykh al-Ḥasan, who shortly thereafter experienced his own dream involving the dead girl. In his dream, however, the daughter's condition was much improved, and she was seen in Paradise reclining on a bed and wearing a crown. When the daughter told the shaykh who she was, he inquired as to the cause of this fortunate change in her circumstances. She explained that a righteous man had prayed for the Prophet while walking near her grave, and the baraka from that prayer alone freed all 550 people buried in the cemetery from the punishments of the grave.[41]

Further insight into how the living might help the dead in this way is provided in an account noted in several of the pilgrimage guides. The story is told that a group of zuwwār once discovered a leg protruding from a grave in al-Qarāfa. They carefully covered the leg with earth, but when they returned later, they were amazed to see the leg sticking out of the ground once more. The reason why the leg would not stay properly buried, they learned, was that it belonged to someone who had kicked and cursed his mother. The zuwwār performed the duʿāʾ, seeking God's forgiveness on behalf of the irreverent son, and then carefully covered the leg once more. God accepted their prayers, and thereafter the leg remained buried.[42] Although adab al-ziyāra permitted offering prayers on behalf of the dead, as well as the living, the guides do not directly deal with the issue of shafāʿa, or intervention of the dead, especially the holy dead, with God, on behalf of the living. Yet this was clearly a major objective of duʿāʾ, as we will discuss in Chapter 4.

Recitation of the Qur'ān by zuwwār at the grave was also encouraged, according to Ibn ʿUthmān's eighth waẓīfa. He points to a statement made by Aḥmad Ibn Ḥanbal (d. 855), the eponymous founder of one of the four schools of Sunnī jurisprudence, which expressly sanctions this activity. The sixteenth waẓīfa similarly permits relatives and friends of the dead to sit near their graves and

[41] Ibid., 58–59.

[42] Ibn al-Zayyāt, *al-Kawākib*, 156–57. See also Ibn ʿUthmān, *Murshid*, 269–70; and al-Sakhāwī, *Tuḥfat*, 276.

dedicate recitations of the Qur'ān on behalf of the dead.[43] Ibn al-Zayyāt tells us of a zā'ir who was unsure of what to do when visiting the tomb of Yaḥyā, the brother of al-Sayyida Nafīsa. Suddenly the visitor heard a voice coming from the tomb behind him commanding him to recite the second half of the thirty-third verse of the thirty-third Sūra of the Qur'ān: "Allāh's wish is but to remove uncleanness far from you, O Folk of the Household, and cleanse you with a thorough cleansing." This was apparently a verse commonly recited by zuwwār at the tombs of descendants of the Prophet Muḥammad (the ashrāf).[44] The pilgrimage guides also mention that the thirty-sixth Sūra, "Yā Sīn," was commonly recited by zuwwār at graves.[45] The significance of this Sūra was tied to a ḥadīth relating that the Prophet instructed Muslims to recite "Yā Sīn" over their dead. Ibn al-Zayyāt and Ibn 'Uthmān also mention another, far less authoritative, ḥadīth, which reported that the Prophet said "Yā Sīn" was the heart of the Qur'ān.[46] The eleventh Sūra, "Hūd," was also commonly repeated by zuwwār. For example, Shaykh 'Alī al-Jabbās, while visiting the cemetery one Friday evening, came to Turbat Banū al-Lahīb. He read there from Sūrat Hūd until he reached the end of the one hundred and fifth verse describing the Day of Judgment: "On the day when it cometh no soul will speak except by His permission; some among them will be wretched, (others) glad." Suddenly the shaykh heard a voice say, "Ibn al-Jabbās, shame on you! None of us are wretched, all of us are glad."[47] Shaykh Ibrāhīm al-Mālikī al-Dūkālī confirmed in a dream that zuwwār at his tomb should read the Qur'ān and never recite poetry.[48]

Zuwwār are frequently cautioned against levity in the cemetery. In his eighteenth waẓīfa, Ibn 'Uthmān abjures the zā'ir not to laugh in the cemeteries, "a place where weeping is more appropriate."[49] Such admonitions notwithstanding, it is clear that al-Qarāfa was often the site of considerable festivity and socializing. The sources collectively leave little doubt that the sort of social intercourse that Ibn

[43] Ibn 'Uthmān, *Murshid*, 38, 62.
[44] Ibn al-Zayyāt, *al-Kawākib*, 94.
[45] Ibn al-Nāsikh, *Miṣbāḥ*, fols. 16r°–16v°, 49v°, 59v°; and Ibn al-Zayyāt, *al-Kawākib*, 159.
[46] Ibn al-Zayyāt, *al-Kawākib*, 16, 159. See also Ibn 'Uthmān, *Murshid*, 274.
[47] Ibn al-Zayyāt, *al-Kawākib*, 251.
[48] Al-Sakhāwī, *Tuḥfat*, 363–64.
[49] Ibn 'Uthmān, *Murshid*, 62.

al-Ḥājj was so concerned about was also a significant aspect of the ziyāra, albeit a troubling one for the ʿulamāʾ, regardless of whether they attacked or defended the institution as a whole. For example, Muḥammad al-Manbijī, the author of *Tasliyat ahl al-maṣāʾib fī mawt al-awlād wa-al-aqārib* (The Consolation of the People of Misfortune in the Death of Children and Relatives), who is generally supportive of the ziyāra, complains in much the same terms as Ibn al-Ḥājj about women dressing up and embellishing their beauty before going out on the ziyāra.[50] He also charges that licentious young men wait for women in the cemeteries and then mingle freely with them there. In addition, the author of the *Tasliya* decries women who go out to the cemetery and sit on tombs. As we have seen, the cemetery clearly provided an important place where men and women might meet each other without too much concern about social supervision. Ibn al-Nāsikh relates a report from al-Qurashī that a man once kissed a woman while the two were perched on the tomb of Shaykh Abū al-Qāsim ʿAbd al-Raḥmān. Suddenly they heard a voice intone from the grave: "Shame! You are in a place where one weeps not laughs."[51] This couple may have been quickly chided, but most young lovers probably escaped such rapid detection in private and secluded corners of the cemetery. Al-Manbijī also criticizes rabble who go to the cemetery simply to enjoy good food, buy and sell things, and chatter about inappropriate topics. Vignettes such as this repeatedly illustrate the liminal quality of al-Qarāfa.

Not only was the Qarāfa liminal space, but the ziyāra was what Victor Turner would describe as a "liminoid" ritual process. Building from the earlier work of Arnold van Gennep on rites of passage, Turner defined full "liminality" as "the state and process of mid-transition in a rite of passage." While they are in the liminal state, "liminars," the subjects of a ritual process, he explains, are "ambiguous, for they pass through a cultural realm that has few or none of the attributes of the past or coming state. Liminars are betwixt and between." Furthermore, while in this intermediary state, liminars are "removed from social structure maintained and sanctioned by power and force."[52]

---

[50] Al-Manbijī, *Tasliyat*, 102.
[51] Ibn al-Nāsikh, *Miṣbāḥ*, fol. 52vº.
[52] See Turner and Turner, *Image and Pilgrimage*, 249, and Turner, *Process*, 149.

Turner went on to describe pilgrimage as a "liminoid" or "quasi-liminal" phenomenon characterized by

> release from mundane structure; homoginization of status; simplicity of dress and behavior; communitas, both on the journey, and as a characteristic of the goal, which is itself a source of communitas, healing, and renewal; ordeal; reflection on the meaning of religious and cultural core-values; ritualized reenactment of correspondences between a religious paradigm and shared human experiences; movement from a mundane center to a sacred periphery which suddenly, transiently, becomes central for the individual, an *axis mundi* of his faith; movement in general (as against stasis), symbolizing the uncapturability and temporal transience of communitas; individuality posed against the institutionalized milieu; and so forth.[53]

Although it shares all these qualities with rites of passage, Turner argued, pilgrimage is not fully liminal in that it is voluntary and "marks no transition from one state or status to another within the mundane sphere."[54] The ziyāra seems to have served as an important medium through which participants entered the liminoid state and experienced the spontaneous communitas Turner describes. For it was in the ziyāra, as we have seen, that powerful sultans donned simple Ṣūfī garments, the rich mixed with the poor, men mixed with women, and the living mixed with the dead as a broad cross-section of medieval Cairene society journeyed out from the "mundane center" of the city to the "sacred periphery" of al-Qarāfa—that "great medium of divine blessing." It was here, too, in the vast, dusty, and liminal expanse of the cemetery that the zuwwār probably experienced something of the communitas Turner delineates as they sought to heal and renew themselves, or simply to engage in "reflection on the meaning of religious and cultural core-values."

The guides make little mention of the abuses that critics of the ziyāra frequently charged were taking place in the cemeteries. These disturbing practices were said to include performing Ṣūfī dhikr, fasting, slaughtering livestock, offering sacrifice and votive offerings, making vows at graves, and decorating tombs with coverings or fancy drapes like the Kaʿba. Exactly how prevalent such activities may have been is unclear. While noting the hostile intentions of the authors of some of these reports, we cannot simply dismiss them out of hand. At the

[53] Turner and Turner, *Image and Pilgrimage*, 253–54.
[54] Ibid., 254.

same time, however, it is important that we consider these practices in the larger context of the ziyāra as a whole. Such a perspective suggests that this institution consisted of a range of activities, some authorized and consistent with even the most conservative and sober interpretations of Islamic doctrine on the one hand, and activities which were, on the other hand, clearly suspect. Taken collectively, these actions defined the ziyāra.

One important activity that the zuwwār were deeply engaged in during their frequent visits to the Qarāfa was listening. While participating in the ziyāra, visitors to the cemetery heard thousands of stories (qiṣaṣ) about the saints whose tombs they came to visit. The pilgrimage guides have preserved for us many of these wonderful qiṣaṣ, and by analyzing them we gain not only a better sense of the ziyāra as an important expression of Muslim piety, but also critical insight into what I will describe in the next chapter as the moral imagination of Islamic society in late medieval Egypt.

CHAPTER THREE

IMAGES OF RIGHTEOUSNESS AND PIETY

The stories and qualities of the saints recorded in the four surviving medieval pilgrimage guides to the cemeteries of Cairo provide invaluable information about the broader significance of the saints (awliyāʾ, s. walī) in the later Middle Ages. Through the stories of the awliyāʾ recounted to the zuwwār in the context of their visits to the cemeteries, we gain essential access to both their thought-world and the texture of their faith. These qiṣaṣ al-awliyāʾ are especially informative about two vital roles of the saints. First, they reveal that the saints served as important models of exemplary piety, specific examples of righteousness that were transmitted to generations of pious visitors through the ziyāra. This is the role we examine in this chapter. Second, the stories of the saints tell us a great deal about the kinds of intercession and miraculous powers attributed to the awliyāʾ. In this sense the ziyāra provided a kind of map of sacred space in al-Qarāfa, pinpointing the specific locations of great reservoirs of baraka where the zuwwār might come to seek the active assistance and intercession of the saints, or simply to benefit from close physical proximity to the divine blessing that engulfed their tombs. This aspect of the awliyāʾ, as agents of mediation, we will take up in the next chapter.

The basic meaning of the verb *waliya* is "to be near" or "to be close to" someone or something. From this sense of proximity the word also comes to mean "to be friends with" or "to have power or authority over." The noun *walī* may thus mean "friend" or "close associate" as well as "protector." In the Qurʾān walī appears in several different contexts. For example, the singular occurs forty-four times, most commonly to assert that the believer has no "friend" or "protector" save God, or alternately that God is the "friend" or "protector" of the believer.[1] In several instances it is said that the

[1] Qurʾān: 2:107, 2:120, 2:257, 2:282, 3:68, 3:122, 4:45, 4:75, 4:89, 4:119, 4:123, 4:173, 5:55, 6:14, 6:51, 6:70, 6:127, 7:155, 7:196, 9:74, 9:116, 12:101, 13:37, 16:63,

unbelievers have "no protecting friend."[2] In at least two cases, however, the word refers instead to an "heir" or "successor."[3] The plural noun, *awliyāʾ*, is found forty-two times in the Qur'ān,[4] of which the most significant instance, in terms of the later development of Ṣūfī doctrine on sainthood in Islam, is Sūra 10:62: "Indeed, there is neither fear nor regret for the friends of God." The largest number of occurrences of the plural, however, involves injunctions that believers should not take unbelievers as friends.[5] The verbal noun, *walāya*, which later came to indicate the function of sainthood, occurs only twice in the Qurʾān (8:72 and 18:44).[6] Although these examples and other Qur'ānic uses of the root *w*l*y* would later form the basis of Ṣūfī notions of sainthood, the Qur'ān itself does not provide an unambiguous concept of either saints or of sainthood. The development of a clearly articulated Islamic doctrine of sainthood, therefore, although drawing upon both Qur'ānic inspiration and sources in ḥadīth, belongs to a later period. This is not to suggest that the earliest Muslims were unaware of saints, or that there were no Muslim saints in the early Islamic period, only that a coherent and systematic theory of saints and sainthood cannot be traced specifically to either the Qur'ān or the Prophetic period.

The first person credited with introducing the notion of walāya in a technical doctrinal sense into Islamic mystical thought is the great ninth-century mystic Abū ʿAbd Allāh Muḥammad b. ʿAlī b. al-Ḥasan al-Ḥakīm al-Tirmidhī (d. 898), who authored the famous *Kitāb khatm al-awliyāʾ* (The Book of the Seal of the Saints) around 873. As Chodkiewicz has demonstrated, in the nearly three centuries between al-Tirmidhī's composition of *Kitāb khatm al-awliyā* and the first truly comprehensive and systematic Ṣūfī doctrinal exposition of a theory of walāya by Ibn ʿArabī (1165–1240), the concept seems

17:33, 17:111, 18:17, 18:26, 19:5, 19:45, 27:49, 29:22, 32:4, 33:17, 33:65, 34:41, 41:34, 42:8, 42:9, 42:28, 42:31, 42:44, 45:19, and 48:22.

[2] Ibid., 4:123, 4:173, 9:74, 18:17, 33:65, 42:8, 42:44, and 48:22.

[3] Ibid., 17:33 and 19:5.

[4] Ibid., 2:257, 3:28, 3:175, 4:76, 4:89, 4:139, 4:144, 5:51 (twice), 5:57, 5:81, 6:121, 6:128, 7:3, 7:27, 7:30, 8:34 (twice), 8:72, 8:73, 9:23, 9:71, 10:62, 11:20, 11:113, 13:16, 17:97, 18:50, 18:102, 25:18, 26:41, 33:6, 39:3, 41:31, 42:6, 42:9, 42:46, 45:10, 45:19, 46:32, 60:1, and 62:6.

[5] Ibid., 3:28, 4:89, 4:139, 4:144, 5:51 (twice), 5:57, 5:81, 9:23, and 61:1.

[6] The alternative form *wilāya* is frequently found in other classical sources, but in only one of the seven authoritative readings of the Qur'ān. See Chodkiewicz, *Seal of the Saints*, 23 on this point.

to have undergone a subtle but complex evolution, which is unfortunately obscured by the fact that the major intervening mystical thinkers were deliberately circumspect in not addressing the matter of walāya in a direct or extended manner in their surviving writings.[7] Generally in Ṣūfī doctrine, the awliyā' are "seekers" who, having entered on a mystical Path (ṭarīqa, pl, ṭuruq), have proceeded through a series of "stations" or "waystations" (which they earn), and "states" (which are bestowed upon them by God), and have achieved one of a series of hierarchical ranks. Ṣūfī theoreticians themselves rarely agreed on the ranks, the exact manner in which the hierarchy of saints was ordered, or on the precise number of saints in each rank. Among some of the categories of sainthood they discuss, however, we find: the the "outstanding" (akhyār), the "substitutes" (abdāl), the "devoted" (abrār), "stakes," such as those used to hold tents firmly to the ground (awtād), the "chiefs" (nuqabā'), and at the summit the unique the "axis" or "pole" (quṭb), also referred to as the "source of help" (ghawth). In Ibn ʿArabī's thought, the highest station of sainthood was the "Station of Proximity" (maqām al-qurba), which the greatest saints (the afrād), share with the prophets (anbiyā'), who are themselves also saints. Here Ibn ʿArabī distinguished between notions of legislative and general prophethood, with the understanding that the saints were the heirs of the prophets in general though not legislative prophethood. And, as Chodkiewicz explains, just as legislative prophethood was sealed by Muḥammad, the "Seal of Muḥammadan Sainthood" was none other than the greatest systematic Ṣūfī thinker, the Shaykh al-Akbār, Ibn ʿArabī himself.[8]

The present study is not concerned with the development or exposition of these technical Ṣūfī doctrines on saints or sainthood.[9] Our aim here is rather to provide a sense of who the saints were, what roles they filled, and what meanings they held for the wider population of Egyptian Muslims in the period between 1200 and 1500 A.D.

In Roman Catholicism the process through which saints are authenticated became the sole prerogative of an institutionalized clerical hierarchy, formalized in the procedures of papal beatification and

---

[7] On al-Tirmidhī's role in the devopment of Ṣūfī doctrines of walāya see Chodkiewicz, *Seal of the Saints*, 27–32; on the intervening thinkers see ibid., especially 59.

[8] Ibid., 137–38.

[9] Readers interested in these questions are referred to the excellent works of Michel Chodkiewicz, as well as Böwering, *The Mystical Vision of Existence in Classical Islam*; Radtke, *Al-Ḥakīm at-Tirmiḏī*; Frederick M. Denny, "God's Friends;" and *The Encyclopedia of Religion*, s.v. Walāyah.

canonization. In the Islamic world, by contrast, this level of formal and centralized institutional control over the certification of sainthood has never existed. The manner in which Muslim saints are identified and acknowledged, therefore, remains, as was the case in early Christianity, very much a matter of local initiative. Muslim saints have traditionally been identified through the acknowledgment and acclamation of believers in a particular region. Because the process of establishing Muslim saints has always been so informal, saints in Islam have generally remained more local in their appeal than have many of their Christian counterparts. There have always been unofficial saints in the Christian world with largely local appeal just as there are a few special individuals in the Islamic experience who have attracted pilgrims from distant lands.

The institutional apparatus of the Church succeeded, albeit with greater or lesser degrees of success regionally, in asserting its control over the process of recognizing and legitimating saints, supervising their veneration, and manipulating the cult for its own ends. Since no comparable clerical institutional hierarchy existed, at least in the Sunnī world, Muslim religious authorities never enjoyed the same type of influence or control over the cult of the saints that their counterparts in Western Christendom often did. To some extent the great Ṣūfī brotherhoods probably did play some role in managing and shaping the production of saints during the period between 1200 and 1500 A.D., but the exact dynamics of their involvement remain unclear. The cult of saints generally, and the ziyāra in particular, were important factors in encouraging the mass popular followings that grew up around the ṭarīqas in this same period, but, it remains to be determined to what extent the ṭarīqas themselves controlled the process whereby saints were identified and subsequently venerated. The pilgrimage guides to medieval Cairo suggest that many of the awliyā' venerated in Egypt were, in fact, prominent Ṣūfīs or otherwise significant religious and legal scholars. Other saints, however, while clearly enjoying an enduring popularity in contemporary public imagination, have left no evidence to suggest that their elevation to sainthood was the product of anything other than spontaneous popular acclamation.[10] Furthermore, we must bear in mind that the production and widespread veneration of saints in the Islamic world long antedates the rise of the great Ṣūfī ṭarīqas in the early thirteenth

[10] An excellent example of one spontaneous popular acclimation of a saint's shrine is presented in Shoshan, *Popular Culture*, 9.

century. Thus, although the leadership of the brotherhoods may have sought to influence the process whereby saints were identified in the popular imagination, it is doubtful that they were able, or even consciously sought, to direct it in any formal or systematic sense.

One might reasonably ask whether the pilgrimage guides themselves are not evidence of an effort by certain elite strata of society to shape and control the ziyāra. It is true that the guides can be quite blunt on occasion in their derision of certain popular practices and beliefs. Furthermore, the preoccupation with adab al-ziyāra and the proper conduct of the zuwwār while visiting the cemetery might similarly suggest efforts to control both the content and form of the institution. On the whole, however, one is struck by a general impression of how inclusive the guides are. One detects, for example, no underlying agenda to replace one set of popular tombs with another, or to guide the veneration of saints along certain predetermined paths. As a rule, the guides speak of what the general populace believes and does at certain tombs without betraying any hint of either disapproval or incredulity. The overriding impression one comes away with is that the primary goal of the guides' authors was to be as comprehensive as possible. As we will show in Chapter 6, their interest in adab al-ziyāra probably arose more as a reflexive response and desire to insulate the ziyāra from the implacable hostility of certain vocal and articulate critics among their fellow ʿulamāʾ than from any conscious design to manipulate the cult of the saints for narrow sectarian or political purposes. Here again the two-tier model of cultural discourse seems far too static and facile to explain adequately a dynamic socio-cultural process such as saint production in late medieval Egypt.

A good example of how eclectic and inclusive the cult of Muslim saints might be is again illustrated by the case of the woman saint named Āsiya, who, the guides tell us, was consistently venerated by segments of the Egyptian populace during the later Middle Ages. Āsiya is the name that the early Qurʾānic exegetes assigned to the figure identified in Sūras 28:8 and 66:11 only as "the wife of Pharaoh" (imraʾat firʿawn).[11] According to the version of the story of Āsiya recounted by Ibn al-Zayyāt, a maid servant of Pharaoh's daughter was once combing her mistress's hair, when the comb accidentally

[11] See *EI*², s.v. Āsiya.

slipped from her hands. Under her breath the servant said "In the name of God," as she stooped to retrieve the fallen object. Her young mistress then asked if the maid was speaking of Pharaoh when she invoked God's name, but the servant explained that the god of whom she spoke was the master of all, including Pharaoh. When Pharaoh's daughter realized that the maid worshiped another god above her father, she denounced the unfortunate woman.

When the servant was brought before Pharaoh, and questioned about her beliefs, she courageously admitted her monotheism. The enraged tyrant then commanded that the servant and all of her children be burned alive in a large brass cow. Just before her children were cast into the flames the servant secured from Pharaoh a promise that their bones would be gathered and buried together. The maid then watched silently as each of her children was consumed by the fire, until they came to her infant son. For a moment it seemed that she might waver in her faith as she stared helplessly at her condemned child. Then God, in His infinite mercy, made the infant speak, and the child urged his mother to be firm in her resolve, "for the punishments of this life are far more bearable than those of the hereafter."

When Āsiya, Pharaoh's wife, discovered what punishment her husband had cruelly imposed on the poor servant and her family, she tried in vain to intercede and stop him. Pharaoh in his blind rage refused her pleas, and accused his wife of adhering to the same heretical beliefs as the condemned woman. At this point Āsiya admitted that she too believed in Allāh. According to some views she also was then martyred at the hand of Pharaoh, while others suggest that her soul miraculously ascended to heaven before she was killed.

Although the authors of the pilgrimage guides reject outright the proposition that the mashhad in al-Qarāfa popularly identified as belonging to Āsiya "the wife of Pharaoh" actually contained her remains, they are not in agreement as to the real identity of the Āsiya who was indeed buried there. Ibn ʿUthmān and al-Sakhāwī identify her as the daughter of an official of Aḥmad b. Ṭūlūn (r. 868–884); Ibn al-Nāsikh argues that she was the granddaughter of Ibn Ṭūlūn himself; Ibn al-Zayyāt accepts the proposition that she is the daughter of a certain Muzāḥim b. Abū al-Riḍa b. Simnūn Khāqān.[12] This

[12] Ibn al-Zayyāt, *al-Kawākib*, 42; Ibn ʿUthmān, *Murshid*, 20; Ibn al-Nāsikh, *Miṣbāḥ*, fol. 7v°; and al-Sakhāwī, *Tuḥfat*, 140, 142–43, and 177.

example of a simple confusion in names, and the uncertain identity of a tomb, demonstrates the remarkably flexible manner in which the cult of Muslim saints expanded in Egypt throughout the Middle Ages. Among the thousands of tombs listed in the pilgrimage guides, we find significant figures representating virtually every period of Islamic history.

The informal and largely unmediated process that frequently produced saints in the Islamic world helps to explain both their proliferation and their generally limited geographical appeal. It also suggests that a contextual understanding of saints and of sainthood in various Islamic societies must be flexible and sensitive to subtle variations in local meaning. At the same time, the veneration of saints in specific Islamic milieus may offer greater insight into local religious sensibility than might be the case where external institutional interference in the articulation and elaboration of the cult is a significant factor.

Since there was no transcendent institutional framework to promote the cult of the saints, in many instances the record of the lives and works of the saints relied exclusively on oral transmission. The intergenerational transfer of hagiographic material was, therefore, often dependent on collective communal memory. Much of this oral tradition has now disappeared, which is why the pilgrimage guides to the cemeteries of Egypt are so important. They capture for us otherwise lost information based on the body of primarily oral material that existed when the guides were composed.

The ziyāra, as we have seen, included a wide range of individual and collective activities centering around the practice of visiting graves in general. Pilgrimage guides, however, were specifically intended to promote and facilitate the ziyāra to the graves of the holy dead. The practice of visiting the awliyā' was viewed as an especially efficacious spiritual exercise through which visitors might learn how to perfect their own lives by reflecting on the lives of authentic and recognized models of piety.[13] In this sense the saints were promoted as ideal prototypes of exemplary piety worthy of contemplation and emulation.

Were all of the individuals mentioned in the guides necessarily "saints?" And what did the term walī mean in this context? The

[13] Ibn al-Zayyāt, *al-Kawākib*, 275–76.

manner in which the pilgrimage guides employ the word suggests that it had a far less precise meaning than it does in technical Ṣūfī manuals. For example, al-Sakhāwī tells us that his work only deals with shaykhs and saints. In another instance, he pleads with God not to "deprive us" of the baraka "of the saints mentioned in this book."[14] Ibn al-Zayyāt makes an almost identical appeal at the conclusion of his own guide.[15] In the context of the pilgrimage guides, then, the word walī implies any holy or righteous person perceived as enjoying a special relationship with God, and it is in this same broad sense that I employ the term here.

The pilgrimage guides generally classify the individuals they consider by association or occupation, in categories called ṭabaqāt (s. ṭabaqa). Ibn al-Zayyāt tells us, for example, that there were ten ṭabaqāt of which the ṣaḥāba, or companions of the Prophet, come first, the ahl al-bayt, also called the ashrāf, or descendants of the Prophet, come next, and the tābiʿūn, or second generation of the faithful, come third. He then skips to the tenth division, which he identifies as the principal intermediaries (arbāb al-asbāb).[16] Although Ibn al-Zayyāt never enumerates the remaining six ṭabaqāt in their proper order, references throughout the text indicate that these included: the viziers (wuzarāʾ), the judges (quḍāʾ), the amirs (umarāʾ), the martyrs (shuhadāʾ), the mystics (ṣūfiyya), the devout (ʿubbād), and finally the jurists more generally (fuqahāʾ). Other categories such as preachers (khuṭabāʾ), Qurʾān reciters (qurrāʾ), relators of prophetic ḥadīth (muḥaddithūn), teachers (mutaṣaddirūn), and public prayer leaders (a'imma), are generally classified with the jurists, or alternately with the mystics. Unfortunately, Ibn al-Zayyāt and the authors of the other guides are not systematic in their use of these ṭabaqāt. For example, while dealing with a Shaykh Abū Muḥammad b. ʿAmr al-Ḥaddād (d. 940/41),

---

[14] Al-Sakhāwī, *Tuḥfat,* 376, 402.

[15] Ibn al-Zayyāt, *al-Kawākib,* 321.

[16] Ibid., 5 and 196. This last is a difficult phrase to translate because without further explanation in the text it is hard to tell exactly what the author intends. Louis Massignon notes that the word *sabab* (pl. *asbāb*) means "intermediary" (*Passion of al-Hallāj,* 1:201, 297, 309, 538, and 3:127). However, Professor Hossein Modarressi (personal communication) informs me that in some Ṣūfī thought the sense of sabab conveys more than "intermediary"; see, for example, Qurʾān 38:83–84. Based on these verses some Ṣūfī thinkers have held that certain saints known as sabab also have power and discretion from God to dispose of affairs in the world. I have translated asbāb here as "intermediaries" because it is not clear if Ibn al-Zayyāt also means special intermediaries with discretionary authority.

Ibn al-Zayyāt speaks of al-qurrā', al-muḥaddithūn and al-fuqahā' as clearly separate and distinct ṭabaqāt.[17]

These occupational and associational distinctions help us to delineate broad categories of sainthood in the late medieval Egyptian imagination, but the guides tell us much more. They reveal a great deal about the individual attributes and qualities of the awliyā' that played an important role in defining the ideal image of piety for the zuwwār. From them it is possible to collect information about the exemplary traits of the saints, and then to reconstruct the essential outlines of these ideal images.

Various aspects of Islamic piety have been stressed in different times and places. For example, heroic contribution to the establishment of Islam, or an especially close association with the Prophet, were clearly emphasized in Egypt during the formative period of Islam. Thus, exceptional figures such as ʿAmr b. al-ʿĀṣ, the Muslim conqueror of Egypt, and ʿUqba b. ʿĀmir al-Juhanī are both buried in al-Qarāfa, and seem to have been venerated from a very early date. During the Fāṭimid era, however, there was a shift in emphasis, at least as far as official patronage was concerned, in the sense that the cult of figures central to the ʿAlid drama was promoted with great zeal. The impressive architectural remains of this policy are still evident in the surviving Fāṭimid monuments in al-Qarāfa.

The pilgrimage guides include a lot of posthumous apocrypha about the saints, but some information in them may well be roughly contemporaneous to the saints themselves. Thus, while we sometimes find mashāhid al-ru'yā established on the basis of a vision experienced long after the death of the person commemorated, we encounter a much larger number of mausolea that are not vision mausolea, such as the tomb of ʿUqba b. ʿĀmir al-Juhanī, and which seem to be genuinely ancient. It appears that subtle changes in the predominant motif of individuals commemorated in the ziyāra occurred over time. While we cannot trace all of these shifts, we can describe the particular motif which characterized the period covered by this study, and what may have prompted its emergence. It appears that between 1200 and 1500 A.D. the earlier motifs of heroic figures from the era of the Islamic conquest, or ʿAlid martyrs, seem to have been at least partially eclipsed and superseded by a new image. This was what might be described as a scholarly and ascetic motif of per-

[17] Ibid., 70.

sonal piety, which came to dominate the cult of Muslim saints in the later Middle Ages. Those individuals whose deaths are identified as occurring after the mid-twelfth century are overwhelmingly described as being scholars and Ṣūfīs. This shift in the dominant motif of new saints seems to have mirrored the increasingly important role of both the ʿulamāʾ generally and the popularization of Ṣūfī ṭarīqas specifically.

The specific qualities and attributes that defined this ascendant paradigm of exemplary piety after 1200 may be loosely grouped into ten general categories: mastery of personal desire, poverty, absence of material need, generosity, honesty, graciousness, eccentricity and special awareness, repentance, resistance to unbelief and hypocrisy, and commitment to the pious life.

Mastery of personal desire

Ascetic denial was a central feature of the Islamic image of exemplary piety in the later Middle Ages. The essence of the ascetic path involved attainment of pure and absolute devotion to God through a personal transcendence of all temporal concerns and distractions. Many ascetics were known for austere lives of fasting, abstinence, and mastery over worldly desires. Ibn Ṭūghān al-Shāfiʿī (d. 1204) was famous, for example, because he fasted forty years, except on feast days when fasting is specifically prohibited in Islam.[18] Yūnis al-Wariʿ fasted for twenty-five years, breaking his fast only at night to eat a loaf of wheat bread. He then fasted an additional twenty-five years, breaking his fast at night only to consume a loaf of barley bread.[19] ʿAbd al-Raḥmān b. al-Qāsim al-ʿUtaqī (d. 806/7) fasted so much that the white of his bones and the green herbs that he ate were clearly visible through his translucent skin.[20]

The exacting standards of the ascetic life were usually beyond the reach of even the most devout. ʿAlī b. Muḥammad al-Muhalabī once encountered a group of twelve ascetics. He wandered with them for two days without eating or drinking. When they finally asked what

[18] Al-Sakhāwī, *Tuḥfat*, 334. Ibn al-Zayyāt, *al-Kawākib*, 225. Virtually the same story is told about Ismāʿīl al-Maflūḥ in Ibn al-Nāsikh, *Miṣbāḥ*, fol. 7r°.

[19] Ibn al-Zayyāt, *al-Kawākib*, 305–6. See also al-Sakhāwī, *Tuḥfat*, 387, and Ibn ʿUthmān, *Murshid*, 606.

[20] Ibn al-Nāsikh, *Miṣbāḥ*, fols. 14v°–15r°, and Ibn al-Zayyāt, *al-Kawākib*, 39–40. See also al-Ṣafadī, *al-Wāfī bi-al-wafayāt*, 18:219.

was troubling him, ʿAlī explained that he was hungry and thirsty. His companions then pronounced him unfit to be counted among them, and ʿAlī was instantly transported back to his home.[21] Shaykh Abū al-Ḥasan b. al-Fuqāʿī (d. 964) also once joined a group of twelve ascetics living in the Jabal al-Muqaṭṭam. Each night one of them would pray and a table containing twelve loaves of bread and a fish would miraculously appear before them. When it was Abū al-Ḥasan's turn to pray he asked God not to disgrace him in the eyes of his new companions, and a table with thirteen loaves of bread and a fish appeared in due course. Abū al-Ḥasan then wished to himself that there was some salt to enhance the flavor of the fish, and the salt instantly appeared. The twelve companions looked at each other in surprise when the table was brought before them, and they asked Abū al-Ḥasan if the salt simply had appeared by itself or because he desired it. He proudly announced that no sooner had he wished for the salt than it appeared. His twelve companions then explained that there was no place for desire among them and Abū al-Ḥasan was compelled to leave their company.[22]

Constant vigilance against the relentless and often imperceptible force of temptation and personal desire was essential among ascetics. Shaykh Abū al-Khayr al-Tīnnātī (d. c. 961) once made his way to Antioch on the Byzantine frontier in search of a hospice (ribāṭ). He was armed with a sword, a shield, and a lance so that he might wage both the physical jihād against the infidel and pursue the ascetic path in conducting an inner jihād of the soul. Abū al-Khayr found a cave to live in, and he made a covenant with God that he would only eat what God placed before him. Thus, he received each night only what he needed to survive. One day, however, he forgot his promise when his eye was attracted by some ripening fruit still glistening with dew. Abū al-Khayr reached out, took the fruit, and started to eat it before suddenly realizing that his desire had overcome him. He immediately discarded the partially eaten fruit and spat out what still remained of it in his mouth. He then sat with his hand on his head deeply distressed by his failure. Suddenly, a detachment of soldiers came upon him. When they saw his sword, lance, and shield they immediately seized the shaykh and took him

---

[21] Ibn al-Zayyāt, *al-Kawākib*, 148–49; see also al-Sakhāwī, *Tuḥfat*, 270, and Ibn al-Nāsikh, *Miṣbāḥ*, fol. 51r°.

[22] Ibn al-Zayyāt, *al-Kawākib*, 130; see also Ibn ʿUthmān, *Murshid*, 318–21.

before their amir. Abū al-Khayr then learned that the soldiers had arrested him because they were rounding up a group of Sudanese highwaymen plaguing the district, and they mistook him for one of them, since his complexion was dark. When the amir asked the rest of his prisoners if they knew Abū al-Khayr, they all said no, which convinced the amir that the shaykh was actually their ringleader. On the orders of the amir, the soldiers then proceeded to amputate the hands and feet of all their prisoners until they came to Abū al-Khayr. They ordered the shaykh to extend his hand, which he did, and they chopped it off. As the soldiers prepared to cut off his leg, Abū al-Khayr raised his face to heaven and pleaded with God saying, "My hand was possessed, so it was amputated, but what is wrong with my leg?" Through God's mercy a knight suddenly came upon the gathering, recognized Abū al-Khayr, and threw himself upon the shaykh with a great shout. When the knight was asked what he was doing he revealed Abū al-Khayr's true identity, whereupon the amir himself, and all those around him, shouted in dismay. The amir threw himself down before the shaykh's foot, kissed it, and wept for forgiveness. Abū al-Khayr assured the amir that he had done nothing wrong.[23]

The world was filled with dangerous distractions, and the truly pious were often forced to go to great lengths to escape them. A shaykh, known only as Muẓaffar, lived in an abandoned monastery called Dayr al-Ṭīn, where he constantly recited the Qur'ān and refused to accept any gifts. Abū al-Qāsim "the mute" spoke only when reciting the Qur'ān. The jurist Abū al-Samrā' "the Blind" went so far as to ask God to make him blind until death, at which time the saint hoped to see his Maker. After his death Abū al-Samrā' confirmed through a dream that God had indeed commanded Abū al-Samrā' to open his eyes, thus fulfilling his wish.[24] When Abū Aḥmad the jurist was appointed as a judge he fled and hid for years to avoid threatening entanglements in worldly affairs.[25]

Many ascetics extended the rigorous standards by which they lived right to the grave. For example, Abū Bakr al-Musāfir asked that when he was laid to rest in his tomb even the shroud he was wrapped

---

[23] Ibn al-Zayyāt, *al-Kawākib*, 110–13. For his biography see al-Ṣafadī, *al-Wāfī*, 13:445.

[24] Al-Sakhāwī, *Tuḥfat*, 277; Ibn al-Nāsikh, *Miṣbāḥ*, fols. 53r°–53v°; Ibn al-Zayyāt, *al-Kawākib*, 308–9; (see also Ibn ʿUthmān, *Murshid*, 608).

[25] Ibn al-Zayyāt, *al-Kawākib*, 144.

in be removed.[26] Self-denial of material goods and pleasures, mastery over personal desire, and seclusion from the corruption of the world were important aspects of the ascetic quest. Satan often sought to dissuade the devout from their contemplation of God, especially through profane distractions. Shaykh Abū al-Ḥasan b. al-Fuqāʿī, for instance, related how once while he and his associates were performing duʿāʾ at the Cave of the Blacks to commemorate the waqfa, a handsome youth wearing beautiful clothes and riding a wonderful horse approached them.[27] The group was distracted from their prayers by this event, and Ibn al-Fuqāʿī expressed his fear that this youth might actually be Satan trying to distract them from God. Even as he spoke, the youth and his horse suddenly plunged into the depths of the earth, thereby proving him right.[28]

Fear of corruption arising simply from routine interaction with others resulted in a strong desire among certain ascetic saints to remain in seclusion as hermits. The mundane world sometimes forced itself upon those wishing to escape its grasp, however. For example, Abū al-Dhikr Muḥammad b. Yaḥya (d. 951/52) was compelled to accept the position of chief judge of Egypt even after he, and more than sixty other jurists, initially refused the position. Abū al-Dhikr desperately sought some way to escape the official responsibility thrust upon him, so he began selling dates at night. Eventually someone warned Abū al-Dhikr that if the caliph discovered that one of his high judicial officials was selling dates at night, he would immediately dismiss the offender. Abū al-Dhikr patiently explained that he was hoping for precisely such an outcome. When the caliph finally did learn of these nocturnal activities he secretly sent his agents to buy dates from the shaykh. When the dates were delivered to the caliph he saved them and offered them to people afflicted with fever because the fruit had been touched by the baraka of Abū al-Dhikr. Those who ate the dates were miraculously cured; as a result, Abū al-Dhikr was brought before the caliph, who commanded the shaykh request a favor. Abū al-Dhikr asked only to be removed from his position as judge, and the caliph reluctantly consented.[29]

---

[26] Ibn al-Nāsikh, *Miṣbāḥ*, fol. 15v°.

[27] Waqfa is the ninth day of the Islamic month of Dhūl Ḥijja, when Muslim pilgrims performing the ḥajj stand for the day on Mount ʿArafāt outside Mecca.

[28] Ibn al-Zayyāt, *al-Kawākib*, 130.

[29] Ibid., 81. Ibn ʿUthmān presents a slightly different account; see *Murshid*, 476.

Mastery over sexual desire was an important reflection of the sort of exacting standards of personal self-control and denial that typically characterized the awliyāʾ. Although the Qurʾān and Prophetic tradition specifically encourage marital procreation and discourage celibate life, sexual desire and attraction have proven no less powerful obstacles to the pursuit of the ascetic life among Muslims than among followers of other religious traditions.[30] Shaykh al-Ghāfiqī dealt with this problem by avoiding the marketplace for twenty-five years, and he never passed a woman without averting his eyes.[31] When Abū al-Faraj Aḥmad (d. 1071/72) once went to visit his teacher, he was attracted by the sight of a woman. When he realized what he was doing he was suddenly ashamed. Later, while reciting the Qurʾān with his master, Abū al-Faraj lost his concentration and the shaykh asked what was wrong. Then the shaykh looked at Abū al-Faraj more closely and pronounced, "This is the result of that glance on your way here." Thereafter Abū al-Faraj never again lifted his eyes from the ground when walking.[32] Abū al-Rabīʿ also kept his eyes fixed on the ground after once gazing upon a woman and subsequently experiencing a dream in which he was warned, "Do not disgrace us." Abū al-ʿAbbās Aḥmad never again left his mosque after once coming across an impoverished woman bathing while he was out fetching some water.[33]

Sometimes the problem of physical attraction required a more drastic solution. Abū al-Baqāʾ Ṣāliḥ b. al-Ḥusayn (d. c. 1145/46) was so handsome that women always stared at him when they saw him. Finally he asked God to disfigure him so that he would not be so attractive. God granted his wish and women began to avert their eyes whenever they passed him.[34] Shuqrān b. ʿUbayd Allāh was so handsome that women became infatuated with him whenever they saw him. When a girl once told an old woman of her love for Shuqrān, the woman declared that she would find some way to bring

[30] Qurʾānic verses cited by jurists as making marriage a duty in Islam include: 2:187, 2:223, 4:25, 24:32–33, and 30:21. Marital sex is viewed by some as a form of worship, and celibacy is generally forbidden. See Denny, *An Introduction to Islam*, 115 and 273.

[31] Al-Sakhāwī, *Tuḥfat*, 351–52; see also Ibn al-Zayyāt, 250.

[32] Ibn al-Zayyāt, *al-Kawākib*, 163; see also Ibn al-Nāsikh, *Miṣbāḥ*, fol. 39v°.

[33] Ibn al-Nāsikh, *Miṣbāḥ*, fols. 74r°–74v°. Ibn al-Zayyāt, *al-Kawākib*, 250; see also al-Sakhāwī, *Tuḥfat*, 351; and Ibn al-Nāsikh, *Miṣbāḥ*, fol. 69v°.

[34] Ibn al-Zayyāt, *al-Kawākib*, 307; see also al-Sakhāwī, *Tuḥfat*, 388–89, and Ibn ʿUthmān, *Murshid*, 614–17.

the two of them together. The old woman made her plans carefully, and when Shuqrān passed by the door to her house one day she called out to him, saying that her son was away and a letter had just arrived which her daughter wanted to hear very much. The old woman first asked Shuqrān if he would be kind enough to stand by the doorway and read the letter, and when he agreed, the old woman exploited his kindness further by urging him to enter her house for the sake of privacy. As soon as Shuqrān entered the house, however, the old woman bolted the door behind him, and the young girl rushed out to grab him. Horrified, Shuqrān sought desperately to avert his eyes as the infatuated girl madly expressed her desire for him. He immediately requested some water so that he could cleanse himself. Then Shuqrān prayed and asked why God had given him such an attractive countenance. In response Shuqrān was suddenly disfigured so that the girl was repulsed by his looks, and she ordered him out of the house. After escaping, however, Shuqrān regained his good looks once more.[35]

Abū Bakr Aḥmad b. Naṣr al-Zaqqāq (d. 904/5) was in Mecca when he was overcome by a desire for milk. He went to the outskirts of the city in search of some, and there he saw a beautiful woman to whom he was attracted. When he expressed his desire for her, the woman chided Abū Bakr, telling him that if he had been concentrating on God he would never have gone in search of milk in the first place. In shame Abū Bakr plucked out the eye that had first beheld the woman, and he returned to Mecca weeping. That night the Prophet Joseph came to Abū Bakr in a dream and restored his eye.[36] In a similar story, the beautiful saint known as al-ʿAynāʾ ("the one with the eyes") was plagued by a particularly insistent suitor. Finally she inquired what attracted the man to her, and he explained that it was her eyes. Some say that upon hearing this, al-ʿAynāʾ plucked out her beautiful eyes and sent them to the man, who promptly died of shock at the sight of them.[37]

Physical beauty was not the principal quality that attracted most people to saints, of course. Al-Qurashī, who suffered a disfiguring

---

[35] Ibn al-Zayyāt, *al-Kawākib*, 238; see also al-Sakhāwī, *Tuḥfat*, 343, and Ibn ʿUthmān, *Murshid*, 369.

[36] Ibn al-Zayyāt, *al-Kawākib*, 80; see also al-Sakhāwī, *Tuḥfat*, 202–3. Ibn ʿUthmān relates different stories, see *Murshid*, 470–73.

[37] Ibn ʿUthmān, *Murshid*, 361; see also Ibn al-Nāsikh, *Miṣbāḥ*, fol. 73v°.

physical affliction, for example, always refused to marry, saying he had no desire to do so. One night in a dream, however, the Prophet Muḥammad came to al-Qurashī and told him about the beautiful woman he would soon marry. The Prophet also visited the prospective bride and told her about al-Qurashī. As a result of these dreams the engagement between al-Qurashī and his bride was soon arranged. Before the wedding al-Qurashī asked God to restore his physical health, and so it came to pass. When the time came to consummate the marriage, however, al-Qurashī went to his wife and found her veiled. When he asked why she was concealing herself from him, the bride explained that the Prophet had promised that she would marry a man with a physical affliction, but al-Qurashī was clearly healthy. So al-Qurashī begged God, once again, to return him to his former condition, and his wish was fulfilled.[38]

Although complete sexual renunciation was not commonly practiced among Muslim ascetics, nor is it frequently reported in the pilgrimage guides, there are several instances where it is mentioned. For instance, Khadīja (d. 1295), the daughter of Shaykh Hārūn b. ʿAbd Allāh b. ʿAbd al-Razzāq, performed the pilgrimage fifteen times and died a virgin, a fact that was noted on her tombstone.[39] On the night of the consummation of her marriage, the sister of Abū al-Ṭayyib b. Ghalbūn (d. 997) begged God to allow her to die a virgin, and her prayer was immediately answered.[40] The woman known only as the "maiden of the desert" had never been seen by a man other than her father, until the night of her wedding. When her husband-to-be, who was also her cousin, came to consummate the marriage, he lifted her veil so as to gaze upon his bride. She was suddenly overcome with embarrassment and she began to sweat excessively. The maiden prayed to God asking that she might never be seen again by a man. Her plea was rewarded, and she died that very moment. Zuwwār to her tomb reported that even when they touched her grave in the dead of winter their hands would begin to sweat.[41] Shaykh ʿAdiyy b. Musāfir was celibate, but he asked God to carry on his line through his brother, and his request was granted.[42]

---

[38] Ibn al-Zayyāt, *al-Kawākib*, 270–71; see also Ibn al-Nāsikh, *Miṣbāḥ*, fols. 65v°–66r°.
[39] Ibn al-Zayyāt, *al-Kawākib*, 226–27; see also al-Sakhāwī, *Tuḥfat*, 334–35.
[40] Ibn ʿUthmān, *Murshid*, 294–97.
[41] Ibn al-Zayyāt, *al-Kawākib*, 143. See also al-Sakhāwī, *Tuḥfat*, 265.
[42] Ibn al-Zayyāt, *al-Kawākib*, 186–87; see also al-Sakhāwī, *Tuḥfat*, 300. The shaykh

Poverty

Although a few saints are portrayed as possessing great wealth, indigence is more consistent with the rejection of material satisfaction, and poverty is a common characteristic of the saints. The theme of saints barely sustaining themselves through the toil of their own labor recurs frequently. For example, Shaykh Abū al-ʿAbbās Aḥmad b. al-Khaṭiyya al-Lakhmī lived in the streets with his daughter, sustaining the two of them on his earnings as a scribe. He refused to accept charity from anyone, even sultans. Someone once swore to divorce his wife if Shaykh Abū al-ʿAbbās refused to accept the gift of a robe. When confronted with such a drastic threat, the shaykh reluctantly accepted the robe but then left it hanging unused for thirty years.[43]

Even what little money some saints received for their work was frequently given away as charity to those less fortunate. Shaykh Shāwir al-Ḥabashī used to sew shirts, using only a single thread. He gave away most of the money he made from his labor as charity.[44] Ibrāhīm b. Aḥmad al-Khawwāṣ (d. 903/4) used to make three baskets each day. He lived off the money he made from one, purchased the materials needed for his work from the sale of the second, and threw the third into the Nile in the hope that God might deliver it to a needy person. People urged Ibrāhīm instead to sell the third basket and give the proceeds from its sale as charity and he finally agreed to try this approach. Shortly thereafter, however, while walking along the riverside, he came across a poor woman and her children who depended for their survival on the baskets Ibrāhīm had traditionally cast into the river. He immediately resolved that henceforth he would bring the poor woman the value of the third basket directly each day.[45]

---

is ʿAdiyy b. Musāfir b. Ismāʿīl al-Hakkārī (d. 1162) the founder of the ʿAdawiyya Ṣūfī ṭarīqa. For his biography see al-Ṣafadī, *al-Wāfī*, 19:534–35 and Ibn Khallikān, *Wafayāt al-aʿyān*, 3:254–55; see also note 89 below. I am most grateful to Wadad Kadi for bringing this to my attention.

[43] Ibn al-Zayyāt, *al-Kawākib*, 232; see also Ibn ʿUthmān, *Murshid*, 390.

[44] Ibid., 192. For his biography see al-Ṣafadī, *al-Wāfī*, 5:305. See also Ibn ʿUthmān, *Murshid*, 74 and 560–61, where different stories are told. Ibn ʿUthmān also tells a story similar to that related by Ibn al-Zayyāt but about a different saint, the tailor Abū al-ʿAbbās Aḥmad b. Muḥammad (d. either 983/84 or 1002/3), *Murshid*, 312.

[45] Ibn al-Nāsikh, *Miṣbāḥ*, fols. 21v°–22r°. See also Lane, *Arabian Society in the Middle Ages*, 52–3, where he tells a variation of this story in the notes to his translation of the *Thousand and One Nights*.

Some saints were actually repulsed by the thought of accepting money in exchange for their services. Abū al-Barakāt ʿAbd al-Muḥsin once turned down twenty dīnārs from someone who traveled from a great distance to consult with him about a legal decision, saying: "I do not sell knowledge for dīnārs."[46] Muḥammad b. al-Muthannā al-Ṣadafī routinely refused money offered him, reacting in horror as if someone was attempting to give him a corpse.[47] The jurist Abū al-Ḥasan ʿAlī b. Ibrāhīm b. Muslim (d. 1168/69) began his career as a cloth merchant, but he left the world of business as the result of a vision. After he and an associate were sitting and discussing business one day, the two men suddenly implored God to cultivate in each of them a loathing of buying and selling. That night Abū al-Ḥasan experienced his strange dream, in which he saw himself making his way to his shop. Upon reaching the entrance to the bazaar, however, he saw a Christian with a reed making a black mark on everyone who entered the market. Abū al-Ḥasan awoke suddenly from his dream so terrified that he never left his house again, devoting himself instead to the pursuit of religious knowledge.[48]

The absence of material need

Although the pious were usually very poor, they were rarely in need of basic necessities. Whenever they did require something it generally appeared, often miraculously. For example, when the jurist Abū al-Qāsim ʿAbd al-Raḥmān b. Muḥammad b. Raslān was building a mosque he ran out of funds before the well was built. When he performed the morning prayers he found under his prayer rug a purse containing twenty-five dīnārs with a message that the money was for the completion of the well. Abū al-Qāsim was never sure if the gold was put there by men or by jinn.[49]

Shuqrān b. ʿUbayd Allāh once asked his assistant for some water with which to perform a major ritual ablution. There was no water to be found, so the shaykh looked skyward and prayed to God, and suddenly the sound of water filling an empty container could be

[46] Al-Sakhāwī, *Tuḥfat*, 354.
[47] Ibn al-Zayyāt, *al-Kawākib*, 104.
[48] Ibid., 252. See also al-Sakhāwī, *Tuḥfat*, 352; and Ibn ʿUthmān, *Murshid*, 342–44.
[49] Al-Sakhāwī, *Tuḥfat*, 392; see also Ibn al-Zayyāt, *al-Kawākib*, 311–12, and Ibn ʿUthmān, *Murshid*, 636.

heard. The water was cold because it was a chilly night, so Shuqrān simply moved his lips and the water warmed instantly to the touch. Since it was also a dark night Shuqrān wished for a lamp to see by, and that too suddenly appeared.[50] Similarly, the famous woman mystic Rābiʿa al-ʿAdawiyya (d. 801) once came to Shaybān al-Rāʿī (d. c. 786/87) and mentioned that she wanted to go on the pilgrimage to Mecca. Shaybān reached into his pocket and pulled out a piece of gold to help pay for the trip, but Rābiʿa reached into the air and suddenly her hand was filled with gold. She declared, "You take from your pocket, and I will take from that which is transcendent."[51]

Umm Aḥmad al-Qābila, who lived in the Muqaṭṭam hills, once told her son to light a lamp on a cold, dark, and rainy night. He explained that there was no oil, so his mother instructed him to fill the lamp with water, invoke the name of God, and light the wick. When Umm Aḥmad's son did as his mother instructed, the wick caught fire immediately. When he asked his mother how water could burn, Umm Aḥmad replied that everything obeys those who submit completely to God.[52]

A certain Abū al-Ḥusayn was once preparing to leave on a trip to Mosul, and he passed by Shaykh Abū al-Khayr al-Tīnnātī. Abū al-Khayr knew that Abū al-Ḥusayn would not accept any money, so the shaykh handed the traveler two apples and told him to carry them with him on his journey. Abū al-Ḥusayn accepted the gift and put the fruit in his pocket. After going for three days without finding anything to eat, Abū al-Ḥusayn reached into his pocket and pulled out one of the apples. After finishing the first apple, Abū al-Ḥusayn reached back into his pocket to retrieve the second apple, but he discovered to his amazement that there were still two apples in his pocket. As he continued his trip Abū al-Ḥusayn discovered that each time he took an apple from his pocket there always remained two more.[53]

Even in death the truly pious were provided for. When Shaykh ʿImrān b. Dāwūd b. ʿAlī al-Ghāfiqī was brought to his grave for

---

[50] Ibn al-Zayyāt, *al-Kawākib*, 237; see also Ibn al-Nāsikh, *Miṣbāḥ*, fol. 74r°.

[51] Al-Sakhāwī, *Tuḥfat*, 304; Ibn ʿUthmān, *Murshid*, 503; Ibn al-Zayyāt, *al-Kawākib*, 192–93. Ibn al-Nāsikh tells almost the same story about another saint, see *Miṣbāḥ*, fol. 83r°. For the biography of Shaybān al-Rāʿī see al-Ṣafadī, *al-Wāfī*, 16:201.

[52] Ibn al-Zayyāt, *al-Kawākib*, 294; see also al-Sakhāwī, *Tuḥfat*, 378.

[53] Ibn al-Zayyāt, *al-Kawākib*, 111; see also al-Sakhāwī, *Tuḥfat*, 241, and Ibn ʿUthmān, *Murshid*, 399.

burial, the mourners discovered that the tomb would not accommodate him because of the shaykh's height. Before they could lift him out of the grave to make it larger, however, the tomb suddenly expanded by itself.[54]

Generosity

The saints were invariably generous with whatever they had in the way of material possessions. The pilgrimage guides are filled with accounts of their open-handedness and charity. For example, Muḥammad b. ʿAbd Allāh b. al-Ḥusayn was famous for urging his customers to buy from his competitors if he had already made a sale that day.[55] Several stories are told about the charity of the wealthy merchant ʿAffān b. Sulaymān al-Miṣrī. ʿAffān had no children, and distributed vast sums of money as charity, reportedly feeding five hundred families daily. He also used to meet the annual pilgrimage caravan on its return from Mecca, at the port of ʿAqaba, with food. ʿAffān also once sold a thousand camels and distributed the profits to widows and the poor.[56]

There are differing accounts about how ʿAffān first acquired his wealth. According to one version he was originally a tailor living and working in al-Fusṭāṭ. One night he was instructed in a dream to go to Baghdad, where he would find his fortune. After experiencing the same dream for three consecutive nights, ʿAffān finally decided to set off for Baghdad. When he reached his destination he began working as a tailor. ʿAffān remained in Baghdad for a month with no result other than that each day his anxiety over the dream increased. Finally his employer asked what was wrong, and ʿAffān explained that he had come to Baghdad because of his vision but he had failed to find his fortune. After ʿAffān recounted the details of his dream his employer exclaimed that he too had experienced a similar dream for many years in which he was instructed to go to Egypt where he would become rich. ʿAffān inquired about the

---

54 Ibn al-Zayyāt, *al-Kawākib*, 250–51.

55 Ibid., 132. See also al-Sakhāwī, *Tuḥfat*, 259–60; Ibn al-Nāsikh, *Miṣbāḥ*, fols. 46v°–47r°; and Ibn ʿUthmān, *Murshid*, 315.

56 Al-Sakhāwī, *Tuḥfat*, 144–48. See also Ibn ʿUthmān, *Murshid*, 182 and 656–61; and Ibn al Nāsikh, *Miṣbāḥ*, fol. 9r°.

details of his employer's dream and the man explained that he was told to go to a certain house where he was to dig for a great sum of money. From the description of this house ʿAffān recognized it as his own, so he immediately left Baghdad and returned to Egypt. ʿAffān dug where his employer instructed him to and there he found his fortune.[57] This wonderful parable of traveling far only to discover that which you seek was back home all along is virtually the same as that of "the man who sought for treasure," found in the *Maṣnavī* of the great Persian mystical poet Jalāl al-Dīn Rūmī (1207–1273).[58] The fact that this story appears in the work of Ibn ʿUthmān, who died in Cairo only eleven years after the birth of Rūmī in Balkh, raises intriguing questions about the role of the ziyāra as a possible source of inspiration and material for Rūmī and other great Ṣūfī poets.

In an alternate version of how ʿAffān became wealthy, the tailor purchased a young black slave. One day ʿAffān ordered his servant to light the oven so they could prepare their meal. The boy lit the fire as ʿAffān instructed, but when the flames leapt up, the servant became so captivated by them that he gathered up all the fabric ʿAffān was working on, as well as ʿAffān's turban, and all his possessions, and threw everything into the roaring fire. Poor ʿAffān then returned home to discover what his young servant had done. But God bestowed great patience and forbearing on ʿAffān, and instead of becoming angry he simply manumitted the young slave, provided him with supplies, and sent the boy on his way. When people learned what had happened to ʿAffān, and of how magnanimously he had reacted to the disaster, they were greatly moved by his forgiving kindness and generosity.

Not long thereafter, one of the great merchants of Egypt came to ʿAffān and asked if he would serve as the merchant's agent in taking some goods to India to sell. The two men agreed on a partnership, and ʿAffān set off for India. He sailed down the Red Sea to Aden, where he remained for some time. Afterwards, ʿAffān sailed on to India, where he conducted his partner's business at great profit. On the return voyage, however, a fierce storm arose and the ship

---

[57] Al-Sakhāwī, *Tuḥfat*, 145. See also Ibn ʿUthmān, *Murshid*, 656–61. A different story is told in Ibn al-Zayyāt, 90.

[58] See Arberry, *More Tales from the Masnavi*, 227–29. Margaret Case brings to my attention that an almost identical Hassidic parable is related by Martin Buber, and cited in Zimmer, *Myths and Symbols*, 219–21.

carrying ʿAffān was blown off course toward the East African coast, the "land of the Blacks." Fearing that they might drown, all the merchants, including ʿAffān, decided to abandon ship and take their goods and money ashore with them. But as soon as they reached land the merchants were seized by soldiers. Eventually they were led before the local king, who was silent until ʿAffān was summoned before him. The king rose suddenly in great excitement at the sight of ʿAffān, kissed ʿAffān's hands and feet, and stood before the startled merchant, who still did not recognize his captor. The king then asked: "Are you not ʿAffān, the tailor from al-Fusṭāṭ, who once purchased a young black slave, a slave who later burned all your clothes in a moment of excitement and whom you forgave, manumitted, and provisioned for the trip home even after he caused you great harm?" ʿAffān acknowledged the account, whereupon the king announced: "I was that slave." ʿAffān thanked God for His mercy and the king offered his entire realm to his former master, the humble tailor from al-Fusṭāṭ. ʿAffān expressed his gratitude, but explained that although he thought of the king as a son it would not be suitable for either himself or those traveling with him to remain in the king's realm for very long. The king reluctantly accepted this decision, but he insisted that ʿAffān accept a boat filled with a great sum of money in return. ʿAffān agreed and then set sail with his fellow travelers for Yemen. When he finally reached Egypt once again he used all of his money to build houses, shops, and baths, among other things. All of these things he endowed, in perpetual trust to God, for the benefit of the poor and unfortunate.[59]

Generosity was an integral part of the pious life, and it was a virtue the saints found impossible to control. The merchant and jurist Abū al-Ḥasan ʿAlī b. Muḥammad b. ʿAbd al-Ghanī consistently gave the profits of his trading activity away as alms for forty years. When he finally married, however, Abū al-Ḥasan suddenly realized that his duty to provide for his wife must take precedence over giving to others. This realization greatly saddened him and he came to his new wife with the profits of his business, weeping. She was deeply puzzled by her husband's distress and asked why he was so upset. Abū al-Ḥasan explained that he was troubled because he was so accustomed to distributing the profits of his trade as charity (ṣadaqa).

---

59 Al-Sakhāwī, *Tuḥfat*, 147–48.

When his new bride wondered how Abū al-Ḥasan had managed to survive with such a habit he explained that he had always placed his trust in God and was never disappointed. Abū al-Ḥasan's wife then instructed him to continue distributing his profits as ṣadaqa, and they both placed their trust in God. The same night while they were sleeping there came a knock at the door. Abū al-Ḥasan went to the door and found a man with a thousand dīnārs claiming that the money belonged to Abū al-Ḥasan. When the shaykh asked what the source of the money was, the man explained that he was simply returning a deposit left with him by Abū al-Ḥasan's father. Abū al-Ḥasan refused to accept the money, and the confused man departed. Later, however, the man experienced a dream in which he was told to return once more to Abū al-Ḥasan and explain, "This is from God in whom you and your wife placed their trust yesterday." The man did as he was instructed and Abū al-Ḥasan finally accepted the money.[60]

Bushrā b. Saʿīd was so generous that he gave away all his money, a hundred thousand dīnārs, as ṣadaqa. When Bushrā no longer had any money to offer, he took out loans whenever Ṣūfīs came to him, until his debts reached a thousand dīnārs. At this point Bushrā's wife interceded and urged her husband simply to hide when people came asking for money. His daughter, however, disagreed and argued that her father should continue borrowing money to give away as ṣadaqa because God would always provide for them. When Bushrā went to pray in the mosque one Friday, there came a knock at the door of his house. When Bushrā's son went to open the door, a purse of money was thrown in and someone said, "Tell your father to borrow without fear." When Bushrā returned home he opened the purse and discovered that there was enough money to cover all of his debts with about fifty dīnārs to spare.[61]

Generosity was such a basic and pervasive characteristic of the pious life that we encounter it even among saints so poor that they had virtually nothing of material value to give. Abū al-Qāsim Yaḥyā b. ʿAlī b. Muḥammad, a descendant of Alī b. Abī Ṭālib, was once approached by a poor man who asked for money. Although Abū al-Qāsim had no money himself, he suggested the man try selling

[60] Ibn al-Zayyāt, *al-Kawākib*, 258; see also al-Sakhāwī, *Tuḥfat*, 356.

[61] Ibn al-Zayyāt, *al-Kawākib*, 68. See also Ibn al-Nāsikh, *Miṣbāḥ*, fols. 18r°–18v°; and Ibn ʿUthmān, *Murshid*, 452–54.

the saint himself. The poor man took Abū al-Qāsim to the vizier, who gave the man a thousand dīnārs with an apology that it would be impossible to find enough money to equal the value of Abū al-Qāsim.[62] The saint, known only as the "beggar for the mystics" (shaḥādh al-fuqarā'), had no money of his own to give, so he used to beg among the wealthy on behalf of Ṣūfīs. Shaḥādh al-fuqarā' would then distribute the money he gathered among all of the Ṣūfīs, each according to his need, so that none of them was left wanting.[63]

Accounts of great individual generosity are frequently noted in connection with moments of particular hardship. Sayyid al-Ahl b. Ḥasan, known as "the grain merchant," for example, maintained five hundred families during a famine in the reign of the Fāṭimid caliph al-Mustanṣir (r. 1036–1094).[64] A destitute woman once came to Shaykh Abū Muḥammad Ismā'īl b. 'Amr, "the blacksmith," seeking assistance. She explained that her husband had left on a journey without leaving anything for her or her two daughters to live on. Abū Muḥammad took pity on the woman, immediately put down his work, and went to buy food and provisions for them. When Abū Muḥammad and the woman arrived at her house, the two daughters came out to greet them. One of the daughters prayed that God might protect the blacksmith from fire in this life as well as the next. Soon thereafter, the generous blacksmith discovered that he was able to take hot iron from the fire with his bare hands without fear of being burned. Abū Muḥammad thanked God for answering the first half of the girl's prayer and he prayed that the second portion of her plea might also be fulfilled. Abū Muḥammad then ceased his work as a blacksmith and devoted the rest of his life to the search for religious knowledge.[65]

In a similar story a poor widow once passed the shop of a generous merchant. As she was weeping, he inquired why. The woman explained that she had only ten dirhams and her daughter was supposed to marry in three days' time but still had no trousseau. The merchant promptly gave the woman the money she needed to marry her daughter properly. In return, he asked only that if the girl was

---

[62] Ibn al-Zayyāt, *al-Kawākib*, 61; see also Ibn 'Uthmān, *Murshid*, 248.

[63] Ibn al-Zayyāt, *al-Kawākib*, 232; see also Ibn 'Uthmān, *Murshid*, 391–92.

[64] Ibn al-Nāsikh, *Miṣbāḥ*, fol. 51v°. See also Ibn al-Zayyāt, *al-Kawākib*, 149.

[65] Ibn al-Zayyāt, *al-Kawākib*, 70; see also Ibn 'Uthmān, *Murshid*, 474–76, and Ibn al-Nāsikh, *Miṣbāḥ*, fol. 21v°. An almost identical story is told about al-Muzanī; see Ibn al-Zayyāt, *al-Kawākib*, 194, and al-Sakhāwī, *Tuḥfat*, 305.

pleased with his gift she should pray for his salvation on the Day of Judgment. After the generous merchant died, he confirmed in a dream that God had answered the girl's prayer.[66] The generosity of Abū ʿAbd Allāh, known as "the gravedigger," was also famous. He provided the trousseaus of twelve hundred brides. In addition, he paid for the circumcision of twelve hundred orphan boys, and provided the burial shrouds for sixteen hundred indigents.[67]

Generosity was not always demonstrated in such sweeping gestures. More often it was reflected in simple acts of hidden selflessness. Shaykh ʿAbd al-Khāliq, "the coppersmith," always took the food his wife prepared for him each day and distributed it as ṣadaqa. His wife discovered what he was doing, and she secretly began adding her own portion of food to her husband's before giving it to him. In place of all the food they gave away, the generous couple ate salt.[68] Similarly, the jurist Abū ʿAbd Allāh Muḥammad, known as "the weasel" used to take his meal to his less fortunate neighbors. Just as he entered their house he would wipe his mouth as if he had just finished eating and say, "there is no food better than this." Abū ʿAbd Allāh's wife once asked him why he did not eat with his children, and he lamented that he was not able to. After his death, the neighbors told Abū ʿAbd Allāh's family what he had secretly been doing with his portion of food. Abū al-Barakāt was never able to return from the public oven without having given away all of his bread as ṣadaqa on the way home.[69]

The truly generous found it impossible to refuse requests for charity no matter how frequently they came. For instance, Shaykh Abū ʿAbd Allāh Muḥammad, who was actually quite wealthy, once decided to eat a good meal to help him recover from an illness. An expensive chicken worth two dīnārs was accordingly prepared for him. Just as the feast was placed before Shaykh Abū ʿAbd Allāh there suddenly came a knock at his door. The shaykh ordered his servant to see who it was and what they wanted. The servant found a poor widow at the door seeking charity. Without hesitating Shaykh Abū ʿAbd Allāh gave his chicken dinner to the poor woman. She gratefully accepted the shaykh's gift and took the chicken home to her

---

[66] Ibn al-Zayyāt, *al-Kawākib*, 165; see also Ibn ʿUthmān, *Murshid*, 282; and Ibn al-Nāsikh, *Miṣbāḥ*, fols. 41r°–41v°.
[67] Al-Sakhāwī, *Tuḥfat*, 179 and 294.
[68] Ibn al-Zayyāt, *al-Kawākib*, 249; see also al-Sakhāwī, *Tuḥfat*, 350.
[69] Ibn al-Zayyāt, *al-Kawākib*, 199; al-Sakhāwī, *Tuḥfat*, 353.

children. Just as her family was sitting down to eat the feast, however, there was a knock at the door. An agent of the owner of the house had come to collect their rent. The poor widow told the rent collector she had nothing to offer him except the wonderful chicken meal they were just about to eat. The chicken was so impressive that the rent collector was sure that his employer would be pleased by it, so he agreed to take the chicken in place of the rent. As it turned out, the rent collector worked for Shaykh Abū ʿAbd Allāh, who owned the poor widow's house without knowing it. When the shaykh saw the chicken return to his table once again he was surprised. He asked how his agent obtained it, and the man told the story of the poor widow who could not afford to pay her rent but offered this wonderful chicken in its place. Abū ʿAbd Allāh promptly instructed the man to return immediately to the woman and inform her that the house she lived in henceforth belonged to her. The shaykh also made arrangements that each year the woman would receive what she and her children needed to live on.

This act of generosity accomplished, the shaykh prepared once more to eat his chicken meal. Before he could begin, however, there came yet another knock at the door. This time it was a poor neighbor seeking assistance. Once again, Abū ʿAbd Allāh told his servant to take the chicken meal from the table and offer it to the needy man. The neighbor gratefully accepted the fine chicken, but on his way home he decided that he was not fit for such a great feast. Just then he passed someone on the road, and the poor man asked if the passer-by would like to purchase the chicken. The stranger was pleased by the sight of the splendid chicken, and he bought it for two dīnārs. He then exclaimed to himself: "This is a meal fit for my father!" and he took the chicken home to Abū ʿAbd Allāh. When the shaykh saw the chicken returning yet another time, he asked his son where it had come from. The son told of how he bought the chicken from someone he passed on the way to his father's house. Abū ʿAbd Allāh asked his son how much he paid in exchange for the chicken and his son said two dīnārs. The shaykh then instructed his son to go to their unfortunate neighbor and offer him another fifty dirhāms.

With this second act of generosity completed, Shaykh Abū ʿAbd Allāh sat down to eat his meal for the third time, but once again there came a knock at his door. Abū ʿAbd Allāh instructed his servant to answer the door, but vowed that if it was another poor person seeking help, the shaykh would manumit his servant on the spot. She returned and confirmed that there was indeed another needy person at the door seeking the shaykh's help. Shaykh Abū ʿAbd Allāh, true to his word, asked his servant to take the chicken once again to the person at the door and afterwards she herself was free.[70]

Generosity did not necessarily cease with the death of a saint. A man from Baghdad once came in search of Shaykh Abū ʿAbd Allāh al-Nabbāsh. The traveler reached Egypt after his long journey only to discover that Abū ʿAbd Allāh was already dead. The disheartened visitor went to the shaykh's tomb and wept bitterly before finally falling asleep. While he slept he saw Abū ʿAbd Allāh in a dream. The shaykh told the visitor that if only he had arrived while Abū ʿAbd Allāh was still alive, he would certainly have offered him a gift. Taking pity on the visitor from Baghdad, the shaykh told the man to go to a certain al-Mukhtār, and ask him for fifty dīnārs on behalf of Abū ʿAbd Allāh. When the visitor awoke from his sleep he went in search of al-Mukhtār, whom he found waiting for him with fifty dīnārs.[71] A similar story is reported about three men known only as "the sugar makers" (al-sukkariyūn). When a poor man came to the marketplace seeking alms from them he was informed that they were already dead. He made his way to their tombs, where he collapsed in grief and hunger. While the poor man slept by the graves of the sukkariyūn one of them came to him in a dream. The poor man was instructed to go to the home of the dead saint and tell his son to dig in a certain place, where he would find money. When the man awoke he followed these directions. The saint's son dug where his father had instructed, and he found a clay pot containing three hundred dīnārs. He then gave the poor man even more money than he requested.[72]

Honesty

Honesty was another important quality commonly attributed to the awliyāʾ. Two men came to the judge al-Khayr b. Nuʿaym b. ʿAbd

[70] Ibn al-Zayyāt, *al-Kawākib*, 164–65; see also al-Sakhāwī, *Tuḥfat*, 281, and Ibn al-Nāsikh, *Miṣbāḥ*, fols. 40v°–41r°.

[71] Al-Sakhāwī, *Tuḥfat*, 179.

[72] Ibn al-Zayyāt, *al-Kawākib*, 230–31; see also Ibn ʿUthmān, *Murshid*, 393–94.

al-Wahhāb b. ʿAbd al-Karīm al-Ḥaḍramī (d. 753/54) concerning a dispute over a sick camel. The qāḍī had just finished washing his robe, and it still had not finished drying when the two men arrived. Khayr b. Naʿīm's daughter greeted the men when they knocked at the qāḍī's door, but she told them that the jurist would not be available until the next morning. During the night the disputed camel died. When the two men returned the next day to ask Khayr b. Naʿīm which of them should incur the loss for the animal, the jurist declared that neither of them was responsible, rather the burden should fall instead on the judge who had wrongly eluded them the day before. Therefore, Khayr b. Naʿīm paid for the camel himself.[73]

Maymūn, "the weaver," always used to mark the fabric he made with a red dot wherever a thread broke. He instructed the merchant who sold the cloth for him to inform customers that under each dot there was an imperfection in the cloth.[74] Muḥammad b. ʿAbd Allāh b. al-Ḥusayn was married to an honest wife. One day a beautiful woman came to Muḥammad's shop and he inquired if she was married. The woman said that she was not, so he asked her to marry him on the condition that he would only see her during the day. The woman agreed and they were married. When Muḥammad suddenly stopped coming home during the day, as was previously his custom, his first wife asked her maid servant to follow him secretly and see where he went from his shop during the day. The servant waited close to Muḥammad's shop, and she followed him as he left. When he entered a house, the servant asked the neighbors about Muḥammad. They explained that this was his house, and he lived there with his wife. The servant returned to Muḥammad's first wife and reported this news about Muḥammad's second wife. Muḥammad's first wife never told her husband that she knew he had taken a second wife. When Muḥammad died, his first wife collected together all of his money and divided it into two equal parts. She gave half of the money to her servant and told her to take it to Muḥammad's second wife and inform her of his death. The servant did as she was told, but when she offered the money to the second wife the woman explained that Muḥammad had divorced her before he died, so she could not accept the money. Abū al-Faraj b. al-Jawzī, who

[73] Ibn al-Nāsikh, *Miṣbāḥ*, fol. 26v°; see also Ibn ʿUthmān, *Murshid*, 229–33.
[74] Ibn al-Zayyāt, *al-Kawākib*, 131.

related this story, said that he did not know which of the two women was more honest.[75]

The saints were not only honest, but they could also count on God's assistance in fulfilling their obligations. Yūnis ʿAbd al-Aʿlā b. Maysara b. Ḥafṣ b. Jābir al-Ṣadafī, known as Abū Mūsā (d. 877), related the story of an unidentified man who once asked someone to borrow a thousand dīnārs. When the lender inquired of the man who would act as his guarantor for the loan, the borrower responded that God would. The lender then provided the money requested and the borrower set off on his travels to conduct business. Through his trade the borrower made a great deal of money, but when the time approached to repay his loan he could not find a ship on which to return home. With no other alternative in sight, the borrower took a piece of wood and hollowed out a cavity in it. In this space he placed one thousand dīnārs. He then sealed the cavity and threw the wood into the sea saying to God, "I have fulfilled my obligation with your guarantee, so deliver it to him." The wood was then carried to the lender, who retrieved it one day while performing his ablutions by the sea. He took the wood home with him, and when he broke it open he found the thousand dīnārs in it with a note saying: "I have redeemed the guarantee of God." Meanwhile, the borrower was able to make an additional thousand dīnārs from his business ventures, and he told himself that if the first thousand he sent in the piece of wood never arrived he would repay his creditor with the second thousand dīnārs. When the borrower finally arrived home he made his way to his creditor to see if the man had in fact received the money sent in the piece of wood. The lender acknowledged that the money had arrived, but he added that he refused to touch it until the borrower arrived to explain what had happened. So the borrower recounted the entire story and his creditor saw how God had delivered the money and redeemed the guarantee.[76]

[75] Ibid., 132. See also Ibn ʿUthmān, *Murshid*, 315; Ibn al-Nāsikh, *Miṣbāḥ*, fols. 46v°–47r°; and al-Sakhāwī, *Tuḥfat*, 259–60.

[76] Ibn ʿUthmān, *Murshid*, 405–8.

Eccentricity and special awareness

The exclusive concentration of the saints on spiritual matters sometimes manifested itself as unusual distraction regarding earthly realities. When we consider some of the miracles associated with saints in the next chapter, we will note a number of examples of saints walking on water, a phenomenon that was often indicative of precisely this sort of distraction. For example, the story of Shaykh ʿAbd Allāh b. al-Barrī al-Naḥawī (d. 1186/87), once started to walk across the water when he failed to realize that the boat on which he was a passenger had not yet reached land.[77] This act reflects a degree of absorption with spiritual matters so complete that the saint was both oblivious to and unaffected by surrounding reality.

The innocent naiveté and eccentricity reported about certain figures mentioned in the pilgrimage guides was often humorous. For example, Shaykh ʿAbd Allāh b. al-Barrī was also famous for wearing a robe with one narrow and one wide sleeve. When he bought things in the market, the shaykh would place them in the wide sleeve of his robe. One day Shaykh ʿAbd Allāh purchased some bread, grapes, and firewood, all of which he placed together in his sleeve. Not surprisingly, the wood crushed the grapes, but as the juice poured from his sleeve the puzzled shaykh asked one of his pupils if it had rained. The student responded: "The rain cloud is in the shaykh's sleeve!" On still another occasion Shaykh ʿAbd Allāh's family announced that they were going to the public bath. The shaykh asked them to hurry home afterward because he was going to the market to purchase provisions for their evening meal. After buying eggs, rice, meat, and firewood, Shaykh ʿAbd Allāh returned to find his family still away and the house locked. He threw all the food and fuel through a small window and went to the mosque to pray. That evening the shaykh asked that the food he had purchased be prepared. He was shocked to learn that upon returning from the public bath his family found only firewood and some eggshells waiting for them. Shaykh ʿAbd Allāh's wife explained that some cats had discovered and eaten all the food he left. The shaykh declared: "There is no god but God! I never imagined that cats would eat forbidden food. Until today I

[77] Ibn al-Zayyāt, *al-Kawākib*, 221–22; see also Ibn ʿUthmān, *Murshid*, 642–45.

was never acquainted with anyone who would eat something that was stolen."[78]

Some of the awliyā' demonstrated a level of eccentricity that clearly bordered on insanity. Shaykh Nujaym, "the simple minded" responded to any greeting with the words, "kishk and meat."[79] Shaykh Mūsā earned the appellation "Cover your hand!" because whenever he saw a woman he would strike her and shout "Cover your hand!"[80] Another shaykh was known as "the mumbler" because he was frequently seen talking to himself.[81] When the famous early Islamic mystic Thawbān b. Ibrāhīm, known as Dhu 'l-Nūn al-Miṣrī (d. 860), learned of a devout woman named Maymūna, "the black," living in the Muqaṭṭam hills he wished to meet her. On his way to find her, however, people asked Dhu 'l-Nūn why he was searching for a woman who was known to be crazy. The great mystic was about to abandon his search when he decided that he had nothing to lose by just seeing her. When Dhu 'l-Nūn finally came upon Maymūna she called him by name and assured him that she was not crazy, as people claimed, just "captivated" by God.[82] The line between absolute devotion to God and insanity was sometimes exceedingly fine. Ibn al-Zayyāt specifically rejects the charge that some saints were touched by madness. Instead, he asserts, saints were sometimes characterized by a sort of overwhelming trance arising from their complete rapture with God.[83]

As unaware, or unconcerned, with trivial realities as saints may have sometimes been, they just as often exhibited a special knowledge of the unknown and unknowable. This quality might manifest itself as an ability to predict the future or to report on the status of the dead. In this sense saints frequently tapped into sources of knowledge to which those around them were not privy. Muslims in the medieval world knew in the very fiber of their beings that the portion of reality readily discernable to the five physical senses constitutes only a fraction of the total universe. But the saints were different,

[78] Ibn al-Zayyāt, *al-Kawākib*, 221; see also al-Sakhāwī, *Tuḥfat*, 331.

[79] Ibn al-Zayyāt, *al-Kawākib*, 43. Kishk is a dish made from flour and meat broth with the consistency of gelatin.

[80] Ibid., 74–75 and 244; see also al-Sakhāwī, *Tuḥfat*, 196 and 347.

[81] Ibn al-Zayyāt, *al-Kawākib*, 150; see also Ibn 'Uthmān, *Murshid*, 290, and al-Sakhāwī, *Tuḥfat*, 271.

[82] Ibn al-Zayyāt, *al-Kawākib*, 40–41; see also Ibn 'Uthmān, *Murshid*, 424, and Ibn al-Nāsikh, *Miṣbāḥ*, fols. 15v°–16r°.

[83] Ibn al-Zayyāt, *al-Kawākib*, 163.

they knew what others could not know. Take, for example, the deaf carpenter who was unable to hear the call to prayer (adhān). He always knew when it was time to pray, however, from the wood with which he worked.[84] There was a fuller, buried near "the mumbler," who was also said to know the precise moment of prayer without actually hearing the adhān.[85] Dīnār al-ʿĀbid always knew when a plate of food offered to him contained something forbidden under Muslim dietary law, because he would see the image of a snake sitting in the plate as if poised to strike him.[86] Khuzayrāna was able to read people's thoughts. When someone once charged that she was a witch, her accuser became ill. The unfortunate man went to Khuzayrāna seeking forgiveness. After explaining that she was not a witch, Khuzayrāna took pity on the man and asked God to cure him. The instant she told her repentant accuser to go about his business he was cured.[87]

On many occasions saints predicted the future. For instance, Abū ʿAbbās Aḥmad (d. 983/84), known as "the tailor," was able to foretell events. The great jurist Imām al-Shāfiʿī himself is said to have told his disciples what would become of each of them after his death. For example, al-Shāfiʿī told Yūsuf b. Yaḥya (d. 845/46), known as al-Buwayṭī, that he would die in a great ordeal, thereby foreshadowing the latter's death in Baghdad during the controversy over the doctrine of the created Qurʾān. Al-Shāfiʿī is also reported to have told Ibn ʿAbd al-Ḥakam, the famous Egyptian historian, that he would return to the Mālikī madhhab, which also occurred. Abū ʿAbd Allāh al-Qurashī correctly predicted the future when he warned his companions to leave Egypt because of a great plague that would afflict the country. Abū ʿAbd Allāh b. ʿAbd Allāh Muḥammad b. Masʿūd (d. 964) prophesied that the people of Egypt would pay for their corruption with hunger, plague, and the tyranny of heretical rule which, from the hindsight of the Fāṭimid conquest, was viewed as an accurate prediction of the victory of the "heretical" Ismāʿīli dynasty.[88]

Access to extraordinary kinds of knowledge extended even to unborn saints, as in the case in the amazing story of Sīdī ʿAdiyy b.

[84] Ibid., 160; see also al-Sakhāwī, *Tuḥfat*, 278.
[85] Ibn al-Zayyāt, *al-Kawākib*, 150; see also al-Sakhāwī, *Tuḥfat*, 271.
[86] Ibn al-Zayyāt, *al-Kawākib*, 131; see also Ibn al-Nāsikh, *Miṣbāḥ*, fols. 45v°–46r°, and Ibn ʿUthmān, *Murshid*, 317–18.
[87] Ibn ʿUthmān, *Murshid*, 608.
[88] Ibn al-Zayyāt, *al-Kawākib*, 139, 65–66, 270, and 131 respectively.

Musāfir. His father was an itinerant shaykh known as "the traveler." Shaykh Musāfir had been wandering for thirty years when he experienced a dream in which he was instructed to return home and sleep with his wife. In the dream he was informed that anyone who slept with their wife on this night would be blessed with a son, and his wife in particular would give birth to a virtuous son. So, after a thirty-year absence, Shaykh Musāfir returned home. When his startled wife asked what her long missing spouse wanted, Shaykh Musāfir told her that he had been instructed to return home and sleep with her that very night, and afterward she would bear him a virtuous son. Not surprisingly, his wife insisted that before he share her bed Shaykh Musāfir climb to the top of a nearby hill and shout to the whole town that he had returned to sleep with his wife and that she would bear him a pious son. When Shaykh Musāfir hesitated, his wife explained that this was necessary so that later, after he left again to resume his wandering, people would not wonder how she became pregnant when her husband was known to have been away for many years. Shaykh Musāfir complied with his wife's request, and Sīdī ʿAdiyy b. Musāfir was thus conceived. During the seventh month of her pregnancy, the spirits of the famous mystical masters Maslama and ʿAqīl passed Sīdī ʿAdiyy's mother while she was fetching water. Maslama paused and urged his companion ʿAqīl to greet the saint. The perplexed ʿAqīl asked: "Where is the friend of God?" Shaykh Maslama told ʿAqīl to look at the woman fetching water and observe the light emanating from her abdomen. Both saints greeted Sīdī ʿAdiyy and then went their way. When Sīdī ʿAdiyy was approximately seven years old, Shaykh Maslama and Shaykh ʿAqīl came upon the young saint once again while he was playing with his friends. Again Maslama asked ʿAqīl if he recognized the child, and ʿAqīl admitted that he did not. Shaykh Maslama patiently explained again that the young boy was ʿAdiyy b. Musāfir. When the two shaykhs went to greet him, the boy responded by saluting each of them twice. Somewhat confused, they asked the child why he repeated his greeting. Sīdī ʿAdiyy responded that this was to compensate for their earlier greeting while he was still in his mother's womb and unable to respond.[89]

[89] Ibid., 187–88. Maslama b. Mukhallad (d. 681/82) and ʿAqīl al-Manbijī, were two of the most important links in the chain of mystical masters through whom ʿAdiyy b. Musāfir traced his spiritual heritage to the Prophet Muḥammad.

The night on which Abū al-Ḥasan al-Dīnawarī (d. c. 942), known as "the son of the jeweler," was born in the city of Dīnawar in western Iran, fell at the end of Shaʿbān, which ushers in the month-long Islamic fast of Ramaḍān. However, since people had not yet sighted the new moon, no one was certain if it was actually the end of the month of Shaʿbān or not. Shaykh Aḥmad al-Kabīr b. al-Rifāʿī announced that anyone who wanted to know whether or not the fast of Ramaḍān had begun should go to Dīnawar and seek out a certain jewler and inquire if his newborn son was nursing or not. If the child was taking his mother's milk, then no one should keep the fast. If, on the other hand, the child was not nursing, the fast had truly begun. When the jeweler was asked if his son was taking nourishment, he responded that he was not informed about the affairs of women, so he led them to the child's mother, who confirmed that the infant had indeed refused to eat since before dawn. Everyone then knew that the fast of Ramaḍān had begun.[90]

Knowledge of future events might even include a saint receiving forewarning of his or her own imminent death. The jurist Abū al-Qāsim ʿAbd al-Raḥmān b. ʿAbd Allāh b. al-Ḥusayn al-Mālikī (d. 1232) predicted on the eve of his death that the next day his associates would pray over his body. No one believed him at the time, but the next morning when they came to the shaykh's house, they found him dead. They prayed over his body and buried him, just as he had predicted they would. Some saints are reported to have dug their graves with their own hands as the hour of death approached. For example, al-Sayyida Nafīsa suddenly felt a great pain on the first day of the month of Rajab. She wrote a final letter to her husband and then began to dig a grave inside her house. When the grave was finished, Nafīsa lowered herself into the tomb and prayed there for a long time. She also recited the Qurʾān in her grave 190 times. When she became too weak to rise, Nafīsa continued to say her prayers while seated in her tomb. She also wept a great deal and persevered in reciting the Qurʾān. Finally, on the first Friday of the month of Ramaḍān, while she was reciting the 127th verse of the sixth Sūrat al-Anʿām: "For them is an abode of peace with their Lord. He will be their defender as reward for what they did," al-Sayyida Nafīsa slipped into unconsciousness and died.[91]

---

[90] Ibid., 285; see also Ibn ʿUthmān, *Murshid*, 572.
[91] Ibn al-Zayyāt, *al-Kawākib*, 244. See also al-Sakhāwī, *Tuḥfat*, 348.

The moment of conception or death of a saint frequently sent ripples through the spiritual dimension of the cosmos. When Abū al-Ḥasan al-Dīnawarī was conceived, for instance, Shaykh Aḥmad al-Kabīr b. al-Rifāʿī, who was with his students at the time, suddenly dropped his head between his knees and shouted, "The mother of the jeweler is pregnant with a noble son whose reputation will be widespread in both the east and west."[92] Shortly before the jurist ʿAbd al-Wāḥid b. Barakāt b. Naṣr Allāh al-Qurashī died, he asked his son not to inform people of his death. The shaykh was ashamed of his sins and did not want anyone to attend his funeral. When ʿAbd al-Wāḥid passed away his son respected his father's wishes and told no one that the shaykh had died. Nevertheless, everyone came to the funeral because they all heard a voice telling them to attend. When Abū al-Ḥajjāj Yūsuf died in 1198/99, his companion Abū al-Ḥasan al-Raffā experienced a dream in which the fetus in his wife's womb was moaning. When Abū al-Ḥasan asked his unborn child what was wrong, the fetus responded, "I am mourning the death of Abū al-Ḥajjāj Yūsuf." Abū al-Ḥasan awoke from this dream to discover that his friend had, in fact, died.[93]

The heightened level of awareness that frequently characterized saints also enabled them to inform the living about the condition of the dead. For instance, whenever Abū Ṭālib b. Abū al-ʿAshāyir passed a grave he was able to report whether the person in the tomb was in agony or resting in peace.[94] The saints who possessed this kind of special awareness were cognizant of a much larger portion of reality than most people and seemed able to transcend the boundaries of the cosmos.

Repentance

This was a world in which the records of good deeds and transgressions were meticulously kept and evaluated. The jurist Ḍiyāʾ al-Dīn ʿAbd al-Raḥmān b. Muḥammad al-Qurashī (d. 1219/20) used

---

[92] Ibn al-Zayyāt, *al-Kawākib*, 33–34; see also Ibn ʿUthmān, *Murshid*, 174; and Ibn al-Nāsikh, *Miṣbāḥ*, fol. 6v°. A similar story of a saint digging his own grave is told about Abū al-Ḥasan ʿAlī Ibrāhīm al-Ḥūfī (d. 1038/39); see Ibn al-Zayyāt, 162. See also Ibn ʿUthmān, *Murshid*, 279, concerning the Khūlāniyīn.

[93] Ibn al-Zayyāt, *al-Kawākib*, 285, 259–60, and 257 respectively.

[94] Ibn al-Nāsikh, *Miṣbāḥ*, fol. 86v°.

to make a list each day of all his actions. In the evening he would thank God for helping him to choose good more frequently than evil.[95] Keeping track of this information was important because however imperfect justice might be in this world, the truly pious knew that there would be a final and inescapable accounting for every action on the Day of Judgment. Things always evened out and they generally did so sooner rather than later. When a woman came to purchase some jewelry from a saint known in the pilgrimage guides only as one of "the jewelers," he was suddenly overcome by desire and kissed her hand as she extended it to try on a bracelet. Recognizing his transgression, the jewler was immediately filled with remorse, and that same night, when he returned home, his wife inquired what it was that he had done wrong. The startled husband sheepishly asked why she was posing such a question, and his wife explained that during the day the water carrier had suddenly kissed her hand as she extended it from behind the door to pay him. The only explanation the jeweler's wife could think of to account for the water carrier having behaved so uncharacteristically was that her own husband had done something wrong. The jeweler then admitted to his wife what had happened when his customer was trying on a bracelet.[96]

One of the most powerful and recurring themes in the Qur'ān is the promise of a certain and final accounting for the deeds of each and every individual on the Day of Judgment. The image of the great scale upon which the good and evil works of every believer would eventually be weighed was not easily dismissed. It is, therefore, not surprising that repentance is a common theme in the life of those described in the pilgrimage guides. Thus Abū al-Dalālāt was understandably alarmed when in a dream he saw a man announcing the names of people going to Paradise and his own name was not among them. When he asked why, he was told it was because he was known to frequent a place where dancing was common. Abū al-Dalālāt repented immediately, and was assured that his name would be duly added to the register of those entering Paradise.[97]

Salvation was never impossible, no matter how awful the crime or sin, as long as the perpetrator repented sincerely. Maḥmūd b.

---

[95] Ibn al-Zayyāt, *al-Kawākib*, 246–47.
[96] Ibid., 232; see also al-Sakhāwī, *Tuḥfat*, 339.
[97] Ibn al-Nāsikh, *Miṣbāḥ*, fol. 37r°.

Sālim b. Mālik, known as "the tall," was originally a soldier in the retinue of the Amīr al-Sarī b. al-Ḥakam. When a man once blocked the path of the amīr and his troops and complained of injustice, the amīr ordered Maḥmūd to execute the man on the spot. Maḥmūd dutifully followed his orders and cut off the petitioner's head. Later, however, when Maḥmūd returned home he reflected on what he had done, and he realized that the man had been justified in his complaints. Maḥmūd began to wonder how he would answer for his crime on the Day of Judgment. Finally he repented, wept bitterly, and determined to end his career as a soldier. After announcing his decision to the amīr, Maḥmūd devoted the rest of his days to leading a pious life. Among other things he restored a mosque, which later became known by his name. In a dream after his death, Maḥmūd confirmed that he had indeed entered Paradise.[98]

Repentance for one's own sins was always laudable, but so was praying for and encouraging others to repent. When ʿAbd Allāh, the husband of Khadīja (d. 932), the daughter of Muḥammad b. Ismāʿīl b. al-Qāsim al-Rassī b. Ibrāhīm Ṭabāṭabā, once arrived at his house accompanied by his wife to discover someone stealing all of their possessions. ʿAbd Allāh made no effort to stop the thief, and when she asked him why, he assured her that this theft would result in the thief's repentance. Not long thereafter a stranger arrived at their home with slaves and a large retinue of servants. The man asked the saint if he remembered the thief who had robbed their house, and Khadīja's husband acknowledged that he did. The stranger then introduced himself as the same thief, and explained that he had made a great deal of money. He offered the saint a thousand dirhams, two slaves, and two slave girls in compensation for his crime. After refusing all of these things Khadīja's husband explained that from the moment he first witnessed the theft he prayed that God might bless the perpetrator. Seeing his prayer answered, Khadīja's husband refused to accept anything from the man in recompense.[99]

Repentance was always within the power of individuals, but judgment and forgiveness were ultimately only God's to grant. For example, when the coffin of a homosexual passed Abū Muḥammad "the blind," he refused to rise in the traditional token of respect for the

---

[98] Ibn al-Zayyāt, *al-Kawākib*, 282; see also al-Sakhāwī, *Tuḥfat*, 373, and Ibn ʿUthmān, *Murshid*, 603–4.

[99] Ibn al-Zayyāt, *al-Kawākib*, 61–62; see also Ibn al-Nāsikh, *Miṣbāḥ*, fols.112v°–113v°.

dead. That night the dead man came in a dream to Abū Muḥammad, who asked what punishment God had imposed. The dead man announced that God had forgiven his sins, which left Abū Muḥammad confused. Until the moment Abū Muḥammad refused to stand as the coffin passed, the dead man explained, he had been condemned to Hell. However, because Abū Muḥammad passed judgment in this way, God had forgiven the dead man's sins. The message was clear: final judgment is God's prerogative alone.[100]

Resistance to unbelief and hypocrisy

A life devoted completely to God produced a unique clarity of vision that made the saints especially potent warriors in the endless struggle with unbelievers and heretics. When two soldiers from an invading army of Franks tried to dig their way under city fortifications during a siege, Abū Jaʿfar "the eloquent" called out: "Where to, O enemy of God?" One of the soldiers died instantly from fright at the sound of Abū Jaʿfar's voice, and his companion converted to Islam on the spot.[101] Shaykh ʿAbd Allāh al-Darwīsh was famous for, among other things, having crucified a pig on the Bāb al-Qarāfa as an act of jihād against the Franks.[102] Although we can rarely pinpoint specific events recounted in the pilgrimage guides, the fact that this shaykh died in 1372 suggests that the crucifixion of the unfortunate animal may have occurred seven years earlier, in response to the sack of Alexandria by Pierre I de Lusignan, the king of Cyprus, in 1365.[103]

There were, of course, many ways in which individuals might contribute to the jihād. The Ayyūbid jurist ʿAbd al-Raḥīm al-Baysānī (d. 1199/1200) devoted the proceeds of a large endowment for the purpose of freeing Muslim prisoners taken captive by the Crusaders.[104] Some saints even gave their lives as martyrs in the struggle against the infidel. Abū al-Fatḥ ʿUmar b. Abū al-Ḥasan ʿAlī b. Abū ʿAbd

---

[100] Ibn ʿUthmān, *Murshid*, 99.

[101] Ibn ʿUthmān, *Murshid*, fol. 208r°. This account should appear on page 425 of the printed edition but does not.

[102] Ibn al-Zayyāt, *al-Kawākib*, 185–86.

[103] For a discussion of this attack on Alexandria, see Aziz Suryal Atiya, *The Crusade in the Later Middle Ages*, especially 319–44.

[104] Ibn ʿUthmān, *Murshid*, 624.

Allāh b. Ḥamawiyya was killed at the Battle of Manṣūra in 1249, and his body was returned to al-Qarāfa for burial.[105]

The unbeliever was not, however, always an invader from a far-off land. There were plenty of Christians and Jews living in Egypt. These communities were ostensibly protected in the Islamic community and granted significant autonomy over the conduct of their own intracommunal affairs through an institution in Islamic law known as the dhimma. The dhimma was essentially a contractual agreement, sanctioned by Prophetic example, which involved the exchange of the limited tolerance and protection of the dominant Islamic community for Christians and Jews in return for their submission, symbolized by certain sumptuary laws and the annual payment of a poll tax. In practice, however, the continued presence of sizable communities of Christians and Jews within the Islamic world frequently served as an irritant to the various Muslim communities in which dhimmis lived. Egypt was no exception in this regard, and in the period between 1200 and 1500 Christians and Jews living in Egypt frequently experienced official repression. This situation was exacerbated by centuries of Crusading effort. The pilgrimage guides reflect this heightened tension between the Muslim and dhimmi communities. For instance, we find a number of examples of saints emerging victorious over their dhimmi antagonists.

Shaykh Abū Ḥafṣ ʿUmar al-Dhahabī was once vexed by a Jew who asked him fifty difficult questions concerning the Qur'ān. After Abū Ḥafṣ successfully answered each question, his Jewish interlocutor realized that there was no way to demonstrate the falsehood of the Qur'ān. In desperation, the Jew quoted the sixty-fourth verse of the fifth Sūra, "The Jews say: Allah's hand is fettered. Their hands are fettered and they are accursed for saying so." When Abū Ḥafṣ acknowledged that this was indeed God's revelation to the Muslims, the Jew held up his hand and declared, "This hand is not fettered." Abū Ḥafṣ struck the Jew in anger for his impudence, saying that the blow would serve as a substitute. When the Jew remained firm in his disbelief, Abū Ḥafṣ declared that from this day forth the Jew's hand would be fettered. The Jew left smiling, but he awoke the next day surprised to find that his hand was indeed fettered.[106]

---

[105] Ibn al-Zayyāt, *al-Kawākib*, 216; see also al-Sakhāwī, *Tuḥfat*, 326.

[106] Ibn al-Zayyāt, *al-Kawākib*, 256; see also Ibn ʿUthmān, *Murshid*, 352–54, and al-Sakhāwī, *Tuḥfat*, 354–55.

The mere physical presence of Christians or Jews was often enough to disturb the delicate aura of baraka surrounding the saints. The jurist Abū ʿAbd al-Raḥmān Raslān (d. 1175/76) once passed a wheat merchant outside Bāb Zuwayla, the main southern gate of the walled city of Cairo, and the seller asked the great jurist if he would put his hand into the wheat as a blessing. The shaykh did as the vendor asked, and the merchant experienced great success in selling his wheat until a Jewish customer came, touched the wheat, and disturbed the residual baraka of Abū ʿAbd al-Raḥmān.[107] Abū al-Ḥajjāj Yūsuf was once praying in a mosque when a Christian masquerading as a Muslim came to pray behind the shaykh. Abū al-Ḥajjāj suddenly declared that there was an awful smell in the mosque, as he turned to face the Christian. Abū al-Ḥajjāj motioned with his eyes for the Christian to leave before he was denounced publicly. As a result, the man converted to Islam on the spot.[108]

Although pious individuals were always prepared to challenge unbelief when it confronted them, conversion to Islam was certainly the preferred outcome of these encounters. There was once a Christian known for his great personal generosity living near Abū al-Ḥasan ʿAlī b. Ibrāhīm b. Muslim. When the shaykh was informed that his Christian neighbor was dying, Abū al-Ḥasan composed a message to the dying man that included the shahāda, the Islamic profession of faith ("There is no god but God, and Muḥammad is the messenger of God"). When the Christian read the message he asked his family to remove him from their presence. When they asked why, he responded, "Because I testify that there is no god but God. And I testify that Muḥammad is the messenger of God." The dying man's stunned family asked why he was suddenly converting to Islam on his deathbed. He showed them the message from Abū al-Ḥasan, and everyone who read the words also converted to Islam. The dying man then requested that the message be placed in the burial shroud with him, and it was. After his death he was seen in a dream and was asked what judgment God had rendered on him. The man explained that when he came into God's presence he was questioned as to which faith he believed. The dead man held out the message from Abū al-Ḥasan and replied that he came professing the same faith as contained in the message. The writing was immediately

[107] Ibn al-Zayyāt, *al-Kawākib*, 311; see also Ibn ʿUthmān, *Murshid*, 634–36.
[108] Ibn al-Zayyāt, *al-Kawākib*, 259; see also al-Sakhāwī, *Tuḥfat*, 357.

recognized as belonging to Abū al-Ḥasan, and the dead man was told: "This is the writing of one who begged us not to punish you. Therefore, go with it to Paradise."[109]

In another instance, al-Mufaḍḍal b. Faḍāla (d. 797/98) one night overheard the loud insults of a Jewish neighbor. Although al-Mufaḍḍal heard the slurs clearly he ignored them. Finally his daughter became upset at her father's inaction, and she asked why he did not respond. Al-Mufaḍḍal patiently explained to his daughter that when he first heard the insults he had intended to respond, but before he could he fell asleep and experienced a dream that made him change his mind. In the dream, al-Mufaḍḍal first saw the Prophet Muḥammad on the Day of Judgment, and also saw his Jewish neighbor entering Paradise before himself. In this way al-Mufaḍḍal discovered that his neighbor would convert to Islam before his death.[110]

Heretics and backsliding Muslims presented a similar problem. When ʿAbd al-Karīm was speaking once about the first caliph, Abū Bakr, a Shīʿī jeered him. As a result of his insolence, the man soon contracted leprosy. When the afflicted man came to ʿAbd al-Karīm seeking his assistance, the saint explained that God would not heal the man except through the love of Abū Bakr. The Shīʿī then repented and was cured.[111]

Graciousness

The saints were not always preoccupied as ardent and potent defenders of the faith. There were many occasions when a softer and gentler side of their personalities became apparent. They were known for a certain discreet politeness and a simple graciousness. Ḥamza b. ʿAbd Allāh swore to himself that he would not eat anything while visiting the home of Abū al-Khayr al-Tīnnātī. During the visit, Abū al-Khayr somehow knew not to press Ḥamza to accept food and thus force him to test his resolve. But as soon as Ḥamza walked out the door of Abū al-Khayr's house, he turned to discover the shaykh running after him with a plate of food. Abū al-Khayr explained to

---

[109] Ibn al-Zayyāt, *al-Kawākib*, 252–53.

[110] Ibid., 125; see also Ibn ʿUthmān, *Murshid*, 328–29, Ibn al-Nāsikh, *Miṣbāḥ*, fol. 42r°, and al-Sakhāwī, *Tuḥfat*, 253–54.

[111] Ibn al-Zayyāt, *al-Kawākib*, 260.

his departing guest that since he had left the shaykh's home Ḥamza was now free to accept a plate of food without hesitation.[112]

Khalaf al-Kattānī (d. 968) was known for turning a deaf ear when he heard ugly or embarrassing sounds. A woman once came to purchase something from him and she accidentally passed gas loudly. Khalaf made no indication that he had heard the unpleasant sound, and when the embarrassed woman spoke to him, Khalaf was so polite that he asked her to raise her voice because he was hard of hearing.[113]

In an extraordinary act of kindness, Abū ʿAbd Allāh Muḥammad b. Muḥammad b. Abū al-Qāsim ʿAbd al-Raḥmān b. ʿĪsa b. Wardān married a woman who gave birth to a child on the very night their marriage was consummated. He said nothing about the incident but went instead to fetch her a wet nurse. The shaykh then renewed the marriage contract with the woman. He loved and raised her son among his own children, and before Abū ʿAbd Allāh died, he bequeathed an equal portion of his estate to this child.[114]

The woman preacher al-Ḥijāziyya, known as Umm al-Khayr, was famous for her kind and noble character. One day a merchant selling fresh dates outside the door of her mosque decided to encourage his customers by falsely advertising that al-Ḥijāziyya herself had purchased four raṭls of dates, worth over a dirham, from him. Al-Ḥijāziyya was just inside the door of the mosque preparing to depart with her attendants when she heard the merchant making his false claim. She paused before leaving the mosque and sent one of her assistants to summon the man. When he came to her, al-Ḥijāziyya gave him a quarter of a dirham and asked him not to use her name. The merchant kissed her hand and promised that he would honor her request.[115]

Commitment to the pious life

For most people prayer and other expressions of piety accounted for only a part of their daily routines. The pious life was different,

112 Ibid., 111.
113 Ibid., 63; see also Ibn ʿUthmān, *Murshid*, 234.
114 Ibid., 70. This would have been a clear violation of Islamic laws of inheritance.
115 Al Maqrīzī, *Khiṭaṭ*, 2:450. A measure of weight, approximately equal to 450 grams or 1 pound.

however. It was a life in which worship and various other expressions of piety became the central organizing feature of daily existence. The pious life was carefully structured so that the demands of routine physical survival would not overwhelm or interfere unduly with the rhythm of endless worship, contemplation, and study. The saints were sometimes so zealous and diligent in pursuit of this objective that they could not even be distracted by the unfolding stages of the life cycle. Shaykh Abū al-ʿAbbās Aḥmad al-Andalusī al-Khazrajī (d. 1203/4), for example, was said to have begun worshiping God while still a fetus in his mother's womb. And it was reported that Shaykh Abū al-Qāsim ʿAbd al-Raḥmān could be heard reciting the Qur'ān from within his grave.[116]

There was seemingly no threshold that the saints were unwilling to cross in denying themselves food, water, sleep, and other material comforts in their pursuit of the truly pious life. And the feats of personal devotion and piety accomplished by the saints were often extraordinary. The grammarian Abū al-Ḥasan ʿAlī b. Bābashādh (d. 1076/77) is said to have recited the Qur'ān two hundred times by each column of the Mosque of ʿAmr before he died in a fall from the roof of the mosque.[117] Abū Yaḥyā Zakariyya was also known for the numerous times he recited the Qur'ān.[118] Khadīja (d. 1295), the daughter of Hārūn b. ʿAbd Allāh b. ʿAbd al-Razzāq, was reported to have made the pilgrimage to Mecca fifteen times.[119] Nājiyya al-Maghribiyya (d. 1261/62) performed the ḥajj no fewer than thirty times. She walked the entire way each time.[120] Jaʿfar al-Mūsawī went to Mecca eighty times on the pilgrimage, but this may not have been so exceptional, since he was a camel trader with business interests in the Ḥijāz.[121]

There was no place in the pious life for frivolity or levity. Khadīja, the daughter of Muḥammad b. Ismāʿīl b. al-Qāsim, was so pious that she was never seen to laugh.[122] Abū al-Ḥasan al-Khalʿī reported that he never saw Shaykh ʿAlī laughing, or even smiling.[123] Weeping

---

116 Al-Sakhāwī, *Tuḥfat*, 394; Ibn al-Zayyāt, *al-Kawākib*, 189.
117 Ibn al-Zayyāt, *al-Kawākib*, 168; see also Ibn ʿUthmān, *Murshid*, 283, Ibn al-Nāsikh, *Miṣbāḥ*, fols., 38v°–39r°, and al-Sakhāwī, *Tuḥfat*, 284.
118 Ibn al-Nāsikh, *Miṣbāḥ*, fol. 15v°.
119 Ibn al-Zayyāt, *al-Kawākib*, 226–27.
120 Ibn al-Nāsikh, *Miṣbāḥ*, fol. 55v°.
121 Ibn al-Zayyāt, *al-Kawākib*, 95–96.
122 Ibn ʿUthmān, *Murshid*, 252, and Ibn al-Zayyāt, *al-Kawākib*, 61–62.
123 Ibn al-Zayyāt, *al-Kawākib*, 162–63.

was much more appropriate to the rigors of constant piety than was laughter. The woman saint known as Zahra "the weeper," for instance, is reported to have wept so much that she went blind.[124] Shaykh Abū al-Ḥasan ʿAlī Ibrāhīm al-Ḥūfī was always seen weeping, as was the jurist Tāj al-Dīn Abū al-ʿAbbās Aḥmad b. Yaḥyā. After his death Tāj al-Dīn was asked in a dream if all his weeping had benefited him. He responded that his tears had doused the fires of Hell. Shaykh Nūr al-Dīn ʿAlī preferred to weep at night rather than sleep.[125]

From the hagiographic material contained in the pilgrimage guides we can trace the main characteristics that broadly defined the awliyāʾ in the collective imagination of late medieval Egypt. Denial of personal desire—whether material or sexual—courage of conviction, exclusive concentration on the pursuit of the pious life, detachment from the world of mundane reality, boundless generosity, honesty, and graciousness all contributed to shaping the exceptional piety for which the saints were renowned. These were the qualities that were related to succeeding generations of zuwwār on their visits to the graves of the saints. As we read these contemporary accounts of the virtues of the saints, the dusty plateau of al-Qarāfa seems less distant and alien, and the world of the ziyāra becomes more immediate. But the saints, their stories, and the institution of the ziyāra also tell us something about the nature and formation of religious and moral imagination in Muslim society during the later Middle Ages.

Scholars frequently describe Islam as an "orthopractic" tradition, in other words, Islam tends to place greater emphasis on the correctness of action among believers than it does on the specific details of doctrine to which they adhere. The word "orthopractic" was coined as a way of contrasting religions such as Islam to "orthodox" traditions, most notably Christianity, whose followers have historically paid particular attention to whether or not their co-religionists accept certain doctrinal positions. This does not mean either that doctrine is irrelevant to Muslims or that Christians are unconcerned with deeds. The point is rather that orthopractic systems generally tend to place greater emphasis on conduct and actions as the plane on which ultimate salvation is determined, whereas orthodox traditions

---

[124] Ibid., 117; see also al-Sakhāwī, *Tuḥfat*, 248, and Ibn al-Nāsikh, *Miṣbāḥ*, fol. 43v°.

[125] Ibn al-Zayyāt, *al-Kawākib*, 161–62; al-Sakhāwī, *Tuḥfat*, 353; Ibn ʿUthmān, *Murshid*, 446.

stress the specific content of doctrine held as the critical factor.

As with other orthopractic faiths, Islam is characterized by an elaborate and complex legal framework. For Muslims, in fact, the mere existence of the sacred Law of God, the Sharīʿa, is the greatest proof of God's infinite mercy. For it is through the divine guidance of the Sharīʿa that God offers salvation, at least for those who pay heed.[126] The ʿulamāʾ have traditionally viewed the Sharīʿa as a theoretically comprehensive framework of divine law. The elucidation and application of God's law to virtually every sphere of daily life has, in turn, consumed the energy and thought of the ʿulamāʾ over the centuries. The results of their efforts fill vast libraries throughout the Islamic world, and bear eloquent testimony to a profound religious vision in which the entire domain of human activity becomes, at least potentially, the arena of divine worship. For it is through their struggle better and more sincerely to conform the conduct of their daily lives to the guidelines of the Sharīʿa that the vast majority of the world's Muslims have historically sought to achieve and perfect their submission to the will of God (islām). In the context of Islamic law every human action falls into one of five distinct categories: actions that are specifically commanded by God (wājib), actions that although not commanded are encouraged by God (mandūb), actions to which God is indifferent (mubāḥ), actions that although not strictly forbidden are reprehensible (makrūh), and finally, actions that God forbids (ḥarām).

The centrality of the Sharīʿa and the orthopractic quality of Islam are clearly reflected in the most basic expression of Muslim spirituality. The famous "five pillars" of Islamic faith are all actions, which themselves affirm the view that correct belief flows most directly and sincerely from proper practice. The word *islām* is itself a verbal noun, one that describes a religion as well as an action. Great attention has thus always been devoted to the effort of Muslims to embody and live their submission to the will of God in every sphere of life. This is obviously not to reduce the sum total of Muslim spirituality to the narrow confines of law—nothing could be further from the truth. Mysticism, for example, encompasses a vast, complex, and

[126] The Islamic notion of salvation is substantially different in this sense from the Christian concept of redemption. As Gerhard Endress cogently explains: "The doctrine of salvation in Islam is the doctrine of men being 'rightly guided by God' to temporal and eternal bliss through God's commands." See his *Einführung in die islamische Geschichte* translated into English as *An Introduction to Islam*, 33.

essential dimension of spirituality in the Islamic tradition. Speculative theology (kalām) and the related endeavor of Islamic philosophy reflect still other ways in which Muslims have historically sought to approach and know God, and each of these is rightfully the province of extensive and important modern scholarship. Without diminishing the importance of mysticism, or other manifestations of Muslim spirituality, however, we can acknowledge that the sacred Law, its interpretation, and its application have historically lain at the heart of what, borrowing from Clifford Geertz, I term the moral imagination of Islamic societies.[127] What I mean by this phrase is the sum of collective social notions and sensibilities of right and wrong—more broadly, of moral order. Moreover, I contend that the orthopractic nature of Islamic societies renders an understanding of the manner in which their moral imagination is constructed, altered, and diffused at the broadest social level essential to appreciating the unique genius of social order in these societies.

The moral imagination of specific Islamic societies has a universal dimension, created through the accumulated efforts of individual thinkers, themselves products of their own specific Muslim communities, as they interact with both the realities of their own age and an international and ever-expanding legacy of legal discourse across time. Through the contributions of its own legal scholars, each Islamic community, therefore, participates in a great historical conversation that ties it to countless other Muslim communities. Through this discourse, which relies upon certain shared paradigms, assumptions, vocabulary, and understandings, each age and community draws upon, reinterprets, and contributes to a mutually intelligible and distinctive Islamic framework as it arrives at its own collective notions of moral order. The unfolding of this great historical dialogue is readily available to us through a diachronic textual analysis of the legal discourse itself.

But how does the social construction of moral imagination take place within a specific society in a distinct historical period? Are there hierarchical structures through which certain elite strata of the ʿulamāʾ generate understandings that are then somehow filtered down and diffused to other levels of society? Or is there a more fluid and dynamic process through which collective notions of moral order are socially constructed? And if the latter situation prevails, what are the

[127] Geertz, *Local Knowledge*, 36–54.

mechanisms through which this consensus on normative moral order is established, revised, and diffused at the broadest societal level? In the cult of saints we find, I think, one important key to resolving these questions.

By identifying saints, and then venerating them through visits to the sites of their tombs, where accounts of their distinctive actions or qualities were related, a broad cross-section of Egyptians in the later Middle Ages collectively participated in identifying exemplars of probity, righteousness, honesty, mercy, generosity, and other virtues that were deemed worthy of widespread contemplation and emulation. The saints personified these values in readily comprehensible and tangible ways, and their tombs marked the exact locations where pious visitors might go to reflect upon those qualities. Thus we find here one important answer to the larger question of how the social construction of moral imagination occurred in Mamlūk society.

But the ziyāra was not simply a vehicle for transmitting information about the saints. Participation in the ziyāra was an important expression of late medieval Muslim piety, focusing on the cultivation of one's character and personal qualities. By improving oneself through this activity, the zuwwār might ultimately hope to grow in both their devotion to God and in their relationship with the divine. At the same time, they shared in larger social notions of ideal moral conduct.

The stories of the awliyā' also offer insight into another dimension of the contemporary imagination—understandings of the saints as both vital repositories of baraka and as critical agents of mediation. We examine these two closely related roles in the next chapter.

CHAPTER FOUR

BARAKA, MIRACLE, AND MEDIATION

As repositories of divine blessing (baraka) the saints frequently performed miracles (karamāt) and served as vital agents of mediation (shafāʿa). In this nexus of baraka, miracles, and mediation, therefore, we find further clues to understanding both the range of meanings attached to the awliyāʾ and the many ways saints assisted Muslims in the medieval world to negotiate the often capricious and treacherous currents of daily existence.[1]

On issues of mediation and intercession between humanity and the divine medieval Muslim theologians and jurists were divided. Those who argued that there could be no intercession between man and God looked to Qurʾān 2:48: "And guard yourselves against a day when no soul will in aught avail another, nor will intercession be accepted from it, nor will compensation be received from it, nor will they be helped." They also pointed to Sūra 2:254: "O ye who believe! Spend of that wherewith We have provided you ere a day come when there will be no trafficking, nor friendship, nor intercession. The disbelievers, they are the wrong-doers." Opponents of the concept of shafāʿa between mankind and God also found support in verses such as 74:48: "The mediation of no mediators will avail them then."

Close reading of these verses, however, does not seem to support an all-encompassing denial of the possibility of human intercession with the divine, except perhaps at the Day of Judgment. And even at the Hour, other verses seem to confirm the role of the Prophet Muḥammad as an intercessor for his community. There are also verses which indicate the reality of human intercession with God more broadly. Proponents of this view acknowledged that such intercession could only take place with divine permission. However, to

[1] Mediation and intercession were important and pervasive features of life generally in the medieval Islamic world, which makes it all the more surprising that neither has yet received the full scholarly attention they deserve. Two notable exceptions that deserve particular mention are Mottahedeh, *Loyalty and Leadership*, and Shaun Marmon, *Eunuchs and Sacred Boundaries*.

deny the possibility of human intercession with God seemed not only to contradict Qur'ānic revelation but also dangerously to constrain God's power. Supporters of the position that in God resides all power, including the power to accept or reject intercession, point to verses such as 39:44: "Say: Unto Allah belongeth all intercession. His is the Sovereignty of the heavens and the earth. And afterward unto Him ye will be brought back." Sūra 2:255 states: "Allah! There is no God save Him, the Alive, the Eternal. Neither slumber nor sleep overtaketh Him. Unto Him belong whatsoever is in the heavens and whatsoever is in the earth. Who is it that intercedeth with Him save by His leave?" Finally, Sūra 43:86 is: "And those unto whom they cry instead of Him possess no power of intercession, saving him who beareth witness unto the Truth knowingly."

Despite persistent efforts in certain strains of Islamic thought to deny human intercession or mediation with God, the majority position, as well as the overwhelming evidence of widespread practices throughout the Islamic world, actively supports human agency as mediators and intercessors with the divine. Although the pilgrimage guides to the cemeteries of medieval Cairo do not discuss the concept of shafā'a itself—in fact the word is notable for its absence in these texts—they do contain extensive accounts of the miracles attributed to saints. The performance of miracles is not a prerequisite of sainthood in Islam, but miracles do offer important confirmation of someone's status among the awliyā' Allāh, "the friends of God." Referred to in the sources as manāqib (feats) and karamāt (miracles), these were fantastic and supernatural occurrences arising from the intervention of divine power. Miracles normally involved a dramatic alteration or transformation of some aspect of reality in a manner perceived as impossible, or at least unlikely, without divine intervention. Gardet has argued that a better translation of karāma is "marvel" because it helps to underline a distinction made in Islamic thought between mu'jizāt, which may only be performed by a prophet and are offered as signs of divine proof of prophethood, and the karamāt of the saints.[2] The latter, Gardet suggests, is "a simple, personal favour" that should be kept secret. Many of the manāqib and karamāt associated with the saints and related in the pilgrimage guides seem hardly secret, however, and they are ultimately indistinguishable from supernatural actions and happenings associated

[2] See *EI*², s.vv. Karāma and Mudjiza.

with prophetic miracle. As Ibn al-Zayyāt observes: "The ulamā', may God be pleased with them, have said that everything which is a muʿjiza for a prophet is permitted as a karāma for a saint (walī) except that which was unique to the Prophet [Muḥammad], God bless him and grant him salvation!"[3] Clearly medieval Muslims distinguished between prophetic (muʿjiza) and saintly (karāma) miracle. The distinction lay not in the nature of the event or in its public character, but in its underlying significance. For prophets miracles were a sign of prophecy, whereas for the awliyā' the same actions merely indicated proximity of the saint to the divine. This subtle but important difference is not clarified by simply referring to muʿjiza as "miracle," and karāma as "marvel."[4]

Miracles were the most dramatic and tangible indication of the presence of baraka associated with the saints. It is important to stress that God is ultimately the source of all baraka. In this sense saints are not the primary cause of miracles, but are able to perform miracles as an attribute of the special blessing God bestows on them. It is through these miracles, therefore, that we can trace the existence and operation of baraka and gain greater insight into the function of saints as mediators between man and God.

In surveying the extensive material in the pilgrimage guides relating to miracles, it seems most appropriate to organize the information into three primary categories, each of which is defined by a complicated series of relationships. These three divisions involve: relationships between humanity and the natural world; interactions among human beings; and finally, relationships between the human and metaphysical realms. To the first category we assign miraculous activity ranging from such obvious examples as preventing the scourge of disease or natural disaster to more enigmatic themes such as the

---

[3] Ibn al-Zayyāt, *al-Kawākib*, 224. The primary muʿjiza associated with the Prophet Muḥammad was the revelation of the Qur'ān. In fact, this is frequently held up as his only prophetic miracle—a view with substantial Qur'ānic evidence to support it. See also al-Sakhāwī, *Tuḥfat*, 333.

[4] I have also chosen to use the word "miracle" instead of "marvel" to describe the manāqib and karamāt of the awliyā' because, as Le Goff points out, the word "marvel," as it was understood in the medieval world, requires greater semantic precision than normally prevails in modern scholarship. In this regard he makes the interesting observation that although medieval Muslims possessed a rich vocabulary—in several languages—for describing "the marvelous," they had no word comparable to *mirabilis* with which to express what was referred to in the West as "the marvelous." See Le Goff, "The Marvelous in the Medieval West," in his *The Medieval Imagination*, 27.

unusual, even fantastic, capacity to transcend normative physical laws that is frequently attributed to saints. In the second category we will consider those miracles which involve the mediating agency of saints in some aspect of human relations. With respect to the metaphysical realm, we examine miracles relating to saintly intercession involving supernatural dimensions of reality.

Miracle and the natural world

As we might expect in an age when immediate physical survival was less frequently taken for granted than is generally true today, the saints were regularly called upon for assistance. In instances where the saints responded, their actions were often credited with making the difference between life and death. This was an age in which such issues still dominated the lives of most people, as the disproportionate percentage of miracles reflecting such concerns clearly demonstrates.

Egypt is a land where the rhythm of life has always been tightly bound to the Nile River. Historically, when the river failed to flood sufficiently, or alternately, when its waters rose too high, the results were usually disastrous. The most famous and certainly the most repeated account of miraculous intervention to bring about a needed or overdue Nile inundation is related about al-Sayyida Nafīsa (d. 824), the great-granddaughter of al-Ḥasan, the son of ʿAlī b. Abī Ṭālib. The story is told that the populace came to al-Sayyida Nafīsa to ask for her intervention when the river failed to rise. She offered them her veil to cast into the Nile. No sooner had the veil touched the water than the river began to rise.[5] Al-Sayyida Zaynab (d. 854/55), the niece of al-Sayyida Nafīsa, was also thought to be particularly effective in ending draught. In years when the river was particularly low, people would come to her tomb and pray there for relief. Frequently their efforts met with success.[6] The Ḥanbalī jurist Abū ʿAmr ʿUthmān b. Marzūq (d. 1168/69) succeeded in making the Nile rise when it was low, or recede when it was too high, simply

[5] Ibn al-Zayyāt, *al-Kawākib*, 32. See also Ibn ʿUthmān, *Murshid*, 166; Ibn al-Nāsikh, *Miṣbāḥ*, fol. 6r°; al-Sakhāwī, *Tuḥfat*, 132–33; and al-Maqrīzī, *Khiṭaṭ*, 2:442.

[6] Ibn al-Zayyāt, *al-Kawākib*, 88; and al-Sakhāwī, *Tuḥfat*, 214.

by going to the river's edge and performing his ritual ablutions there.[7] A ḥawsh, that belonged to the Banū ʿUthmān was another location known to be an effective place for people to offer their prayers to God when the Nile failed to rise. Ibn al-Zayyāt relates that during a particular low Nile, Shaykh Sharaf al-Dīn Ibn al-Jabbās reported that after he had given up all hope he was instructed in a dream to lead people to the turba of the Banū ʿUthmān. On Friday evening he guided a mixed crowd of men, women, and children to this place, and they offered prayers there for deliverance. The next morning the river began to rise. Al-Sakhāwī mentions that ʿAbd Allāh b. al-Ḥasan b. ʿAbd Allāh b. Ḥājil al-Ṣadafī, a companion of the Prophet, whom people believed settled in Egypt, read a letter from the second Muslim caliph, ʿUmar, while standing at the banks of the river during a low Nile, and the water began to rise.[8]

Water, and the often critical need for it, are themes that recur repeatedly. There is, for example, the story of ʿAmr b. Muṭīʿ al-Kindī (d. 767) who gave ṣadaqa throughout the year from his productive garden. One day the well from which he watered his plants suddenly dried up and his trees and crops began to wither. ʿAmr wept and prayed. Later, while he was sleeping, a voice assured him that he would no longer have to worry about his garden. When ʿAmr awoke from this dream his trees were green again and full of ripening fruit. From that day forth he never again had to water his garden, for whenever ʿAmr's trees needed water the rains always came.[9] There are a number of stories about saints known for providing thirsty travelers with water from pitchers that never emptied. Thus the devout ascetic Muḥammad b. Ismāʿīl once provided an entire caravan with water from a single jug.[10]

Saints were often called upon to protect travelers from the violent forces of nature. Once there was an old widow and her four daughters who lived from week to week on the yarn that they spun. Each Friday the old woman would take the week's yarn to market for sale. With half of the money earned she would purchase the raw

---

[7] Ibn ʿUthmān, *Murshid*, 518; Ibn al-Zayyāt, *al-Kawākib*, 197, only mentions this jurist without providing any details of his miracles.

[8] Ibn al-Zayyāt, *al-Kawākib*, 309; al-Sakhāwī, *Tuḥfat*, 231.

[9] Ibn al-Zayyāt, *al-Kawākib*, 98; see also al-Sakhāwī, *Tuḥfat*, 227.

[10] Ibn al-Zayyāt, *al-Kawākib*, 290; see also Ibn al-Nāsikh, *Miṣbāḥ*, fol. 82r°. Somewhat different accounts may also be found in Ibn ʿUthmān, *Murshid*, 437; and Ibn al-Zayyāt, 158, 294–95.

flax needed for spinning the next week's quota of yarn. With the other half she would buy food. One Friday the woman wrapped her yarn in a red rag to take to market. On the way, however, a bird suddenly swooped down from the sky and stole her bundle of yarn. The old woman fainted from surprise, and when she recovered she began to weep and wonder how she would ever feed her daughters. People gathered around her and asked what was wrong. When the old woman related what had happened, she was directed to al-Sayyida Nafīsa, who, she was told, might pray to God with great effect to solve any problem. The woman did as they suggested, making her way to Nafīsa's home. The saint took pity on the old woman and prayed to God on her behalf. When Nafīsa was finished praying she told the woman to sit and wait, "for God is almighty." The woman sat by the doorway, her heart deeply troubled at the thought of her children starving. Not more than an hour later some men approached and asked to enter the house. Al-Sayyida Nafīsa bade them enter and asked on what business they came. The men responded that they were a group of merchants who had been traveling at sea for some time. When they approached the Egyptian coast their boat suddenly began to leak and, despite all of their efforts, they were unable to prevent the sea from rushing in. As their ship was foundering the merchants implored God to come to their aid. Just then a bird appeared and dropped a bundle of yarn wrapped in a red cloth. The men took the bundle and stuffed it into the breech in their vessel, and, by the will of God, and through the baraka of al-Sayyida Nafīsa, the leak was sealed. The merchants then explained, "We have come to you with five hundred silver dirhams, thankful to God for our safety." Al-Sayyida Nafīsa wept and thanked God for His kindness and mercy. Then she called the old woman to her and asked how much her yarn would normally sell for. The woman responded "twenty dirhams," and Nafīsa told her, "Rejoice, for God has replaced each dirham with twenty-five!" The woman took the money and returned home to tell her daughters how God had responded to her grief through the baraka of al-Sayyida Nafīsa.[11]

Pilgrims performing the ḥajj often relied on the protection of the saints from the elements of nature. Abū ʿAbd Allāh once wished to make the pilgrimage, so he visited Shaykh al-Musaynī and asked the

[11] Ibn al-Zayyāt, *al-Kawākib*, 32–33; Ibn ʿUthmān, *Murshid*, 168; and al-Sakhāwī, *Tuḥfat*, 133–34.

shaykh to pray for his safety during the ḥajj. Al-Musaynī told him to call out if anything went wrong during the trip. While Abū ʿAbd Allāh was traveling a strong wind began to batter his boat so fiercely that it almost sank. He called out to Shaykh al-Musaynī for assistance, and suddenly the frightened pilgrim heard the shaykh's response in his ear, "Here I am," and immediately the wind died down. When Abū ʿAbd Allāh returned to Egypt, the shaykh inquired how the trip had gone. Abū ʿAbd Allāh told the shaykh that thanks to his prayers no serious threat had occurred. Shaykh al-Musaynī responded, "Not even on the day you were sailing and you called out to me?"[12]

Illness and disease were constant companions in the medieval world, and the saints were often called upon for assistance in restoring good health. The list of medical problems for which the intervention of the saints was sought ranged from simple toothaches, to life threatening illness.[13] Again the most famous account of miraculous cure is attributed to al-Sayyida Nafīsa. The story is told of the daughter of a Jewish family living near Nafīsa who was so badly crippled that she could not walk. One day her family decided to go to the public bath and they proposed to carry her there with them. The lame girl refused, suggesting instead that she be allowed to stay with their kind neighbor, Nafīsa, who agreed to watch over the girl. While performing her ritual ablutions in preparation for the noon prayers, Nafīsa accidentally splashed water on the crippled girl who was sitting nearby. The child was suddenly cured, and when her family returned home they were amazed to find her walking. Her entire family converted to Islam on the spot, and, according to some accounts, more than seventy Jews living in the area also converted to Islam on this occasion.[14]

The simple touch of a saint was often enough to result in fantastic cures. Abū Bakr Muḥammad, once passed a crippled woman who was begging. He told her that he had nothing to give her but commanded her to give him her hand. When she put her hand into his, Abū Bakr told the woman to rise, and she did "by the will of

---

[12] Ibn al-Zayyāt, *al-Kawākib*, 218.

[13] See the tomb referred to as belonging to raqqāʾīn al-ḍurūs (the teeth magicians) in al-Sakhāwī, *Tuḥfat*, 265; and as "al-Ḍarrāsīn," in Ibn ʿUthmān, *Murshid*, 294.

[14] Ibn al-Zayyāt, *al-Kawākib*, 32; Ibn ʿUthmān, *Murshid*, 163–65; Ibn al-Nāsikh, *Miṣbāḥ*, fol. 6r°; al-Sakhāwī, *Tuḥfat*, 130–31; and al-Maqrīzī, *Khiṭaṭ*, 2:442.

God."[15] When two young boys fought with each other in a Qur'ān school, one plucked out the eye of the other. Their teacher picked up the eye and replaced it without any damage to the boy's sight.[16] Similarly, when two men fought and one knocked out the tooth of the other, the famous mystic Dhu 'l-Nūn al-Miṣrī put some of his own spittle on the broken tooth and then reattached it successfully to the owner's jaw.[17]

At the grave of the Ḥanafī jurist Bakkār b. Qutayba (d. 884), the story is related that when the Caliph al-Mutawakkil (r. 847–861) appointed Bakkār as the qāḍī of Egypt, the caliph sent his messenger to Baṣra to inform the jurist of his appointment. To the envoy's disdain, the shaykh arrived from a trip to the baker dressed in only a simple robe and carrying a plate of warm bread. Bakkār gave the caliphal messenger two loaves of bread before he returned to Baghdad. When the messenger reached the city, he informed the caliph of his meeting with Qāḍī Bakkār. The caliph anxiously asked for the two loaves of bread, but the courier explained that only one loaf remained. The caliph quickly took the loaf in exchange for one hundred dīnārs, and told the surprised messenger that had he kept the other loaf he would have received another hundred dīnārs for it. The caliph then pulverized the loaf and added it to some kohl. Shortly thereafter, the same envoy was summoned to perform another errand. On this occasion, however, the caliph was informed that his messenger had gone almost blind as the result of a serious eye infection. The nearly sightless envoy was then brought before the caliph who applied the mixture made from Bakkār's loaf of bread to the man's infected eyes. The eyes quickly healed, whereupon the grateful courier asked how he might obtain some of this wondrous medication. The caliph informed him that it was made from the very loaf of bread supplied by Bakkār, and the courier deeply regretted having not saved the second loaf.[18]

The faqīh Abū ʿAbd al-Raḥmān (d. 1175/76) is reported to have written a line on a mirror and then commanded a woman having difficulty in childbirth to look into the mirror. When the woman did

---

[15] Ibn al-Zayyāt, *al-Kawākib*, 294, and al-Sakhāwī, *Tuḥfat*, 378.

[16] Ibn al-Zayyāt, *al-Kawākib*, 241; al-Sakhāwī, *Tuḥfat*, 344–45; Ibn ʿUthmān, *Murshid*, 361; and Ibn al-Nāsikh, *Miṣbāḥ*, fol. 73v°.

[17] Ibn al-Zayyāt, *al-Kawākib*, 233–34; see also Ibn ʿUthmān, *Murshid*, 378.

[18] Ibn al-Zayyāt, *al-Kawākib*, 49; see also Ibn ʿUthmān, *Murshid*, 214–19, and Ibn al-Nāsikh, *Miṣbāḥ*, fols. 24v°–26r°.

as the jurist told her, she gave birth immediately.[19] Such miraculous powers of healing were not restricted to living saints. For instance, an ill man on the verge of death was instructed in a dream to make his way to the tomb of Abū Muḥammad ʿAbd al-ʿAzīz al-Khawārizmī (d. 1010/11). He went to the tomb, prayed there, and was cured. Much the same story is told about another deathly ill person who was instructed in a dream to stand between the tomb of ʿAbd Allāh b. ʿAbd al-Raḥmān b. ʿAwf and the tomb of a descendant of the Prophet (sharīf) named al-Farīd, and pray to God. Again, the patient heeded the advice and was promptly cured.[20]

Saints frequently transcended the laws of nature. We find, for example, a number of instances of saints walking on water. When al-Fusṭāṭ burned and the populace fled across the river to Gīza, Shukr "the simple minded" boarded a boat that sank in the middle of the Nile. When those who did not drown reached the safety of the river bank, they found the shaykh standing there with his clothes still perfectly dry.[21] The jurist Abū al-Qāsim told of a journey he once made by sea. As the ship passed a certain island, the passengers saw a black woman performing the ritual prayer (ṣalāt) incorrectly. They told her this was not the right way to pray, and she asked them to show her the correct procedure. They taught her the Fātiḥa, the first Sūra of the Qurʾān, and also demonstrated the proper way to perform the prayers. As the ship sailed away, however, the passengers were startled to see the woman racing after them across the surface of the water. She implored them to teach her again how to pray because she had already forgotten. The passengers urged her to continue praying in her accustomed manner as this was clearly pleasing to God.[22]

Many saints seemingly possessed telekinetic powers. Such ability was occasionally manifested in ways that revealed the perfection of a saint's submission to the will of God. For example, the great mystic Dhu 'l-Nūn was once attempting to demonstrate that when a person was completely obedient to God everything else in the world,

---

[19] Ibn al-Zayyāt, *al-Kawākib*, 311. For the biography of this saint see al-Ṣafadī, *al-Wāfī*, 10:185.

[20] Ibn al-Zayyāt, *al-Kawākib*, 126–27, 241; see also Ibn ʿUthmān, *Murshid*, 327, 371.

[21] Ibn al-Zayyāt, *al-Kawākib*, 163; see also al-Sakhāwī, *Tuḥfat*, 280, and Ibn ʿUthmān, *Murshid*, 278–79.

[22] Ibn al-Zayyāt, *al-Kawākib*, 269–70; see also al-Sakhāwī, *Tuḥfat*, 363.

in turn, became subservient to that believer. In making this point to some of his companions, Dhu 'l-Nūn ordered a bed to move by itself around the house and return to its place. As soon as he spoke, the bed moved to each corner of the house before going back to its original position.[23] Complete submission to God's will, therefore, freed saints from laws normally governing the physical world. On a number of occasions this characteristic took the form of a kind of alchemy whereby saints transformed objects or substances from one thing into another and then back again. Shaykh Abū al-ʿAbbās Aḥmad used to gather firewood. Each day he would give away as charity the proceeds of the wood he sold. Once someone threw a purse of money at his feet and told the shaykh to take it. Abū al-ʿAbbās refused the money, explaining that God forbade His servants from accepting worldly goods as He already provided them with all of their needs. The shaykh then explained that anything he might require he obtained through the wood he collected. This fact he demonstrated by converting some wood into gold and then back again into wood.[24] In another example, a vizier once ordered his agents to compel everyone to buy his nitrate. When they came to Shaykh ʿAbd Allāh al-Khāmī, who lived in the Qarāfa, however, he refused to accept anything from a tyrant. The vizier's agents explained that the shaykh had no choice in the matter and then dumped the nitrate in his house. As they turned to leave they were suddenly unable to find the exit from his house. The agents begged the shaykh to let them go, and he responded that if they wanted to leave his house they would have to take the nitrate with them. When the agents returned with ʿAbd Allāh's portion of nitrate, the vizier demanded an explanation. The men explained what had happened, but the vizier refused to accept their story and accused them of accepting a bribe from the shaykh. The vizier himself then went to ʿAbd Allāh's house, along with his agents and the nitrate, and asked the shaykh why he refused to purchase it even at a fair price. ʿAbd Allāh told the vizier that it was not common for people to force others to purchase stones. In anger the vizier commanded his agents to dump the contents of the containers before him. When they did as he asked, the vizier suddenly sought God's forgiveness because all of the nitrate had, in fact, turned to stone. From that day forth the vizier commanded that no one in

---

[23] Ibn al-Zayyāt, *al-Kawākib*, 234.

[24] Ibid., 139; see also al-Sakhāwī, *Tuḥfat*, 262.

al-Qarāfa, or anywhere else, would be compelled to buy his nitrate.[25]

When Abū ʿAbd Allāh Muḥammad Zurbihān al-ʿAjamī, known as Shaykh Zurbihān, first arrived in Egypt he slept by the shop of a brass merchant. That night the shop was robbed. The police accused Shaykh Zurbihān of the crime, but the owner of the shop was himself skeptical of the charge. He told the police that if they harmed Shaykh Zurbihān, then God would surely punish the shop owner himself. At this point Shaykh Zurbihān proved his piety by converting an ordinary plate into gold and then back again. The shop owner asked the shaykh to pray for him. Shaykh Zurbihān asked God to replace the man's poverty with wealth, and through the baraka of the shaykh, the shop owner became one of the wealthiest people in all of Egypt.[26]

Shaykh Abū Ṭarṭūr was a brick maker and a close companion of Shaykh Abū al-Saʿūd. One day a group of people came to Shaykh Abū Ṭarṭūr and told him that when they visited Abū al-Saʿūd he offered them food in broken potsherds. They scoffed that the shaykh did not own a single vessel in good condition. Abū Ṭarṭūr became impatient at this observation and said, "If my shaykh had chosen the things of this world, then he would simply say to this brick, 'Become gold!' and it would have turned to gold." As he spoke, the brick turned to gold before them. Abū Ṭarṭūr then commanded the brick to return to its original form, explaining that he only wanted to make a point.[27]

In still another instance of transmutation, a man came from the countryside to visit Abū ʿAbd al-Raḥmān Raslān and brought the shaykh a jar of milk as a gift, which he gratefully accepted. The next day, when the visitor came to bid farewell to the shaykh, Abū ʿAbd al-Raḥmān took the empty jar and filled it with water. He sealed the vessel and gave it to his visitor, asking him not to open it until he reached his family. When the man returned to his home he opened the jar to discover that it was filled with honey.[28]

The ability of some saints to travel great distances instantaneously further demonstrates their immunity from physical laws. Saints known

---

[25] Ibn al-Zayyāt, *al-Kawākib*, 195–96; see also al-Sakhāwī, *Tuḥfat*, 307.

[26] Ibn al-Zayyāt, *al-Kawākib*, 224; see also Ibn al-Nāsikh, *Miṣbāḥ*, fol. 87v°, and al-Sakhāwī, *Tuḥfat*, 332–33.

[27] Ibn al-Zayyāt, *al-Kawākib*, 318.

[28] Ibid., 311, and Ibn Uthmān, *Murshid*, 636.

for this sort of magical travel are often called the "masters of concealment" (arbāb al-ṭayy). Abū al-Ḥasan ʿAlī, the baker, used to perform the pilgrimage to Mecca and return in a single day. Once an old woman brought him two loaves of bread to bake. When Abū al-Ḥasan took the loaves out of his oven the woman sighed and began to weep. When he inquired why she was upset, the old woman told Abū al-Ḥasan that her son was absent on the pilgrimage in Mecca and she wished he could taste the warm bread. The baker told her to wrap the bread in a kerchief and leave it with him, which she did. This was on the eve of the waqfa, when all Muslims making the pilgrimage stand on Mount ʿArafāt for the day. When the son returned from the pilgrimage he brought the kerchief with him and gave it to his mother. She invoked God's name and asked when he had received the kerchief. He told her that it arrived the eve of the waqfa wrapped around two loaves of warm bread.[29]

This sort of magical travel was fairly common among the saints. For instance, Abū Bakr b. ʿUtba told of sitting in a mosque once when a man entered and someone asked him where he had been in the middle of the night. The man said he had been in Mecca, and that he started the evening in Medīna. Abū al-Khayr al-Tīnnātī told a similar story of an Ethiopian who was sitting in a mosque in Tripoli with his head in his cloak when he said to himself, "O God, if only I was at the [Masjid] al-Ḥarām [in Mecca]." When he pulled his head out from his cloak he found his wish answered. The jurist Abū al-Ḥasan ʿAlī b. Marzūq Abū ʿAbd Allāh, known as al-Rudaynī (d. 1145/46), is reported to have flown through the air like a bird to speak with his arch rival Abū ʿAmr ʿUthmān b. Marzūq al-Ḥūfī (d. 1168/69). Another saint actually assumed the form of a bird in order to visit a colleague. Thus, we read of ʿAbd al-Qādir al-Kīlānī interrupting a sermon once to talk to a bird. When he finished, he explained to his perplexed students that the bird was actually Shaykh ʿAdiyy b. Musāfir, who had come from Syria in the form of a bird.[30]

The freedom that saints frequently enjoyed from the routine laws of physics was one example of their special relationship with the natural world. Another aspect is reflected in the numerous accounts of interactions between saints and animals, particularly with wild ani-

[29] Ibn al-Zayyāt, *al-Kawākib*, 149. See also al-Sakhawī, *Tuḥfat*, 270; Ibn ʿUthmān, *Murshid*, 292–93; and Ibn al-Nāsikh, *Miṣbāḥ*, fols. 51r°–51v°.

[30] Ibn al-Zayyāt, *al-Kawākib*, 270, 149, 302 (see also Ibn Uthmān, *Murshid*, 605–6), and 188 respectively.

mals. Two animals that appear repeatedly in the hagiographic material are lions and snakes. For example, two jurists once traveled to visit Shaykh Abū al-Khayr al-Tīnnātī. On the way they stopped to perform the evening prayer, but one of the men recited the Fātiḥa incorrectly. When they slept that night both men experienced wet dreams. As a result, the next morning they went in search of a place to bathe themselves completely, since they were both in a state of ritual impurity. While they were cleansing themselves, however, a lion came and sat on their clothing. As the two men waited in the cold water, wondering in fear what they might do, Shaykh Abū al-Khayr approached and shouted at the lion, who backed away, gently wagging his tail. While rubbing its ear, Abū al-Khayr scolded the lion for meddling with his guests. As the two frightened jurists quickly dressed themselves, Abū al-Khayr chided them for being frightened and preoccupied with concern for outward reality (ẓāhir). He explained that he, on the other hand, was more concerned with understanding inner meaning (bāṭin).[31] Another of the awliyā', Shaykh Abū al-Qāsim b. Naʿma, was famous for riding on the back of a lion.[32] It was said of Umm Hayṭal that vipers drank from her hand and snakes slept by her head. Umm al-Ḥusayn was known to pray on the Jabal al-Muqaṭṭam at night surrounded by wild animals.[33]

Evil and corrupt men sometimes attempted unsuccessfully to use lions to kill saints. For instance, Khumārawayh, the son of Aḥmad b. Ṭūlūn, became angry with Abū al-Ḥasan Bunān (d. 928/29) because the shaykh protested the ruler's decision to appoint a Christian vizier. Khumārawayh threw Bunān to a lion, but the animal would only lick the saint.[34] While Ḍiyā' al-Dīn ʿAbd al-Raḥmān b. Muḥammad al-Qurashī was traveling in various lands, he once spent a night in a mosque. The imām of the mosque was a Shīʿite and, when he learned that Ḍiyā' al-Dīn was a Sunnī, the imām expelled the shaykh from the mosque, hoping a lion who lived in the area would kill him. Instead, however, the lion entered the mosque and killed the Shīʿite imām himself.[35]

---

[31] Ibn al-Zayyāt, *al-Kawākib*, 111. See also al-Sakhāwī, *Tuḥfat*, 241–42; Ibn ʿUthmān, *Murshid*, 400; and Ibn al-Nāsikh, *Miṣbāḥ*, fol. 82v°–83r°.

[32] Ibn al-Zayyāt, *al-Kawākib*, 207–8. See also al-Sakhāwī, *Tuḥfat*, 319.

[33] Al-Sakhāwī, *Tuḥfat*, 293; Ibn al-Nāsikh, *Miṣbāḥ*, fol. 84r°.

[34] Ibn ʿUthmān, *Murshid*, 552; see also Ibn al-Zayyāt, *al-Kawākib*, 290–91, and al-Sakhāwī, *Tuḥfat*, 377. For the biography of this saint see al-Ṣafadī, *al-Wāfī*, 10:289.

[35] Ibn al-Zayyāt, *al-Kawākib*, 246–47.

Many stories told about the saints recount their kindness to wild animals. Al-Sayyida ʿĀʾisha, the daughter of Hishām, was known for healing birds. Once when she passed a man grilling a lamb she wept because it reminded her that although animals go into the fire dead, people go into the inferno of Hell alive.[36] Shaykh ʿImād, the servant of Shaykh Abū Zakariyya Yaḥyā al-Sabtī, told the story of how once while in the service of his master there was a knock at Shaykh Abū Zakariyya's door. Abū Zakariyya asked ʿImād to go and see who was at the door, and when he opened the door ʿImād found an enormous lion standing before him. ʿImād returned to his master pale with fright. Abū Zakariyya chided his assistant for being frightened of the lion, and the saint placed his hand on ʿImād's heart, telling him to go back and see what the lion needed. When ʿImād returned to the lion, the animal stretched out its leg and ʿImād immediately noticed that there was a large abscess on the animal's paw filled with puss. He lanced the abscess and removed all the puss from the wound. The lion then licked the lintel of Abū Zakariyya's house and rubbed himself against ʿImād's leg before departing.[37]

Shaykh Abū al-Faḍl Muḥammad was known as al-ʿAṣāfīrī because he loved small birds (al-ʿaṣāfīr). Whenever Abū al-Faḍl earned three dirhams, he would give two away as charity and use the third to buy sparrows, which he promptly set free. He is reported to have freed one bird thirty different times. When the saint died, birds came to his funeral and fluttered over his coffin.[38] There were even certain tombs that animals were known to visit in search of baraka. Wild creatures used to come to the tomb of Shaykh Abū al-Ḥasan ʿAlī al-Lakhmī when they were sick or injured, and rub against his tomb. They were blessed and cured through the dust of his tomb.[39]

Just as the saints cared for animals, animals in turn often watched over or assisted saints. For instance, whenever the blind shaykh, Abū al-Samrāʾ, who lived to be 120 years old, took off his clothes, the

---

[36] Ibn ʿUthmān, *Murshid*, 473, see also Ibn al-Zayyāt, *al-Kawākib*, 79.

[37] Ibn al-Zayyāt, *al-Kawākib*, 206 and 229.

[38] Ibid., 145. See also al-Sakhāwī, *Tuḥfat*, 266; Ibn ʿUthmān, *Murshid*, 291; and Ibn al-Nāsikh, *Miṣbāḥ*, fol. 50r°.

[39] Ibn al-Zayyāt, *al-Kawākib*, 79 and 121. He appears to be confused about the location of this tomb, as he notes this same story in two different places. See also Ibn al-Nāsikh, *Miṣbāḥ*, fol. 42v°. Although Ibn ʿUthmān, *Murshid*, 474, notes this saint he make no mention of this story. Al-Sakhāwī, *Tuḥfat*, 203–4 and 250, seems to make the same mistake as Ibn al-Zayyāt, identifiying the same tomb in two different places.

birds would delouse them for him.[40] Abū al-ʿAbbās Aḥmad al-Andalusī was originally the son of a great king in the Maghreb, but he was born blind while his father was away on a journey. The infant's mother feared that her husband would be displeased with his sightless child, so she took the baby to the desert and abandoned him there. When her husband returned from his trip she told him that his son had died. The king simply responded: "Perhaps God will compensate us." Meanwhile, God sent a gazelle to nurse the child in the desert. One day while the king was out hunting he followed the tracks of a gazelle until he suddenly came upon the animal nursing a human child. The king's heart was moved to compassion "by the blood of kinship," and he said: "I will take this child in compensation for my dead son." He took the infant home and with great happiness said to his wife, "God has compensated us with this boy, so take him and raise him. He will be our son." When the woman saw the child she wept bitterly and admitted, "I swear by God this is my child!" She then told her husband the entire story of how she had abandoned the blind infant in the desert. The king then praised God for returning their son safely.[41]

Shaykh Zurbihān had a cat that used to meow once each time a visitor approached. One day the cat meowed forty times, but when the guests arrived the shaykh counted and found there were forty-one. Shaykh Zurbihān rubbed the cat's ear and chided, "Why did you lie?" The animal rose and circled each visitor in turn carefully, suddenly leaping up on the head of one of the visitors and urinating. The shaykh then realized the man was actually a Christian, whom the saint reproached for pretending to be a Muslim. The man admitted he had been deceiving people for some time without being detected, and he then promptly converted to Islam in the presence of Shaykh Zurbihān.[42]

Miracle and mediation among human beings

Saints played a special role in the medieval Islamic conception of the cosmos; they transcended central fissures defining the universe,

---

[40] Ibn al-Zayyāt, *al-Kawākib*, 308–9; see also Ibn ʿUthmān, *Murshid*, 608.
[41] Ibn al-Zayyāt, *al-Kawākib*, 314; see also al-Sakhāwī, *Tuḥfat*, 393–94.
[42] Ibn al-Zayyāt, *al-Kawākib*, 224–25.

and their unique gifts and powers made saints effective intermediaries in helping people to negotiate critical relationships with the forces of nature. The saints also bridged great chasms among people, most notably between rulers and subjects and between the rich and the poor.

When the actions of the Aḥmad b. Ṭūlūn's administrators became too oppressive, a man once left his family and fled to the grave of Ḥamdūna daughter of al-Ḥusayn (d. 850/51). The physical and social liminality of al-Qarāfa clearly offered a measure of sanctuary from those fleeing the often oppressive arm of medieval secular justice. While sleeping near the grave the man was suddenly awakened by the sound of an approaching horse. He rose to meet the stranger on horseback, who inquired why the man was hiding. The hapless exile explained he was fleeing the agents of the ruling tyrant. The visitor pressed the man to explain about whom he was speaking, to which the fugitive replied "Ibn Ṭūlūn." The visitor then asked the man to relate what had happened to make him flee. When the exile finished his story, the stranger on horseback promised to intercede with the authorities. So the fugitive climbed onto the horse behind the stranger, and they made their way together back to the city. Upon arriving at the head of the hippodrome, the exile suddenly realized that some nearby soldiers were dismounting in order to honor his companion. Suddenly realizing the stranger on horseback was none other than Aḥmad b. Ṭūlūn himself, the hapless fugitive was filled with fear. Once they reached the palace Ibn Ṭūlūn noted the man was pale from fright, so he reassured his guest saying: "I would not have come to you without the intervention of the woman at whose grave you were seeking refuge. I saw her in a dream and she told me to help this troubled man." Ibn Ṭūlūn then instructed his administrators to issue the man a pardon and gave him five hundred dīnārs before sending him on his way.[43] Ibn ʿAbbūd was likewise famous for conveying the needs of the people to amirs and kings.[44]

There are also several accounts of saints concealing people who were fleeing from the police. For instance, Abū Bakr al-Anbārī was once sitting outside the door of his mosque when a man running from the police begged the jurist for his help. Shaykh Abū Bakr

---

[43] Ibid., 67–68; see also Ibn ʿUthmān, *Murshid*, 450, and Ibn al-Nāsikh, *Miṣbāḥ*, fol. 18r°.

[44] Ibn al-Zayyāt, *al-Kawākib*, 281.

instructed the man to go into the mosque. When the police arrived they asked the shaykh where the man had gone and Abū Bakr told them: "inside the mosque." The fugitive was filled with fright as he heard the shaykh reveal his location, but suddenly the wall of the mosque miraculously opened so that the fugitive could escape. When the police entered the mosque they found it empty. After they left the man returned to Shaykh Abū Bakr, who told him: "God will not forsake whoever seeks refuge with Abū Bakr al-Anbārī."[45] A similar story is told about Abū al-Ḥasan al-Fuqāʿī. A man pursued by the police came to the shaykh seeking protection. The fugitive was instructed to enter the door located behind the shaykh. As the police approached, the shaykh waved his hand and the door vanished as the wall behind him suddenly became solid. After the police left, Shaykh Abū al-Ḥasan al-Fuqāʿī waved his hand once more and the door reappeared. The fugitive then emerged and went safely on his way.[46]

When a house near the jurist Abū Isḥāq Ibrāhīm, also known as Ibn Khallāṣ al-Anṣārī, was robbed, all the people living in the quarter came to Ibrāhīm and asked him to pray on their behalf. He prayed to God that those who were innocent would not be punished by oppressors. Then everyone went to the head of the police, who ordered that each man be beaten. Each time the police raised their hands to strike, however, they were mysteriously restrained from delivering the blow. This sequence was repeated until the police came to the last man, who quickly confessed his crime. When the police asked the guilty man why he had confessed, he explained that he had heard Abū Isḥāq Ibrāhīm pray that the innocent would not be punished, so the thief, knowing he was guilty, repented and confessed. The chief of police, fearing that he might be counted among the oppressors mentioned by Ibrāhīm in his supplication to God, did not order the culprit beaten.[47]

For those in positions of secular power who failed to respect the intervention of saints, the consequences could be severe. Shaykh ʿAbd al-Jabbār, also known as Ibn al-Farrāsh, for instance, attempted to

---

[45] Ibid., 146–47. See also al-Sakhāwī, *Tuḥfat*, 268; Ibn ʿUthmān, *Murshid*, 291–92; and Ibn al-Nāsikh, *Miṣbāḥ*, fols. 50r°–50v°.

[46] Ibn al-Zayyāt, *al-Kawākib*, 131; see also al-Sakhāwī, *Tuḥfat*, 258, and Ibn al-Nāsikh, *Miṣbāḥ*, fol. 45v°. Another story along much the same lines is told about Abū Bakr Aḥmad b. Naṣr al-Zuqqāq (d. c. 905 or 912/13). See Ibn al-Zayyāt, 80; al-Sakhāwī, 203; and Ibn ʿUthmān, *Murshid*, 470–73.

[47] Ibn al-Zayyāt, *al-Kawākib*, 255.

intervene in the case of a man captured by the police. The chief of police refused the saint's plea, and ʿAbd al-Jabbār sent word that the police chief would be killed the same night. The man confidently asserted that he would bring down ʿAbd al-Jabbār's house on top of him if the saint's prediction failed to occur. As the saint predicted, however, at midnight a group of men arrived from Baghdad with orders to execute the chief of police.[48]

Attempts by those in positions of authority to deal unfairly with the saints themselves were never successful. When a caliph seized some gallnuts of Shaykh Abū ʿAbd Allāh Muḥammad b. Yūsuf al-Takrūrī, for example, the shaykh told his servant not to worry because they would be returned shortly. As soon as the caliph discovered that the expropriated gallnuts had turned to stone he promptly returned them to the saint, whereupon the stones reverted immediately back to gallnuts.[49]

Problems arising from poverty were another important area in which the saints were often called upon for assistance. In this regard the inability to repay debt is a particularly prevalent theme. Maʿn b. Zayd b. Sulaymān once made his way to the tomb of Abū al-Ḥasan ʿAlī b. Marzūq, also known as al-Rudaynī, while on the ziyāra. Maʿn b. Zayd slept next to the tomb and in a dream al-Rudaynī came to him. Maʿn asked for help with a ten thousand-dirham debt he was unable to pay. Al-Rudaynī instructed Maʿn to pray to God for assistance in the name of the bond between God and al-Rudaynī. When Maʿn awoke a blind shaykh came to him asking, "Are you the one who beseeched God with the blessings of Shaykh Abū al-Ḥasan al-Rudaynī?" Maʿn responded, "yes," and the shaykh said, "Take these ten thousand dirhams and settle your debt with them."[50]

Once in the days of Aḥmad b. Ṭūlūn a man inherited some money from his father. Before long, however, the man spent all of his inheritance. He continued spending and borrowing money, and when he was unable to repay the loan a warrant for his arrest was issued and he was seized. Although he was granted a three-day reprieve to find the money needed to settle his debts, by the last day the

---

[48] Ibid., 295–96; see also Ibn ʿUthmān, *Murshid*, 602–3, and al-Sakhāwī, *Tuḥfat*, 379.

[49] Ibn al-Zayyāt, *al-Kawākib*, 129.

[50] Ibid., 302; see also Ibn ʿUthmān, *Murshid*, 605, and Ibn al-Nāsikh, *Miṣbāḥ*, fols. 85v°–86r°.

man was still at a loss as to how he would satisfy his creditors. The hapless debtor finally went to al-Qarāfa and visited most of the tombs there seeking help. When he came to the tomb of Abū al-Qāsim al-Farīd he fell asleep. In his dreams Abū al-Qāsim handed him a cucumber, of which there was a shortage in those days. When the man awoke from his dream he was amazed to find a cucumber in his lap. Before he could recover from the shock, Ibn Ṭūlūn himself suddenly appeared and said, "I have passed this way many times but I have never seen you before today." The debtor jumped to his feet, related to Ibn Ṭūlūn what had happened, and handed him the cucumber. Ibn Ṭūlūn gave the man some money and told him to settle his debt with it. Abū al-Qāsim then became known as "the possessor of the cucumber" (ṣāḥib al-khiyār).[51]

A certain al-Ḥamīdī also once had a debt of seventy dirhams that he was unable to repay. He went to the Mashhad of al-Sayyida Nafīsa, where he recited from the Qur'ān and wept by the tomb of Muḥammad b. al-Ḥasan b. al-Ḥusayn. A wealthy woman nearby heard this petition and handed the man her necklace, urging him to settle his debt with it for the sake of the saint. Al-Ḥamīdī gratefully accepted the necklace and turned around to leave, but before he had taken many steps his creditor approached him and told him to return the necklace. Al-Ḥamīdī did as he was told, but asked his creditor why he was forgiving the debt. The man told al-Ḥamīdī that he had seen Muḥammad b. al-Ḥasan b. al-Ḥusayn in a dream and the saint promised al-Ḥamīdī's creditor a palace in heaven if he canceled the debt. The creditor then compounded his generosity by putting into al-Ḥamīdī's hand even more silver than the original debt had amounted to.[52]

A wealthy man was once going on the ḥajj to Mecca and left a box containing ten thousand dīnārs with a venerable old shaykh for safekeeping. The shaykh had four daughters, and when his wife found the box of money she spent all of it providing trousseaus for her daughters, without the shaykh's knowledge. When the old shaykh saw his wife purchasing so many expensive items, he asked her where she had obtained the money. She told him it was from God, so he asked no further questions. When the owner of the money returned from his pilgrimage he came to the shaykh to retrieve his property.

---

[51] Ibn al-Zayyāt, *al-Kawākib*, 67; see also Ibn 'Uthmān, *Murshid*, 448.
[52] Ibn al-Zayyāt, *al-Kawākib*, 36; see also al-Sakhāwī, *Tuḥfat*, 138–39.

When the shaykh went to fetch the box he discovered, to his horror, that it was empty. He confronted his wife and asked what she had done with the money. She explained that she had used it to prepare her daughters for their marriages. The old shaykh struck his face in exasperation and told her that the money had only been deposited with him for safe-keeping. He returned to the owner of the box and asked if the man would come back the next day to receive the box, and the man agreed.

The shaykh immediately went to ʿAffān b. Sulaymān al-Baghdādī and told him the whole story. ʿAffān, who was known for his great generosity, told the shaykh to bring the box to him and not to worry. ʿAffān filled the box with money and sealed it. The next morning when the owner of the box returned to the shaykh's house to collect his money he noticed that the cord and seal around the box were different. He inquired if the shaykh had opened the box. The shaykh evaded the question, asking instead if the man was unsure of the weight and amount of money he had left in the box originally. The owner responded that although of course he knew how much money he had left in the box, he would not take his money until the shaykh answered his question directly. At last the shaykh narrated the story and the owner of the box rose, kissed the shaykh's head and said, "May God bless you for it!" The man then went on to explain that he had dedicated the money to assisting needy religious scholars, the poor, or widows. So he left the box, satisfied that his money had been spent as intended. The old shaykh then took the box back to ʿAffān in order to return his money, but ʿAffān also refused to take the money once it had been devoted to God's service. The devout shaykh then took the box of money and returned home with it.[53]

Besides debts, the saints also helped to alleviate other needs of the destitute and unfortunate. A poor man caught at the onset of winter without proper clothing went to the tomb of Shaykh Muḥammad b. ʿAbd Allāh b. al-Ḥusayn, known as al-Bazzāz, and begged for assistance. The next day the man's mother came to him with a shirt and trousers, saying that some of her friends had given her the clothing for him. He took the clothes and thanked God. Remembering

[53] Al-Sakhāwī, *Tuḥfat*, 145–46; see also Ibn ʿUthmān, *Murshid*, 431–32. Ibn ʿUthmān's account involves only one daughter and 200 dīnārs, but the essence of the story is the same.

that he still lacked a cloak, however, the poor man returned to the saint's tomb and prayed once more. On the road home someone handed him a cloak and the man thanked God once more. After this he never ceased visiting the tomb of al-Bazzāz.[54]

For most people the pilgrimage to Mecca was probably the single greatest expense of their lives. It is not surprising, therefore, that the saints were called upon to assist pilgrims in securing the financial means necessary for making the ḥajj. For example, those who lacked the money for this purpose were encouraged to visit the tomb of Abū al-Ḥasan al-Dīnawarī and dedicate the reward of one hundred repetitions of "God is One" to him.[55] Abū Ḥafṣ b. Ghazzāl b. ʿUmar al-Ḥaḍramī advised those seeking al-Dīnawarī's help to follow a somewhat more elaborate procedure. He told them to perform a major ritual ablution by washing their entire body, anoint themselves with perfume, go to the tomb of Abū al-Ḥasan, and pray there. The zāʾir was supposed to perform four rakaʿāt (the sequence of bowing and prostration of which the ritual of worshipful prayer, or ṣalāt, consists). During the first rakʿa the visitor was to recite the first Sūra of the Qurʾān, al-Fātiḥa, and the 255th verse of the second Sūra, known as the "Throne Verse."[56] During the second rakʿa the pilgrim should repeat the Fātiḥa and also recite the first verse of the 97th Sūra.[57] While performing the third rakʿa the petitioner was instructed to recite again the Fātiḥa and the first verse of the 102nd Sūra.[58] In the fourth and final rakʿa, the visitor should repeat the Fātiḥa and then conclude with Sūrat al-Ikhlāṣ.[59] After this the visitor should declare:

[54] Ibn al-Zayyāt, *al-Kawākib*, 132–33.

[55] Ibn ʿUthmān, *Murshid*, 344 and 593. Al-Sakhāwī identifies this saint as Abū al-Ḥasan al-Ṭawīl; see *Tuḥfat*, 359.

[56] This verse is: "Allah! There is no God save Him, the Alive, the Eternal. Neither slumber nor sleep overtaketh Him. Unto Him belongeth whatsoever is in the heavens and whatsoever is in the earth. Who is he that intercedeth with Him save by His leave? He knoweth that which is in front of them and that which is behind them, while they encompass nothing of His knowledge save what He will. His throne includeth the heavens and the earth, and He is never weary of preserving them He is the Sublime, the Tremendous."

[57] This verse is: "By the snorting coursers."

[58] The verse reads: "Rivalry in worldly increase distracteth you."

[59] Sūra 112: "Say: He is Allah, the One! Allah, the eternally Besought of all! He begetteth not nor was begotten. And there is none comparable unto Him."

> O One without equal, O Master of spirits and of souls, O Loving One, O Loving One, O possessor of the Glorious Throne, O Originator, O Restorer, O He who accomplishes whatever He wishes, I ask You, by the light of Your face, which illuminates the corners of Your throne, and by Your omnipotence, through which You master all of creation, and by Your mercy, which encompasses everything, O One who helps, assist me! O One who helps, assist me! O One who helps, assist me!

Finally the zāʾir was supposed to point to the grave, before sunrise, and say: "Oh Lord, grant the recompense for this prayer to Shaykh Abū al-Ḥasan al-Dīnawarī, the one in this grave." With this the zāʾir was to remove his clothing, except for his undergarments, and roll on the tomb, while making sure to keep his feet off of the tomb itself. God willing, the visitor could then expect to make the pilgrimage to Mecca during the course of the following year.[60] The same sort of assistance might be obtained from Fāṭima al-ʿĀbida if one visited her tomb and circumambulated it seven times.[61] A man who once was unable to visit the tomb of the Prophet Muḥammad in Medina experienced a dream one night in which the Prophet instructed him to visit the tomb of ʿAbd Allāh b. Aḥmad b. Ṭabāṭabā (d. 959/60), a descendant of ʿAlī b. Abī Ṭālib, instead. If the man did so, he was promised, he would be counted among those who had actually visited the Prophet's tomb.[62]

The saints were not only helpful in providing whatever people were lacking but they also helped to find lost or stolen articles. One day, for example, a man came to Shaykh Sālim al-ʿAfīf in great despair. Sālim asked what was wrong, and the man explained that he had lost a notebook with all of his accounts in it while in the company of an unscrupulous person. The petitioner then explained that he had been directed to Shaykh Sālim who, the man hoped, would pray on his behalf. The shaykh told the man to go to the market and purchase a measure of sweets for them to eat while the shaykh prayed. While the shaykh was occupied with his prayers the man went as instructed to the sweet shop and purchased a raṭl

[60] Ibn al-Zayyāt, *al-Kawākib*, 287–88; see also Ibn al-Nāsikh, *Miṣbāḥ*, fols. 81v°–82r°.

[61] Ibn al-Zayyāt, *al-Kawākib*, 122.

[62] Ibid., 61. See also Ibn ʿUthmān, *Murshid*, 242. For the biography of ʿAbd Allāh b. Aḥmad b. Ṭabāṭabā see al-Ṣafadī, *al-Wāfī*, 17:42–43. The foundations of the Mashhad of Ṭabāṭabā may still be seen approximately 500 meters west of the tomb of al-Shāfiʿī (see Map 2). For discussion and plan of this structure see Creswell, *MAE*, 1:11–15 and Grabar, "The Earliest Islamic Commemorative Structures, 10–11.

(approximately 450 grams or one pound) of sweets. The merchant weighed out the sweets and took a piece of paper to wrap up the purchase for his customer. Suddenly, the man recognized the paper as a page from his own account book. He asked the merchant how he had obtained the paper and the owner of the sweet shop explained that it was a page from an old notebook he had recently purchased. The customer examined the notebook and discovered that it was indeed his. He paid the sweet merchant for the notebook and for the raṭl of sweets and returned to Shaykh Sālim. The happy owner of the notebook recounted how he had recovered his property as he offered Shaykh Sālim the sweets. The shaykh refused them, explaining that his only aim in sending the man to buy sweets in the first place was so that he might recover his property.[63]

The saints also thwarted theft. For example, a merchant was once traveling with his wares near the tombs of al-Sayyida Fāṭima al-Ṣughrā al-Qurashiyya and ʿĀtika, the daughter of ʿĪsā al-Makiyya, descendants of ʿAlī b. Abī Ṭālib. Suddenly a group of men blocked the path ahead in an attempt to rob him. The merchant quickly sought refuge at these tombs and implored God for assistance. Then he heard a voice telling him to recite, "There is no God but He, the Living, the Everlasting." The frightened merchant did as instructed, and the bandits were unable to find him in the dark even when they touched him with their hands. Eventually, they gave up and left.[64]

Thieves who attempted to steal from saints themselves were equally unsuccessful. A highwayman once blocked the road as Shaykh Abū al-Faḍl al-Sāʾiḥ approached. The robber ordered the shaykh to take off his clothes. Abū al-Faḍl stripped down to his trousers, whereupon the bandit told him to take off his trousers as well. The shaykh did as he was told, and throwing his clothes at the thief in disgust, he said: "Take them and go to the sea." No sooner had the highwayman taken the clothes than his horse suddenly dashed off like the wind. The bandit found he was unable to control his mount as the animal continued on its course, rushing headlong into the sea until it reached deep water. Fearing for his life, the thief realized that his predicament was the result of having stolen the shaykh's

[63] Ibn al-Zayyāt, *al-Kawākib*, 120. See also Ibn ʿUthmān, *Murshid*, 232–33; Ibn al-Nāsikh, *Miṣbāḥ*, fol. 43r°; and al-Sakhāwī, *Tuḥfat*, 249.

[64] Ibn al-Zayyāt, *al-Kawākib*, 43; see also Ibn al-Nāsikh, *Miṣbāḥ*, fol. 23r°.

clothes. The thief promptly repented sincerely on the spot, and he emerged safely from the water. He immediately made his way to al-Qarāfa to search for Shaykh Abū al-Faḍl. The shaykh told the repentant thief to leave the clothing and go on his way, with the explanation that the saint had prayed for the man's repentance.[65] While ʿAbd al-Karīm was at the mosque a thief entered his house to steal his cloak. When the scoundrel attempted to leave the shaykh's house, however, he was unable to find the door. The thief put the cloak back in its proper place, and suddenly the door reappeared. He tried several more times to take the cloak, but each time he found the exit had vanished. Near the tomb of Shaykh Rasm al-Qudūrī is a turba containing the remains of some of the descendants of the Prophet (ashrāf). One day a thief came in search of things to steal from the mausoleum. He found nothing there, but when he tried to leave he too was unable to find the exit. The thief eventually fell asleep in the mausoleum and while sleeping he experienced a dream in which he saw the ashrāf who were buried there. They scolded him for wronging the living as well as the dead and then ordered him out of the mausoleum.[66]

Sometimes the obstacles to wronging the friends of God were less benign than a vanishing door. While traveling to Mecca in a boat, for example, Shaykh al-Dirʿī lost some gold. A bedouin taking passage on the same boat found the gold but decided to keep it for himself. While sleeping, the bedouin's dreams were interrupted by a visitor who instructed him to return the gold to Shaykh al-Dirʿī. The bedouin awoke from his dream but dismissed it, saying: "I will not return anything." When the man went back to sleep he experienced a second dream. This time the visitor carried a lance in his hand and he told the bedouin to return the money to al-Dirʿī or he would die. The startled man asked his visitor where he could find Shaykh al-Dirʿī and he was told: "He is with you on the boat." When he awoke the bedouin asked his fellow passengers about Shaykh al-Dirʿī until he found the shaykh and returned the gold.[67]

Attempts to cheat the saints were also unsuccessful. For example, Shaykh Rasm al-Qudūrī, who sold clay cooking pots, once sold a

---

[65] Ibn al-Zayyāt, *al-Kawākib*, 140; see also al-Sakhāwī, *Tuḥfat*, 262–63, and Ibn ʿUthmān, *Murshid*, 313–14.
[66] Ibn al-Zayyāt, *al-Kawākib*, 260, 281.
[67] Ibn ʿUthmān, *Murshid*, 351–52.

pot to a customer for a dirham. The man took his pot home and placed it on the fire only to discover that it was broken. He returned to Shaykh al-Qudūrī with the broken pot and complained. The shaykh held out the dirham the man had used to pay for the pot and told him to look at it. The coin was made of copper rather than silver, and the shaykh informed his customer: "If you had given us a good [dirham], you would have taken a good [cooking pot]." The customer then offered another coin and he received a sound pot in exchange.[68] A similar story is told about the jurist Abū ʿAbd Allāh Muḥammad b. Raslān, who worked as a tailor. Customers who paid with bad coin found that the neck openings of their garments were still closed when they tried to wear them. If the customer returned with a good coin for the shaykh, he always received a garment with a proper neck opening in exchange.[69] The jurist Muḥammad al-Murābiṭ, who was also a tailor, was even more demanding of his customers. He only made clothes for people who promised not to disobey God, and he bound them to their word. If people went back on their promises they would discover, to their surprise, that the garment Muḥammad had made would choke them to the verge of death until they repented.[70]

It was always wise to keep one's promise to a saint. For instance, a man who made his livelihood from his horse vowed when the animal suddenly collapsed one day that if his horse rose again he would dedicate the day's earnings to Shaykh Abū ʿAbd Allāh al-Muṣaynī. When the animal did get up, however, its owner failed to keep his pledge. The next day the animal fell a second time and the owner once more swore that if his horse would only regain its feet he would give the day's earnings to Shaykh al-Muṣaynī. However, when the horse got to its feet a second time the owner again failed to fulfill his promise. The same thing occurred on the third day, but this time the man finally went to the shaykh with the money. When he arrived at Shaykh al-Muṣaynī's home and knocked on his door, the shaykh called out: "Why did you not come the first day?" Then the shaykh

---

[68] Ibn al-Zayyāt, *al-Kawākib*, 281; see also al-Sakhāwī, *Tuḥfat*, 372, and Ibn al-Nāsikh, *Miṣbāḥ*, fol. 80r°.

[69] Ibn al-Zayyāt, *al-Kawākib*, 311; see also Ibn ʿUthmān, *Murshid*, 634–36, and al-Sakhāwī, *Tuḥfat*, 392.

[70] Ibn al-Zayyāt, *al-Kawākib*, 255. Ibn ʿUthmān mentions this saint but not this story; see *Murshid*, 344–46.

told him to take his money and asked that God bless him with it.[71] In a similar instance, a butcher purchased a ram that became ill the same night. When he was sure the animal would die the butcher swore to God that if it lived he would give the skin and head to Shaykh al-Muṣaynī. The next day he awoke to find the ram fully restored to health. The butcher then slaughtered the ram but he took only the skin to the shaykh. The shaykh asked: "And where is the head?" The startled butcher promised to bring it immediately.[72]

Crimes committed against saints were never left unpunished. The jurist Abū al-Manīʿ Rāfiʿ b. Daghsh al-Anṣārī (d. 1139) was murdered one night while sitting in the miḥrāb of his mosque awaiting the sunrise. No one knew who had killed the shaykh, whose passing was greatly mourned. Various amirs and even the sultan attended his funeral. A week after Abū al-Manīʿ was murdered a Jew was also mysteriously killed near the same mosque. On the night of his burial the murdered Jew came to one of his neighbors in a dream. The neighbor asked the murdered man who had killed him, and the Jew explained that it was the same person who killed Shaykh Abū al-Manīʿ. He then revealed the name of the man who had committed both crimes. When the neighbor awoke from the dream he went to the police, who quickly apprehended both the suspect and his servant. The servant protested his innocence and denounced his master, explaining that the previous day when his master had held out the knife used to commit the murders the weapon had groaned. The culprit then admitted his deeds and was crucified for his crimes.[73]

The saints were not only helpful in finding lost objects, or in preventing objects from being stolen, but they were also called upon to rescue missing or captured people. The son of a man from the al-Maghāfir clan, born to his dhimmi wife, was once captured by the Byzantines. Although the mother made the ransom payment demanded to secure his release, her son failed to return. The distressed women then told her husband that she had heard of a woman named al-Sayyida Nafīsa who might be prevailed upon to pray to God on behalf of their son. The father went to Nafīsa, as his wife had asked,

---

71 Ibn al-Zayyāt, *al-Kawākib*, 218; see also Ibn ʿUthmān, *Murshid*, 646–48.

72 Ibn al-Zayyāt, *al-Kawākib*, 217.

73 Ibn al-Zayyāt, *al-Kawākib*, 203; see also Ibn ʿUthmān, *Murshid*, 638–39, and al-Sakhāwī, *Tuḥfat*, 316.

and he told the saint what had happened. Nafīsa took pity on them and prayed that God might soon bring their son back to them. That same evening there was a knock at their door and the women opened it to find her son standing there. She asked him what had happened, and he explained: "I was standing at work when I suddenly felt a hand on the shackles and a voice say, 'Release him!' I was instantly freed from the manacles and fetters, after which I felt nothing until I crossed the threshold of our home." The mother rejoiced at her son's miraculous return, converted to Islam, and went into the service of al-Sayyida Nafīsa. News of the miracle spread quickly, and seventy dhimmi families living nearby converted to Islam the same night through the baraka of al-Sayyida Nafīsa.[74]

Another woman was with her young son by the river's edge one day when a group of "blacks" (al-sūdān) abducted her child and took him to their boat. At the same moment Shaykh Abū ʿAbd Allāh Muḥammad b. Yūsuf al-Takrūrī ("the West African") was passing by, and people explained to him what had happened. The saint saw the kidnappers in their boat unfolding the sail and preparing to leave, so he commanded the wind to stop, which it promptly did. Then the shaykh called out to the men in the boat to return the child, but they refused. Shaykh Abū ʿAbd Allāh next told the boat to stand still in the water, and it also obeyed his command. Then Abū ʿAbd Allāh walked across the water until he reached the boat. When the kidnappers saw this they wept, repented, and handed the boy over to the shaykh. He took the child and walked back across the water to the shore, where he returned the boy safely to his grateful mother.[75]

Shaykh ʿAbd al-Karīm once passed a well where he found a woman shouting frantically. He asked what was wrong, and she told him that her child had just fallen into the well. ʿAbd al-Karīm placed his hand on the well and a stream of water gushed forth, raising the child safely from the depths of the well. A similar story is told about Abū ʿAbd Allāh Muḥammad b. ʿAbd Allāh b. ʿAbd al-Ḥakam (d. 881/82), who as a young man was a companion of Imām al-

---

[74] Ibn ʿUthmān, *Murshid*, 169–70. See also Ibn al-Nāsikh, *Miṣbāḥ*, fols. 6r°–6v°; al Sakhāwī, *Tuḥfat*, 132; and al-Maqrīzī, *Khiṭaṭ*, 2:442. Al-Maqrīzī's version is somewhat confused because the husband does not appear at all. Therefore, the son and the mother convert to Islam at the conclusion of the story.

[75] Ibn al-Zayyāt, *al-Kawākib*, 129; see also al-Sakhāwī, *Tuḥfat*, 257–58, and Ibn al-Nāsikh, *Miṣbāḥ*, fols. 12v°–13r°.

Shāfiʿī. He once found a woman whose child had fallen from her shoulders into the river as she knelt down to fill a water skin. When the shaykh saw the distraught mother he wept in pity for her and the child was suddenly brought forth safely on the crest of a wave.[76]

Miracle and the realm of spirits and dreams

The saints also played an important role in mediating affairs between people and various supernatural agents. The most significant aspect of this role, of course, involved the relationship between mankind and God. Usually such mediation involved either a living saint supplicating God for assistance on behalf of someone, or a dead saint intervening with God as an advocate. As an example of the former we have the case of Fāṭima, the great-granddaughter of the great Shīʿite imām Jaʿfar al-Ṣādiq. Once, when all of her money was exhausted during a great drought, Fāṭima took a rusted necklace left to her by her dead husband and instructed her servant to sell it in the market and buy whatever food she could with the money obtained. The servant wandered around the market in vain for a long time before she came upon the kind jeweler Bushrā b. Saʿīd, who asked why she was distressed. The servant told him the story and the jeweler took the necklace to examine it. When he returned he asked if she would sell it for two hundred dīnārs. The servant was amazed at such an offer and thought the jeweler was jesting with her. He left her again for a short time and returned saying that the necklace's value was not more than two hundred and fifty dīnārs. When the servant heard this figure she scolded the jeweler for mocking her mistress, a pious and noble woman known for the efficacy of her prayers. The man insisted that he was not joking, so the servant asked him to bring the money and follow her to al-Sayyida Fāṭima. The servant told her mistress what had happened in the market and then Fāṭima, who was standing behind the door of her house, asked the jeweler if the servant's story was true. He confirmed that it was, so she then instructed him to divide the money into two equal portions and keep half for himself. He told the saint that the money would not benefit him, but that he would gain much more if al-

---

[76] Ibn al-Zayyāt, *al-Kawākib*, 260, 214. For the biography of this saint see al-Ṣafadī, *al-Wāfī*, 3:338.

Sayyida Fāṭima would agree to pray for him and his descendants. She asked God to bring virtuous people from his line, and it came to pass. Among his descendants were Abū ʿAbd Allah al-Ḥusayn and his son Abū al-Faḍl b. Abū ʿAbd Allāh al-Ḥusayn b. Bushrā b. Saʿīd, the generous jeweler.[77]

The hagiographic literature also yields many examples of interaction between the saints and jinn. It was known, for example, that jinn came to the zāwiya of the jurist Abū al-Ḥasan ʿAlī b. al-Ḥusayn al-Khilaʿī (d. 1099) to recite the Qurʾān and learn ḥadīth from him.[78] It was also said that during the day the great imām al-Mufaḍḍal b. Faḍāla judged between men and at night he dispensed justice among the jinn. Whenever people were possessed by jinn they would swear by Shaykh Ibn Faḍāla, and the jinn would quickly leave them. Once Ibn Faḍāla passed someone who had succumbed to an epileptic fit. The saint rebuked the female jinn who caused the seizure and commanded her to leave the man alone. But when the jinn explained that the man had just insulted the caliphs Abū Bakr and ʿUmar, the imām instead urged the jinn to increase the man's torment.[79]

Ibn Rifāʿa once visited the tomb of Ibn Faḍāla at night and found there a flickering figure that came into view one moment and was gone the next. Ibn Rifāʿa asked the phantom its identity, and he was told that henceforth he should not visit the tomb of Ibn Faḍāla alone at night because this is when jinn visited the tomb.[80] Shaykh Abū Isḥāq Ibrāhīm, known as al-Qarāfī, used to deliver such wonderful khuṭbas in a loud and firm voice that jinn came each Friday to hear him. Muḥammad b. Muḥammad al-Qurashī told of how once, on his way to al-Fusṭāṭ, he passed by a group of people reciting the Qurʾān so beautifully that he decided to pray the early morning ṣalāt with them. While talking to them after completing the prayers, he suddenly realized that they were spirits and not corporal beings. He asked them who they were, and they explained that

---

[77] Ibid., 66–67. See also Ibn ʿUthmān, *Murshid*, 443–46; and Ibn al-Nāsikh, *Miṣbāḥ*, fols. 17r°–17v°. Ibn ʿUthmān states that the father, Abū ʿAbd Allāh al-Ḥusayn, died in 998 and his son, Abū al-Faḍl b. Abū ʿAbd Allāh al-Ḥusayn, died in 1087/88, which seems highly unlikely.

[78] Ibn al-Zayyāt, *al-Kawākib*, 164; see also Ibn al-Nāsikh, *Miṣbāḥ*, fol. 40v°, and al-Sakhāwī, *Tuḥfat*, 281. For his biography see Ibn Khallikān, *Wafayāt al-aʿyān*, 3:317–18.

[79] Ibn al-Zayyāt, *al-Kawākib*, 124.

[80] Ibid. Accounts of this saint may also be found in al-Sakhāwī, 253–54; Ibn al-Nāsikh, *Miṣbāḥ*, fol. 42r°; and Ibn ʿUthmān, *Murshid*, 328–29.

they were Muslim jinn who came each Friday to hear the khuṭba of Abū Isḥāq.[81] Just as the birds used to delouse the clothes of Abū al-Samrā, the jinn used to serve him.[82] Once Muḥammad al-Udfūwī was performing the pilgrimage to Mecca with a group of Ṣūfīs. They had no provisions so the shaykh held out a bowl and took up a collection from among them saying, "whoever has something and hopes for a divine reward in recompense should put it in this bowl." A large snake suddenly came forward with a dirham in its mouth and dropped it into the bowl saying, "We are jinn who have come to make the pilgrimage with you this year."[83]

There are similar accounts of communication between saints and ḥūr (s. ḥūriyya), the so-called "maidens of Paradise," who are said to greet the believer when he enters heaven and are always at his disposal. When Abū al-Ḥasan ʿAlī b. al-Ḥasan b. ʿAlī, another of the Ṭabāṭabā family, saw Paradise in a dream he found there a beautiful ḥūriyya, and he asked for whom she was designated. She told him that she belonged to whoever paid her price. When he asked what that price was, the ḥūriyya told him it was staying awake all night rather than during the day. After that Abū al-Ḥasan never slept at night. He saw her once again and she warned him not to fall asleep or his covenant would be broken. According to Ibn ʿUthmān's version of this story, the ḥūriyya instead requested one hundred recitations of the Qur'ān. After the saint completed the recitations he saw the ḥūriyya once again, and he told her he had accomplished what she had demanded of him. She promised Abū al-Ḥasan that the next night he would be with her in Paradise. When he awoke from the dream, Abū al-Ḥasan prepared himself and informed everyone that he would die that same day, which he did.[84]

The wandering mystic Zayn al-Dīn b. Musāfir once became very thirsty on his travels. When he saw a water jug hanging in an arch and swaying gently in the breeze he sat down in the archway, hoping that someone from the house would come out so he might ask for a drink. While he was sitting there Zayn fell asleep, and in his dream he saw a wonderful ḥūriyya. When he asked her for whom

---

[81] Ibn al-Zayyāt, *al-Kawākib*, 267–68; see also al-Sakhāwī, *Tuḥfat*, 361.

[82] Ibn al-Nāsikh, *Miṣbāḥ*, fol. 89v°.

[83] Ibn al-Zayyāt, *al-Kawākib*, 157–58. See also Ibn ʿUthmān, *Murshid*, 271–72; al-Sakhāwī, *Tuḥfat*, 276–77; and Ibn al-Nāsikh, *Miṣbāḥ*, fols. 33v°–34v°.

[84] Ibn al-Zayyāt, *al-Kawākib*, 62; Ibn ʿUthmān, *Murshid*, 247–48.

she was intended, she told Zayn that she was destined for the one who overcame his wants and abandoned his desire for water. Zayn then told the ḥūriyya that he had no need of water, so she reached out her hand and struck the water jug so that it shattered. Zayn awoke to the sound of the jug smashing on the ground, and he thanked God for compensating him for the drink of water with the beautiful ḥūriyya.[85]

Once the Ṣūfī Abū Isḥāq Ibrāhīm (d. c. 1106/7) was speaking to his associates about the ḥūr during a gathering in the Jawsaq al-Udfūwī. That night each of his Ṣūfī companions experienced a dream in which a ḥūriyya came to him and said, "I am your companion in heaven."[86] Shaykh Abū al-Ḥasan al-Ṭarā'ifī was known for the great affection he had for Ṣūfīs. When ten Ṣūfīs visited his shop one day, the shaykh treated them very graciously. He invited them to his home, where he offered them all they could possibly eat. One of the Ṣūfīs, however, refused to eat anything, so Shaykh Abū al-Ḥasan asked why. The Ṣūfī told the shaykh that his only desire was to marry Abū al-Ḥasan's beautiful daughter. Abū al-Ḥasan went to his daughter and informed her that the Ṣūfī had requested her hand in marriage. She replied that this marriage would make her very happy, so Shaykh Abū al-Ḥasan brought nice clothes for the Ṣūfī and the marriage took place that evening. Later that night, when Abū al-Ḥasan was asleep, he dreamed of the Day of Judgment. As God was passing judgment the shaykh's name was called. He was greeted in the kindest manner and was shown a palace that he was told would be his in return for his generosity to the Ṣūfīs. Next the shaykh was provided with a beautiful robe of green silk, which he was told was in return for the robe which he had given to the Ṣūfī who married his daughter. Tables filled with food on gold and silver dishes were then brought before Abū al-Ḥasan in recompense for the wedding banquet he had prepared for the Ṣūfī. Finally, a ḥūriyya of such extraordinary beauty that if anyone saw her he would surely die from desire was brought to the shaykh in return for the daughter he had married to the Ṣūfī. Shaykh Abū al-Ḥasan awoke from his excitement over this wonderful vision, and he discovered that he was still wearing the beautiful silk robe. The taste of the

---

85 Ibn al-Zayyāt, *al-Kawākib*, 186.

86 Ibid., 158. See also al-Sakhāwī, *Tuḥfat*, 277.

food was still in his mouth, the scent of the perfume from the ḥūriyya still filled his nostrils, and Abū al-Ḥasan found he was still intoxicated from the beauty of the words spoken to him. The shaykh rose from his bed rapidly and rushed to the Ṣūfī to ask how he was passing his wedding night. In response the Ṣūfī inquired how Shaykh Abū al-Ḥasan was passing the night in his palace and in the embrace of the beautiful ḥūriyya. Abū al-Ḥasan wept and pleaded with God to take him to Paradise, so he died the same night.[87]

Death clearly presented no obstacle for the saints. Living saints as well as dead ones were routinely called upon to intervene with God to affect change in the lives of the people who venerated them. Communication with dead saints was thus very common, and the primary medium for such communication was dreams. Through dreams dead saints offered their advice, gave instructions, listened to complaints, and promised help. For instance, the Ḥanbalī jurist Abū al-Faraj ʿAbd al-Wāḥid al-Anbārī was seen in a dream after his death, and he confirmed that God had sent him to Paradise.[88] A man who once fell asleep near a tomb said to belong simply to "the miracle worker" experienced a dream in which the entire area around the tomb was converted into a beautiful vineyard filled with rivers, trees, and vines. The unknown saint buried in this tomb visited the man's dream and asked: "Have you not heard what the Prophet, may the blessings and peace of God be upon him, said? 'The grave of the believer is a garden among the gardens of Paradise.'" When the visitor to the tomb awoke the next morning, he wrote on the tomb: "The owner of the vine."[89]

Dead saints sometimes also made requests through dreams. Shaykh ʿAlī b. al-Jabbās used to visit al-Qarāfa on a regular basis. Once while he was dreaming someone asked why he never visited their tomb. Shaykh ʿAlī asked: "Who are you?" The response was: "We are the descendants of al-Ṣayrafī." When he awoke the next morning, Shaykh ʿAlī promptly went and visited their mausoleum. Shaykh Khalaf b. ʿAbd Allāh al-Ṣarfandī told a zā'ir in a dream to visit the

[87] Ibn al-Zayyāt, *al-Kawākib*, 201–2; see also Ibn ʿUthmān, *Murshid*, 529–31, and al-Sakhāwī, *Tuḥfat*, 314.

[88] Ibn al-Zayyāt, *al-Kawākib*, 226; see also al-Sakhāwī, *Tuḥfat*, 334. For similar accounts involving other saints see Ibn ʿUthmān, *Murshid*, 294, and Ibn al-Zayyāt on Shaykh Ibrāhīm al-Mālikī, 271.

[89] Ibn al-Zayyāt, *al-Kawākib*, 172; see also Ibn ʿUthmān, *Murshid*, 288; and al-Sakhāwī, *Tuḥfat*, 288.

tomb of his shaykh, Abū al-Ḥasan ʿAlī al-Arṣūfī first.[90] The custodian of the Mashhad of al-Sayyida Āmina, the granddaughter of Jaʿfar al-Ṣādiq, once accepted a consignment of twenty raṭls of lamp oil from a stranger. When he put the oil into the lamps of the mausoleum they would not light. That night al-Sayyida Āmina came to the custodian in a dream and told him to return the oil because "we only accept what is good." She also told him to ask where the oil came from. The next day the custodian returned the oil, and when the owner of the oil asked why the custodian was returning it, he responded that it would not light. He added that the saint had come to him in a dream and told him only to accept that which is good. The man believed what the custodian told him, saying, "you speak the truth; I am a tax collector."[91]

When Yaʿqūb al-Muhtadī was on his deathbed he converted from Judaism to Islam. His family, however, ignored his deathbed conversion. When they placed his corpse facing east he turned back toward the qibla. Nevertheless, his family wrapped his body in a shroud and buried it in the Jewish cemetery. Yaʿqūb then came to the sultan in a dream and complained that although he died a Muslim he was buried among the Jews. Yaʿqūb asked the sultan to move the corpse to a Muslim graveyard when he awoke. Concerned that he be able to confirm this unusual story, the sultan asked Yaʿqūb if he had any distinguishing mark that would lend credence to the account. Yaʿqūb told the sultan of a mole he had in a certain place. The next morning the sultan went to Yaʿqūb's relatives and told them the story of his dream. They confirmed that Yaʿqūb converted to Islam just before his death, so his body was exhumed, washed, and the proper prayers said before it was reburied in the Muslim cemetery. Yaʿqūb's relatives also then converted to Islam and were eventually buried near him.[92]

Saints often foretold the future through dreams. When al-Fāḍil ʿAbd al-Raḥīm fell asleep near the tomb of Abū al-Baqāʾ Ṣāliḥ b. al-Ḥusayn b. ʿAbd al-Ḥamīd al-Mubtalā, the saint came to him in a

---

[90] Ibn al-Zayyāt, *al-Kawākib*, 196, 216; see also Ibn ʿUthmān, *Murshid*, 646, and al-Sakhāwī, *Tuḥfat*, 326.

[91] Ibn al-Zayyāt, *al-Kawākib*, 92. See also Ibn ʿUthman, *Murshid*, 420; Ibn al-Nāsikh, *Miṣbāḥ*, fol. 77v°; and al-Sakhāwī, *Tuḥfat*, 219–20. Taxcollecting was not viewed as a noble profession because taxcollectors were routinely directed by Muslim rulers to exact taxes not authorized under Islamic law.

[92] Ibn al-Zayyāt, *al-Kawākib*, 230; see also al-Sakhāwī, *Tuḥfat*, 337.

dream and asked what was wrong. Al-Fāḍil ʿAbd al-Raḥīm explained that he was poor, so Abū al-Baqāʾ showed him a chamber with Saladin reclining on a high bed. The saint told al-Fāḍil to enter, and he did. Saladin rose and seated al-Fāḍil next to him on the bed and poured dīnārs into al-Fāḍil's open lap. Saladin then motioned to the officials of his government, and they approached and kissed al-Fāḍil's hand. As the dream ended the saint assured al-Fāḍil that, although he was sleeping, these things would truly come to pass. When al-Fāḍil did awake, everything he had seen in his dream subsequently occurred.[93] When al-Qarqūbī destroyed a small mosque so as to build a larger one in its place, he experienced a dream. In the dream he was told to dig under the site of the mosque in a certain place and at a certain depth where he would find a treasure (*kinz*). Al-Qarqūbī awoke from this dream and decided it must have been caused by Satan, but he experienced the same dream twice more that night. The next morning, therefore, al-Qarqūbī ordered some of the workmen to dig where he had been instructed in his dream. As they dug, the workmen came across a large and wonderful tomb. When they opened the tomb they found a shroud wrapped around the pristine body of a saint. Al-Qarqūbī announced that this must be the treasure foretold in his dream, so he replaced the cover of the tomb and marked it clearly. This is how the Mosque al-Kinz received its name.[94]

A host of central figures from early Islamic history transcended death and were able to communicate through dreams with Muslims across the ages. All of the great founders of Islamic jurisprudence, for example, made use of dreams to communicate with the living long after their own deaths. The Ḥanbalī jurist Waththāb b. al-Mīzānī was said to have seen Imām Aḥmad b. Ḥanbal in a dream in which the imām handed him an apple.[95] The Ḥanafī jurist Abū al-Qāsim ʿAbd al-Raḥmān b. Abū ʿAbd Allāh Muḥammad b. Sulaymān al-Lakhmī (d. 1242/43) wished desperately that he might see Imām Abū Ḥanīfa, and he subsequently did see the imām in a dream. He asked Abū Ḥanīfa to pray for him, and the imām asked Abū al-Qāsim what he specifically wanted. Abū al-Qāsim responded that

[93] Ibn al-Zayyāt, *al-Kawākib*, 307–8.
[94] Ibid., 231–32. See also al-Maqrīzī, *Khiṭaṭ*, 2:456; Ibn ʿUthmān, *Murshid*, 392; and al-Sakhāwī, *Tuḥfat*, 338–39.
[95] Ibn al-Zayyāt, *al-Kawākib*, 304; see also al-Sakhāwī, *Tuḥfat*, 386.

he hoped to go to heaven. Abū Ḥanīfa replied that he would pray on behalf of Abū al-Qāsim if the jurist promised to abide faithfully by the five basic religious obligations of Islam, and if he would devote himself only to those people who came to him in search of religious knowledge. Abū al-Qāsim answered that he had already done so, and Abū Ḥanīfa told Abū al-Qāsim that his wish would be fulfilled.[96] When the jurist Ḥamīd al-Mālikī was in a dispute with some of his fellow Mālikī jurists, one of them told Ḥamīd that he incorrectly attributed something to Imām al-Mālik. That night the imām confirmed in a dream to Ḥamīd's opponent that Ḥamīd had correctly attributed the statement to the great jurist.[97] Imām al-Shāfiʿī visited al-Rabīʿ b. Sulaymān al-Murādī (d. 883/84) in a dream and announced that God had seated the imām on a bed of gold after his death and spread pearls over him.[98]

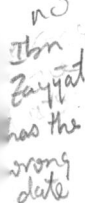

The Prophet Muḥammad himself made his way into a large number of dreams. He was, for example, supposed to have designed the Turba of Shihāb al-Dīn al-ʿUmarī (d. 1231/32), a descendant of the Caliph ʿUmar b. al-Khaṭṭāb, for him in a dream.[99] Similarly, the Prophet instructed the Ṣūfī shaykh Ibn Ḥawshab al-Saʿūdī (d. 1307/8) to build a turba and a zāwiya in 1305/6.[100] Shaykh Fakhr al-Dīn al-Fārisī (d. 1263/64) related that he once experienced a dream in which he was standing by the tomb al Abū al-Khayr al-Tīnnātī, looking toward the desert. Suddenly the expanse was filled with men dressed in white robes, and among them stood the Prophet. Fakhr al-Dīn kissed the hand of the Prophet, who then asked Fakhr al-Dīn why he did not build a mosque on this site. Fakhr al-Dīn responded that he had nothing with which to build a mosque. The Prophet told Fakhr al-Dīn to instruct the Muslims to build the mosque, and then the Prophet went to the tomb of the famous mystic Dhu 'l-Nūn and greeted him. The tomb suddenly split open, and the great mystic rose from it and saluted the Prophet in return. Fakhr al-Dīn, the

[96] Ibn al-Zayyāt, *al-Kawākib*, 225–26.

[97] Al-Sakhāwī, *Tuḥfat*, 271. ʿAbd al-Malik al-Būhalī also claimed to have seen Imām Mālik in a dream sitting in a palace garden in the middle of a desert. See Ibn ʿUthmān, *Murshid*, fol. 42v°. In the printed version of Ibn ʿUthmān, the saint listed is al-Mūṣulī, 98.

[98] Ibn al-Zayyāt, *al-Kawākib*, 212–13; see also 211–12 and 232–33, and Ibn ʿUthmān, *Murshid*, 484 for different but similar accounts. For the biography of this saint see al-Ṣafadī, *al-Wāfī*, 14:81.

[99] Ibn al-Zayyāt, *al-Kawākib*, 116; see also al-Sakhāwī, *Tuḥfat*, 247.

[100] Al-Sakhāwī, *Tuḥfat*, 32.

Prophet, and Dhu 'l-Nūn then returned to the tomb of Abū al-Khayr al-Tīnnātī, where the Prophet again instructed Fakhr al-Dīn to build the mosque. When Fakhr al-Dīn awoke from this dream he related it to a wealthy patron, who believed the dream and sold a house he owned in order to build this vision mosque requested by the Prophet.[101]

In a number of visions the Prophet was seen visiting certain graves and other locations. For instance, in the month of Rajab of 1352, the market inspector Ibn Abū Ruqayba had a vision in which the Prophet was seen visiting the tombs of al-Ḥalāwī and al-Ghaffārī. At a miḥrāb near the tomb of Abū al-Fatḥ al-Farghānī the Prophet was seen in a dream praying. The Prophet was supposedly seen a thousand times at the miḥrāb by the grave of Abū al-Qāsim al-Ḥijār.[102] The jurist Abū Bakr Muḥammad also built a mosque on the site where he saw the Prophet.[103]

Through these dream visits the Prophet, like the saints, offered advice and instructions on a variety of subjects. For example, a student from far away once came to Abū al-Ḥasan b. Ṭāhir b. Ghalbūn (d. 1008/9) to learn the seven ways of reciting the Qur'ān. When the student had learned how to recite the Qur'ān properly he asked Abū al-Ḥasan for a certificate (ijāza) certifying his competency. Abū al-Ḥasan was not sure of his own ability as a teacher and he feared his student might make a mistake, so he refused to provide the document. That night the Prophet came to Abū al-Ḥasan in a dream and told him to give his student, and anyone else who came to him to learn how to recite the Qur'ān, an ijāza.[104] The famous Shāfiʿī jurist ʿIzz al-Dīn ʿAbd al-ʿAzīz b. ʿAbd al-Salām (d. 1262) received numerous requests for fatāwā (legal opinions) from east and west. Muḥammad b. ʿAbd al-Raḥmān al-Uṣūlī once requested a fatwā from ʿIzz al-Dīn, but Muḥammad b. ʿAbd al-Raḥmān was unhappy with the decision he received. That night in a dream the Prophet asked to see ʿIzz al-Dīn's fatwā, and Muḥammad b. ʿAbd al-Raḥmān

---

[101] Ibn al-Zayyāt, *al-Kawākib*, 109; see also Ibn ʿUthmān, *Murshid*, 396, and al-Sakhāwī, *Tuḥfat*, 238–39.

[102] Ibn al-Zayyāt, *al-Kawākib*, 294; Ibn ʿUthmān, *Murshid*, 283; Ibn al-Nāsikh, *Miṣbāḥ*, fol. 73r°.

[103] Ibn al-Zayyāt, *al-Kawākib*, 296. We assume here that Abū Bakr "saw" the Prophet in a dream. For other accounts of visions of the Prophet see Ibn al-Zayyāt, 118; Ibn ʿUthmān, *Murshid*, fol. 163r°; and Ibn al-Nāsikh, *Miṣbāḥ*, fols. 83r°–83v°.

[104] Al-Sakhāwī, *Tuḥfat*, 264–65; see also Ibn al-Nāsikh, *Miṣbāḥ*, fols. 48v°–49r°. For the biography of this saint see al-Ṣafadī, *al-Wāfī*, 16:404.

showed it to him. The Prophet read the decision and said three times that the jurist had not made a mistake.[105] When ʿAbd Allāh b. Saʿīd made an error in reciting ḥadīth, the Prophet came to him in a dream and told him that Shaykh Abū al-ʿAbbās Aḥmad b. al-Khaṭiyya al-Lakhmī would correct it. When Abū Faḍl b. al-Jawharī and his wife had a dispute they separated for several nights. The Prophet came to each of them in their dreams and advised them "not to trouble the heart of a saint," so they patched up their differences.[106] When ʿAbd al-Muḥsin b. Sulaymān asked the Prophet in a dream who was the best man then living in the Muslim community, the Prophet told him to visit Abū al-Ḥasan ʿAlī, also known as Ibn Qifl. When ʿAbd al-Muḥsin awoke he went to visit Abū al-Ḥasan, on whose face could be seen the light of sainthood.[107]

Dreams were not always clear in their meaning, and at times they required expert interpretation. For example, Abū Bakr b. ʿAbd al-Ghaffār al-Muhallabī al-Ḥamdānī (d. 1214/15) used to love memorizing poetry. One night he experienced a strange dream in which he saw a man holding a bowl filled with fire. The man then took fire from the bowl and put it into his own mouth. Abū Bakr b. ʿAbd al-Ghaffār was so startled by this dream that he awoke suddenly. Realizing that the dream must contain a warning, he went to a religious scholar and recounted the dream. The scholar asked Abū Bakr if he had recently received any illicit money, to which Abū Bakr responded that he had not. The shaykh then asked if Abū Bakr had memorized any poetry, and he acknowledged that he had. The scholar then explained that this was the message of the dream. So from that day on Abū Bakr abandoned poetry and sought only religious knowledge.[108] Shaykh Abū al-Ḥasan al-Irtājī was known for his ability to interpret such visions, as were a group of saints buried south of the tomb of the jurist Ibn Khamīs.[109]

Dreams were the preferred medium of communication for dead saints, but they were not the only way. As we saw in Chapter 1, when two lovers sat on the tomb of a saint and kissed each other,

[105] Ibn al-Zayyāt, *al-Kawākib*, 272; see also al-Sakhāwī, *Tuḥfat*, 366–67. For the biography of this saint see al-Ṣafadī, *al-Wāfī*, 18:520.
[106] Ibn al-Zayyāt, *al-Kawākib*, 232; Ibn ʿUthmān, *Murshid*, 297–303.
[107] Ibn al-Zayyāt, *al-Kawākib*, 181; see also Ibn al-Nāsikh, *Miṣbāḥ*, fols. 35vº–36rº.
[108] Ibn al-Zayyāt, *al-Kawākib*, 228; see also al-Sakhāwī, *Tuḥfat*, 336.
[109] Ibn al-Zayyāt, *al-Kawākib*, 70–71, 219. See also Ibn ʿUthmān, *Murshid*, 631 for another example.

the indignant occupant of the tomb simply spoke up in protest. We also noted how a voice emanating from the tombs of Fāṭima and ʿĀtika saved the merchant who was set upon by thieves. A number of other examples of dead saints speaking from the grave confirm that this mode of communication was common. Shaykh Abū al-Ḥasan ʿAlī was known for his frequent visits to the Mashhad of Imām al-Ḥusayn. Each time he entered the mausoleum, Shaykh Abū al-Ḥasan would greet al-Ḥusayn with: "Peace be upon you, O grandson of the Prophet!" and each time the shaykh heard a response. However, one day Shaykh Abū al-Ḥasan entered the mausoleum and greeted the saint as usual, but heard no response. Consequently, Shaykh Abū al-Ḥasan was greatly saddened until later that night he experienced a dream in which al-Ḥusayn explained he had been busy conversing with his grandfather, the Prophet Muḥammad, when Abū al-Ḥasan had entered the mosque.[110] While digging near the grave of Abū Jaʿfar, a workman once heard the shaykh speaking. According to some accounts the saint told the workman to stop, and his hands were suddenly transfixed. Other versions claim the workman heard the shaykh reciting the Qurʾān.[111] While transferring the grave of Khalaf b. ʿAbd Allāh al-Ṣarfandī in order to make room for the new mausoleum of Imām al-Shāfiʿī, people also heard a voice. Ibrāhīm b. al-Ṣimma al-Muhallabī related that he was told of a certain grave from which people heard the sound of the Qurʾān being recited.[112]

When the Qurʾān was recited by the living at graves, as was common practice, the saints were also known to speak from the tomb. For example, when someone reciting the Qurʾān near the grave of Fāṭima, the daughter of al-Qāsim al-Ṭayyib, made a mistake the saint quickly mentioned it from her tomb.[113]

Regardless of whether problems arose in the natural, human, or spiritual spheres, the saints provided an important avenue of recourse

---

[110] Ibn al-Zayyāt, *al-Kawākib*, 65. Ibn al-Nāsikh, *Miṣbāḥ*, provides an abbreviated version of this story; see fols. 15r°–15v°. See also Ibn ʿUthmān, *Murshid*, 438.

[111] Ibn al-Nāsikh, *Miṣbāḥ*, fol. 7r°. See also Ibn al-Zayyāt, *al-Kawākib*, 41. According to Ibn al-Zayyāt's version the workman was a prisoner. He may have confused the story with another tomb which he simply identifies as belonging to al-nāṭiq (the speaker), 172. This version is much the same as that told by Ibn ʿUthmān, *Murshid*, 287; see also al-Sakhāwī, *Tuḥfat*, 140.

[112] Al-Sakhāwī, *Tuḥfat*, 326; Ibn ʿUthmān, *Murshid*, 98.

[113] Ibn al-Zayyāt, *al-Kawākib*, 88.

for the perplexed. There was virtually no dimension of human experience from which the assistance of the awliyāʾ was precluded. But above all, saints functioned as quintessential cosmic go-betweens. Through their appeals to the saints in the course of the ziyāra, late medieval Egyptian Muslims expressed their need for assistance in bridging the vast distance they sometimes perceived separating them from an omnipotent God.

According to the Qurʾān the Almighty is at once everywhere and yet dwells nowhere specifically. He is, by His own account, both immanent in the world and also uniquely transcendent. This abstract "is/is not" explanation may capture the ambiguity of the Real in the rarefied atmosphere of esoteric Ṣūfī speculation, but it provided little comfort for those facing the immediate and concrete problems of mundane daily existence. The reassuringly certain proximity of the saints helped to fill that disquieting void. Even when the awliyāʾ failed to respond positively, those seeking their intercession and mediation were comforted by the assurance that their petitions had at least been delivered to the right address. The exact locations of the saints' tombs were known and readily accessible through the ziyāra. Fear that the saints might not respond favorably was tolerable. It was, on any account, preferable to the possibility that the relatively inconsequential pleas of average people might never reach an all-powerful God of whose specific address no one was sure. The reassurance of delivering the message in person to the right place was no insignificant matter for the zuwwār. In their capacity as intermediaries, therefore, the saints represented the last best hope that the message would reach the ears of the All Merciful. This was, after all, a world in which the resolution of most important matters in life was closely bound to proper mediation.

Modern Egyptians still carefully cultivate and assiduously tend vast networks of mediation which they regularly mobilize and rely upon in negotiating many of life's obstacles. It is often through such wisāṭa, mediation, that issues great and small are determined. The evidence of the pilgrimage guides suggests that in this respect little has changed. Essential to the smooth operation of what in Egyptian colloquial Arabic is called wasṭa (influence) is the promise of reciprocity. Those who receive must always be prepared to give—even when the chance of having to request a reciprocal favor seems remote or unlikely. Genuine and important requests for assistance are, therefore, usually refused only after serious deliberation and with great hesitation, as one never knows upon whom or upon which networks of mediation one may have to call for help in the future.

Visiting the tombs of the awliyā' in the context of the ziyāra was also a vital part of establishing and maintaining these important bonds of wisāṭa. Although it may be obvious to modern observers that people would visit the tombs of the holy dead seeking their mediation and intercession with the divine when the situation demanded it, it is probably less evident that zuwwār might also visit the tombs of the awliyā' simply to sustain their relationships to the holy dead by offering prayers on their behalf, thereby reinforcing the bonds of reciprocal obligation and duty that lie at the heart of wisāṭa. The saints were always there to listen. Even when the most fervent human hopes and desires go unanswered, there is generally some solace to be found in the knowledge that someone listened sympathetically. This role, too, the saints fulfilled with great patience and effect.

Finally, analysis of their miracles illustrates at least four ways in which the saints were routinely expected to help those seeking their assistance. First, problems might be resolved through direct contact with the powerful baraka associated with the awliyā'. Second, saints might intercede on behalf of the petitioner and invoke God's mercy and aid. Third, the petitioner might hope that his or her own invocation of God's help would be more favorably received when made in the vicinity of the saint's tomb. Fourth, and most problematic from a theological perspective, some petititioners appealed directly to the saint with the anticipation that the saint might grant the petition.

The significance of the saints in contemporary imagination, however, went far beyond any simple calculus of utilitarian benefit. As we have seen, saints also functioned as models of exemplary piety and of the righteous life worthy of both contemplation and emulation. And even in their roles as beacons marking the location of great stores of highly charged divine blessing, the awliyā' fulfilled other functions. For example, their tombs were eagerly sought by people wishing to bury their dead near the saints. Pious visitors were attracted by the opportunity to dwell for a few moments in the reflected baraka that enveloped the tombs of the "friends of God." In assessing the overall significance of the saints in the collective imagination of late medieval Egyptian society, therefore, we must resist any temptations to distill what was clearly a complex host of interconnected meanings to some essential core.

The tendency to reductionism is by no means an exclusively modern phenomenon. The ziyāra was as bitterly contested as it was pervasive and broadly popular. And in the heated polemic of attack upon and defense of the ziyāra, we find important additional clues in our inquiry into the broad collective meanings that the veneration of Muslim saints held for Egyptian society in the later Middle Ages.

CHAPTER FIVE

"IDOLATRY AND INNOVATION": THE LEGAL ATTACK ON ZIYĀRAT AL-QUBŪR

The centrality of the Sharīʿa and the orthopractic emphasis of the Islamic tradition make texts of Islamic jurisprudence (fiqh) an invaluable source of historical information about many aspects of medieval life and thought. There are few areas of human activity on which the jurists have not commented at one time or another, and the ziyāra in late medieval Egypt is no exception.

Although the Sharīʿa may be understood as an ideally comprehensive framework for conduct, it is not a uniform code of law. The early Muslim jurists agreed that God's Law is comprehensive, but never reached consensus over its details. They identified the two primary sources of Law as Qur'ānic revelation and ḥadīth—reports about the sunna (actions, words, and unspoken acquiescence) of the Prophet Muḥammad and his closest companions.[1] An essential latitudinarianism also emerged in Islam, which made it possible for Muslims to accept a degree of diversity in the exact interpretation and implementation of fine points of the Law. Defining the limits of this flexibility has sometimes proven problematic for specific Muslim communities, but a general willingness to accept varying interpretations of specific details of the Sharīʿa and even differences regarding subsidiary sources of the Law has not only contributed to the global spread of Islam, but has also assured a remarkable degree of cohesion and transcendent sense of unity within the Muslim community (umma) over more than fourteen centuries. Divergence in theological dogma and legal doctrine—which certainly occur in Islam—have usually not carried the same weight as similar differences have entailed in religious traditions that emphasize orthodox over orthopractic considerations.

Flexibility in Islamic jurisprudence is clearly reflected in a number of recognized legal schools, and each of the three primary sectarian divisions within Islam, Sunnī, Shīʿi, and Ibāḍī, has its own legal rites.

[1] In Shīʿite jurisprudence the ḥadīths of the Imāms are also included.

Among Sunnīs, for example, four great schools, or madhhabs, survive into the present: the Ḥanafī, Shāfiʿī, Mālikī, and Ḥanbalī, each of which takes its name from the school's earliest expositor. Within Shīʿism each major subsect also has its own schools of law. Furthermore, even within these legal schools there is frequently a diversity of opinion on a variety of legal matters and approaches. Islamic jurisprudence, then, is the product of a complex diachronic process of dialogue within and among various schools of law. Essentially, this impressive body of legal discourse is produced as jurists respond to legal questions and problems by referring both to the principles of jurisprudence within their own school and to the accumulated body of previous discourse, in a manner remarkably similar to Responsa (*sheʾeloth uteshuboth*) in Jewish law. Although some questions considered by Muslim jurists are abstract and theoretical in nature, others are specific and clearly relate to concrete concerns. Disagreement among individual jurists over interpretation, or the specific method to be employed in applying legal sources, is frequent.

Of particular interest for this study are the rigorously contested positions taken in the first half of the fourteenth century by prominent jurists on the meaning and function of the ziyāra. In this period an extended debate ensued after the great Ḥanbalī jurist Taqī al-Dīn Aḥmad ibn Taymiyya (1263–1328), and later one of his most famous students, Shams al-Dīn Abū Bakr Muḥammad b. Abū Bakr al-Zarʿī ibn Qayyim al-Jawziyya (1292–1350), vigorously attacked the ziyāra. In response to this challenge the famous Shāfiʿī chief qāḍī of Damascus, Taqī al-Dīn al-Subkī (d. 1355), eventually authored an extensive response. It is the debate between these two sides that we now consider. Ibn Taymiyya and Ibn Qayyim were prolific critics of the cult of the saints, and we consider their unrelenting assault on the ziyāra and the veneration of Muslim saints in this chapter. The response of their critics in defense of the ziyāra, primarily through the work of al-Subkī, will occupy us in the next chapter. At the heart of the legal controversy lay two central theological issues: the purpose and thus the permissibility of ziyāra itself, and a related question of the acceptability of prayer offered in cemeteries generally, and at certain venerated tombs specifically. It is with this latter concern that we begin.

The English word "prayer" is widely used to translate a host of Arabic words that describe different aspects of human communication with God. For example, the Arabic term *ṣalāt*, when used alone and not in compound, generally refers to the ritual of worshipful prayer which devout Muslims are called upon to perform at five designated times each day.[2] The mechanics of ṣalāt consists of a combination of formal, distinct, and precisely structured actions and formulaic expressions. Beginning with ablution (wuḍūʿ), the series of prescribed steps that make up ṣalāt leads the worshiper through contemplation and expression of intention (niyya), the recitation of formulaic statements and passages from the Qurʾān, combined with bowing and kneeling (rakʿa), and prostration (sujūd), with the toes, knees, both palms, nose, and forehead resting either on the mosque floor or on a prayer mat of some sort. The exact number of rakʿas as well as the wording in which the prayer is expressed vary from one prayer period to the next. For example, the predawn prayer calls for two rakʿas whereas the noon and afternoon prayers both involve four rakʿas. The content of prayer itself includes brief formulas, recitation of the Fātiḥa, the opening Sūra of the Qurʾān, and other brief Qurʾānic passages that may vary in length. Islamic legal texts devote considerable attention to the details of both the actions and content of the ṣalāt ritual. Some schools of Islamic law prescribe their own minor variations in the ritual, which typically seem to be of greater consequence to the jurists than to average believers.

Each of the five daily ṣalāt usually concludes with individual and personal supplication and petition to God known as duʿāʾ.[3] Although duʿāʾ routinely accompanies the formal prayer ritual, however, personal supplications to God may also take place at almost any time. There are, in fact, a number of terms in Arabic that describe different types of supplication. For example, istighfār refers to petitions requesting God's forgiveness; istisqāʾ denotes a petition for rain; istighātha and istinjād both refer to requests for aid or assistance, and so forth. In employing the word "prayer," therefore, it is important to bear in mind that the more general English term does not reveal distinctions made in Islamic faith between formalized ritual worship of God and supplications to God, which may be either personal and individual or offered by or on the behalf of a whole community. The type of prayer most closely associated with the ziyāra was, of course, the supplicatory variety, or duʿāʾ.

---

[2] *EI*[2], s.v. Ṣalāt.

[3] Ibid., s.v. Duʿā; see also Padwick, *Muslim Devotions*.

Ibn Taymiyya and Ibn Qayyim on the performance of duʿāʾ at graves

Ibn Taymiyya, scion of a prominent family of Syrian Ḥanbalī jurists, was a harsh and relentless critic of numerous aspects of contemporary social and religious practice. His doctrine, which Laoust describes as "conservative reformism," was hostile both to Ashʿarī kalām (speculative theology), which he saw as too dependent upon reason and to Ṣūfī mysticism, which he viewed as tied to unacceptable notions of freewill and doctrines of monism, antinomianism, and esotericism.[4] Ibn Taymiyya's legal approach involved qualified jurists determining current legal questions by returning to a close reading of the precise text of the Qurʾān and ḥadīth, rather than by relying on the received wisdom of the founders of the four recognized madhhabs of Sunnī jurisprudence and their successors. His ideas have continued to resonate and have had an important impact upon subsequent thinkers and movements seeking the revival (tajdīd) and reform (iṣlāḥ) of various Islamic societies up to the present. Ibn Taymiyya's thought was, for example, the central inspiration behind the doctrines of the Wahhābī movement in eighteenth- and nineteenth-century Arabia, and his thought has also enjoyed great prominence among radical Islamist thinkers and polemicists during the second half of the twentieth century.[5]

His predilection for adopting strident, inflexible, and adversarial positions frequently made for bad relations between Ibn Taymiyya and his scholarly colleagues. Their hostility, in turn, contributed to his being compelled to defend the soundness of his writings before courts of his peers on several occasions. At the same time, his obvious brilliance and charisma occasionally also prompted Mamlūk sultans, such as al-Malik al-Nāṣr ibn Qalawūn, to seek the great jurist's advice and counsel.[6] His weakness in the area of collegial diplomacy, however, and his proclivity for participating in direct, even violent action to rectify perceived abuses and innovations to the Sharīʿa, landed Ibn Taymiyya in jail more than once.[7] He died, in fact, as

[4] *EI*^{2}, s.v. Ibn Taimīya.

[5] See for example, Sivan, *Radical Islam*, and Voll, "Renewal and Reform in Islamic History: *Tajdid* and *Islah*."

[6] On Ibn Taymiyya's relation with Sultan al-Malik al-Nāṣr see Muhammad Umar Memon, *Ibn Taimīya's Struggle*, 47.

[7] Of special interest in this regard are the tombs and relics that Ibn Taymiyya and his followers smashed in the cemeteries around Damascus. See Ibn Qayyim,

a prisoner in the Damascus Citadel in 1328, having spent the last two years of his life there. What precipitated this final arrest in 1326 was a tract Ibn Taymiyya authored against ziyārat al-qubūr.[8]

Ibn Qayyim al-Jawziyya was among Ibn Taymiyya's most important pupils and closest associates, and is often viewed as his successor. Like his master, Ibn Qayyim was a prolific writer and influential jurist.[9] He had his own run-ins with colleagues, including the Shāfiʿī chief judge of Damascus, Taqī al-Dīn al-Subkī, whose writing in defense of the ziyāra we take up in the next chapter. Ibn Qayyim was arrested along with Ibn Taymiyya in 1326, and was released only after the latter's death in 1328.

Ibn Taymiyya and Ibn Qayyim both described supplicatory prayer (duʿāʾ) as "the essence of worship" (mukh al-ʿibāda).[10] And it was the close association between duʿāʾ and tombs arising from the ziyāra that particularly provoked their ire and wrath. The practice of deliberately seeking out the graves of prophets, or other venerable individuals for the purpose of making petitions there must, from a legal position, Ibn Taymiyya asserted, be either better or worse than offering such supplications elsewhere. From his interpretation of the Sharīʿa this widespread practice constituted a flagrant violation of divine Law.[11] However, he denied the contention of some jurists that the prohibition against praying at graves is connected with the ritual impurity of the soil in graveyards, caused by the mixing of the earth with decaying flesh. Ibn Taymiyya finds no prophetic tradition supporting this position and in the case of prophets, he points out, there is a ḥadīth that proves to the contrary that the problem

---

Ighāthat al-lahfān, 212. See also Little, "The Historical and Historigraphical Significance of the Detention of Ibn Taymiyya," and his "Did Ibn Taymiyya Have a Screw Loose?"; Memon, *Ibn Taimīya's Struggle*, especially 80–87; and Makdisi, "Ibn Taimīya"; and Laoust, "Quelques opinions," 431–38. For the most authoritative account of Ibn Taymiyya's thought see H. Laoust, *Essai sur les doctrines sociales et politiques.*

[8] *EI*², s.v. Ibn Taimīya. The printed text of this tract is found in *Majmūʿ rasāʾil*, 103–22.

[9] *EI*², s.v. Ibn Ḳayyim al-D̲jawziyya.

[10] Ibn Taymiyya, *Majmūʿ fatāwā*, 27:86. The term *ʿibāda* is translated here as "worship," although it should be noted that the word refers more specifically to the broad range of acts and actions associated with the worship of God; see Ibn Qayyim al-Jawziyya, *Ighāthat al-lahfān*, 202.

[11] Ibn Taymiyya, *Kitāb iqtiḍāʾ*, 337, 340–42, 365, 368–700. See also Memon, *Ibn Taimīya's Struggle*, 267, 269–70, 286, and 289–90. Here Ibn Taymiyya cites Ṣūras: 42:21, 7:33, and 6:80–83, as well as the sunna of the Prophet and the practice of the righteous early generations of Islam, as the basis for his understanding of the holy Law as precluding duʿāʾ at places such as tombs.

of ritually impure soil associated with graves could not affect prophets, since the flesh of their bodies does not decompose in the tomb.[12] Ibn Qayyim concurs in this position in his *Ighāthat al-lahfān min maṣāyid al-shayṭān* (Assistance for the Grieving from the Snares of Satan), noting that the graves of prophets are among the purest of places.[13] He also notes that the ḥadīths identifying the whole earth as a place of prayer except graveyards and public baths make no mention of ritual impurity as the reason behind the prohibition. If this was the issue, Ibn Qayyim argues, then other ritually impure sites such as slaughterhouses and privies would have been noted in the ḥadīths as well. Ritually impure soil might also simply be covered over with loads of clean soil, thus eliminating the problem altogether. Furthermore, he points out, the Prophet's mosque in Medina was built over a preexisting graveyard from the days of polytheism, after the bodies were exhumed and the tombs leveled with the surrounding earth. The real problem with praying in graveyards, therefore, was not ritual impurity but the similarity of praying near the dead with the abhorrent practices of pre-Islamic polytheism, which the Prophet condemned and forcefully abrogated. In his great collection of legal opinions (fatāwā), Ibn Taymiyya explains that the only places Muslims are supposed to seek out with the intention of praying there are mosques and sites connected with the rituals of the ḥajj.[14] Accidental prayers uttered spontaneously while visiting or passing a grave are not a problem, but deliberately going to tombs in order to offer duʿāʾ is reprehensible. As is frequently the case in Islamic jurisprudence, the intention of the believer is the decisive factor in distinguishing between lawful and forbidden actions.[15]

When asked whether there were certain times or places that were more efficacious for the offering of supplications to God, Ibn Taymiyya acknowledged that there clearly were. For example, the last third of each night is an especially good time for making appeals to God, because it is during this period, according to a prophetic ḥadīth, that the Almighty descends to the lowest of the seven heavens, which is also the earth's sky. According to this ḥadīth qudsī God pledges

---

[12] Ibn Taymiyya, *Majmūʿ fatāwā*, 27:59–60; *al-Jawāb al-bāhir*, 8; *Kitāb iqtiḍāʾ*, 333. See also Memon, *Ibn Taimīya's Struggle*, 264.

[13] Ibn Qayyim, *Ighāthat al-lahfān*, 186–89.

[14] Ibn Taymiyya, *Majmūʿ fatāwā*, 27:138.

[15] Ibn Taymiyya, *Kitāb iqtiḍāʾ*, 336–37, 364, and 370. See also Memon, *Ibn Taimīya's Struggle*, 267, 286, and 290.

to respond to requests for assistance and forgiveness made in the period just prior to the break of dawn.[16] In terms of specific places, Ibn Taymiyya mentions only Mount ʿArafāt, the Valley of Minā, and other places near Mecca where the ḥajj rituals are performed, as well as any mosque. Although all mosques are appropriate for both ṣalāt and duʿāʾ, Ibn Taymiyya acknowledges another prophetic tradition identifying three mosques as especially favorable for prayer, to which Muslims are also permitted to travel with the specific aim of offering prayer. These are the Masjid al-Ḥarām in Mecca, the Prophet's mosque in Medina, and the al-Aqṣā Mosque in Jerusalem.[17] Other locations, such as the tomb of the Prophet or the friends of God (awliyāʾ Allāh), are not mentioned by the most righteous early generations of Islam as being more efficacious than any other place and are, therefore, forbidden as destinations of travel if the primary purpose is to pray at them.[18]

Whatever is not explicitly enjoined must be evaluated as either legally permissible or not. With regard to making graves a destination for the purpose of offering duʿāʾ, Ibn Taymiyya argues unequivocally that such practice constitutes recent and proscribed innovation in Islam. Why, then, is it that people persist in this activity, despite the fact that it enjoys no sanction in the sunna of the Prophet and his companions, or the generation that followed them? In answering this question Ibn Taymiyya shares his own insights and understanding of the actions of his contemporaries. The heart of the problem, he argues, lies in people's inability to accept that God could or would hear the prayers of anyone as insignificant as themselves without the agency of intermediaries in closer proximity to God.[19] In reflecting on the logic underlying this fear, Ibn Taymiyya disapprovingly relates an illuminating analogy made by his contemporaries between the role of saints as intermediaries with God and the well-known practice of employing human intermediaries to secure favors from temporal political powers: "If one says: 'I ask [the saint or prophet], on account

[16] Ibn Taymiyya, *Majmūʿ fatāwā*, 27:129–30. According to some versions of this tradition the entire second half of each night is especially recommended for the offering of duʿāʾ. The term *ḥadīth qudsī* refers to traditions of the Prophet that contain the non-Qurʾānic speech of God to Muḥammad. See Graham, *Divine Word.*

[17] Ibn Taymiyya, *Majmūʿ fatāwā*, 27:130. On this tradition see also Kister, "You Shall Only Set Out."

[18] Ibn Taymiyya, *Majmūʿ fatāwā*, 27:130, and *Kitāb iqtiḍāʾ*, 338 and 368–70. See also Memon, *Ibn Taimīya's Struggle*, 268–69 and 289–90.

[19] Ibn Taymiyya, *Majmūʿ fatāwā*, 27:72, 74–75, 145, and 151.

of his being closer to God than me, to intercede on my behalf in these matters because I implore God through him just like the sultan is implored through his intimate associates and attendants.' then this is among the actions of the polytheists and Christians."[20]

In responding to this widespread perception, Ibn Taymiyya explains that even if a prophet were closer and more important to God than are average individuals, that only means that God would give the prophet or saint a greater reward than He would give others. It does not imply that God would give individuals anything more than they deserved in their own right, simply because they beseeched Him through the agency of a prophet rather than appealing to Him directly.[21] Appeals for assistance that are warranted and appropriate will surely find a divine response, with or without the intervention or help of saints and prophets. Furthermore, the friends of God would never collude in seeking God's assistance for anything that would not find divine favor anyway. Thus, either one has a legitimate request for God's help or one does not. If a plea is proper and justified, then the assistance of a saint or prophet in making needs known to God is unnecessary. If, on the contrary, one seeks something inappropriate, the friends of God would hardly involve themselves in advancing the case. So the appeal to intermediaries in reaching God is meaningless from a pragmatic vantage and thoroughly reprehensible from a proper legal standpoint.

Ibn Qayyim offers a somewhat different analysis of why people persist in venerating tombs despite the absence of any Qurʾānic or prophetic mandate. The foremost problem, according to Ibn Qayyim, is ignorance of God's revelation, particularly a lack of awareness both of God's messages confirming His absolute oneness and those terminating the root causes of polytheism. The cost of this ignorance is high, according to Ibn Qayyim, not only because it lessens people's share in God's mercy but also because it makes them susceptible to the devil's enticements. Defense against the duplicity of Satan is thus a direct corollary of one's knowledge of God's will. Another factor contributing to the proliferation of tomb veneration, according to Ibn Qayyim, was falsified ḥadīth that encourage people to glorify tombs and their residents. An example of one such fabricated

---

[20] Ibid., 72. See also Ibn Qayyim, *Ighāthat al-lahfān*, 219, where exactly the same analogy is made.

[21] Ibn Taymiyya, *Majmūʿ fatāwā*, 27:75.

prophetic tradition is: "If matters vex you, then go to residents of tombs." Similarly, fantastic stories about the efficacy of certain tombs as related by custodians and other tomb folk have a profound impact upon those desperate souls in distress who hear these miraculous accounts of proven remedies and fulfilled needs. Satan is both subtle and patient in luring such ignorant and vulnerable folk to the veneration of tombs in progressive stages. First he urges them simply to supplicate at tombs. Then, when God in His infinite mercy responds to the sincerity of their pleas, these ignorant and unfortunate souls incorrectly attribute the fulfillment of their requests to the efficacy of the tombs rather than to God Himself. Such people are oblivious to the fact that God answers the prayers of the destitute wherever they are uttered, even in unlikely places such as taverns, public baths, or the market. Repeating this tactic in stages, Satan convinces the vulnerable that supplication offered before tombs is more effective than duʿāʾ offered in other times and places. Supplication offered at tombs is progressively and subtly transformed, thereby, into duʿāʾ made directly to the dead themselves.[22]

Lack of fortitude on the part of the common folk was another problem contributing to the glorification of graves, from Ibn Qayyim's perspective. In another passage he favorably quotes the famous ninth- and tenth-century Iraqi Ḥanbalī scholar Abū al-Wafāʾ ʿAlī b. ʿAqīl (1040–1119) to the effect that whenever the commandments of God become burdensome on the ignorant and common folk, they deviate from the sacred Law and extol a law of their own making, which they adopt of their own volition and which is easier for them to follow.[23] Ibn ʿAqīl specifically goes on to mention tomb veneration as an example of the tendency among the masses to pursue the easiest course rather than adhere strictly to the commands of God.

The widespread perception of the efficacy of duʿāʾ performed at certain tombs was, judging from the amount of space he devoted to this problem, clearly a significant obstacle Ibn Taymiyya confronted in his unsuccessful campaign to end the practice.[24] In a long passage he responds to the question of whether the fact that duʿāʾ offered at graves is, in fact, sometimes answered may be taken as evidence

[22] Ibn Qayyim, *Ighāthat al-lahfān*, 214–16.
[23] Ibid., 195.
[24] Ibn Taymiyya, *Majmūʿ fatāwā*, 27:71–78; *Kitāb iqtiḍāʾ*, 342–43 and 347–58. See also Memon, *Ibn Taimīya's Struggle*, 270–72 and 275–82.

of the legal acceptability of this activity. Ibn Taymiyya explains resolutely that efficacy is never a justification for making supplicatory prayers at tombs, for several reasons. First, he points to the fact that many of the supplications of polytheists and non-Muslim monotheists (ahl al-kitāb) that are made to idols, statues of saints, and venerated sites are also granted. Yet, Ibn Taymiyya asks rhetorically, is the fact that these prayers are sometimes answered to be taken as evidence of the permissibility of actions unanimously recognized among Muslims as prohibited in Islam? Proscribed innovation (bidʿa) arises from unbelief, and it is a slippery slope best avoided by the faithful. Bidʿa does not promote proper belief or action; if it did it would be lawful in the first place. One of the most seductive and dangerous aspects of bidʿa, in fact, is that it contains elements of both truth and elements of falsehood, as do the religions of the polytheists and ahl al-kitāb.[25] Perfection of belief, therefore, is to be found in doing what God and His prophet commanded and in abstinence from what they prohibited. Emulation of the mixed practices of unbelievers should not be taken as a guide for Muslims.

Another reason Ibn Taymiyya offers to explain why seeming efficacy does not justify supplication to God at tombs, relates to the fact that a great deal of outright lying is connected with the veneration of tombs. Falsehood, he warns, is tied to polytheism, just as fidelity to God is linked to truth. The believers are those of truth and sincerity, whereas the unbelievers are people of prevarication and polytheism. Among the examples of fabrication associated with the veneration of tombs Ibn Taymiyya cites falsely identified tombs (such as those erroneously attributed to Noah, Abraham, and the Prophet Muḥammad's daughters Umm Kalthūm and Ruqayya); tombs said to hold the relics of prophets; graves and other sites where visions of the Prophet have been manifested, or where the permanent vestiges of his footprints may be viewed; claims about proven remedies at certain tombs, which are later usually misidentified as belonging to prophets even though they may actually contain the remains of sinners and unbelievers; all sorts of assertions about the supposedly miraculous powers of those buried in a given tomb; invented accounts of miracles performed and needs met at specific tombs; and the outrageous claims made by the custodians of certain tombs that they are the lineal descendants of those buried there, frequently tying

[25] Ibn Taymiyya, *Majmūʿ fatāwā*, 27:172–73.

themselves thereby to the family of the Prophet himself.[26] Here Ibn Taymiyya pauses to single out the Fāṭimid founders of Cairo for special rebuke. Living in the afterglow of the Sunnī restoration in Egypt and Syria, when the Fāṭimids were frequently portrayed as the originators of a host of religious practices viewed as dangerously heterodox and unacceptable, Ibn Taymiyya was in keeping with the spirit of his age when he denounced the Fāṭimids for such abuses as the veneration of the tombs of the holy dead. Echoing a common theory of the period, Ibn Taymiyya asserted that, contrary to their claims, the Fāṭimids were not even remotely genuine heirs of the Prophet, descending instead from either Jews or Zoroastrians.[27]

Closely associated to the Ismāʿīlīs in Ibn Taymiyya's typology of heretical Islamic movements promoting falsehood were the philosophers, from among whose ranks he specifically mentions Ibn Sīnā (Avicena, d. 1037) and the great mathematician Ibn Haytham (Alhazen, d. c. 1039) by name. The worst offenders of the prohibition against the glorification of tombs, however, were, in Ibn Taymiyya's view, the Imāmiyya or Twelver Shīʿites, whom he accuses of being the most deceitful sect in the Muslim community.[28]

In articulating his third reason for rejecting efficacy as a justification for the practice of performing duʿāʾ at tombs, Ibn Taymiyya asks what makes people assume that there is actually any connection between tombs and the granting of a petition made at them. He points out that vows made in hopes of securing divine assistance have no impact on whether or not those requests are ultimately realized, and tombs are even less effective than vows. Needs are fulfilled either with or without supplication. In the latter instance there is obviously no question of the impact of a tomb, whereas in the former great personal exertion characterizes fruitful duʿāʾ. It is, therefore, the effort involved in supplication which explains its ultimate realization, not the tomb. If the same plea had been made anywhere else it would have been fulfilled in the same manner.[29]

In concluding his renunciation of efficacy as a justification of duʿāʾ offered at graves, Ibn Taymiyya returns to the matter of ends and means. Even if God ordains that tombs possess some sort of power

---

[26] Ibid., 113–14, 134–36, 141, 145, and 494.

[27] Ibid., 174.

[28] Ibid., 175. Ibn Taymiyya, refers here to the rāfiḍa, and it is presumed that he means Imāmī Shiʿites. *EI*², s.v. Rāfiḍites.

[29] Ibn Taymiyya, *Majmūʿ fatāwā*, 27:175–76.

or effect in the realization of petitions made at them, the jurist warns, there is no assurance that this fact would make it licit for people to tap such power. Specifically, Ibn Taymiyya tackles here the contention of some philosophers, such as Ibn Sīnā, and certain speculative theologians, such as al-Ghazālī, that the disembodied spirits of the dead are somehow able to connect with the souls of petitioners who are in close proximity to the graves of the dead in such a manner as to fortify or magnify the supplication of the living. Similarly, Ibn Taymiyya reminds his followers, there are numerous examples of other sorts of available and effective, albeit illicit, power in the cosmos: sorcery, astral worship, conjuring with jinn, soothsaying, various sorts of divination, and the casting of lots, to name a few. The mere existence of supernatural or spiritual forces does not necessarily imply divine sanction for their manipulation by human beings.[30] In his *Kitab iqtiḍāʾ al-ṣirāt al-mustaqīm li-mukhālafat aṣḥāb al-jaḥīm* (Book of the Necessity of the Straight Path in Opposing the Associates of Hell), Ibn Taymiyya adds the warning that God may even grant improper petitions only to punish ultimately those who make them, either because of the substance of the request or because of the manner in which it is made. In acknowledging that duʿāʾ offered by certain righteous individuals near graves may be efficacious, he warns that they should not be imitated by the average believer. Only God knows why some supplicatory prayers made in the vicinity of tombs are fulfilled. And although duʿāʾ offered at graves may occasionally be answered, the devout are advised to bear in mind that many more petitions that are appropriately made far from tombs are also fulfilled. If the benefit of praying at graves outweighed the harm done, the Prophet would have made it lawful and we would know about it from the practice of the righteous forebears (salaf) who followed him.[31] Instead, the Prophet forbade ṣalāt facing tombs, the making of tombs into mosques, and all similar actions leading to Hell. Both Ibn Taymiyya and Ibn Qayyim note reports that when the salaf did visit the Prophet's grave to greet him, they were always careful to turn their backs to his grave and face the qibla when offering duʿāʾ on his behalf.[32]

---

[30] Ibid., 177.

[31] Ibn Taymiyya, *Kitāb iqtiḍāʾ*, 335–36, 348–53 and *Majmūʿ fatāwā*, 27:123–24. See also Memon, *Ibn Taimīya's Struggle*, 266, and 274–79.

[32] Ibn Taymiyya, *Majmūʿ fatāwā*, 27:223 and Ibn Qayyim, *Ighāthat al-lahfān*, 200–1.

During times of trouble Muslims are encouraged to pray, supplicate, and ask God's forgiveness in ways that He has made known, either directly through revelation or through the practice of the Prophet Muḥammad. Invoking created beings, such as angels, prophets, and apostles, or places, such as the Kaʿba or the sacred well of Zamzam near the Kaʿba, in making oaths while supplicating God is not permitted. Making angels and prophets into lords is blasphemy, warns the jurist, so what of those who take lesser beings, such as venerated shaykhs, as lords?[33] Ibn Taymiyya distinguishes here three degrees of prohibited action in descending order of their repugnance.[34] First, there is supplication directly to the buried prophet or saint requesting that he or she resolve a problem, such as curing an illness. This, he affirms, is outright polytheism. Somewhat less egregious is the practice of asking the intercession of a prophet or saint with God, in the belief that this supplication will be more powerful than one's own. This practice is similar to the Prophet's companions (ṣaḥāba) requesting his prayers on their behalf in times of communal trial during the first years of the Islamic community. However, although it was perfectly acceptable for the ṣaḥāba to seek the Prophet's intercession during his lifetime, it is not legal to ask dead prophets and saints for such assistance. To prove his point Ibn Taymiyya cites a ḥadīth from the Prophet's companions relating to a drought during the caliphate of ʿUmar b. al-Khaṭṭāb (634–644). In this instance the community did not go to the Prophet's tomb seeking his intervention; instead they faced Mecca and supplicated God directly as a community. Least objectionable of the three degrees of prohibited duʿāʾ involving saints and prophets was the practice of supplicating God directly, but doing so while simultaneously invoking the blessing or sanctity of a saint or prophet. Ibn Taymiyya notes that many people engage in this sort of supplication, but it too is improper, finding no sanction in the practice of the righteous early generations of the Islamic community. These descending ranks of unacceptable duʿāʾ offered at the graves of the venerated dead

---

[33] Ibn Taymiyya, *Majmūʿ fatāwā*, 27:67, 89–90 and 133.

[34] Ibid., 27:72–86. Ibn Qayyim in his account of Ibn Taymiyya's levels or degrees of bidʿa reflected in the veneration of tombs identifies four degrees in the same descending order: supplicating the dead directly to fill one's needs, imploring the dead to ask God on one's behalf, asking God oneself but at the tomb of a saint, and believing that duʿāʾ offered at a tomb is more efficacious than supplication offered in a mosque. See Ibn Qayyim, *Ighāthat al-lahfān*, 217–18.

reveal Ibn Taymiyya's emphasis on direct unmediated interaction between individuals and God; and his analysis reinforces the fact that there was a range of contemporary practice involving duʿāʾ at the graves of the holy dead. Although some people were directly calling upon the dead to take action themselves, others were either seeking the aid of the dead in reaching God or simply invoking the name of the dead in their own direct appeals to the Almighty.

There is, Ibn Taymiyya tells us bluntly, no merit in offering duʿāʾ on behalf of the dead at or near graves.[35] Prayers for the dead offered at their funerals are better than supplication for them at their tombs, and there is no reason why duʿāʾ on behalf of the dead should be offered at their graves.[36] Furthermore, more prayers are offered on behalf of Muḥammad than for anyone else.[37] In keeping with the logic of his argument, then Ibn Taymiyya condemns the practice of going to the Prophet's tomb for the purpose of offering duʿāʾ there. He repeatedly cites a prophetic ḥadīth found in the *Sunan* of Abū Dāwūd (d. 888) which states: "Do not make my tomb into a celebration (īdan). Pray for me wherever you are, for your prayers will reach me."[38] Ibn Taymiyya also notes the practice of the Rāshidūn, or first four caliphs who succeeded Muḥammad after his death, who he says used to greet the Prophet in his Mosque in Medina rather than go to his grave for that purpose.[39] He and Ibn Qayyim cite a number of Qurʾānic verses and prophetic ḥadīths to support their case.[40]

Ibn Taymiyya also tackled the building of monumental funerary edifices in the cemeteries of Mamlūk Egypt and Syria. Islamic law is virtually unanimous and unambiguous in its prohibition against the construction of large commemorative monuments over graves,

---

[35] Ibn Taymiyya, *Kitāb iqtiḍāʾ*, 334; see also Memon, *Ibn Taimīya's Struggle*, 265.

[36] Ibn Taymiyya, *al-Jawāb al-bāhir*, 46.

[37] Ibid., 23. Theoretically, the formula: "God bless our master Muḥammad and grant him salvation!" (*ṣallā Allāh ʿalā sayyidinā Muḥammad wa-sallam*), or a similar variation of this expression, should be recited whenever supplications are made to God. In addition, prayers for the Prophet should be offered during the five ritual performances of prayer each day, as well as whenever one enters or leaves a mosque. Most devout Muslims routinely invoke God's blessing on Muḥammad, and even his direct descendants, at every mention of the Prophet's name.

[38] Ibid., 8, and *Kitāb iqtiḍāʾ*, 109–10; see also Memon, *Ibn Taimīya's Struggle*, 160–61 and 289. On Ibn Taymiyya's definition of this term see *Ibn Taimīya's Struggle*, 11–22.

[39] Ibn Taymiyya, *al-Jawāb al-bāhir*, 9.

[40] Ibn Qayyim, *Ighāthat al-lahfān*, 220–23. He identifies a series of Qurʾānic verses which, he argues, preclude either tomb veneration or appeals for mediation. These include 2:123, 2:254–55, 5:16, 6:51, 18:10, 20:109, 21:28, 32:4, and 39:43–44.

as the doctrine of the leveling of graves with the surrounding earth (taswiyat al-qubūr) makes clear.[41] The most generous legal interpretations allow for a simple construction of unfired brick, low enough in height that it might be stepped over. Most scholars recommend nothing more than the placement of an uninscribed stone marker, or a circle of stones around the grave. In theory, the less imposing a grave marker the better. The breech between legal theory and actual practice, however, is as wide as it is general, and by the later Middle Ages large-scale commemorative funerary architecture was prevalent throughout most of the Islamic world. Nowhere was this more evident than in the great cemetery of al-Qarāfa, which had become by the later Middle Ages the prime example among jurists throughout the Islamic Middle East and North Africa of precisely what proper Muslim burial should *not* be.[42] Janine Sourdel-Thomine speculates that the dichotomy between theory and reality in Muslim burial practice is due to the fact that although the jurists are virtually unanimous in their condemnation, their injunction falls into the technical legal category of makrūh, or reprehensible actions, as opposed to ḥarām, or absolutely forbidden actions.[43] Thus, the legal scholars rarely involved themselves in anything more than a passing condemnation of this extensive practice.

Building mosques over tombs was the most serious violation of the wider prohibition against monumental commemorative funerary architecture, and Ibn Taymiyya exploited the abundant examples of this transgression with particular enthusiasm. One ḥadīth quoted the Prophet as declaring shortly before his death: "Verily, those before you took tombs as places of prayer, however, do not take tombs as mosques as I forbid you from that." Another tradition quotes the Prophet as forbidding the plastering of tombs, the placing of domed vaults over them, or building any other sort of structure over them.[44] Both jurists approvingly cite the example of the second caliph, ʿUmar b. al-Khaṭṭāb, whose troops found the perfectly preserved body of a prophet named Daniel, who had been dead three hundred years, lying on a bed with his holy book placed near his head, in the treas-

---

[41] *EI*², s.v. *Ḳabr.*

[42] See, for example, the great compendium of legal opinions from North Africa and Andalusia authored by Aḥmad ibn Yaḥyā al-Wansharīsī, *al-Miʿyār*, 1:318. See also Ibn Taymiyya, *Kitāb iqtiḍāʾ*, 377; and Memon, *Ibn Taimīya's Struggle*, 295.

[43] *EI*², s.v. *Ḳabr.*

[44] Ibn Taymiyya, *al-Jawāb al-bāhir*, 12; Ibn Qayyim, *Ighāthat al-lahfān*, 195–96.

ury of al-Hurmuzān during the conquest of Tustar. On the caliph's order thirteen graves were dug by day, and during the night the prophet's body was secretly deposited in one of them. All the graves were then leveled to prevent the tomb from subsequently becoming a place of pilgrimage.[45] Based on these and other traditions, Ibn Taymiyya and Ibn Qayyim argued that all mosques built over tombs were strictly forbidden, and furthermore that all existing mosques of this sort should be destroyed.[46] Ibn Qayyim cites the example of a sinful mosque mentioned in Sūra 9:107–8 and later destroyed by the Prophet as proof that any mosque built in violation of the holy Law should be demolished, tomb-mosques being foremost among them.[47] Ibn Qayyim goes on to mention further ḥadīths that reject even the use of inscribed grave markers.

In locating the emergence of dangerous innovations arising from the veneration of tombs, such as long-distance journeys undertaken with the object of performing pilgrimage to them, Ibn Taymiyya and Ibn Qayyim al-Jawziyya were certain that the first three and most pristine centuries of Islamic history were free of such abominations.[48] Gradually, however, Satan duped people into venerating the graves of righteous individuals. Tombs thus became idols as people began to worship and celebrate them in place of God, and with each successive generation such innovations became worse and more numerous. This deterioration from the prophetic model after the first three centuries of Islam closely parallels reports from al-Bukhārī and other early collectors of prophetic ḥadīth about the emergence of tomb veneration prior to Islam among the generations after Noah, which is blamed for the origin of idol worship.[49] The rise of the cults of pre-Islamic idols such as al-Lāt, Yaghūth, Yaʿūq, and Nasr

[45] Ibn Taymiyya, *Kitāb iqtiḍā'*, 339; and Memon, *Ibn Taimīya's Struggle*, 268–69. Ibn Qayyim, *Ighāthat al-lahfān*, 203. One suspects that if this had been Egypt, all thirteen graves would have subsequently become sites of veneration and pilgrimage.

[46] Ibn Qayyim, *Ighāthat al-lahfān*, 210; see also Ibn Taymiyya, *Kitāb iqtiḍā'*, 330, and *Majmūʿ fatāwā*, 27:77; Memon, *Ibn Taimīya's Struggle*, 262.

[47] Ibn Qayyim, *Ighāthat al-lahfān*, 195–96 and 210. For an account of the destruction of the "opposition mosque" see Ibn Isḥāq, *Sīrat al-nabī*, translated by Guillaume as *The Life of Muhammad*, 609–10.

[48] Ibn Taymiyya, *al-Jawāb al-bāhir*, 50; see also Ibn Qayyim, *Ighāthat al-lahfān*, 202–3.

[49] Ibn Taymiyya, *al-Jawāb al-bāhir*, 12. Ibn Taymiyya's comments here are tied to his explanation of Qur'ān 71:22–23. See also Ibn Qayyim, *Ighāthat al-lahfān*, 182–84, 191, 197, and 212–13.

are specifically traced to the veneration of the tombs of pious people.[50]

In analyzing the reemergence of tomb veneration among Muslims after the first three centuries of Islamic history, the roles of both Shiʿites and Christians figure prominently in Ibn Taymiyya's and Ibn Qayyim's explanations. For example, Ibn Taymiyya attributes the emergence and spread of the practice of building mausolea over tombs to the decline of the ʿAbbāsid empire in the tenth century A.D. and the rise of powerful and assertive Shiʿite states such as the Būyids, the Qarmatians, and the Fāṭimids.[51] The Fāṭimids are especially singled out for criticism because of their patronage of and pilgrimage to mausolea, which, Ibn Taymiyya claims, became even more important for them than the ḥajj. Ibn Qayyim blames Shiʿites more generally for the glorification of mausolea and the resulting neglect and deterioration of mosques.[52]

Christians too are cited on numerous occasions for their notorious habit of venerating saints and turning their tombs into sanctuaries, an activity for which the Prophet specifically condemned them.[53] Ibn Qayyim makes note of a ḥadīth related on the authority of the Prophet's wife ʿĀʾisha questioning churches containing reliquaries and icons that had been observed by Muslims seeking refuge in Ethiopia prior to the hijra. The Prophet acknowledged this evil practice, explaining that when a righteous person among them dies, Christians build places of prayer over their graves and put icons in them. Ibn Taymiyya singles out St. Paul here for special blame in deceiving Christians into corrupting their religion, a role comparable to that which Shiʿites played among Muslims. In an extended discourse on Christian deception, which he claims exploited the veneration of tombs among Muslims, Ibn Taymiyya offers a revealing glimpse into the sort of religious syncretism that clearly characterized dimensions of religious life in Egypt during the later Middle Ages. For example, some Christians are accused of intentionally trying

---

[50] Ibn Taymiyya, *Kitāb iqtiḍāʾ*, 333–34, and Memon, *Ibn Taimīya's Struggle*, 264–65. See also Ibn Qayyim, *Ighāthat al-lahfān*, 182–84.

[51] Ibn Taymiyya, *Majmūʿ fatāwā*, 27:161–64, 167, and 465–66.

[52] Ibn Taymiyya, *al-Jawāb al-bāhir*, 19. Ibn Taymiyya cites a book entitled *Manāsik ḥajj al-mashāhid* (Rituals of Pilgrimage to Mausolea) by Ibn Nuʿmān as proof of this emphasis on pilgrimage to mausolea. Ibn Qayyim, *Ighāthat al-lahfān*, 198.

[53] Ibn Taymiyya, *Majmūʿ fatāwā*, 27:72, 130, 145, 460–61, and 464; *Kitāb iqtiḍāʾ*, 332, and *al-Jawāb al-bāhir*, 11. See also Memon, *Ibn Taimīya's Struggle*, 264, and Ibn Qayyim, *Ighāthat al-lahfān*, 184, 186, and 191–92.

to encourage the glorification of tombs among Muslims in an effort to blur distinctions between Christianity and Islam.[54] Jesus and Mary were supposedly compared to al-Ḥusayn and Sayyida Nafīsa, his great-granddaughter, over whose apocryphal tombs Egyptians built impressive mausolea. In such ways these duplicitous Christians are charged with presenting Christianity and Islam as simply two paths to the same truth. The deliberate blurring of distinctions, and the effort to present the differences between Christianity and Islam as being of no greater significance than the internal divisions among the various schools of Islamic jurisprudence, according to Ibn Taymiyya, explains the ease with which many hypocritical and insincere "converts" from Christianity had made their way into Islam, bringing with them their lies and abhorrent practices.[55] Furthermore, by encouraging prohibited actions in Islam, such as the glorification of tombs, he asserts, Christians managed to strengthen the position of their own religion vis-à-vis Islam. Additional charges against Christians include tricking ignorant Muslims into venerating Christian tombs, baptizing their children in hopes of prolonging their lives, visiting and making vows to churches and sacred Christian sites, and even seeking communion from priests and monks. It is precisely such duplicitous activities as these which, Ibn Taymiyya tells us, necessitated the Sharīʿa.

Ibn Taymiyya and Ibn Qayyim occasionally drew upon a multitude of activities regularly occurring in the cemeteries of Egypt and greater Syria to illustrate their denunciations of proscribed innovation. Although their descriptions of many of these abuses are brief, and clearly colored by an underlying agenda of hostility to the veneration of the holy dead, they nevertheless offer useful information on the sorts of activities taking place in the graveyards. Among the expressions of tomb veneration condemned by these two jurists are dismounting from afar and approaching tombs on foot while bowing, uncovering the head and kissing the ground before the tomb, shouting and moaning to the point that sobbing may be heard, touching and embracing tombs, kissing them, rubbing cheeks with their dust, prostrating before and praying to them, lighting candles or oil lamps over them at night, circumambulating them, hanging

[54] Ibn Qayyim, *Ighāthat al-lahfān*, 184; Ibn Taymiyya, *Majmūʿ fatāwā*, 27:161, 460–64.

[55] Ibn Taymiyya, *Kitāb iqtiḍāʾ*, 344, and Memon, *Ibn Taimīya's Struggle*, 273.

drapes on them (perhaps imitating the kiswa, or richly embroidered cloth that is draped over the Kaʿba in Mecca), leaving notes requesting assistance, and anointing tombs with perfume or rose water.[56] Ibn Qayyim observes that many activities associated with the veneration of tombs clearly mimic actions associated with the ḥajj.[57] For example, besides circumambulating the tomb as if it were the Kaʿba, and touching and kissing the tomb as if it were the sacred black stone, zuwwār sometimes even cut their hair, shaved, offered sacrifices to the tomb, and congratulated each other at the conclusion of their visitation rituals, in emulation of the same actions performed at the conclusion of the ḥajj. He claims that the zuwwār valued the garments worn in these ziyāras so highly that they would refuse to trade them even if they were offered robes worn on a proper pilgrimage to Mecca in exchange.

What benefits, according to these critical jurists, did people hope to gain from their veneration of the graves of the holy dead? Ibn Qayyim identifies several objectives behind the ziyāra including appeals for success, sustenance, good health, relief from debts, release from troubles, and assistance in various concerns. Not all zuwwār sought such benign goals, however, as Ibn Taymiyya also found it necessary to criticize those who made their way to certain tombs in order to invoke divine wrath and pronounce curses there on their enemies.[58]

Vows and votive offerings made by the zuwwār were another important aspect of the ziyāra. Ibn Taymiyya notes critically that offerings of items such as silver and gold candelabra and lamp oil were regularly made to the tombs and their custodians.[59] He also notes that some people even pray at and make vows to springs and trees considered sacred, hanging bits of cloth and the like on trees, or taking their leaves for the baraka they supposedly confer. In condemning these actions he draws the obvious parallel to practices associated with the pre-Islamic worship of idols, many of which were also trees, rocks, and springs. Ibn Qayyim is also critical of vows

---

[56] Ibn Taymiyya, *Majmūʿ fatāwā*, 27:91–92. See also Ibn Qayyim, *Ighāthat al-lahfān*, 194–95, 197, and 217.

[57] Ibn Qayyim, *Ighāthat al-lahfān*, 194.

[58] Ibid. See also Ibn Taymiyya, *Kitāb iqtiḍāʾ*, 353, and Memon, *Ibn Taimīya's Struggle*, 279.

[59] Ibn Taymiyya, *Majmūʿ fatāwā*, 27:77 and 146–50, and *Kitāb iqtiḍāʾ*, 360 and 383 see also Memon, *Ibn Taimīya's Struggle*, 283–84 and 299.

and votive offerings of candles and oil lamps. Likewise, he asserts, waqfs established with the object of keeping candles and lamps illuminated over tombs, or for any other purpose, are not lawful.[60] The butchering of livestock, presumably in sacrifice, near tombs in al-Qarāfa apparently occurred, since both Ibn Taymiyya and Ibn Qayyim found it necessary to criticize this practice as well.[61] Neither should offerings of money, lamp oil, candles, livestock and the like be made to the custodians of tombs, or to the host of people who earned all or part of their livelihood by attaching themselves to various tombs. We do not know a great deal about the identity of these individuals associated with tombs, but they probably included beggars, Qur'ān reciters, Ṣūfīs residing in zāwiyas, itinerant religious story tellers and preachers, street entertainers, pilgrimage guides, mendicant ascetics, the insane, and various petty merchants selling flowers, rose water, perfume, incense, candles, water, food, sweets, and other items required by visitors to the cemeteries.

Ibn Taymiyya took a strong stand against tomb custodians and all others who derived an income from the pilgrimage trade in cemeteries. In one fatwā he argued not only that it was lawful for responsible political authorities to forbid people from earning money in this way but that the expropriation of money earned from the ziyāra was also sanctioned.[62] This particular fatwā was prompted by a dispute over the performance of mystical concerts (samāʿ) performed next to the tomb-mosque of the patriarch Abraham in Hebron, and the role of the mosque's prayer announcer (mu'adhdhin) in these concerts. The term *samāʿ*, which technically means "hearing," describes gatherings in which dhikr, mystical chanting, or dancing takes place with or without musical accompaniment. In this case the samāʿ was probably connected with the Mevlevī (or Mawlawiyya) Ṣūfī order of "whirling dervishes," since both the playing of reed flutes and dancing are mentioned in the fatwā. Specifically, Ibn Taymiyya responds in his legal opinion to whether or not the political authorities have the right to compel this mu'adhdhin to stop participating in these gatherings or face dismissal, and furthermore, whether or not they can forbid the samāʿ and seek to obstruct it by relocating it to a

---

[60] Ibn Taymiyya, *Majmūʿ fatāwā*, 27:136–37. Ibn Qayyim, *Ighāthat al-lahfān*, 195 and 210.

[61] Ibn Taymiyya, *Majmūʿ fatāwā*, 27:495. See also Ibn Qayyim, *Ighāthat al-lahfān*, 217.

[62] Ibn Taymiyya, *Majmūʿ fatāwā*, 27:77, 106–11.

place too confined to permit dancing. His predictably uncompromising responses reveal the low threshold of his tolerance for the specific activities described in the fatwā as well as his general distaste for the larger host of activities involved in the ziyāra in the later Middle Ages. Not only was there no divine or prophetic sanction for these practices from his vantage point, but they also bore the dangerous hallmarks of forbidden innovation, echoing the idolatry of the pre-Islamic jāhiliyya. Dhikr, Qur'ānic recitation, fasting, charity, vows, and offerings were all analogous to du'ā' for Ibn Taymiyya in the sense that none should be performed at graves. Although he concedes that he is willing to forgive and pray for the divine pardon of ignorant people who engage in the various abuses associated with the ziyāra, Ibn Taymiyya cautions that an important distinction must be maintained between forgiveness of the individual violator and sanctioning the transgression itself.[63]

Clear and substantial prophetic sanction in ḥadīth for some form of ziyāra, however, obliged Ibn Taymiyya to wage his campaign against the popular veneration of graves by emphasizing a distinction between what he described as lawful ziyāra (al-ziyāra al-shar'iyya) and forbidden ziyāra (al-ziyāra al-bida'iyya). In grappling with the Prophet's example, Ibn Taymiyya sought to circumscribe closely those activities that constituted permissible ziyāra and to demarcate acceptable practices from prohibited innovation. Based on the sunna of Muḥammad, licit actions associated with proper ziyāra included greeting the dead, supplicating God on behalf of the dead (assuming, of course, that the visit itself to the tomb had not been undertaken with the specific purpose of offering du'ā' there), and visiting the dead for the purpose of reminding oneself of the transitory nature of life and contemplating the warning of inevitable death represented by the grave. In terms of this final cautionary function of visiting tombs, Ibn Taymiyya even goes so far as to permit visits to the graves of unbelievers, as long as the visitor does not ask God's forgiveness on behalf of dead infidels.[64]

Ibn Qayyim likewise distinguishes between proper and forbidden ziyāras, although in terms somewhat different from those employed

[63] Ibn Taymiyya, *Kitāb iqtiḍā'*, 351–52, 378, and Memon, *Ibn Taimīya's Struggle*, 278, 296.
[64] Ibn Taymiyya, *Majmū' fatāwā*, 27:70–71, 119–20, and 164–66.

by Ibn Taymiyya. The proper or permitted ziyāra Ibn Qayyim terms "the visit to graves of those who profess the unity of God" (ziyārat al-muwaḥḥidīn li-l-qubūr) which he contrasts with "the visit of the polytheists" (ziyārat al-mushrikīn).[65] The goals of the lawful ziyāra are threefold in Ibn Qayyim's analysis. First, permitted ziyāra allows the zā'ir to remember, contemplate, and be admonished about the hereafter. The Prophet urged this sort of visit through the ḥadīth attributed to him which states: "Visit tombs because they remind you of the hereafter." The second goal of the proper ziyāra is to perform a good deed for the person buried there. For if one's acquaintance with the dead is not maintained one forgets them, just as the living are forgotten if we do not visit them for an extended time. And if the living enjoy being visited, the dead do so even more because in the place they inhabit they are separated from their family, friends, and acquaintances. And in a remark reminiscent of Ibn Abī Ḥajala's concern with good neighborliness, Ibn Qayyim observes that should the visitor come bearing a gift, such as supplication for the dead, alms offered on their behalf, or a righteous act bringing one closer to God (qurba) dedicated on behalf of the dead, their happiness is magnified, just as the living are especially pleased when a visitor arrives bearing a gift. In terms of duʿā' offered on behalf of the dead, Ibn Qayyim notes that the Prophet permitted only supplications seeking God's forgiveness and mercy for the dead and requests for their well-being. The third and final objective of the lawful ziyāra is for the visitor to perform a good deed for himself by adhering closely to the sunna and not going beyond what Muḥammad made lawful in this, as in every other action. By conducting the ziyāra in keeping with the Prophet's example, the visitor performs a good deed both for himself and the dead.

In contrast to the proper ziyāra of those who profess the oneness of God, Ibn Qayyim describes the ziyāra of the polytheists. The origins of these forbidden visits lie in the worship of idols, which closes the circle since, as we noted earlier, the genesis of idol worship itself lies in the veneration of the holy dead from the time of Noah. The polytheists believe that the soul of the venerated dead is closer to God and, therefore, possesses a higher rank and greater merit in the eyes of God. Furthermore, the blessings and kindness of God continue to flow over the souls of the holy dead without interruption.

[65] Ibn Qayyim, *Ighāthat al-lahfān*, 218–19; see also 198–99 and 202.

Thus, the polytheists believe that if the soul of the visitor draws near to and connects with the soul of the holy dead it may share in the beneficence of the Almighty through the mediation of the soul of the holy dead in exactly the same manner as rays of light are reflected from a clear mirror or water onto the body facing them. The perfection of such visits is achieved when pilgrims direct their faces, souls, and all of their zeal toward the dead, thereby channeling all their aspirations and attention exclusively toward the dead. And the more one's zeal and heart are united in their focus on the dead, the better and the more likely is one to benefit from them. This, according to Ibn Qayyim, is the sort of ziyāra described by the great Muslim philosophers Ibn Sīna and al-Farābī (d. 950). If rational spirits are connected to higher spirits in this way, they argue, light emanating from the latter will flood the former. And through this connection between the soul of the visitor and the soul of the venerated dead, the pilgrim shares in some portion of the blessing God bestows on the saint. Rejecting this theory of the mingling of souls and the benefits achieved therefrom through the veneration of the dead, Ibn Qayyim sees only a dangerous link with the worship of stars and idols that characterized the polytheistic "Age of Ignorance" before the advent of Islam. Furthermore, it is through such seductive and dangerous ideas that the polytheists succeed in transforming the limited ziyāra that focuses on contemplation of the hereafter and supplication on behalf of the dead into latter-day idol worship, where the faithful are misled either into supplicating God through the mediation of the venerated dead or even worse, trying to siphon off a measure of the baraka which God has bestowed on the saints.

Ibn Taymiyya was frequently charged by his opponents with being unconditionally opposed to any manifestation of the ziyāra, an accusation that carried the not-so-subtle implication that he was himself guilty of unlawful innovation. Frequent denials indicate clearly how sensitive the great Ḥanbalī jurist was to this dangerous charge.[66] In response to a request by the Mamlūk sultan, al-Nāṣir Muḥammad, and the leading notables of the Mamlūk empire for clarification of a fatwā on the ziyāra that Ibn Taymiyya had written seventeen years earlier, he wrote *al-Jawāb al-bāhir fī zuwwār al-maqābir* (The Splendid Response Concerning Visitors to the Cemeteries). Ibn Taymiyya casts

---

[66] Ibn Taymiyya, *al-Jawāb al-bāhir*, 14–22, and *Kitāb iqtiḍā'*, 327 and 364, and Memon, *Ibn Taimīya's Struggle*, 261 and 286.

himself in this interesting little tract as a tolerant moderate on this issue, in contradistinction to important jurists who denied the legitimacy of the ziyāra altogether.[67] He points out that a number of early authorities viewed the Prophet's initial prohibition against visiting graves as not having been abrogated by later ḥadīth supposedly legitimating it. The most notable example of this refusal to acknowledge prophetic sanction for ziyāra was Muḥammad b. Ismāʿīl al-Bukhārī (d. 870), the collector of one of the two greatest canonical collections of ḥadīth, who failed to relate the traditions most widely accepted as abrogating the Prophet's initial blanket prohibition against visiting graves. Despite Ibn Taymiyya's obvious sympathy for this position, he was compelled to acknowledge that the weight of legal opinion classified the most acceptable forms of ziyāra as either mubāḥa (neutral actions devoid of either merit or harm), or as mustaḥabba (recommended action to which divine rewards accrue). He carefully staked out his own position in this disputed legal terrain by identifying three types of ziyāra: those which are absolutely forbidden, such as visits involving lamentation, wailing, falsehood, or polytheism; visits which are merely neutral, such as those undertaken in grief, to contemplate the inevitability of death, or simply out of a desire to be close to the deceased; and, finally, visits which are mustaḥabba, a category that he limits strictly to the offering of duʿā' on behalf of dead Muslims. Ibn Qayyim explains that the dead are in need of the supplication and intercession of the living because while in the grave they face the terrifying ordeal of questioning by the two angels Munkar and Nakīr, who examine the dead on their beliefs and actions and punish them there if necessary. The Prophet's example of what proper supplication on behalf of the dead should include is preserved in a ḥadīth transmitted on the authority of ʿAwf b. Mālik:

> O God, forgive him. Have mercy on him. Excuse him and protect him. Honor his descent and make wide his entrance. Bathe him with water, snow, and hail. Cleanse him from sin just as the white shroud is cleansed of filth. Exchange his house with a better house; his family with a better family; and his wife with a better wife. Admit him

[67] Ibn Taymiyya, *al-Jawāb al-bāhir*, 2, 5, 22–24, and 43–47. He cites important transmitters of traditions among the tābiʿūn (the second Muslim generation after the Prophet), such as Ibrāhīm al-Nakhaʿī (d. 714 or 715), Abū ʿAmr ʿĀmir b. Sharāḥīl b. ʿAmr al-Shaʿbī (d. c. 728), and Muḥammad b. Sīrīn (d. 728), as among those who absolutely abhorred the ziyāra.

> to Paradise and protect him from the punishments of the tomb and the agony of Hell.[68]

Even in this instance of duʿāʾ offered on behalf of dead believers, however, Ibn Taymiyya is quick to negate the practical impact of ziyāra by reminding us that duʿāʾ offered on behalf of the dead at their graves is in no way inherently better than supplication for them offered in a mosque or at home. Furthermore, since one should not undertake ziyāra to graves specifically for the purpose of offering duʿāʾ there, Ibn Taymiyya has so narrowly constructed the category of ziyāra mustaḥabba as to make it meaningless.

Much criticism of Ibn Taymiyya, as well as his response to it, centered around visits to the tomb of the Prophet in Medina.[69] For example, the future Shāfiʿī chief qāḍī of Damascus, Muḥammad b. Abū Bakr b. ʿĪsā b. Badrān al-Akhnāʾī (d. 1332), accused Ibn Taymiyya of forbidding visits to all graves, including ziyāra to the tomb of Muḥammad and those of other prophets.[70] However, in his *al-Jawāb al-bāhir* Ibn Taymiyya points out that if visiting the tombs of average believers is lawful, then visits to the graves of prophets and other righteous individuals must certainly be even more so—the Prophet Muḥammad, as one would anticipate, being especially privileged over everyone else in this regard.[71] Although Ibn Taymiyya did not assert that visits to the Prophet's tomb were unacceptable, he did take a strong stand against making any grave, including that of the Prophet, the object of travel. In defending this position, Ibn Taymiyya cites the custom of the Prophet's companions who, the jurist tells us, never traveled to Medina for the sake of visiting Muḥammad's grave. While they were in Medina, Ibn Taymiyya relates, the companions never went to the house of ʿĀ'isha, the Prophet's wife, where he was buried for the purpose of greeting him. Instead they greeted Muḥammad during their prayers as well as while entering and exiting his mosque.[72] As the Prophet's mosque is one of three places to which Muslim pilgrimage is specifically permitted, from Ibn Taymiyya's position, if a believer undertakes travel in order to pray in the Prophet's mosque, it is then acceptable to visit Muḥammad's tomb and to greet him.

---

[68] Ibn Qayyim, *Ighāthat al-lahfān*, 201.

[69] On the cult of the Prophet's tomb, see Shaun Marmon, *Eunuchs and Sacred Boundaries*.

[70] Ibn Taymiyya, *Majmūʿ fatāwā*, 27:182–92, 228, 235–36, 243, and 292–94.

[71] Ibn Taymiyya, *al-Jawāb al-bāhir*, 15.

[72] Ibid., 18. Idem, *Majmūʿ fatāwā*, 27:243.

How significant such distinctions between the Prophet's tomb and his mosque were in the contemporary imagination are hard to gauge, of course, since the Prophet's mosque had by Ibn Taymiyya's day long since been expanded to encompass his tomb, thus making it the most notable violation of the prohibition against building mosques over burial sites. In fact, Ibn Taymiyya faults al-Akhnāʾī for comparing travel for the purpose of visiting Muḥammad's tomb with travel undertaken for ziyāra to other graves precisely because the Prophet's tomb is within his mosque, to which travel is specifically permitted.[73] Denying the legality of travel to any of the three designated mosques to which the Prophet specifically permitted travel, Ibn Taymiyya explains, would clearly constitute unbelief, for which the guilty party must either repent or face death.[74] By extension, therefore, any ziyāra that is incidental to travel or authorized pilgrimage is perfectly legitimate, even encouraged. What is not acceptable, in contrast, is travel undertaken exclusively or primarily for the purpose of visiting tombs, regardless of whether the tomb contains the Prophet himself or someone else. Likewise, supplicatory praying at graves is not itself wrong, as long as it is genuinely spontaneous in nature and strictly ancillary to the primary goal of the visit.

The decisive factor in determining the permissibility of actions here is clearly the traveler's intention and not the actions themselves. The act of undertaking long-distance travel, therefore, became an important factor for Ibn Taymiyya because it helped to clarify the intention behind the ziyāra. Travel inevitably involves a certain degree of preparation and planning, and it is generally undertaken with a clear goal in mind. Recognizing that he was on firmer ground here, Ibn Taymiyya devotes considerable attention to condemning travel with the aim of performing ziyāra. Except for certain contemporary Shāfiʿī and Ḥanbalī scholars with whom he disagreed, Ibn Taymiyya argued that many jurists supported his own position, at least on this limited point.[75] If one of the goals of travel was to visit a tomb, then this fact was sufficient to make the trip itself unlawful, thus nullifying abridgment of the noontime, afternoon, and dusk performances of the worshipful prayer rituals that Muslims are normally permitted during lawful travel.[76]

---

[73] Ibn Taymiyya, *Majmūʿ fatāwā*, 27:243.
[74] Ibn Taymiyya, *al-Jawāb al-bāhir*, 22.
[75] Ibid., 24.
[76] Ibn Taymiyya, *Majmūʿ fatāwā*, 27:139.

Analysis of Ibn Taymiyya's and Ibn Qayyim's strategy reveals the centrality of the link between duʿāʾ and ziyāra at the foundation of the cult of Muslim saints in the later Middle Ages. Rather than waste his energies attacking the many obvious symptomatic excesses of the cult, Ibn Taymiyya goes to the heart of the matter. The cult of the saints, with all of its monumental funerary architecture, its elaborate and largely fabricated hagiography, its extensive pilgrimage networks and practices, and its liminoid social mixing, formed a vast superstructure of dangerous innovation that Ibn Taymiyya and his associates found deeply offensive. And underlying this complex institution lay the basic connection between duʿāʾ and the ziyāra; it was at this target that Ibn Taymiyya aimed the well-crafted arrows of his impressive legal mind. He realized that if he could successfully disentangle duʿāʾ from the ziyāra, and then pare the ziyāra back as far as the prophetic ḥadīth would allow, he would seriously undermine the legal basis and justification upon which the cult of Muslim saints rested. The logic of his strategy reveals both his own penetrating legal acumen and an essential contemporary insight into the nature of the cult of the saints—and the complex legal basis upon which it rested. But the long imprisonment he and Ibn Qayyim endured and Ibn Taymiyya's tragic death as a prisoner in the Damascus citadel clearly bespeak the limitations of their perspective in terms of the larger collective contemporary understanding of the veneration of Muslim saints.

CHAPTER SIX

"TO REMEMBER, PERFORM GOOD DEEDS, AND RECEIVE BLESSING": THE LEGAL DEFENSE OF ZIYĀRA

Ibn Taymiyya's prominence in the history of late medieval Islamic legal thought is responsible for the considerable attention his uncompromising attacks on the ziyāra and the cult of Muslim saints have attracted from modern scholars.[1] It is important that we bear in mind, however, that the ideas of Ibn Taymiyya and Ibn Qayyim al-Jawziyya, particularly as they relate to the ziyāra, constituted a minority and distinctly unpopular position among the ʿulamāʾ of their time. The opposing and dominant legal interpretation of the ziyāra has been preserved especially in the response of the great Shāfiʿī chief qāḍī of Damascus, Taqī al-Dīn al-Subkī (d. 1355), to the writings of Ibn Taymiyya. This work, which bears the title *Shifāʾ al-siqām fī ziyārat khayr al-anām* (The Remedy for the Ill in Visiting the Best of Mankind), was primarily intended to refute Ibn Taymiyya's ideas, although it was not written until after his death in 1328. Al-Subkī informs us in his introduction that the title he originally proposed, in fact, was *Shann al-ghāra ʿalā man ankara safar al-ziyāra* (Launching the Attack on the One Who Denies Travel for the Ziyāra).[2] The work focuses on the question of visiting the grave of the Prophet in Medina, but this was primarily a tactical decision, an attack on his famous adversary where al-Subkī detected the greatest weakness.

Visiting the mosque and tomb of the Prophet in Medina is routinely a part of the itinerary of those making their way to or from Mecca while performing the ḥajj. Ibn Taymiyya's argument challenging the licitness of travel undertaken with the purpose of visiting tombs, including the Prophet's tomb, was, therefore, a deeply shocking proposition for the vast majority of Muslims, and al-Subkī clearly intended to make the most of that fact. But although his book centers on the question of visiting the Prophet's tomb, al-Subkī

---

[1] See for example Memon, *Ibn Taimīya's Struggle* and Niels Henrik Olesen, *Culte des saints*.

[2] Al-Dīn al-Subkī, *Shifāʾ al-siqām*, 2.

makes it clear in a number of places that many of his observations and arguments are more broadly applicable to the ziyāra as a whole.

The *Shifāʾ* is divided into ten chapters, the first of which includes a lengthy examination of fifteen ḥadīths clearly supporting the ziyāra to the grave of the Prophet. Most of these ḥadīths are variations of the same report. For example: "My mediation is assured for whoever visits my grave," and several variants such as: "Whoever intentionally visits me will stand near me on the Day of Judgment." Another ḥadīth states: "Whoever performs the ḥajj and visits my grave after my death, it will be as if they visited me during my life." An alternative version states: "Whoever performs the ḥajj and does not visit me has offended me."[3]

In the next chapter al-Subkī considers a number of ḥadīths which, while not directly mentioning visits to the Prophet's tomb, contain information supporting ziyāra there. These subsidiary ḥadīths revolve around the issue of whether there is any difference between saluting the Prophet at his grave and elsewhere. This question arises because of the tradition that God informs Muḥammad whenever people greet and invoke blessings on him. Ibn Taymiyya and Ibn Qayyim, it will be recalled, used this tradition to prove that there was no reason to go to the Prophet's tomb to greet him, since he is aware of salutations whenever and wherever they are uttered. Al-Subkī acknowledges the same ḥadīth and offers several variant traditions which explain that God has designated a special angel to keep track of whoever extends greetings to and seeks blessings for the Prophet so that he can respond in kind. However, the author of *al-Shifāʾ* goes on to argue, there are in fact two distinct kinds of greetings for Muḥammad. The first type is actually a form of duʿāʾ requesting God's blessings on the Prophet, a good example of which is the formula "God bless him and grant him salvation!" which is routinely invoked by Muslims after each mention of the Prophet's name. There is no difference whatsoever between the enunciation of this formula by one in the immediate vicinity of the Prophet and someone far away, al-Subkī confirms, concurring in this with Ibn Taymiyya.[4]

The second sort of greeting is a direct personal salutation to the Prophet himself, one which should be made in his presence by anyone visiting him either during his life or after his death. This sec-

---

[3] Ibid., 2–3, 20, 27–29, 31–32.
[4] Ibid., 41–49.

ond sort of greeting is different from the first in that it requires a direct response from the Prophet himself. This direct response by the Prophet is confirmed by a tradition that states: "No sooner does one greet me than God sends back my soul so that I can return the greeting." Furthermore, the Prophet responds to this sort of direct salutation whether it is made in person or is transmitted by a messenger. For example, al-Subkī relates that the Umayyad caliph ʿUmar b. ʿAbd al-ʿAzīz (r. 717–720) regularly used to send his personal greetings to the Prophet via a messenger system he established for that purpose. Thus the person who visits Muḥammad's grave and extends his or her greeting in person enjoys a certain advantage of proximity and direct speech with the Prophet, and the merit that results is correspondingly greater than that from a greeting or blessing uttered away from the Prophet's presence. Al-Subkī acknowledges that there is some debate as to whether the Prophet actually hears greetings uttered at his grave or whether he is also informed of them through the mediation of an angel. The jurist offers two contradictory ḥadīths on this matter, with the final evaluation that although both are weak traditions, the one indicating that the Prophet is informed of the greeting by an angel is the weaker of the two. Other evidence also argues in favor of the Prophet's direct awareness of greetings offered at his grave. For example, al-Subkī cites a report from Sulaymān b. Saḥīm that he saw the Prophet in a dream and asked him whether he was aware of the greetings of visitors to his grave. The Prophet confirmed that he was aware of them and that he responded to them. Similarly, there is a report from Ibrahīm b. Bishār that in one of his pilgrimages to Mecca he went to Medina and visited the Prophet's grave. Ibrahīm b. Bishār relates that he stood outside the chamber containing the Prophet's grave and extended his greeting, and heard the response from within.[5]

Al-Subkī next turns to the Prophet's companions and those in the second generation of Islam, and he offers a very different view from the one presented by Ibn Taymiyya and Ibn Qayyim al-Jawziyya. Citing strong authority al-Subkī notes that among the companions the Prophet's personal prayer announcer, Bilāl b. Rabāḥ, was particularly noted for traveling from Syria specifically and exclusively to visit Muḥammad's tomb in Medina after the Prophet once appeared

[5] Ibid., 49–51.

in a dream and scolded Bilāl for not visiting. Among the second generation, the caliph ʿUmar b. ʿAbd al-ʿAzīz was known not only for sending regular messenges of greeting to the Prophet in his grave but also for traveling from Syria to visit the tomb himself and salute Muḥammad. There are many other examples, al-Subkī claims, of companions who traveled to Medina on other business and included a visit to the Prophet's tomb among their objectives for traveling. He also cites instances of people traveling to Medina on business who were asked by others to stop at the Prophet's tomb and extend their greetings to him.[6]

The very fact that ziyāra to Muḥammad's tomb was a well known and established aspect of the pilgrimage from the earliest period is offered as yet further proof of its legitimacy. The early forebears disagreed over whether one should visit Mecca before Medina, or vice versa, but there was no disagreement over the propriety of visiting the Prophet as an integral aspect of the ḥajj. Furthermore, al-Subkī points out, virtually every legal text on rituals offers specific instruction on how to greet the Prophet when visiting his tomb. Interestingly, al-Subkī cites the comments of two early and very prominent scholars from Ibn Taymiyya's own Ḥanbalī madhhab, Abū Bakr al-Ājirī (d. 970) and Ibn Baṭṭa (d. 997), on how to greet the Prophet and the first two caliphs, Abū Bakr and ʿUmar, who are buried next to him.[7] Laoust observes that Ibn Baṭṭa's work in particular influenced both Ibn Taymiyya and Ibn Qayyim.[8] Al-Subkī notes that al-Ājirī and Ibn Baṭṭa were responding to certain heretics of their day who opposed the burial of the two caliphs next to the Prophet; the permissibility of the ziyāra itself, al-Subkī assures us, was never at issue in their time. And who would have imagined, al-Subkī adds rhetorically, that anyone would oppose either the ziyāra or travel undertaken because of it in our own day?

The *Shifāʾ* next considers the work of prominent jurists and religious scholars concerning the ziyāra to the Prophet's tomb. These works, al-Subkī announces from the start, are unanimous in considering visits to Muḥammad's tomb to be a recommended action. In fact, the Ḥanafī and Ḥanbalī schools of law, he says, consider ziyāra to be nearly an obligation for those performing the ḥajj or

[6] Ibid., 52–56.
[7] Ibid., 58–61.
[8] *EI*[2], s.v. Ibn Baṭṭa.

ʿumra, an optional lesser pilgrimage to Mecca. He supports his argument with numerous citations from prominent legal scholars representing all four Sunnī madhhabs. For example, he quotes from the *al-Hidāya fī-al-fiqh* by the great Ḥanbalī jurist Abū al-Khaṭṭāb Maḥfūẓ b. Aḥmad al-Kalwadhānī (d. 1116), to the effect that it is recommended that pilgrims visit the tomb of the Prophet and his companions once they have completed the ḥajj to Mecca. Likewise, the famous Ḥanbalī jurist Ibn Qudāma al-Maqdisī (d. 1223), describes ziyāra to the Prophet's grave as a recommended action in his *al-Mughnī*, which al-Subkī describes as one of the greatest works of Ḥanbalī jurisprudence. The early Mālikī jurist Ibn Abū Zayd (d. 996) and his *Kitāb al-nawādir* are also cited by al-Subkī. In this work Ibn Abū Zayd explains that those visiting the tombs of martyrs should greet them in the same way as one greets the Prophet and his two companions, Abū Bakr and ʿUmar. Ibn Abū Zayd, quoting the even earlier Mālikī scholar Ibn Ḥabīb (d. 853), states that the broader custom of greeting the dead at their tombs arises from the practice of greeting the Prophet, Abū Bakr, and ʿUmar.[9] Although the founder of the Mālikī school generally viewed the ziyāra favorably, al-Subkī admits that Mālik b. Anas opposed repetitive visits to the Prophet's grave, fearing they might lead to certain unspecified dangers. The other three schools of Sunnī jurisprudence, however, encouraged multiple visits to Muḥammad's tomb because "the multiplication of good is good." Al-Subkī also examines various explanations for why Imām Mālik is also reputed to have objected to the phrase: "We visited the Prophet's tomb." Al-Subkī favors the argument that Mālik simply preferred to drop the word "tomb" and say: "We visited the Prophet." A simple semantic problem should not be taken as indicative of Mālik's disapproval of visiting Muḥammad's grave entirely. Al-Subkī himself has no objection to using the expression "we visited the Prophet's tomb," since the ḥadīths related from the Prophet themselves include the phrase "whoever visits my tomb."

The ḥadīth quoting Muḥammad as commanding that his grave not be made into a celebration, which Ibn Taymiyya and Ibn Qayyim focused on so extensively, is problematic from al-Subkī's perspective for several reasons. First, he finds the reliability of the tradition questionable. Second, he sees several possible alternative meanings for

[9] Al-Subkī, *Shifāʾ al-siqām*, 64–66, 68, 71, 76–78.

what the expression actually means. Finally, a prohibition against making the tomb of the Prophet into a celebration is not an attack on the ziyāra itself, only on the excesses sometimes associated with it.[10]

Al-Subkī next comes to a consideration of the larger issue of visiting tombs as a prelude to his systematic response to Ibn Taymiyya's attack on the ziyāra. Al-Subkī states outright that the accepted and agreed-upon sunna of the Prophet commands visiting tombs in general to contemplate the inevitability of death, among other reasons. Furthermore, the righteous forebears never forbade visits to Muḥammad's tomb, and they were also in agreement about visiting the dead generally. Finally, there is a general consensus among the ʿulamāʾ, as attested in the judgment of the great Shāfiʿī jurist and traditionist Muḥyī Dīn Abū Zakariyya Yaḥya b. Sharaf al-Nawawī (d. 1277), that visits by men, at least, are recommended. Although there was no dispute about women visiting the Prophet's grave in al-Subkī's view, he admitted that there was a difference of opinion within his own madhhab about women visiting tombs in general. He identifies four leading views on this matter within the Shāfiʿi law school. The first and best-known position is that women going out to visit tombs is reprehensible but not forbidden. This is the view of the great Shāfiʿī jurist Ibn Abū ʿAṣrūn (d. 1189) and a number of other leading figures. According to al-Subkī, al-Nawawī's explanation for this is the undesirability of women going out on excursions generally. The second view is that women going to visit tombs is not permitted. The third view is that it is indifferent. The fourth position is that if women are visiting graves in order to weep, grieve, and lament the dead, then it is forbidden. The only visits by female mourners that partisans of this view find tolerable are those by old and sexually undesirable women. The difference between male and female visitors to cemeteries is that men supposedly possess the necessary restraint and fortitude to resist ostentatious mourning, unlike women. Those who forbid women from going to visit tombs, al-Subkī tells us, rely on a prophetic ḥadīth stating "God curses women visitors to tombs."[11]

However, there is another, admittedly minority, position that permits women to visit tombs in general. One ḥadīth supporting this view is the Prophet's statement, "I had forbidden you from visit-

[10] Ibid., 78–80.
[11] Ibid., 82–84.

ing tombs, however, visit them." Another tradition is that when the Prophet saw a woman weeping by a grave he comforted her and did not forbid her from performing the ziyāra. Finally, al-Subkī notes, the Prophet's wife ʿĀʾisha received advice from him on how to greet the dead during a joint visit with her husband to the cemetery of al-Baqīʿ. Al-Subkī finds all of these arguments offered by those who support women performing the ziyāra to be credible, and indicates his own support for the practice.[12]

In the sixth chapter of the *Shifāʾ*, al-Subkī examines the various functions of the ziyāra and focuses on its role as a type of qurba—a good deed or pious work, the performance of which brings one closer to God. He contends that confirmation of the ziyāra's status as a form of qurba is attested in all four of the primary sources of the Sharīʿa recognized by the Sunnī legal schools: the Qurʾān, the sunna of the Prophet, the consensus of religious scholars, and by analogy.[13] The Qurʾānic sanction for viewing the ziyāra as a form of qurba is provided by Sūra 4:64, which states, "We sent no messenger save that he should be obeyed by Allāh's leave. And if, when they had wronged themselves, they had but come unto thee and asked forgiveness of Allāh, and asked forgiveness of the messenger, they would have found Allāh Forgiving, Merciful."

This verse, according to al-Subkī, both urges believers to come and ask forgiveness of God in the presence of the Prophet and encourages Muḥammad to seek God's forgiveness on their behalf. As for the sunna of the Prophet, al-Subkī refers readers of the *Shifāʾ* back to his first and second chapters, where he presents all the relevant ḥadīths confirming the legitimacy of ziyāra to Muḥammad's tomb itself. Furthermore, the jurist goes on to state, in the true and agreed-upon sunna of the Prophet lies the instruction to visit tombs in general. The consensus of religious scholars reinforces the position that ziyāra is a recommended action, at least for men, as confirmed by Abū Zakariyya al-Nawawī. Moreover, some literalist interpreters even consider it an obligation in view of the Prophet's ḥadīth commanding visits to his tomb. As for analogy, al-Subkī points to the Prophet's example of visiting the graves of the martyrs of the Battle of Uḥud in the cemetery of al-Baqīʿ just outside of Medina. Since

---

[12] Ibid., 126.
[13] Ibid., 80–85.

this action was not particular to the Prophet, it is recommended for others. And, also by analogy, if visiting the tombs of others is recommended, then visiting the tomb of the Prophet has priority, owing to his position and the obligation of Muslims to exalt him. Glorifying the Prophet is a duty, al-Subkī argues, derived not only from the Qur'ān and the consensus of the learned, but from the practice of the companions, those who came after them, all religious scholars, and the righteous forebears in general. Most importantly, glorifying the Prophet of Islam is not the same thing as worshiping him, so there is nothing to fear of in terms of glorifying Muḥammad through proper ziyāra to his tomb.[14]

In an important passage al-Subkī then pauses to list and consider the four primary objectives behind the ziyāra. The first reason to visit graves is simply to remember death and the hereafter. Merely viewing graves is sufficient for this objective, and there is no need either for knowledge of who is buried there or for any additional action, such as asking forgiveness for them. This is a recommended action because of Muḥammad's statement: "Visit graves because they remind you of the hereafter." A second aim of the ziyāra is to supplicate on behalf of the dead, and this is also a recommended action, and one that every deceased Muslim has a right to expect, as established by the actions of the Prophet in his visits to the cemetery of al-Baqīʿ. The third goal of the legitimate ziyāra is to be blessed by being in the presence of the righteous dead. The fourth aim is to pay one's respects to the dead. Whoever was revered during their lifetime has a right to the same respect after death, and the ziyāra is the summation of reverence. The model for this type of visit is the example of the Prophet's visit to the grave of his mother. Such ziyāras may be intended as an act of mercy, kindness, or companionship toward the dead. In regard to this objective of respecting the dead, there is a prophetic ḥadīth which states that the dead are comforted while in their tombs if they are visited by whoever was close to them in this world. Yet another tradition from the Prophet encourages Muslims to greet fellow Muslims whom they know when passing their graves. No such greeting passes without the dead being aware of it and responding to it, al-Subkī assures us.[15]

---

[14] Ibid., 86.
[15] Ibid., 86–88.

Having established the ziyāra as an authentic manifestation of qurba, al-Subkī turns his attention to the issue of travel (safar) undertaken for the purpose of visiting tombs. Ibn Taymiyya and Ibn Qayyim argued that, if travel was undertaken for the purpose of visiting a grave, that is sufficient evidence of a prohibited ziyāra. In stark contrast, al-Subkī argues that if the ziyāra is a qurba, then travel for the purpose of performing the ziyāra is itself a qurba. Any action that is a means of achieving a qurba is itself a qurba.[16]

In chapter seven, at the heart of the *Shifā'*, lies al-Subkī's analysis and refutation of what he terms the three "judicial errors" of his adversary, Ibn Taymiyya. Al-Subkī divides this chapter of the *Shifā'* into two sections. The first deals with these "judicial errors." In the second half of the chapter there is a point-by-point refutation of a specific fatwā by Ibn Taymiyya dealing primarily with the question of whether or not it is permissible to abbreviate the prayer rituals while traveling to perform the ziyāra.[17] There are, according to al-Subkī, three essential errors in the arguments of Ibn Taymiyya that must be clarified. The first is his understanding of the ḥadīth "Do not undertake travel except to three mosques." Ibn Taymiyya, al-Subkī says, incorrectly imagines that this ḥadīth forbids travel undertaken with the aim of performing the ziyāra. He presents a series of alternative versions of this tradition, and argues that the ḥadīth is only intended to exempt three specific mosques from the general prohibition against traveling to mosques for the purpose of venerating them. The true meaning of the statement, then, is simply that Muslims should not embark on travel to any mosques in order to venerate them, other than the three specifically indicated.

A distinction must thus be made, al-Subkī argues, between the motivation for travel and the destination of travel. Reasons for travel may include the ḥajj, a search for knowledge, waging the jihād against infidels, visiting the graves of one's parents, and emigration, among others. Likewise, destinations of travel may include Mecca, Medina, Jerusalem, or any other place. Thus, traveling to Mount ʿArafāt to conclude the ceremonies of the ḥajj, for example, is an obligation

[16] Ibid., 105.

[17] Ibid., 117–21. The second part of this chapter begins on page 138, and in responding to Ibn Taymiyya's fatwā, al-Subkī stresses that he working from a copy of Ibn Taymiyya's work written in his own hand and marked up with the comments of other jurists.

according to the consensus of Muslims. However, Mount ʿArafāt is not among the three mosques identified in the prophetic tradition. Likewise, travel to any place with the aim of seeking knowledge is permissible and recommended, and may even be viewed as either a collective duty on the community or an individual obligation. The same may be said of travel for the jihād or for emigration from the lands of the infidel to the House of Islam. Visiting the graves of one's parents out of reverence or ziyāra to the graves of friends or the righteous dead is permitted, just as is traveling for business and other purposes. The intention of the ḥadīth, then, is only to limit travel to three specific mosques, and even within this narrow context travel is only interdicted for certain purposes. Travel to any mosque for the purposes of seeking knowledge, for example, is perfectly legitimate. In any event, travel to the tomb of the Prophet has nothing to do with this ḥadīth, because travel in this instance is not connected with glorification of the physical grave site, but is undertaken to visit the person buried there. Through this logic al-Subkī seeks to make a larger distinction between visiting tombs and visiting the occupants of tombs.[18] For if the ziyāra is viewed in terms of visiting the dead themselves, and not the site of their burial, then this ḥadīth on which Ibn Taymiyya places such emphasis has no relevance whatever.[19] The effect of the ḥadīth is thus restricted in two ways, according to al-Subkī: first the intended goal of travel must be a mosque other than the three indicated in the prophetic tradition, and second, the specific goal of travel must be to glorify or venerate the building itself. Furthermore, since travel with the aim of performing the ziyāra to Muḥammad is, in fact, undertaken to one of the three mosques specifically made lawful by the ḥadīth, and since the object of the ziyāra is to glorify the inhabitant of the tomb and not the place itself, how can Ibn Taymiyya possibly deny it?

This brings al-Subkī to a denunciation of what he sees as the real motivation behind Ibn Taymiyya's reasoning. The objective of his adversary, al-Subkī contends, is to forbid the ziyāra altogether.[20] This aim is made clear in Ibn Taymiyya's second and third "judicial errors" which, al-Subkī argues, serve as the basis upon which the fantasy which grips his opponent is built.

[18] Ibid., 125 and 134.
[19] Al-Subkī reinforces this point again on page 125.
[20] Ibid., 128–29.

Ibn Taymiyya's second error was generalizing from a few limited examples of excess, or improper manifestations of the ziyāra, to nullify the ziyāra itself and travel undertaken in connection with its performance. In addition, al-Subkī charges Ibn Taymiyya with relying on a number of weak though convenient ḥadīth, such as "Do not make my tomb into a celebration." In examining Ibn Taymiyya's distinction between lawful and prohibited ziyāra, al-Subkī finds fault with the narrow manner in which his opponent has defined his categories. The lawful ziyāra, from Ibn Taymiyya's perspective, was defined by and restricted to greeting the dead, supplicating God for mercy on their behalf, and visiting graves to contemplate the reality of death and judgment. The forbidden ziyāra, meanwhile, was characterized by a kind of polytheism whereby the dead were associated with God, supplications for assistance being made directly to them, and their tombs venerated by people rubbing them, kissing them, and prostrating before them. Al-Subkī acknowledges the obvious distinction between these two forms of ziyāra, although he repeatedly downplays the significance of the second category, insisting that no real Muslims accept it. Only a few ignorant people, he insists, engage in such abhorrent practices, which are completely rejected by the pious. Thus, the very basis of the ziyāra, and concomitantly travel undertaken for that purpose, should not be denied to the vast majority of people who observe proper etiquette because of the abuses of a few misguided souls.[21]

Between the two categories of lawful and forbidden ziyāra outlined by Ibn Taymiyya, al-Subkī inserts what he sees as another distinct category of lawful visit. He refers to it as ziyāra for the purpose of being blessed by simply being in the proximity of the righteous dead. This type of permitted ziyāra may also include supplicating God on one's own behalf in the presence of the holy dead, without there being a danger of engaging in polytheism of any sort. Although Ibn Taymiyya never fully deals with this sort of ziyāra, al-Subkī charges that it is clear from the import of his opponent's words that he considers it to fall under his second category of unlawful ziyāra. Rejecting the falsity of Ibn Taymiyya's implied position, al-Subkī asserts that the righteous forebears undertook ziyāra to the graves of certain holy people precisely with the aim of benefiting from the

[21] Ibid., 127–28, 131.

baraka associated with them. He returns here to the issue of glorifying the Prophet by noting that if there is a recognized benefit in visiting the graves of certain pious individuals, then how much greater must be the blessing associated with the tombs of prophets and apostles. This observation affords another opportunity to criticize Ibn Taymiyya for comparing the tomb of the Prophet to other Muslim tombs, thereby depreciating his status to a blasphemously mundane level. Ibn Taymiyya's rejection of vows promising to visit graves is a source of further amazement to al-Subkī. He demands evidence of uncontested agreement among earlier authorities that would support the position that vows made to visit the Prophet's tomb need not be fulfilled. Finding no such evidence, al-Subkī takes the exactly opposite stance: that vows made to visit Muḥammad's tomb must be honored.[22]

The third "judicial error," from al-Subkī's perspective, is Ibn Taymiyya's notion that the ziyāra is a form of forbidden innovation (bidʿa). This contention, al-Subkī argues, is not supported by either the views of any religious scholars or examples from the Prophetic period.[23] Al-Subkī reminds his readers of the proofs provided earlier in the *Shifāʾ* which disprove Ibn Taymiyya's claims that both the ziyāra and travel undertaken to perform it constituted forbidden innovation. How, al-Subkī asks rhetorically, could anyone knowledgeable in these matters advance such baseless doubts about the ziyāra, and denounce as bidʿa that which Muslims, east and west, generation after generation, have agreed upon unanimously? Furthermore, he asserts, if Ibn Taymiyya had been called upon to furnish proof for the validity of his general prohibition against the ziyāra he would have been unable to do so.

Ibn Taymiyya's third error arises from his misunderstanding, or misappropriation, of the meaning of early commentary on the Qurʾānic verse 71:23 to the effect that making tombs into places of worship is a variety of polytheism.[24] The verse in question deals with Noah's complaint to God that people refuse to listen and insist on keeping their old gods: "And they have said: 'Forsake not your gods. Forsake not Wadd, nor Suwʿā, nor Yaghūth, Yaʿūq or Nasr." The early commentators on the Qurʾān identified these figures as originally

[22] Ibid., 129–30, 132.
[23] Ibid., 131–32.
[24] Ibid., 136.

being righteous individuals among Noah's people whose graves were so venerated that eventually statues in their likenesses were erected over them and they became worshiped as idols. In forbidding the ziyāra and travel associated with it, al-Subkī complains, Ibn Taymiyya imagines that he is safeguarding belief in the oneness of God (tawḥīd) and preventing that which leads to polytheism. This proposition is absurd, al-Subkī argues, because this Qur'ānic verse deals with such errors as making tombs into places of worshipful prayer, cleaving to them, and placing graven images over them, and not with ziyāra and duʿā'. All of the former clearly lead to polytheism and are also prohibited by relevant ḥadīth, such as: "God cursed the Jews and Christians who have taken the graves of their prophets as places of prayer." Ziyāra, greeting the dead, and duʿā', in contrast, do not lead to polytheism, which is why God made them lawful, in both the words and actions of His Prophet. If these actions lead to polytheism in the same way as making images and the like do, al-Subkī reassures, then surely God would not have made them lawful for any of the righteous forbears, nor would the Prophet or his companions have visited the martyrs of the battle of Uḥud and others buried in the cemetery of al-Baqīʿ. It is not, al-Subkī warns, for us to forbid except that which God has made unlawful.

The Law is clear, al-Subkī pronounces, on what is and what is not permitted. Making tombs into places of prayer, placing graven images over them, and clinging to them are all strictly forbidden. Performing the ziyāra, greeting the dead, and supplicating God, both on behalf of the dead and on the visitor's own behalf are, on the contrary, recommended. Furthermore, every rational person knows the difference between the two, and whoever observes the lawful guidelines of the ziyāra will not be led astray. In forbidding the ziyāra by making it analogous to creating graven images, according to al-Subkī, Ibn Taymiyya is as much at variance with the text of the Qur'ānic verse as is someone who views the making of tombs into places of worshipful prayer as a recommended action.[25]

Ziyāra undertaken with the aim of receiving blessing or glorification does not end in deification, nor does it exceed what the Qur'ān and the sunna make lawful. Such visits are also perfectly in keeping with the practice of the Prophet's companions in regard to glorifying the

[25] Ibid., 137.

Prophet, both during his life and after his death. Therefore, how can Ibn Taymiyya deny the permissibility of the ziyāra, al-Subkī asks rhetorically, as he recites in resignation Sūra 2:156: "Indeed we belong to God, and to Him we shall return." Al-Subkī further protests that all of Ibn Taymiyya's arguments are thus built on the fantasy that people embark on polytheism when they undertake the ziyāra. Here al-Subkī adds that although each piece of evidence that Ibn Taymiyya cites points him in the opposite direction, he persists in these judicial errors. As a result, he reaches faulty conclusions about what motivates people to perform the ziyāra. Unfortunately, there would have been no remedy for this malady, al-Subkī observes, short of God's having inspired Ibn Taymiyya with the truth.[26]

Just as it is acceptable to visit the Prophet and greet him, al-Subkī explains, so is it permitted to glorify him, supplicate God either on the Prophet's behalf or on one's own behalf, and obtain divine blessing simply by being in physical proximity to Muḥammad. It is also proper and acceptable to petition the Prophet or seek his assistance and mediation with God. Seeking the mediation and assistance of the Prophet is sanctioned by the practice of the prophets, the apostles, the righteous forebears, and generations of average Muslims. There was, al-Subkī says, no rejection of this practice among religious authorities in any age prior to Ibn Taymiyya's improper innovation in opposing it. Even Adam, the first man and the first Muslim, beseeched God in the name of Muḥammad, al-Subkī relates.[27]

Ibn Taymiyya was clearly at odds with the practice of the vast majority of his contemporaries on this issue of seeking the mediation of the Prophet or the holy dead at the site of their tombs. The perceived efficacy of supplicating in the vicinity of the saints was related to the widespread perception that the souls of the dead were in some fashion present in the grave and fully conscious of what happened there. There was, however, disagreement among Muslim theologians and philosophers about the exact relationship of the body and the soul between death and resurrection and whether the saints, martyrs, and prophets were any different from other people in this regard.[28]

---

[26] Ibid., 138.

[27] Ibid., 160–62.

[28] Ibid., 194, 205–6, and 209–14. For a diachronic survey of these views see Smith and Haddad, *The Islamic Understanding of Death*. See also Eklund, *Life between Death and Resurrection*.

The great medieval theologian al-Ghazālī, for example, insisted that death was merely an altered state of existence. The soul returns to the body after a brief separation at the time of burial and remains present with the body in the grave after death, rather than waiting until the Resurrection to be reunited with the body. With death, however, al-Ghazālī explained, the soul's capacity to control the movements and actions of the body is terminated. Although the organs of the body inform the soul during life, the soul has the capacity to sense and experience things such as happiness, pain, and grief by itself and without the aid of the bodily organs. And it is through this extrasensory capacity that the soul experiences the awesome questioning of the two angels Munkar and Nakīr, followed by either pleasure or punishment in the tomb while awaiting final Judgment.[29]

Others, meanwhile, speculated as to whether some of the lower bodily spirits might be present in the buried corpse, but not the soul itself. Muslim physicians identified three distinct spirits (arwāḥ) within the body, al-Subkī informs us. Among these arwāḥ were: the physical spirit based in the liver, which controls the various bodily functions; the animal spirit located in the heart, which is our life force; and, finally, the mental spirit which actually triggers our actions and movements, and which is located in the brain. There obviously must be some form of life after burial for the Islamic notion of the "punishment of the grave" to have any meaning. At the same time, however, there was clear evidence from both the Qurʾān and ḥadīth which indicated that some righteous souls at least return to God immediately after death. Perhaps, al-Subkī suggests, it is the animal spirit which is present with the body in the grave. In any event, there is life of some sort in the grave, which both necessitates the same respectful conduct in the presence of the dead as one would accord them in life and also makes the grave a vital physical nexus in the efforts of the living to secure the mediation of the holy dead with God.[30]

In terms of mediation (shafāʿa), angels, prophets, and even righteous believers all had the potential of serving as intermediaries between Muslims and God. There were, according to al-Subkī, however, five distinct types of mediation associated with the Prophet Muḥammad,

---

[29] Al-Ghazālī, *Iḥyāʾ*, 4:493–94.
[30] Al-Subkī, *Shifāʾ al-siqām*, 206, 212, and 214.

some of which were unique to him and others not. The first type is specific to Muḥammad and involves respite from the "standing" or waiting and expediting the Judgment itself. The second type of mediation involves intercession to facilitate the entrance of a whole group of people, namely, the Muslim community, into heaven at the Judgment. This form of mediation is also reserved specifically for Muḥammad. The third variety involves intervention on behalf of people who otherwise deserve to be consigned to Hell. The authorities are unclear, according to al-Subkī, as to whether or not this type of mediation was unique to the Prophet. The next type may be carried out by Muḥammad, any other prophet, angels, or indeed any Muslim, and involves securing the release from Hell for those who have already been dispatched there. The fifth type of mediation listed by al-Subkī entails intervention to increase the rank of those in heaven. Although it is not agreed that this sort of mediation is unique to Muḥammad, al-Subkī approvingly cites authorities who assert that it is.[31]

Ibn Taymiyya and al-Subkī in historical context

As even the most cursory review of contemporary legal and theological works reveals, al-Subkī's perception of the ziyāra was widely shared among his peers. He was perhaps more dismissive than some of them of the obvious excesses that were surely occurring around him in the great cemeteries of Mamlūk Egypt and Syria, but his views on the ziyāra were by far more representative for his age than were those of Ibn Taymiyya. The exceptional quality of Ibn Taymiyya's stance on the ziyāra has, in fact, largely been obscured by the decontextualized attention his work often receives from both modern secular scholarship and Islamic revivalists.[32] When we place his writing and thought alongside that of his colleagues, however, the contrast between his ideas and theirs is striking.

For example, the statements of Muḥammad al-Ghazālī on the ziyāra, although written more than two centuries prior to the work of either Ibn Taymiyya or al-Subkī, reflect this mainstream view

[31] Ibid., 214–20.

[32] For an example of how Ibn Taymiyya is presented in isolation from the larger historical context in which he lived, see Shoshan, *Popular Culture*, 67–69.

within Sunnī Islam on the permissibility of the ziyāra. In his monumental work, *Iḥyā' 'ulūm al-dīn* (Revitalization of the Religious Sciences), al-Ghazālī offers numerous ḥadīth accounts encouraging the ziyāra, and he observes: "Visiting tombs is recommended in general to remember and contemplate, and ziyāra to the tombs of the righteous is recommended for the sake of blessing as well as contemplation."[33] He recognized a reciprocal benefit in the ziyāra for the visitor and the dead. The primary benefit for the visitor, in al-Ghazālī's view, was contemplation of the inevitability of death. The dead, meanwhile, profited from any du'ā' offered by the zuwwār on their behalf. "The visitor should not neglect supplication, either for himself or the dead, nor should the visitor fail to contemplate death by considering the dead," al-Ghazālī warned. Quoting the great early reporter of ḥadīth, Abū Hurayra (d. c. 676–678), the *Iḥyā'* reminds visitors to greet dead acquaintances whenever passing their tombs. Al-Ghazālī, like al-Subkī, saw no threat in a host of activities to which Ibn Taymiyya and his pupil Ibn Qayyim objected so strenuously. In one passage, for example, al-Ghazālī recommends reciting the Qur'ān by graves. In another he encourages women to perform the ziyāra, as long as their visits are limited and not prolonged. Al-Ghazālī also notes that it is important that women be suitably dressed when they go to the cemeteries so as not to attract the undue attention of men. Like most jurists who approved of the ziyāra, al-Ghazālī stressed the importance of proper etiquette during the visit. For example, he states: "It is recommended in the visit to tombs that one stands with one's back to the qibla and facing the dead. While greeting one should not rub, touch, or kiss the tomb, as this is the practice of Christians."[34]

From the standpoint of most medieval jurists the permissibility and underlying value of the ziyāra were well established and accepted facts, and were not matters of great concern. There was, however, genuine anxiety among jurists and religious scholars over certain excesses and improper manifestations. These reservations and concerns were presented not in the sort of inflammatory, revisionist, and radically anti-ziyāra rhetoric of Ibn Taymiyya and Ibn Qayyim al-Jawziyya, but took the form of a sober review and renewed emphasis

---

[33] Al-Ghazālī, *Iḥyā'*, 4:490. Nearly a dozen and a half ḥadīth reports are cited between pages 485 and 492. This section of the *Iḥyā'* is translated by T.J. Winter.

[34] Ibid., 4:490–92.

on the essential role of the proper conduct and attitude of the zuwwār while visiting cemeteries. This interest in adab al-ziyāra is closely related in both tone and content to the sort of material discussed in Chapter 2.

The *Majlis fī ziyārat al-qubūr* (An Exhortation on Visiting Tombs) of ʿAlāʾ al-Dīn ʿAlī b. Ibrāhīm b. Dāwūd al-ʿAṭṭār is an excellent example of this sort of concern. ʿAlāʾ al-Dīn was a prominent Shāfiʿī ḥadīth scholar, a student and associate of Muḥyī al-Dīn al-Nawawī, and director of the Dār al-Ḥadīth al-Nūriyya, a major endowed institution in Damascus for the propagation of ḥadīth study.[35] He died in 1324, only four years before Ibn Taymiyya. The *Majlis*, which exists only in manuscript, is a short, thoughtfully composed, and circumspect treatise focusing on various aspects of adab al-ziyāra.[36] Lacking the hyperbole of either Ibn Taymiyya or al-Subkī, the *Majlis* provides a more sober insight into the mindset of many ʿulamāʾ of this period.

ʿAlāʾ al-Dīn states unequivocally at the outset of his work that the ziyāra is a unanimously recognized part of the sunna and, furthermore, that it is a desirable activity, being among the most important manifestations of actions that bring one closer to God. Like al-Ghazālī and al-Subkī, ʿAlāʾ al-Dīn is careful to reinforce this statement by offering a number of the already familiar prophetic traditions firmly establishing the proper legal basis for the ziyāra. While recognizing that most Shāfiʿī jurists do not favor women visiting tombs, ʿAlāʾ al-Dīn essentially sides with al-Subkī and al-Ghazālī in not rejecting the ziyāra conducted by women. He cautions, however, that certain conditions must apply for the ziyāra of women to be desirable. For example, the visit by an old woman wishing to pray for the dead and contemplate death is generally to be encouraged. If, on the other hand, her intention is to wail and mourn by the grave, then this is unacceptable. The ziyāra by young women is, by and large, not to be encouraged, he states. Ziyāras involving ostentation of any sort or temptation by or of women, of course, are absolutely forbidden as an offense to both the living and the dead.[37]

---

[35] For brief biographies of ʿAlāʾ al-Dīn ʿAlī b. Ibrāhīm b. Dāwūd al-ʿAṭṭār, see: al-Subkī, *Ṭabaqāt al-shāfiʿiyya*, 10:130; Ibn Kathīr, *al-Bidāya*, 14:117; Ibn Ḥajar al-ʿAsqalānī, *al-Durar al-kāmina*, 3:73, and Ibn ʿImād, *Shadharāt al-dhahab*, 6:63.

[36] ʿAlāʾ al-Dīn ʿAlī b. Ibrāhīm b. Dāwūd al-ʿAṭṭār, *Majlis fī ziyārat al-qubūr*, Dār al-Kutub al-Miṣriyya, *Taṣṣawuf* no. 962.

[37] Ibid., 2r°–3v°, 7r°–7v°.

Beginning with the matter of visiting the Prophet's tomb, ʿAlāʾ al-Dīn stresses that the ziyāra to Muḥammad's tomb is made out of respect, admiration, and remembrance for the Prophet. Departing from al-Subkī's view here, ʿAlāʾ al-Dīn denies that one of the proper aims of the ziyāra is to glorify the Prophet, because Muḥammad forbade Muslims from making his grave into an idol or celebration. Such was the practice of Jews and Christians, ʿAlāʾ al-Dīn warns, who turn the graves of their saints into places full of amusement, games, and gaiety.[38]

Seeking the mediation and assistance of the Prophet in asking for God's help is fine, according to the *Majlis*, as long as one is careful not to ask Muḥammad himself to resolve problems. The Prophet's companions sought his mediation in this way both before and after his death. Similarly, ʿAlāʾ al-Dīn points out, the ʿulamāʾ continue to seek the mediation of the saints and righteous dead in securing God's help. The zuwwār must never be fooled into believing that the dead themselves have power over anything, as only God has the power and authority to determine events. Closely connected to the role of mediation is the baraka associated with the holy dead. As did al-Subkī and al-Ghazālī, ʿAlāʾ al-Dīn recognizes the benefit of visiting the dead for the purpose of receiving some of the baraka associated with their persons. The fact that God bestows such baraka on prophets, among others, is demonstrated, he says, by the fact that their bodies are not subject to the physical corruption of the grave.[39]

Just as the example of the Prophet serves as a model in legitimating mediation of the venerated dead, the sort of proper conduct that should characterize the ziyāra to his tomb sets the standard for all tomb visits. Thus, circumambulation of the tomb is forbidden, as are actions such as pressing one's stomach or back against the tomb, or touching and kissing the tomb. Prostration before the tomb is also forbidden, just as the Prophet forbade people from prostrating before him in life. Correct deportment while visiting the Prophet's tomb demands that one maintain a proper distance from the tomb in the same way as one would were Muḥammad still alive. The correct distance, according to ʿAlāʾ al-Dīn, is four cubits. The back of the visitors should be in the direction of prayer while they face and greet the Prophet. Next, they turn to the right and greet the Prophet's

[38] Ibid., 3vº–4vº.
[39] Ibid., 9vº–11vº.

two companions, Abū Bakr and ʿUmar, before returning to the initial position to supplicate God and beseech Him concerning both earthly matters and those of the hereafter. It is forbidden to ask the Prophet himself for these things, ʿAlāʾ al-Dīn reminds us again, as only God may grant such requests. Muslims should also not perform any of the five prescribed rituals of worshipful prayer (ṣalāt) in the direction of tombs, the author of the *Majlis* states, lest they become idols. Greeting the Prophet, on the other hand, is perfectly acceptable, and even those who are simply passing the Prophet's tomb are urged to greet him each time as if he were still alive.[40]

ʿAlāʾ al-Dīn also stresses the contemplatory value of visiting graves in general, regardless of whether they contain the remains of Muslims or unbelievers. For example, the Prophet visited the grave of his mother, who died before the revelation of Islam. Whereas those visiting the graves of Muslims are encouraged both to contemplate death and offer duʿāʾ on behalf of the dead, those visiting the graves of nonbelievers should not offer supplication. There was, ʿAlāʾ al-Dīn conceded, even some question among jurists as to whether or not it was permissible to salute and greet the non-Muslim dead. Those opposed to such greetings, he says, argue that one should not greet unbelievers as a general principle, regardless of whether they are living or dead.[41]

Cemeteries are places of humility and sanctity, according to the *Majlis*, and one should respect the dead just as one would respect the living. For example, riding horses, mules, or other animals among the tombs was improper from ʿAlāʾ al-Dīn's viewpoint. Noting a tradition that the Prophet once instructed someone not to wear sandals while visiting cemeteries, zuwwār are advised to go barefoot during the ziyāra. In addition to not rubbing or kissing tombs, visitors to the cemetery are also urged not to walk on tombs or to sit on them—ʿAlāʾ al-Dīn cites the ḥadīth of Abū Hurayra that it is better to sit on a live ember than it is to sit on a tomb. Approaching tombs should be done in the same way as approaching a living person. In terms of greetings, it is desirable to greet the dead as Muḥammad is reported to have greeted them: "Peace be upon you, [O residents of this] abode of believers!" Activities such as reciting the Qurʾān at graves, sprinkling tombs with water, and placing small

---

[40] Ibid., 4vº–6vº, 11rº.
[41] Ibid., 6vº.

pebbles, rocks, or pieces of wood on the headstone or at the head of a tomb are all recommended. Leaving pebbles as a token of one's visit is reminiscent of Jewish custom, and is supposedly attested to in a tradition that the Prophet placed pebbles on the tomb of his infant son Ibrāhīm, among others, during his own visits to their tombs. When the ziyāra becomes merely a pretext for amusement, pleasure, or sinful activities, ʿAlāʾ al-Dīn warns, then a place of reflection has been converted into a place of foolishness, a place of remembrance has become a place of forgetfulness, and a place of sadness has been transformed into a place of joy.[42]

Likewise, he cautions, strict guidelines in the construction of tombs must be observed, or what should be a place for building a final abode for the hereafter becomes only a wasteland. Here ʿAlāʾ al-Dīn repeats the familiar legal refrain against monumental funerary architecture. The only purpose for elevating a tomb at all, he states, should be to let the visitor know who is buried there. Buildings—especially mosques—should thus not be erected over graves, nor should tombs be plastered or painted.[43] Instead of building a monumental structure in the cemetery, ʿAlāʾ al-Dīn advises, build an abode in the hereafter by using one's money to construct mosques, barrages on the Nile, public water fountains, or simply give money as alms to Ṣūfīs, the poor, or the needy.[44] Furthermore, any inscriptions placed on tombs should be strictly in conformity with the Sharīʿa which, he states, precludes the use of Qurʾānic verses. ʿAlāʾ al-Dīn quotes al-Ghazālī with approval to the effect that tombs should not to made to stand out in any way. He also urges Muslim rulers to appoint custodians in the cemeteries to prevent corruption, transgressions, and depravity. These guardians of the moral order might also ensure that no grave be raised more than one hand's height above the level of the ground and that grave diggers do not disturb other tombs while about their business. In view of both the chaotic placement of graves in al-Qarāfa and the extent of monumental funerary architecture there, ʿAlāʾ al-Dīn's recommendations in this regard seem futile. Nevertheless, his concern reflects the prevailing, albeit resigned, concern of jurists and religious scholars over the great dichotomy between the Sharīʿa's guidelines concerning proper burial

---

[42] Ibid., 7v°–8v°, 11r°–11v°, 12v°–13r°, 15v°–16v°.
[43] Ibid., 8v°–9r°, 12v°, 15v°–16v° and 20r°.
[44] Ibid., 9v°.

customs and actual practice. The *Majlis* rejects the practice of endowing waqfs for the maintenance or construction of tombs or for building additions onto the tombs of the holy dead, presumably either to accommodate more visitors or to make room for additional burials close to the saint. Nor should votive offerings or vows be dedicated to tombs.[45]

In terms of the results of the ziyāra, ʿAlāʾ al-Dīn divides these into benefits for the living and benefits for the dead. In addition to the blessing or mediation achieved through their ziyāras, the living primarily receive benefits in two ways. First, by simply visiting the dead all the problems of this life are put into their proper transitory context; second, as a pious work, the ziyāra increases the reward of the living in the hereafter. The dead also benefit from the ziyāra in two ways. First, the ordeal of the grave is mitigated through the friendship and love conveyed from the living through their greetings; second, the dead earn the benefit of the supplication offered on their behalf by the zuwwār, just as the merit of other pious works and acts of charity performed on their behalf also accrue to them.[46]

It is important to stress that the legal basis in the Sharīʿa for the ziyāra was never seriously in question. Despite the best efforts of the harshest critics of the ziyāra to circumscribe and limit it, even they had to concede that some form of this institution was not only permissible but recommended in the sunna of the Prophet. At the same time, there was widespread recognition among most legal scholars of a persistent and troubling tendency in the actual conduct of the ziyāra for dangerous excess and abuse. Proponents of the ziyāra tended to minimize the significance of the abuses on the one hand, while cultivating a deeper appreciation of and adherence to proper norms of adab al-ziyāra, on the other hand.

For Ibn Taymiyya, Ibn Qayyim al-Jawziyya, and their supporters, the ziyāra was a dangerous institution because it held enormous potential for eroding the firm Islamic commitment to tawḥīd, the assertion of God's absolute uniqueness and unity. Although their views never became those of the majority, among either jurists or the public at large, they enjoyed an importance far beyond the num-

---

[45] Ibid., 14r°–16v°, 18r°–20r°.
[46] Ibid., 12r°–12v°, 13v°–14r°.

ber of people who actually subscribed to their ideas. These two brilliant jurists not only enjoyed great prominence in their own time, but their thought has continued to reverberate in the collective Muslim consciousness across the centuries. Even if most people did not ultimately accept their views on the ziyāra or on duʿāʾ offered near graves, these ideas could not simply be dismissed out of hand. The unequivocal courage and forthright clarity with which Ibn Taymiyya and Ibn Qayyim denounced the cult of the saints inspired enduring respect among both their contemporaries and later generations. They raised troubling questions that had an unsettling effect upon both their legal colleagues and on many people in the larger population. There is a certain defensiveness in the response of their critics, and one suspects that the attacks of Ibn Taymiyya and Ibn Qayyim had a sobering effect, from time to time, on the manner in which the ziyāra was manifested. And although their intention was neither to elaborate more critical notions of adab al-ziyāra nor to encourage more rigorous adherence to norms of proper conduct among zuwwār, their harsh attacks probably had that effect in the long run.

Although the perspective of Al-Subkī and his colleagues prevailed as the dominant one, it has received little attention from modern scholars. For defenders of the ziyāra the institution was not only sanctioned by prophetic practice but encompassed a host of laudable and worthy meanings. In sum, the ziyāra was an act of exemplary piety and a form of qurba—an act bringing one closer to God.

In Islam, as we have said, actions and the correctness of actions, as measured by the supreme standard of the holy Law, carry special significance and meaning. Thus, Ibn Taymiyya's and Ibn Qayyim's assault on ziyāra and the performance of duʿāʾ near graves were profoundly disturbing for many people who routinely participated in visiting graves and offering supplication in their vicinity. The *Shifāʾ* and works such as ʿAlāʾ al-Dīn's *Majlis* were intended to reassure believers that there was no fundamental problem with this ancient and very popular institution. In a religious system that places such emphasis on action, al-Subkī understood the essential significance of an institution that afforded people an opportunity to experience their faith in such a substantive and meaningful way. The ziyāra, as he clearly recognized, fulfilled a variety of personal and psychological needs that could not be ignored. If there were excesses and errors in the way the ziyāra was conducted, the solution was not to reject the whole institution but to minimize these aberrations by encouraging greater awareness of and adherence to acceptable standards of proper conduct.

Ibn Taymiyya viewed the ziyāra as it was manifested in his day as a sinister threat. The only solution in his view was to excise the problem by so thoroughly circumscribing the conditions under which lawful ziyāra might occur that the whole institution would simply wither away. The mindset revealed in his writing is one of radical and idealistic transformation in contemporary social and religious life. Although an understanding of Ibn Taymiyya's views casts important light on the cult of the saints in Mamlūk Egypt and Syria, in evaluating his fierce attack it is useful to remind ourselves that he died in jail in large part because of those ideas. And, perhaps in the greatest irony of all, his tomb subsequently became a greatly revered destination among the zuwwār of Damascus.[47]

[47] *EI*^{2}, s.v. Ibn Taimīya.

CONCLUSION

We end where we began, with the decision of Shaykh Ibn Abī Ḥajala to bury his dead son at the remote southern end of al-Qarāfa al-Kubrā, near the tomb of ʿUqba b. ʿĀmir al-Juhanī, "the companion of the Prophet of God." In this choice of burial sites, and through his book, *Jiwār al-akhyār*, Ibn Abī Ḥajala opens for us important vistas onto a range of meanings that the cult of Muslim saints held for the late medieval imagination. First, he makes clear that the tombs of the awliyāʾ marked those special places on the map of sacred space where there lay great reservoirs positively charged with divine blessing. This baraka was channeled through the saints, and its powerful aura permeated the surrounding area and enveloped the whole vicinity of their tombs. It was to the protective embrace of this soil, blessed by the baraka associated with the saint and all the righteous neighbors buried in the vicinity of Sīdī ʿUqba, that Ibn Abī Ḥajala committed the body of his beloved son Muḥammad, finding thereby some measure of solace. In entrusting Muḥammad to the baraka-infused perimeter of Sīdī ʿUqba's tomb, Ibn Abī Ḥajala wished to secure for his son the blessing of a peaceful rest before the awesome events marking the arrival of the Hour. It was also in this same hallowed ground, the shaykh fervently hoped, that he too would someday find a resting place among the righteous for the duration of the interlude between death and resurrection.

The residents of medieval Cairo did not make their way out to the Qarāfa only in order to bury their dead, however. They also came to the cemetery in large numbers to greet and share in the company of their dead relatives, to lay flowers on and wash their graves, to recite the Qurʾān over them, and to beseech God to have mercy on them. And, in that particular dimension of the ziyāra which has been the focus of this study, a broad cross-section of medieval Egyptians also came to the cemetery to visit the tombs of the saints. In this context the zuwwār hoped to benefit in various ways from coming into the physical presence of divine blessing at those special tombs and mausolea that filled the great plateau of al-Qarāfa like so many "bright stars in a sky whose light not even the full moon can conceal."

Some pious visitors came merely to rest for a moment in the reflected glow of the baraka that was known to infuse the tombs of the holy dead. Other zuwwār offered prayers of supplication in those remarkable places "known for the fulfillment of prayer." A range of motivations seems to have characterized these supplications at the tombs of the saints. Some duʿā', for example, were dedicated to God by the zuwwār on behalf of the dead saint. Other visitors made their own personal pleas to God with the hope that their prayers might be blessed in some general sense if offered in the vicinity of the righteous. On the other hand, some pious visitors clearly saw the awliyā' as powerful transmission stations, acting to boost signals and instantly relaying prayers offered near their tombs directly to God. Still other zuwwār seem to have come not seeking the intercession of the saints with God so much as the direct intervention of the awliyā' themselves in various matters. Although this final objective was shocking to many in a religious system profoundly committed to the absolute and indivisible oneness and omnipotence of the Creator, such requests by pious visitors for the direct intervention of the saints were clearly part of the larger picture. As many of the stories related about the saints during the course of the ziyāra make evident, the saints were seen by many as potent mediators of a whole range of critical boundaries—natural, manmade, and spiritual—that defined the contours of the late medieval universe.

In composing his book, *Jiwār al-akhyār*, about the accomplishments of Sīdī ʿUqba' and the prophetic traditions related on his authority, Ibn Abī Ḥajala reveals important information about the interrelationship of saints, baraka, and supplication offered at their tombs. The shaykh hoped to secure for himself, his son, and those buried near them an endless stream of duʿā' to be made on their behalf by generations of future visitors to the tomb of Sīdī ʿUqba. In his introduction to the *Jiwār*, the author states his intention to leave the book as a waqf, or trust, in the tomb complex of Sīdī ʿUqba.[1] In this brief passage Ibn Abī Ḥajala takes us to the heart of one of the most important aspects of the cult of the saints: in highlighting the nexus of baraka and duʿā' at the graves of the saints, Ibn Abī Ḥajala illuminates the reciprocal character of the relationship between the zuwwār and the awliyā'.

---

[1] Shaykh Ibn Abī Ḥajala, *Jiwār al-akhyār*, fols. 2v°–3r°.

Visitors to the tombs of the saints hoped some of their baraka might rub off. In exchange, zuwwār offered supplications requesting God's mercy on behalf of the saints. Sometimes the zuwwār also made solemn oaths and votive offerings. They might, for example, anoint the saint's tomb with oil or perfume, light candles or oil lamps on the tomb, or, as in the case of Ibn Abī Ḥajala, present a waqf, such as his book. The intensely personal nature of this give-and-take between the saints and those who came to visit them is important for two reasons. First, it underscores the late medieval understanding that the dead were very much aware of their visitors; and the dead frequently demonstrated their cognizance by either speaking up from the grave, or through the medium of dreams. The fact of this presence of the saints necessitated considerable attention to the rules of respect and proper conduct governing visits to the dead, adab al-ziyāra. Second, the direct personal quality of the relationship between saints and their visitors suggests that the fact of death posed no fundamental barrier to interaction between the living and the dead. There seems to have been no substantial difference in how people approached powerful and influential agents of wisāṭa, regardless of whether those patrons happened to be alive or dead. In Ibn Abī Ḥajala's world, proximity to the right people with powerful connections was the best way to ensure desired results: why should the world of the hereafter be any different? Proper attention and due care in choosing one's neighbors and associates was not simply quaint advice from Ibn Abī Ḥajala, it was sound strategy in both life and death. But cultivation of the right sorts of friends and associates could never be one way; it required a certain shared understanding of reciprocity, the willing performance of service with the expectation that one day favors might be returned.

Ibn Abī Ḥajala clearly intended his book to be read or heard by generations of pious visitors to the tomb of Sīdī ʿUqba. In learning about the life and deeds of this saint through Ibn Abī Ḥajala's book, zuwwār might better contemplate the exemplary qualities of the saint and his role as a great champion of early Islamic history. In exchange for the edifying knowledge contained in the *Jiwār*, Ibn Abī Ḥajala specifically obligates those visitors who benefit from his book to supplicate God and seek divine mercy for the author and all those buried near him. Shaykh Ibn Abī Ḥajala was thus not only expressing his own deep piety; he was also forthrightly participating in an important cultural pattern of behavior by forging vital bonds of friendly reciprocity among himself, future zuwwār to the tomb, and the dead saint. In seeking through his book to guarantee that the achievements of Sīdī ʿUqba would never be forgotten, thereby assuring a perpetual stream of duʿāʾ at the site from grateful zuwwār, Ibn Abī Ḥajala was also developing an intensely personal relationship with the saint upon whose influence as an intercessor with God the shaykh hoped to call for both himself and his son on the Day of Judgment. This was precisely the sort of mutual assistance for which good neighbors relied on each other—both in life and after death.

Not all jurists and religious scholars were as comfortable with this kind of reciprocity that Ibn Abī Ḥajala and Taqī al-Dīn al-Subkī saw as natural and healthy. The criticism of Ibn Taymiyya and Ibn Qayyim al-Jawziyya has proven valuable to our inquiry, but not because they reflect the views of "high" as opposed to "popular" culture, as Shoshan might have us believe.[2] In fact, as the works of al-Subkī, Ibn Abī Ḥajala, al-Ghazālī, and ʿAlāʾ al-Dīn make clear, Ibn Taymiyya was hardly the ardent spokesman for the cultural and religious elite; rather, he was the persecuted champion of a minority position among his colleagues and the eloquent spokesman of a lost cause. Ibn Taymiyya's importance for the study of the cult of the saints lies in the way he and his colleagues demonstrate for us the critical link between the act of supplication and visits to the tombs of the holy dead. The image of people offering their prayers of supplication at the tombs of the holy dead was clearly disturbing to Ibn Taymiyya and his associates because it threatened the rigorous monotheism of the Islamic message. But there is strategy as well as doctrinal discomfort at work in Ibn Taymiyya's writing. He saw in the ziyāra the prime agency of the cult of the saints, and the link between ziyāra and duʿāʾ as the factor legitimating the whole edifice of the cult in the minds of his peers. By first circumscribing the ziyāra as much as possible, and then by separating ziyāra from duʿāʾ, Ibn Taymiyya aimed at nothing less than undermining the cult altogether. His ultimate failure in achieving this objective notwithstanding, Ibn Taymiyya and Ibn Qayyim provide us with an important perspective on the larger contemporary meaning of the cult.

What al-Subkī and other legal advocates of the ziyāra make plain for us, however, is that perfectly legal, even laudatory, forms of duʿāʾ

---

[2] Shoshan, *Popular Culture*, 67–69.

also occurred in association with the ziyāra. As an analysis of the work of major proponents of the ziyāra among the ʿulamāʾ makes clear, there were many facets of meaning which the cult of the saints held for the collective imagination of late medieval Mamlūk society. For example, the zuwwār also came to the tombs of the special friends of God to contemplate and to learn. They came to ponder death and the transitory nature of life. They also came to reflect on the exemplary lives of the awliyāʾ. And from the rich evidence of the pilgrimage guides we learn a great deal about the content of what the zuwwār listened to and reflected upon as they heard the stories of the saints.

The didactic significance of these entertaining qiṣaṣ of the awliyāʾ must not be underestimated, I have argued, because of the particular stress that an orthopractic religion like Islam places on action and on the correctness of action. *Al-islām*, peace through submission to the will of God, is not the product of some sudden epiphany; rather it implies for devout believers a life of struggle and ceaseless effort to achieve salvation by living one's entire life in accordance with the Law of God. This is the essence of the oft-repeated statement "Islam is a way of life." Exemplars of right conduct and piety are, therefore, extremely significant in Islamic spirituality. Through his life and actions, of course, the Prophet Muḥammad provides the supreme example of what constitutes correct action. He is al-uswa al-ḥasana, the "beautiful model" that all Muslims are enjoined to emulate.[3] But through the example of their lives, the awliyāʾ provided additional models of ideal piety. The stories recounted about the saints and their lives in the course of the ziyāra offered important lessons about many of the central defining qualities of Islamic faith.[4] These qiṣaṣ did not replace either the Qurʾān or the ḥadīth, of course, but they supplemented them. And in the largely unmediated process whereby Muslim saints were identified and venerated through the ziyāra and the qiṣaṣ al-awliyāʾ, Egyptian Muslims in the later Middle Ages found an important mechanism for the social construction and transmission of their collective moral imagination.

---

[3] Schimmel, *And Muḥammad Is His Messenger*; see especially chapter 2.

[4] The notion of taqlīd (emulation) in Shīʿite thought, especially in the Uṣūlī school, is an obvious parallel here that deserves attention, although in that context emulation was, until recently, usually reserved for living exemplars. See Halm, *Shiʿa Islam*, 104–5, 113, and 155. See also Momen, *An Introduction to Shiʿi Islam*, xxii, 88–89, 175–76, 204, and 340 n. 25.

The ziyāra was, of course, not the only way in which broad social notions of right and wrong, more generally of moral order, were generated, transformed, transmitted, and diffused to a wide spectrum of the population, but it was one very important way that has previously escaped serious scholarly attention. Accounts of the exemplary lives and heroic actions of the saints were simple and direct and, when related orally at the tombs in the rich colloquial dialect of Egypt, they were free of the often intimidating and austere format and classical language of the established legal texts. The great didactic value of these stories was enhanced by the enjoyable, easily accessible, and sociable format of the ziyāra in which they were presented. The Prophet, as the most perfect of men, always set the universal standard, of course, which the ʿulamāʾ interpreted and over which they served as the watchful guardians. But the saints were more immediate, in both a physical and a psychological sense. They never replaced the model of the Prophet, but they reinforced and supplemented it, and they became important beacons of encouragement for everyday people engaged in the difficult everyday struggle to lead their lives in accordance with the will of God.

As Ibn al-Ḥājj is always quick to remind us, however, not everyone in the cemetery was there to supplicate God or to reflect upon the exemplary qualities and piety of the awliyāʾ. His disapproving comments remind us that although al-Qarāfa may have been a "great medium of divine blessing," it was much more than that in the social economy of late medieval urban space. I have argued that al-Qarāfa was a quintessential liminal place located on the margins of a great medieval city. It was here that a lot of vital social mixing took place; here the living mixed with the dead, the rich mixed with the poor, the powerful with the powerless, men with women, the formally educated with the illiterate, believers with nonbelievers, authorities with outlaws, and the mundane mixed with the sacred. And if al-Qarāfa was indeed liminal space, the ziyāra was what Victor Turner called a liminoid phenomenon—an essential instrument of normative communitas, or social antistructure, which played its own important role in integrating the communal life of this great metropolis.

Furthermore, in this extensive mixing that characterized the Qarāfa, and specifically in the institution of the ziyāra, we find important clues to the process whereby the great Ṣūfī brotherhoods that emerged in the early thirteenth century forged bonds with the general populace. It was precisely in the period covered by this study that large mass followings were attracted to the ṭarīqas. The ziyāra was by this point an ancient phenomenon, and all the evidence suggests that by the later Middle Ages Muslims had been venerating the tombs of the holy dead for a very long time indeed. But contemporary observers indicate that in the early thirteenth century, exactly when ṭarīqa-based Ṣūfism emerged and attracted a mass following, the ziyāra first occurs as an organized group event. The convergence of these two developments may be coincidental, but that seems unlikely. The cult of the saints as a whole was unquestionably central to the bond between ṭarīqa Ṣūfism and the populace. As Chodkiewicz reminds us: "Sufism and sainthood are inseparable. In the absence of saints there is no Sufism: it is born of their sainthood, nourished by it, and led to reproduce it."[5] And if the cult of the saints lay at the core of ṭarīqa Ṣūfism, then I hope that this study has demonstrated that the ziyāra, lay at the heart of the cult of the saints. The best evidence suggests that the ziyāra was the critical agency through which the link between the brotherhoods and the population at large was made and solidified. Although the ziyāra was not the invention of Ṣūfism, nor was Ṣūfism the outgrowth of the ziyāra, both seem to have been profoundly affected by their connection with each other in the early thirteenth century. The specific dynamics of this relationship clearly deserve further attention. However, I suspect that it was the product of a fluid two-way process of cultural discourse, rather than either the outgrowth of a reified "popular culture" or the end result of any calculated manipulation by political and spiritual elites.[6]

Finally, what does our consideration of the veneration of Muslim saints in late medieval Egypt reflect more broadly on notions of the holy in the Islamic tradition? On one hand, the universal aspect of the holy in Islam was characterized early on, as Peter Brown observes,

---

[5] Chodkiewicz, *Seal of the Saints*, 13.

[6] Here I note my only objection to Chodkiewicz, who seems to see room for a "deliberate adaptation from above" as a motivating and explanatory factor in the emergence of mass-based Ṣūfī ṭuruq and "the clearer affirmation, in doctrinal teaching, of the reassuring, mediating function of the saints"; see his *Seal of the Saints*, 13–14. I find it difficult to accept either such a one-sided impetus, or the intentional manipulation by a conspiracy of political and religious elite in explaining social phenomena as widespread and polymorphous as ziyāra, the cult of the saints generally, or even ṭarīqa-based Ṣūfism. That various elite participated and sought to direct these things I have no doubt, but I am skeptical of both how extensive or genuine a level of control was actually achieved.

by large and "permanently localized" centers, such as Mecca and Medina.[7] These were places that were forever fixed and where the holy possessed universal significance. On the other hand, through the cult of local saints, the holy in Islam also came to possess a more specific regional character. The universal aspect of the holy has remained a powerful force, permanently tied to unchanging locations, and was never dissipated by the endless division of holy relics. This universal dimension of the holy has had profound implications for the strong sense of communal solidarity that Muslims the world over continue to experience. In other words, the holy, in its universal aspect, speaks to and unites Muslims across both space and time as members of a single community of faith. Through the saints, meanwhile, the holy was also provided a local address. And in this context the holy was given a reassuring and familiar voice—one punctuated by the tones and cadence of regional dialects and local vernacular—that spoke directly to more particular and immediate circumstances. Muslims worldwide have continued to share and participate in the universal dimension of the holy, most notably through the ḥajj, while on the local level the holy has been made accessible through institutions such as the ziyāra and the cult of the saints. This remarkable capacity for combining unifying elements of universal significance with considerable diversity in local expression, in turn, has historically marked the special genius of Islamic civilization as it unfolded from the Strait of Gibraltar to the Strait of Malacca.

---

[7] Brown, *Cult of the Saints*, 90.

APPENDIX

We can divide Ibn al-Zayyāt's guide, *al-Kawākib*, according to his three jihāt. He starts with the westernmost and largest jiha. He takes three shuqaq together, which he collectively calls al-buqʿa al-ṣughrā. The first shuqqa begins with Mashhad al-Ashrāf opposite Bāb al-Qarāfa, and ends with the tombs around Mashhad Ṭabāṭabā (*al-Kawākib*, 37–64). The second shuqqa of the first jiha extends from Turbat Abū al-Ḥasan al-Ṣāyigh to Jawsaq al-Mādhrāʾī (64–74). The third shuqqa, forming the buqʿa al-ṣughrā, runs from the Turba of Imām al-Ḥasān al-Anṣārī to Qubbat al-Ṣadafī (74–83).

The first shuqqa of al-Mashāhid, the second group of three shuqaq in the first of the three jihāt, begins with Qubbat al-Ṣadafī and ends with the tomb of ʿAmr b. al-ʿĀṣ (83–87). The second shuqqa starts from the tomb of ʿAmr b. al-ʿĀṣ and concludes at Turbat al-Qāsim al-Ṭayyib (83 and 87–96). The third shuqqa of Mashāhid runs from al-Qāsim al-Ṭayyib to Masjid al-Amn (83 and 96–114).

The first shuqqa of al-buqʿa al-kubrā, the third set of three shuqaq in the first jiha, begins at the Mosque of al-Amn and ends with the tomb of Ibn ʿAbd al-Muʿṭī (114 and 115–24). The second shuqqa of the buqʿa al-kubrā goes from Turbat al-Mufaḍḍal b. Faḍāla to the grave of Abū ʿAbbās al-Ḥarār (114 and 124–55). Ibn al-Zayyāt starts the last shuqqa of the buqʿa al-kubrā either at Turbat al-Idfūwī or Jawsaq al-Mādhrāʾī, and concludes it with Masjid al-Fatḥ (114 and 155–73). We then conclude the first of the three jihāt into which the cemetery was divided with a review of important tombs and locations south of Masjid al-Fatḥ. This tenth and final shuqqa of the western jiha Ibn al-Zayyāt simply calls al-Qarāfa al-Kubrā (173–85). The first jiha was geographically the largest of the three vertical divisions of the cemetery, and Ibn al-Zayyāt referred to it as al-jiha al-kubrā al-ʾūlā (185).

The second major division of al-Qarāfa, called the jiha al-wusṭā or "middle jiha" by Ibn al-Zayyāt, also consists of ten shuqaq grouped into three sets of three with one remaining at the end (185). The first set of three shuqaq was designated by the most famous tomb in the area, that of Imām al-Warsh (d. 812/13). The second group of shuqaq is known as al-ʿUthmāniyya, and the third set of three shuqaq is identified by the tomb of al-Muṣīnī. The last shuqqa of the second or middle jiha is referred to as Thanā' and Sanā (37 and 185). Ibn al-Zayyāt again uses Bāb al-Qarāfa as the point of departure for the second jiha, and he begins with the tomb of Shaykh ʿAbd Allāh al-Darwīsh (185–86).

The third and easternmost section of the cemetery is referred to as the jiha al-ṣughrā, or "small jiha" (277). Once again, starting from Bāb al-Qarāfa we begin with a nearby tomb, in this case the grave of Aḥmad b. Ṭūlūn (278). At the beginning of the *Kawākib al-sayyāra*, Ibn al-Zayyāt informs us that this jiha, like the previous two, consists of three sets of three shuqaq with a tenth shuqqa at the end (37). The first set of three shuqaq is identified as those of the jabal or mountain. The second set of shuqaq is designated by three sites, Abū al-Saʿūd, Ruzbahān, and Ibn Daqīq. The last group of three shuqaq is identified with the tomb of Abū al-Rabīʿ. The tenth and final shuqqa of the third jiha consists of the tombs near Ibn ʿAṭā' Allāh al-Skandarī. Unfortunately, however, Ibn al-Zayyāt's neat division of the cemetery breaks down to a certain extent in his discussion of this third jiha. Without warning he announces that he has already covered five of its ten shuqaq in his description of the second jiha (277). Clearly the second and third jihas are substantially more compact and less distinct physically than the first jiha. Ibn al-Zayyāt's deliberate mixing of the two sections also suggests that his symmetric division of the Qarāfa into three vertical slices, each subdivided into ten discrete segments, is largely artificial.

NOTE ON SOURCES

Unfortunately, we do not possess much biographical detail about the authors of the four guides used as sources in this book. *Murshid al-zuwwār ilā qubūr al-abrār* (The Pious Visitors' Guide to the Tombs of the Righteous), the earliest of the four works relevant to this study, was apparently written at the end of the twelfth century, or early in the thirteenth century, by al-Muwaffaq Abū al-Qāsim ʿAbd al-Raḥmān b. Abū al-Ḥaram b. ʿUthmān al-Anṣārī al-Saʿdī al-Shāriʿī (d. October, 1218).[1] The work is preserved in a number of manuscripts and has recently been edited and published.[2] *Murshid al-zuwwār* is cited frequently as an authority in subsequent pilgrimage guides. The author, usually referred to simply as Ibn ʿUthmān, was trained in ḥadīth and Shāfiʿī jurisprudence (fiqh). Rāghib points out that Ibn ʿUthmān was from a prominent family of Egyptian legal and religious scholars.

The second of the four guides, *Miṣbāḥ al-dayājī wa-ghawth al-rājī wa-kahf al-lājī* (The Lamp for the Darkness, Aid for the Expectant Seeker, and Haven for the Seeker of Refuge), was compiled by Majd al-Dīn Muḥammad b. ʿAbd Allāh al-Nāsikh, more generally known as Ibn al-Nāsikh, who died around 1297, nearly eighty years after Ibn ʿUthmān.[3] We know relatively little of Ibn al-Nāsikh other than

[1] This work is also sometimes identified as: *al-Dur al-munaẓẓam fī ziyāra*, or *Faḍl al-jabal al-muqaṭṭam*, or the *al-Durr al-manṭūr fī ziyāra al-qubūr*. See Rāghib, "Essai d'inventaire," 265–66. Rāghib has succeeded in identifying this author more precisely than earlier researchers. His work thus serves as an important correction to Brockelmann, Massignon and others. See ibid., 266–68.

[2] Ibn ʿUthmān, *Murshid al-zuwwār*. This work was not edited and published until after the research for this study was completed. I relied, therefore, most heavily on British Library, Oriental Manuscript OR. 3049 and OR. 4635 (especially the latter). I also examined Dār al-Kutub al-Miṣriyya, *Tārīkh* no. 325 (of which the first 52 folios are missing). Rāghib also notes another copy of this manuscript under al-Azhar, *Tārīkh* no. 3974 (see Rāghib, "Essai d'inventaire," 268 n. 3), which I have not seen. Since Ibn ʿUthmān's work is now edited and published, I have adjusted all citations to match the printed edition.

[3] This work is currently available only in manuscript. Rāghib employs the Dār al-Kutub ms. *Tārīkh* no. 1461, whereas I have relied on Princeton University Library, Garrett Collection of Arabic Manuscripts, Yahuda Section, no. 375. Ibn al-Nāsikh is sometimes referred to as Ibn ʿAyn al-Fuḍalāʾ. See Rāghib, "Essai d'inventaire," 272–73.

the fact that he served in the retinue of the vizier and poet Tāj al-Dīn Abū ʿAbd Allāh b. Muḥammad.

More than a century separates Ibn al-Nāsikh from the author of the third guide, Shams al-Dīn Abū ʿAbd Allāh Muḥammad b. Muḥammad b. al-Zayyāt, more commonly referred to simply as Ibn al-Zayyāt, who died in February 1412. He completed his guide, *al-Kawākib al-sayyāra fī tartīb al-ziyāra fī al-qarāfatayn al-kubrā wa-al-ṣughrā* (The Shooting Stars in the Organization of the Visit to the Two Qarāfas, the Greater and the Lesser) in February 1402.[4] Ibn al-Zayyāt was, like his father, a Ṣūfī mystic; in fact, he died and was buried in the khānqāh of Siryāqūs north of Cairo.

Finally, *Tuḥfat al-aḥbāb wa-bughyat al-ṭullāb fī al-khiṭaṭ wa-al-mazārāt wa-al-tarājim wa-al-biqāʿ al-mubārakāt* (The Gem of the Beloved and Desired Object for Those Seeking the Quarters, Shrines, Biographies, and Blessed Places), was written by Nūr al-Dīn Abū al-Ḥasan ʿAlī b. Aḥmad b. ʿUmar b. Khalaf b. Maḥmūd al-Sakhāwī al-Ḥanafī.[5] Of this author we know almost nothing. Even the date of his death is unknown, although we have the fragment of a history of Egypt he wrote which ends abruptly in 1482/83, quite possibly the date of his death. For some time he was even confused with the more famous Shams al-Dīn Abū al-Khayr Muḥammad b. ʿAbd al-Raḥmān al-Sakhāwī, the author of the great biographical dictionary, *al-Ḍawʾ al-lāmiʿ*.[6]

Chronologically the four guides fall roughly around the years 1218, 1297, 1402, and 1483, respectively, a reasonable distribution for the purposes of examining the period 1200 to 1500 A.D. with assurance that we are not missing any significant developments in the genre. Structurally and organizationally the guides are remarkably similar. The later guides rely heavily on the earlier ones and actually reproduce parts of them verbatim. Although we lack information on Egyptian pilgrimage guides prior to the mid-twelfth century, the fact that Rāghib can trace the history of this type of literature in the Islamic world generally to at least the early ninth century makes it doubtful that the four guides considered here reflect the emergence of a fundamentally new category of literature in Egypt. It seems more

[4] Al-Sakhāwī, *Tuḥfat al-aḥbāb*, 209. Also see Rāghib, "Essai d'inventaire," 276.

[5] The latter two of these four guides are available in published form and I have relied here on the published editions of both *al-Kawākib* and the *Tuḥfa*.

[6] Rāghib, "Essai d'inventaire," 277–78.

reasonable to assume that these guides are only the earliest surviving examples of what was probably a substantially older tradition.

The guides routinely begin with an invocation to God and prayers offered on behalf of the Prophet Muḥammad. Ibn ʿUthmān, the author of the earliest surviving guide, then proceeds with a review of the causes of and praises for the special sanctity of the Jabal al-Muqaṭṭam, the Muqaṭṭam hills that overlook the Qarāfa. He also mentions the five companions of the Prophet (ṣaḥāba) who are buried on the plateau of al-Qarāfa below the mountain, and provides a brief catalogue of mosques situated on the Jabal al-Muqaṭṭam. Ibn ʿUthmān next offers a synopsis of ḥadīth related from or about the Prophet Muḥammad, that either encourage or justify the ziyāra. There follows a statement that the dead are fully aware of visitors to their graves, which leads him to a discussion of why proper behavior on visits to the graveyard is essential. Ibn ʿUthmān presents twenty waẓīfas, or guidelines, basic to the correct deportment of pious visitors (zuwwār), which we consider in Chapter 2. After discussion of matters such as resurrection, the ways in which God honors saints in their graves, praying and performing sacrifice on behalf of the dead, and a number of related topics, Ibn ʿUthmān mentions several eminent members of the Prophet's family buried on the edge of the Qarāfa, foremost among them being al-Sayyida Nafīsa (d. 824), the great-grandaughter of the Prophet's grandson, al-Ḥasan (d. 669); Zayd b. Zayn al-ʿĀbidīn (d. 740), the grandson of the Prophet's other grandson, al-Ḥusayn (d. 680); and Muḥammad (d. 658), a half-brother of the Prophet's wife ʿĀʾisha (d. 678) and a participant in the assasination of the third caliph, ʿUthmān (d. 656).

Ibn al-Nāsikh's *Miṣbāḥ al-dayājī*, depends to a great extent on its predecessor, *Murshid al-zuwwār*, and is structurally similar to the latter. After the invocation, Ibn al-Nāsikh praises the vizier he served and he goes on to explain that his purpose in writing the guide was to win the favor of his powerful employer. Ibn al-Nāsikh asserts that the *Miṣbāḥ* not only includes 5,000 important graves not mentioned in the earlier *Murshid al-zuwwār*, but also corrects the errors he found in the works of Ibn ʿUthmān and others.

Al-Kawākib al-sayyāra fī tartīb al-ziyāra of Ibn al-Zayyāt relies on both the earlier works of Ibn ʿUthmān and Ibn al-Nāsikh. Ibn al-Zayyāt opens his guide with a laudatory survey of the merits of Egypt and the Nile, including an account of the Muslim conquest of Egypt. He continues with a discussion of the significance of the

Jabal al-Muqaṭṭam, which is very reminiscent of the earlier work of Ibn ʿUthmān. And, like his predecessor, Ibn al-Zayyāt offers guidelines to ensure the proper conduct of the zuwwār. Following an enumeration of the Prophet's companions who are buried in Egypt, Ibn al-Zayyāt begins his tour of al-Qarāfa.

Tuḥfat al-aḥbāb of al-Sakhāwī starts with a short introduction in which the author reaffirms the legitimacy of the ziyāra. Following a brief linguistic digression concerning various terms employed in Arabic to describe the grave and a statement on the inevitability of death, al-Sakhāwī embarks on his own survey of the cemeteries around Cairo.

The fact that references to pilgrimage guides exist as early as the ninth century indicates that the four guides used in this study are fairly late representatives of this category of pious literature. But the matter of who first wrote them and why still eludes us. It is unfortunate that some scholars have sought to tie the guides to exclusively Shīʿite origins.[7] Even if we accept the proposition that the earliest guides, about which we have no substantive information beyond brief citations, were the first such pilgrimage guides written in the Islamic world, the question remains as to whether they were original creations or merely the first written record of a much older oral tradition. Further, was that tradition Shīʿite, or even Muslim, in origin? As tempting as it may be to equate the earliest surviving citations of pilgrimage guides with the genesis of the genre itself, in the present incomplete state of our knowledge, the origins of the guides remain obscure. Surely we would not contend that Abū ʿAbd Allāh al-Mārīnī, who died only five years before the demise of the last Fāṭimid caliph, actually wrote the first pilgrimage guide to the cemeteries of Egypt, a work known to us only through a brief citation in al-Sakhāwī.[8] And even if al-Mārīnī did prove to be the first author of such a guide, would we be able to assert that the material contained in it was mainly, or even largely, his own creation? Perhaps it is more important to examine why this type of literature enjoyed such lasting, even increasing, popularity throughout the later Middle Ages. The fact that so many guides were composed in Egypt between 1200 and 1500, however, does seem significant and may well suggest that the already ancient institution of the ziyāra under-

---

[7] Ibid., 259. Rāghib states: "This specialized literature, which is considered among the most ancient of Islam, was in its origin specifically Shīʿite."

[8] Ibid., 260–61.

went some important transformations and developments in this period.

It becomes evident from even a quick perusal of the surviving guides that their sources were many and varied. Some of the information is clearly the result of the authors' own observations. A much larger part of the material makes no pretense of being original. Earlier guides and information provided by the spiritual directors of group ziyāras, the mashāyikh al-ziyāra, were additional important sources. Ibn al-Zayyāt, for example, tells us that his own spiritual guide, Shihāb al-Dīn Aḥmad b. Maʿīn b. ʿAlī al-Miṣrī al-Ādamī, was one of the mashāyikh al-ziyāra. He also tells us that he carefully reviewed an impressive list of previous guides and other related works in preparing the *Kawākib*.[9] Tombstones, commemorative funerary inscriptions, and other epigraphic evidence offered still more information. And there were other significant sources that the authors of the pilgrimage guides could and did rely upon. These men were not only literate but were also widely read scholars. The vast and varied literature of Islamic civilization was readily available to them, and they were seemingly well versed in it. Among the scores of works cited we find references to major figures such as the early Islamic historians Ibn Isḥāq (d. 767), al-Wāqidī (d. 823), Ibn ʿAbd al-Ḥakam (d. 871), al-Ṭabarī (d. 923), al-Kindī (d. 961), and al-Musabbiḥī (d. 1029); the great medieval biographer Ibn Khallikān (d. 1282); theologians such as al-Ghazālī (d. 1111) and Ibn al-Jawzī (d. 1200); and great collectors of ḥadīth, such as Muslim b. al-Ḥajjāj (d. 875) and al-Bukhārī (d. 870). The guides were thus produced by scholars who were writing well within the context of Muslim religious scholarship.

For whom were the pilgrimage guides written, and why? Only two of the guides, *Miṣbāḥ al-dayājī* of Ibn al-Nāsikh and the *Kawākib al-sayyāra* of Ibn al-Zayyāt, are explicit on this question. The former author prepared his work, as we have noted, for his employer the vizier Tāj al-Dīn Abū ʿAbd Allāh. Ibn al-Nāsikh informs us that he was attracted to his master by the latter's love of knowledge, and because the vizier wished to follow his grandfather's lead in performing the ziyāra. Ibn al-Nāsikh seized the opportunity to be of service and produced his guide as a way of ingratiating himself to his powerful patron.[10]

[9] Ibn al-Zayyāt, *al-Kawākib*, 4, 220, 225, and passim.

[10] Ibn al-Nāsikh, *Miṣbāḥ al-dayājī*, fols. 1v°–2r°.

Ibn al-Zayyāt, on the other hand, tells us that one of his "brothers," presumably a fellow Ṣūfī, asked him to prepare a book dealing with the arrangement of tombs included in the ziyāra of al-Qarāfa.[11] Thus, Ibn al-Zayyāt set out to identify the graves of the ṣaḥāba, their successors (al-tābiʿīn wa tābiʿīhim), the martyrs (shuhadāʾ), as well as the illustrious religious scholars (ʿulamāʾ), relaters of prophetic tradition (muḥaddithūn), judges (man waliya al-qaḍāʾ), reciters of the Qurʾān (qurrāʾ), teachers (mashāyikh al-risāla wa al-mutaṣaddirīn), preachers (wuʿʿāẓ wa khuṭabāʾ), announcers of the ritual prayer (muʾadhdhinūn), and Ṣūfī mystics (ahl al-taṣawwuf). Ibn al-Zayyāt tells us that his aim was to sort out who was really buried where, and which places were most efficacious for prayer.

Although the guides of Ibn ʿUthmān and al-Sakhāwī do not explicitly state why they were prepared, it seems likely that they were intended for much the same readership as the *Kawākib*. That is to say, they were meant to survey the Qarāfa systematically and to clarify the location of particular sites that mystics and fellow scholars should visit. Thus, among the surviving guides, the *Miṣbāḥ* is unique in terms of its intended audience. None of the other works presents itself as created originally to gain the favor of a powerful or wealthy patron.

Other textual sources employed in this study include medieval legal and theological texts, devotional works, traditional historical chronicles, biographical dictionaries, descriptive and topographical works, and finally the accounts of both Muslim and Western travelers who visited Egypt. Although most of these texts will be familiar to specialists in the field, few of them have been examined before with a view to evaluating what light they shed on either the ziyāra or the veneration of Muslim saints.

[11] Ibn al-Zayyāt, *al-Kawākib*, 4.

GLOSSARY

adab al-ziyāra – Guidelines or etiquette for proper performance of the *ziyāra*.
ʿālim – See *ʿulamāʾ*.
amīr – A general or military commander.
ʿamūd – A column or pole; also a carved and inscribed columnar marble or stone grave marker.
Ayyūbids – The Sunnī dynasty founded by Saladin (Ṣalāḥ al-Dīn) that replaced the Fāṭimids and ruled Egypt between 1171–1250 A.D.
awliyāʾ (s. *walī*) – Saints; also *awliyāʾ allāh*—the "friends of God."
baraka – Divine blessing or charisma.
barzakh – This term designates both the place and the period stretching from death to resurrection.
bidʿa – An innovation—usually in the sense of a forbidden or heretical deviation from Islamic law or doctrine.
dhikr – "Mentioning," or "remembering;" the central Ṣūfī spiritual exercise. It may take various forms but usually involves prolonged repetition of one of the divine names or religious formulas as a means of focusing attention on and contemplating God.
dhimmis – Protected non-Muslims, primarily Christians, Jews, and Zoroastrians.
dinār – A gold coin. Until 1425 the canonical Mamlūk dinār weighed 4.25 grams. In that year Sultan al-Malik al-Ashraf Barsbay minted a lighter dinār (called the al-Ashrafī) that matched the Venetian ducat weighing 3.45 grams.
dirham – A silver coin. Although the weight varied, during much of the Mamlūk period it was supposed to weigh approximately 2.97 grams. Approximately 20 dirhams equalled one gold dinār.
duʿāʾ – Supplicatory prayer.
faqīh (pl. *fuqahāʾ*) – A Muslim jurist. See *fiqh*.
Fātiḥa, al- – The first *Sūra* of the Qurʾān.
Fāṭimids – A powerful dynasty of Ismāʿīlī Shīʿites who ruled Egypt between 969 and 1171 A.D. They built the city of Cairo (*al-Qāhira*) shortly after their conquest of Egypt in 969.
fatwā (pl. *fatāwā*) – A legal opinion issued by a Muslim jurist.
fiqh – Islamic jurisprudence.
furūʿ (s. *farʿ*) – A section or subdivision of something; here of the Qarāfa cemetery. See *shuqqa* below.
al-Fusṭāṭ – The first capital of Islamic Egypt built initially as a garrison city after the Arab conquest in 642 A.D.
ḥadīth – Prophetic traditions; reports of the actions and sayings of the Prophet Muḥammad and his closest companions; the second most important source of Islamic law, after the Qurʾān.
ḥajj – The Muslim pilgrimage to Mecca, one of the "Five Pillars" of Islam which Muslims are obliged to perform at least once during their lives—assuming they have both the financial and physical ability to do so.
ḥawma – A section, or a group of graves within a graveyard. Although the term usually refers to a part of a larger graveyard (*maqbara*), it is also sometimes used interchangeably with *maqbara*.
ḥawsh – Any walled enclosure; here encompassing a group of tombs.
ḥūriyya (pl. *ḥūr*) – Maiden of Paradise.

ʿīd – A "festival" or feast. There are only two canonical feasts in Islam: *ʿId al-fiṭr*, which marks the end of the Ramaḍān fast, and *ʿĪd al-aḍḥa*, or "Feast of the Sacrifice," which marks the end of the *ḥajj*.

imām – The term has a variety of distinct meanings. First, it refers to any leader of the daily rituals of worshipful prayer in Islam. In Sunnī Islam the term is also used as an honorific for a great religious teacher and scholar. Among Shīʿites, the word may either refer to any descendant of the Prophet Muḥammad, through his first cousin and son-in-law (ʿAlī b. Abī Ṭālib), who is recognized as legitimate successor to the Prophet as both religious and political leader of the Muslim community (*umma*); or, more generally, to a great Shīʿi religious leader.

Ismāʿīlīs – One of three major sects of Shiʿism. They are also known as "Seveners" because they believe that Ismāʿīl, the eldest son of the sixth Shīʿī Imām, Jaʿfar al-Ṣādiq was the true successor to his father. See also Fāṭimids.

jawsaq (pl. *jawāsiq*) – Large Fāṭimid period pavilions which seem to have served as rest houses for the Fāṭimid elite during their visits to the Qarāfa cemetery.

jiha (pl. *jihāt*) – A term used by Ibn al-Zayyāt to refer to one of three great north to south vertical sections into which he divides al-Qarāfa.

jihād – Broadly the term means "striving" or exerting great effort, especially in religion. It may also mean a "holy war."

jinn – Referred to as "genies" in English. A category of non-corporeal spiritual beings who, like mankind, possess both a conscience and the capacity to do either good or evil.

karāmāt (s. *karāma*) – Miracles performed by Muslim saints as a sign of the grace God has bestowed upon them. See also *manāqib*.

khānqāh (pl. *khawāniq*) – A Ṣūfī hostel or cloister containing cells where resident and itinerant Ṣūfīs live, learn spiritual discipline from a recognized master, and conduct spiritual exercises and rituals. See also *zāwiya* below.

khuṭba – A homily offered in a congregational mosque immediately before the Friday noon prayer.

lawḥ – A stone grave marker which may or may not be inscribed with an epitaph.

madhhab (pl. *madhāhib*) – A rite or school of Islamic jurisprudence. Among Sunnī Muslims there are four recognized schools: Ḥanafī, Mālikī, Shāfiʿī, and Ḥanbalī. Egypt has historically followed the Shāfiʿī madhhab.

madrasa (pl. *madāris*) – A teaching-mosque for the transmission of the Islamic religious sciences.

manāqib – Amazing feats performed by saints. See also *karāmāt*.

mamlūk – The word means "owned" and refers specifically to slave soldiers. These slave soldiers came to rule Egypt from 1250–1517 A.D., hence giving their name to the Mamlūk Empire.

maqbara (pl. *maqābir*) – A graveyard.

mashhad (pl. *mashāhid*) – A mausoleum. Generally the word means a gathering or, alternately, the place of such a gathering; see Ibn Manẓūr, *Lisān*, 4:2349–50; al-Jawharī, *al-Ṣaḥāḥ*, 2:393. Lane, *Lexicon*, 1611, states: "A funeral assembly or procession. A place a martyr has died or is buried." In the period of this study, however, the term is not confined to the tomb of a martyr. See also *qubba*.

mashhad al-ruʾya – A "vision-mausoleum" usually built in response to instructions or a command received through the medium of a dream.

mashāyikh (s. *shaykh*) *al-ziyāra* – Leaders of the *ziyāra*. More generally the term *shaykh* may refer to any venerated religious scholar, the head of a Ṣūfī brotherhood, or the leader of a tribe.

mawlid (pl. *mawālid*) – A "saint's day." The term means birthday and may mark either the birth of the saint or prophet or their death date—in which case it marks their "birth" into Paradise.

maydān – A hippodrome.

miḥrāb – The niche in the wall of a mosque indicating the direction of prayer (*qibla*).
minbar – The raised seat in a mosque from which the *khuṭba* is offered.
nāẓir – A financial controller or supervisor.
niyya – Means "intention." In order for ritual acts, such as prayer, to be valid the intent of the person performing the act must be pure and proper.
qabr – A simple individual grave.
qāḍī – An Islamic judge officially appointed by established political authority whose legal rulings are binding and enforceable, as opposed to the legal opinions (see *fatwā*) of a jurist which are not.
qibla – The direction of Mecca, towards which Muslims face each day while performing their daily rituals of worshipful prayer.
qiṣṣa (pl. *qiṣaṣ*) – A short narrative, story, or tale.
qubba – Meaning a tent or lodging made of animal skins (see Ibn Manẓūr, *Lisān*, 5:3507; al-Jawharī, *al-Ṣaḥāḥ*. 1:197; and al-Zabīdī, *Tāj*, 1:419. The sense in the current context is "a dome, or cupola, of stone or bricks: and a building covered with a dome or cupola" (Lane, *Lexicon*, 2478).
qurba – A good deed or a pious work through which one seeks to draw near or approach God.
rakʿa (pl. *rakaʿāt*) – The sequence of bowing and prostration composing the *ṣalāt*.
raṭl – A measure of weight, approximately equal to 450 grams or 1 pound.
ribāṭ (pl. *arbiṭa*) – A hospice or retreat, in this period such institutions were frequently for devout widows.
ṣadaqa – Voluntary charity or alms as opposed to obigatory alms (see *zakāt*).
ṣaḥāba – Companions of the Prophet Muḥammad.
salaf – The "righteous forebears," refers to the first three generations of Islam.
ṣalāt (pl. *ṣalawāt*) – The canonical or ritual prayers in Islam which are performed five times each day and are one of the "Five Pillars" of Islamic faith.
samāʿ – Means "listening," but refers to mystical concerts which may consist of music, verse, religious songs, and/or Qurʾānic passages which are used by some Ṣūfī brotherhoods, such as the Mevlevis, in connection either with their sacred dance (*ḥaḍra*), or to achieve an ecstatic state of proximity to the divine.
ṣawm – Fasting from just before sunrise until after sunset during the holy month of Ramaḍān. This annual obligation is considered one of the "Five Pillars" of Islam.
Sayidda, al – An honorific meaning "Lady" or "Mistress" frequently used before female saints.
sharīʿa – The holy Law of God which is primarily based on the Qurʾān and the *sunna* of the Prophet Muḥammad.
sharīf – A descendant of the Prophet Muḥammad.
shaykh – See *mashāyikh* above.
shafāʿa – Mediation or intercession.
shirk – The act of associating anything with God, idolary or paganism. More generally it is the opposite of *al-Islām*, submission to the will of God. It is the one sin God does not forgive.
shuqqa (pl. *shuqaq*) – A term used by Ibn al-Zayyāt to describe the ten horizontal subsections of the three primary vertical sections (*jihāt*) into which he divides al-Qarafa. See also *furūʿ* above which the same author uses interchangeably with *shuqqa*.
Sīdī – An honorific frequently used before the names of male saints; lit. "my master" or "my lord."
sunna – Means "custom" or "practice." The term usually refers to the actions, words, and unspoken acquiescence (of the Prophet Muḥammad and his close companions of the first generation of Muslims), which are preserved in reports known as *ḥadīth*. The *sunna* of the Prophet forms the second most important

source of divine Law (*sharīʿa*) after the Qurʾān. Approximately 85% of all Muslims are referred to as Sunnīs which indicates the centrality they assign to both the authority of the Prophet and his companions as well as their acceptance of the legitimacy of the historical community of Islam (*umma*). Shīʿites, in contrast, recognize the rights of the Prophet's first cousin and son-in-law, ʿAlī b. Abī Ṭālib, and his descendants, to rightful leadership of the *umma*. They also add to the *sunna* of the Prophet the practice and sayings of the Shīʿite *imāms*.

Ṣūfī – A follower of the mystical path in Islam. See also *taṣawwuf*.

Sūra – Any of the 114 chapters of the of the Qurʾān.

ṭabaqa (pl. *ṭabaqāt*) – An associational category.

tābūt – A cenotaph.

ṭāʾifa (pl. *ṭawāʾif*) – A group, faction or sect. In Ṣūfism the term is frequently used interchangeably with *ṭarīqa* to refer to brotherhoods.

taqlīd – In Sunnī Islam the term refers to acceptance and imitation of established legal authority without reference to any independent inquiry. Among Shīʿites the term means emulation or following the guidance of a great religious leader.

taraḥḥum – Pleading for God's mercy.

ṭarīqa (pl. *ṭuruq*) – A Ṣufi brotherhood. See also *ṭāʾifa*.

turba – A tomb. In this period the term is frequently used interchangeably with *qubba*, thus indicating that the *turba* was often a cubical mausoleum surmounted by a dome.

taṣawwuf – Ṣūfism, the mystical path in Islam.

ʿulamāʾ (s. *ʿālim*) – A term referring broadly to religious scholars.

umma – Generally any religious community. Specifically, the Muslim community.

vizier (or *wazīr*) – A chief minister.

walāya – The Ṣūfī doctrine of sainthood.

walī – See *awliyāʾ* above.

wālī – The administrative governor of a province.

waqf (pl. *awqāf*) – An endowed trust, usually to support religious or charitable institutions.

waqfa – An essential aspect of the ḥajj to Mecca which involves pilgrims standing on the plain of ʿArafāt (12 miles/19 kilometers) southwest of Mecca on the 9th of the month of Dhū ʾl-Ḥijja, the second day of the pilgrimage. It is said to symbolize the Day of Judgment.

waẓīfa (pl. *waẓā ʾif*) – A term used by Ibn ʿUthmān to mean guideline, or rule of conduct.

wazīr – See vizier above.

wilāya – See *walāya*. In other contexts this term means sovereignty or rule.

wisāṭa – Mediation or intervention.

zāʾir – See *zuwwār* below.

zakāt – An obligatory tax on most types of property which Muslims must pay as alms to the poor and needy. The amount which must be paid depends on the nature of the property held. Annual payment of such alms is one of the "Five Pillars" of Islamic faith. See also *ṣadaqa*.

zāwiya (pl. *zawāya*) – In this period a flexible term with a variety of meanings. It might refer to anything from the corner of a large mosque to a *khānqāh*. Frequently a *zāwiya* designated a small mosque attached to the tomb of a saint where Ṣūfīs gathered to perform their *dhikr* or other rituals.

ziyāra (pl. *ziyārāt*) – The act of visiting the tombs of the dead. May also refer more specifically to visits to the Prophet's tomb in Medina.

zuwwār (s. *zāʾir*) – Visitors. Here pious visitors to the cemetery.

BIBLIOGRAPHY

Primary Sources

Abū al-Faraj, ʿAbd al-Raḥmān b. Aḥmad b. al-Rajab al-Ḥanbalī. *Ahwāl al-qubūr wa-aḥwāl ahlihā ilā al-nushūr.* Beirut, 1985.

Abū Dāwūd, Sulaymān b. al-Ashʿath. *Sunan* Abī Dāwūd. 4 vols. Beirut, n.d.

ʿAṭṭār, ʿAlāʾ al-Dīn ʿAlī b. Ibrāhīm b. Dāwūd al-. *Risāla fī ziyārat al-qubūr.* Manuscript. Dār al-Kutub al-Miṣriyya, Taṣawwuf no. 962.

Fabri, Félix. *Le voyage en Egypte de Félix Fabri, 1483.* Translated by Jacques Masson. 3 vols. Cairo, 1975.

Ghazālī, Abū Ḥāmid Muḥammad al-. *Iḥyāʾ ʿulūm al-dīn.* 4 vols. Cairo, A.H. 1289. T.J. Winter has translated a relevant portion of this work as *The Remembrance of Death and the Afterlife. Kitāb dhikr al-mawt wa-mā baʿdahu. Book XL of the Revival of the Religious Sciences, Iḥyāʾ ʿulūm al-dīn*, Cambridge, 1989.

——. *Kitāb al-madnūn al-ṣaghīr.* Cairo, A.H. 1303.

——. *Kitāb al-madnūn ʿalā ghayr ahlihi.* Cairo, A.H. 1303.

——. *Mishkāt al-anwār.* Cairo, 1963. See also a translation by W.H.T. Gairdner, *Al-Ghazzālī's Mishkāt al-Anwār* (*The Niche for Lights*). London, 1924.

Ghistele, Joos van de. *Le voyage en Egypte de Joos van Ghistele.* Translated by Renée Bauwens-Préaux. Cairo, 1975.

Harawī, Abū al-Ḥasan ʿAlī b. Abī Bakr al-. *Kitāb al-ishārāt ilā maʿrifat al-ziyārāt.* Edited by Janine Sourdel-Thomine. Damascus, 1953. See also her translation of this work, *Guide des lieux de pèlerinage*, Damascus, 1957.

Ibn ʿAbd al-Ḥakam. *The History of the Conquest of Egypt, North Africa and Spain, Known as the Futūḥ Miṣr of Ibn ʿAbd al-Ḥakam.* Edited by Charles C. Torrey. Yale Oriental Series no. 3. New Haven, 1922.

Ibn Abī Ḥajala, Aḥmad b. Yaḥyā. *Jiwār al-akhyār fī dār al-qarār.* Manuscript. Dār al-Kutub al-Miṣriyya, Taṣawwuf no. 893.

Ibn Baṭṭūṭa, Muḥammad b. ʿAbd Allāh. *Riḥlat Ibn Baṭṭūṭa.* Beirut, n.d. Translated by H.A.R. Gibb, *Ibn Battúta, Travels in Asia and Africa 1325–1354.* London, 1929.

Ibn Duqmāq, Ṣārim al-Dīn b. Aydamar. *Kitāb al-intiṣār li-wāṣitat ʿiqd al-amṣār.* Edited by K. Vollers. 2 vols. Cairo, 1893.

Ibn Ḥajar al-ʿAsqalānī. *al-Durar al-kāmina fī aʿyān al-miʾa al-thāmina.* 5 vols. Cairo, n.d.

Ibn Ḥajar al-Haytamī. *Kitāb al-jawhar al-munaẓam fī ziyārat al-qabr al-sharīf.* Cairo, 1892.

Ibn al-Ḥajj, Muḥammad b. Muḥammad. *Madkhal al-sharʿ al-sharīf.* 4 vols. Cairo, 1929.

Ibn Hishām. *al-Sīra al-nabawiyya.* Edited by Muṣṭafā al-Saqqā et al. 4 vols. in 2. Cairo, n.d. Translated by A. Guillaume as *The Life of Muhammad.* Oxford, 1955.

Ibn ʿImād, ʿAbd al-Ḥayy. *Shadharāt al-dhahab fī akhbār min dhahab.* Cairo, 1931–32.

Ibn al-Jawzī, Abū al-Faraj ʿAbd al-Raḥmān. *Talbīs Iblīs.* Cairo, A.H. 1340. Translated in installments by D.S. Margoliouth, "The Devil's Delusion." *IC* 9–12, 19–21 (1935–1948).

Ibn Jubayr, Abū al-Ḥusayn Muḥammad b. Aḥmad. *Riḥlat Ibn Jubayr.* Beirut, 1964.

Ibn Kathīr. *al-Bidāya wa-al-nihāya.* 14 vols. Beirut, 1982 repr.

Ibn Khallikān, Abū al-ʿAbbās Shams al-Dīn Aḥmad b. Muḥammad b. Abū Bakr. *Wafayāt al-aʿyān wa anbāʾ abnāʾ al-zamān.* Edited by Iḥsān ʿAbbās in 8 vols. Beirut, 1972.

Ibn Manẓūr, *Lisān al-ʿarab*. 6 vols. Cairo, n.d.
Ibn al-Nāsikh, Majd al-Dīn Abū ʿAbd Allāh (Maʿālī) Muḥammad b. ʿAbd Allāh. *Misbāḥ al-dayājī wa ghawth al-rājī wa-kahf al-lājī*. Manuscript. Princeton University Library, Garrett Arabic Manuscript Collection, Yehuda Section no. 375.
Ibn Qayyim al-Jawziyya, Shams al-Dīn. *Kitāb al-rūḥ*. Cairo, A.H. 1357.
——. *Ighāthat al-lahfān fī maṣāyid al-shayṭān*. Cairo, 1939.
Ibn Taghrī Birdī, Abū al-Maḥasan. *al-Nujūm al-zāhira fī mulūk miṣr wa-al-qāhira*. 16 vols. Cairo, 1930–1972. See also the translation of this work by William Popper, *History of Egypt, 1382–1469 A.D.* 8 vols. University of California Publications in Semitic Philology, 13–14, 17–19, and 22–24. Berkeley and Los Angeles, 1954–1963.
Ibn Taymiyya, Aḥmad. *al-Furqān bayn awliyāʾ al-raḥmān wa-awliyāʾ al-shaytān*. Cairo, A.H. 1310.
——. *Jawāb al-bāhir fī zuwwār al-maqābir*. Cairo, n.d.
——. *Kitāb iqtiḍāʾ al-ṣirāṭ al-mustaqīm mukhālafat aṣḥāb al-jaḥīm*. Cairo, 1950.
——. *Majmūʿ fatāwā shaykh al-islām Aḥmad b. Taymiyya*. 36 vols. Beirut, 1978. See in particular volume 27, "al-ziyāra."
——. *Majmūʿ rasāʾil Ibn Taymiyya*. Cairo, 1323 A.H. See especially "*Risāla ziyārat al-qubūr wa-al-istinjād bi-al-maqbūr*," 103–22.
Ibn ʿUthmān, al-Muwaffaq Abū al-Qāsim ʿAbd al-Raḥmān b. Abī al-Ḥaram Makkī. *Murshid al-zuwwār ilā qubūr al-abrār*. Edited by by Muḥammad Faḥī Abū Bakr. Cairo, 1995. See also the following manuscripts: British Library, Oriental Manuscript OR. 4635 and OR. 3049. For a third copy see Dār al-Kutub al-Miṣriyya, *Tārīkh* no. 325.
Ibn al-Zayyāt, Shams al-Dīn Abū ʿAbd Allāh Muḥammad b. Muḥammad. *al-Kawākib al-sayyāra fī tartīb al-ziyāra fī al-qarāfatayn al-kubrā wa-al-ṣughrā*. Edited by Aḥmad Taymūr. Cairo, A.H. 1325.
Jawharī, Ismāʿīl b. Ḥammād al-. *Al-Ṣaḥāḥ*. 7 vols. Beirut, 1984 repr.
Khosrāw, Nāṣer-e. *Book of Travels* (*Safarnāma*). Edited and translated by W.M. Thackston. Albany, 1986.
Manbijī, Muḥammad b. Muḥammad al-. *Tasliyyat ahl al-maṣāʾib fī mawt al-awlād wa-al-aqārib*. Cairo, 1960.
Maqrīzī, Taqī al-Dīn Abū al-ʿAbbās Aḥmad b. ʿAlī al-. *al-Mawāʾiẓ wa-al-iʿtibār bi-dhikr al-khiṭaṭ wa-al-āthār*. 2 vols. Būlāq, A.H. 1270.
——. *Kitāb al-sulūk li-maʿrifat duwal al-Mulūk*. 4 vols. in 12 parts. Cairo, 1934–1973.
Muslim b. al-Ḥajjāj al-Qushayrī. *Ṣaḥīḥ*. 5 vols. Cairo, n.d.
Piloti, Emmanuel. *L'Egypte au commencement du quinzième siècle, d'après le traité d'Emmanuel Piloti de Crète* (*incipit 1420*). Edited by P.H. Dopp. Cairo, 1950.
Qalqashandī, Shihāb al-Dīn. *Ṣubḥ al-aʿshā fī ṣināʿat al-inshāʾ*. 14 vols. Cairo, 1913–1919.
Qurʾān al-. See: Ahmed Ali. *Al-Qurʾān, A Contemporary Translation*. Revised definitive edition, Princeton, 1988. See also Marmaduke Pickthall, *The Meaning of the Glorious Koran, An Explanatory Translation*. 1930; rpt. New York, n.d.
Ṣafadī, Khalīl b. Aybak al-. *al-Wāfī bi-al-wafayāt*. Edited by H. Ritter et al. 22 vols. in print. Istanbul, Damascus, Wiesbaden, and Beirut, 1931–.
Sakhāwī, Nūr al-Dīn Abū al-Ḥasan ʿAlī b. Aḥmad b. ʿUmar b. Khalaf b. Maḥmūd al-. *Tuḥfat al-aḥbāb wa bughyat al-ṭullāb fī al-khiṭaṭ wa-al-mazārāt wa-al-tarājim wa al-biqāʾ al-mubārakāt*. Cairo, 1937.
Sakhāwī, Shams al-Dīn Abū al-Khayr b. ʿAbd al-Raḥmān al-. *al-Ḍawʾ al-lāmiʿ fī aʿyān al-qarn al-tāsiʿ*. 12 vols. Cairo, A.H. 1353.
Subkī, Tāj al-Dīn al-. *Ṭabaqāt al-shāfiʿiyya al-kubrā*. 10 vols. Cairo, 1964–76.
Subkī, Taqī al-Dīn al-. *Shifāʾ al-siqām fī ziyārat khayr al-anām*. 2nd ed. Beirut, 1978.
Ṭabarī, Muḥammad b. Jarīr al-. *Taʾrīkh al-rusul wa al-mulūk* (*Annales*). Edited by M.J. de Goeje et al. 15 vols. (Leiden, 1879–1901).
Tirmidhī, Abū ʿAbd Allāh Muḥammad b. ʿAlī b. al-Ḥasan al-Ḥakīm al-. *Kitāb khatm al-awliyāʾ*. Edited by Othmān I. Yaḥyā. Beirut, 1965.

Untitled index of saints' tombs in Cairo. Anonymous author. Manuscript. Bibliothèque de l'Institut des langues et civilisations orientales, Arabic Manuscript no. 404.
Wansharīsī, Aḥmad ibn Yaḥyā al-. *al-Miʿyār al-muʿrib wa-al-jāmiʿa al-mughrib ʿan fatāwī ahl ifrīqiyya wa-al-andalus wa-al-maghrib*. 14 vols. Rabat, 1981.
Wāqidī, Muḥammad b. ʿUmar b. al-. *Kitāb al-maghāzī*. Edited by Marsden Jones. 3 vols. Oxford, 1966.
Yāqūt al-Ḥamawī, Shihāb al-Dīn Abū ʿAbd Allāh, *Muʿjam al-buldān*. 5 vols. (Beirut, 1957).
Zabīdī, Moḥammad al-Murtaḍā al-. *Tāj al-ʿarūs*. Cairo, A.H. 1306–07.

Secondary Works

Abu-Lughod, Janet L. *Cairo 1001 Years of the City Victorious*. Princeton, 1971.
Amīn, Muḥammad M. *Al-Awqāf wa al-ḥayā al-ijtimāʿiyya fī miṣr, 649–923 A.H./1250–1517 A.D.* Cairo, 1980.
Amīn, Muḥammad M., and Laila A. Ibrahim. *Architectural Terms in Mamluk Documents*. Cairo, 1990.
Arberry, A.J. *Tales from the Masnavi*. London, 1961.
——. *More Tales from the Masnavi*. London, 1963.
Ariès, Philippe. *Western Attitudes toward Death from the Middle Ages to the Present*. Baltimore, 1974.
——. *The Hour of Our Death*. New York, 1981.
——. *Images of Man and Death*. Cambride, Mass., 1985.
Atiya, Aziz S. *The Crusade in the Later Middle Ages*. London, 1938.
Ayalon, David. *Gunpowder and Firearms in the Mamlūk Kingdom*. London, 1956.
——. *Islam and the Abode of War: Military Slaves and Islamic Adversaries*. London, 1994.
——. *Mamlūk Military Society*. London, 1979.
——. *Outsiders in the Lands of Islam: Mamlūks, Mongols and Eunuchs*. London, 1988.
——. *Studies on the Mamlūks of Egypt (1250–1517)*. London, 1977.
——. "The Wafidiyya in the Mamlūk Kingdom." *IC* 25 (1961): 81–104.
Baldick, Julian. *Mystical Islam. An Introduction to Sufism*. London and New York, 1989.
Behrens-Abouseif, Doris. *Islamic Architecture in Cairo: An Introduction*. Leiden, 1989.
——. "Change in Function and Form of Mamluk Religious Institutions." *Annales islamologiques* 21 (1985): 73–93.
Berkey, Jonathan. *The Transmission of Knowledge in Medieval Cairo*. Princeton, 1992.
Bianquis, T. "Ibn al-Nablulusi, un martyr sunnite au IVᵉ siècle de l'hégire." *Annales islamologiques* 12 (1974): 45–66.
Bloom, Jonathan. "The Mosque of the Qarafa in Cairo." *Muqarnas* 4 (1987): 7–20.
Bourdieu, Pierre. *La Distinction: Critique sociale du jugement* Paris, 1979. Translated by Richard Nice as *Distinction*. Cambridge, Mass., 1986.
Bousquet, G.H. "Notes sur deux aspects contemporains du culte de saints chez les musulmans." *RA* 79 (1936): 777–82.
——. "La baraka, le mana et le dunamis de Jésus." *RA* 91 (1947): 166–70.
——. "le rituel du culte des saints. (A propos du livre de T. Canaan)." *RA* 93 (1949): 277–90.
Böwering, Gerhard. *The Mystical Vision of Existence in Classical Islam: The Qurʾānic Hermeneutics of the Ṣūfī Sahl al-Tustarī* (Berlin and New York, 1980).
Bravmann, M.M. *The Spiritual Background of Early Islam*. (See especially "Life After Death in Early Arab Conception") Leiden, 1972.
Brinner, William M. "Prophet and Saint: The Two Exemplars of Islam," in *Saints and Virtues*, Edited by John Stratton Hawley, Berkeley and Los Angeles, 1987: 36–51.
Brown, Peter. "The Saint as Exemplar in Late Antiquity." *Representations* 1.2 (1983): 1–25.

——. *The Cult of the Saints, Its Rise and Function in Latin Chistianity.* Chicago, 1981.
Bulliet, Richard W. *Conversion to Islam in the Medieval Period.* Cambridge, 1979.
Burgoyne, Michael H. *Mamluk Jerusalem. An Architectural Study.* Essex, 1987.
Butler, Alfred J. *The Arab Conquest of Egypt.* 1902; rpt. Oxford, 1978.
Calverley, E.E. "Doctrines of the Soul (Nafs and Rūḥ) in Islam." *MW* 33 (1943): 254–64.
Campo, Juan Eduardo. *The Other Sides of Paradise. Explorations into the Religious Meanings of Domestic Space in Islam.* Columbia, S.C., 1991.
Canaan, T. "Mohammedan Saints and Sanctuaries in Palestine." *Journal of the Palestine Oriental Society* 4 (1924): 1–84; 5 (1925): 163–203; 6 (1926): 1–69 and 117–58.
Casanova, M. Paul. *Essai de reconstitution topographique de la ville d'al Foustât ou Miṣr.* In the Mémoires de l'Institut français d'archéologie orientale du Caire, no. 35 (in 3 fascs.). Cairo, 1913–1919.
Chamberlain, Michael. *Knowledge and Social Practice in Medieval Damascus, 1190–1350.* Cambridge, U.K., 1994.
Chartier, Roger. "Culture as Appropriation: Popular Cultural Uses in Early Modern France," in Steven L. Kaplan, ed., *Understanding Popular Culture: Europe from the Middle Ages to the Nineteenth Century.* Berlin, 1984, 229–53.
——. "La culture populaire en question" *Histoire* 8 (1981): 85–96.
Chittick, William C. *The Sufi Path of Knowledge: Ibn al-ʿArabi's Metaphysics of Imagination.* Albany, 1989.
——. *The Self-Disclosure of God: Principles of Ibn al-ʿArabī's Cosmology.* Albany, 1998.
——. *The Breath of the All-Merciful: Ibn al-ʿArabī's Articulation of the Cosmos.* Albany, forthcoming.
——. *Faith and Practice of Islam: Three Thirteenth Century Sufi Texts.* Albany, 1992.
Chodkiewicz, Michel. *Le sceau des saints, Prophétie et sainteté dans la sainteté dans la doctrine d'Ibn Arabî.* Paris, 1986. Translated by Liadain Sherrard as *Seal of the Saints: Prophethood and Sainthood in the Doctrine of Ibn ʿArabī.* Cambridge, U.K., 1993.
——. *An Ocean without Shore: Ibn Arabi, The Book, and the Law.* Albany, 1993.
Clerget, M. *Le Caire, Etude de géographie urbaine et d'histoire économique.* 2 vols. Cairo, 1934.
Cohen, Mark R. *Jewish Self-Government in Medieval Egypt.* Princeton, 1980.
Combe, E., J. Sauvaget, G. Wiet, et al. *Répertoire chronologique d'épigraphie arabe.* 17 vols. Cairo, 1931–1975.
Crabites, P. "From Marauder to Mystic (A Saint of Rhodes)." *MW* 23 (1933): 77–81.
Creswell, K.A.C. *Early Muslim Architecture.* 2 vols. 1938–1940; rpt. New York, 1978.
——. *The Muslim Architecture of Egypt.* 2 vols. 1952–1959; rpt. New York, 1978.
——. "A Brief Chronology of the Muḥammadan Monuments of Egypt to 1517 A.D." *BIFAO* 16 (1919): 39–164.
Daftary, Farhad. *The Ismaʿilis, Their History and Doctrines.* Cambridge, U.K., 1990.
Daneshvari, Abbas. *Medieval Tomb Towers of Iran, An Iconographical Study.* Lexington, Ky., 1986.
De Jong, F. "Cairene Ziyara-days: A Contribution to the Study of Saint Veneration in Islam." *Die Welt des Islams* (new series) 17 (1976/77): 26–43.
——. *Ṭuruq and Ṭuruq-Linked Institutions in Nineteenth Century Egypt.* Leiden, 1978.
Denny, Frederick M. *An Introduction to Islam.* 2nd ed. New York, 1994.
——. "God's Friends: The Sanctity of Persons in Islam." In *Sainthood.* Edited by Richard Kieckhefer and George D. Bond, 69–97. Berkeley and Los Angeles, 1988.
Dermenghem, E. *Le culte des saints dans l'Islam maghrébin.* Paris, 1954.
Destaing, E. "Un saint musulman au XVe siècle, Sīdi Mahammed el-Haowârī." *JA* 10 (1906): 295–341 and 385–438.

Dickie, J. "Allah and Eternity: Mosques, Madrasas and Tombs." In *Architecture of the Islamic World, Its History and Social Meaning.* Edited by G. Michell. 15–47. London, 1978.
Dodd, Erica C. "The Image of the Word: Notes on the Religious Iconography of Islam." *Berytus* 18 (1969): 35–79.
Dols, Michael. *The Black Death in the Middle East.* Princeton, 1977.
Dopp, P.H. "Le Caire vu par les voyageurs occidentaux du Moyen Âge, premier article." *Bulletin de la Société royale de géographie d'Égypte* 23 (1950): 117–49. "Deuxième article." 24 (1951): 115–62.
Dunlop, D.M. "A Spanish Muslim Saint: Abu'l ʿAbbās al-Mursi." *MW* 35 (1945): 181–96.
Eaton, Richard M. *The Sufis of Bijapur, 1300–1700: Social Roles of Sufis in Medieval India.* Princeton, 1978.
Ehrenkreutz, Andrew S. *Saladin.* Albany, 1972.
Eklund, Ragnar. *Life between Death and Resurrection According to Islam.* Uppsala, 1941.
Eliade, Mircea. *Images and Symbols. Studies in Religious Symbolism.* Princeton, 1991.
——. *The Myth of the Eternal Return; Or, Cosmos and History*, Princeton, 1954.
——. *Patterns in Comparative Religion.* New York, 1968.
——. *The Sacred and the Profane.* New York, 1959.
Endress, Gerhard. *An Introduction to Islam.* Translated by Carole Hillenbrand. Edinburgh, 1988.
Ernst, Carl W. *Sufism: An Essential Introduction to the Philosophy and Practice of the Mystical Tradition of Islam.* Boston, 1997.
——. *Words of Ecstasy in Sufism.* Albany, 1985.
Ewing, Katherine Pratt. *Arguing Sainthood: Modernity, Psychoanalysis, and Islam.* Durham, N.C., 1997.
Fernandes, Leonor. *The Evolution of a Sufi Institution in Mamluk Egypt: The Khanqah.* Berlin, 1988.
——. "Some Aspects of the *Zāwiya* in Egypt at the Eve of the Ottoman Conquest." *Annales islamologiques* 23 (1983): 9–17.
Gaborieau, Marc. "The Cult of the Saints in Nepal and Northern India". In *Saints and Their Cults.* Edited by Stephen Wilson, 291–307. Cambridge, U.K., 1983
Galal, M. "Essai d'observations sur les rites funéraires en Egypte." *REI* 11 (1937): 131–299.
Garcin, Jean-Claude. "Deux saints populaires du Caire au début du XVIe siècle." *BEO* 29 (1977): 131–43.
——. *Espaces, pouvoirs et ideologies de l'Egypte médiévale*, London, 1987.
——. "Histoire et hagiographie de l'Égypte musulmane à la fin de l'époque mamelouke et au début de l'époque ottomane." In *Hommages à la mémoire de Serge Sauneron, 1927–1976*, 2:287–316. Cairo, 1979.
Geertz, Clifford. *Islam Observed.* Chicago, 1971.
——. *The Interpretation of Cultures.* New York, 1973.
——. *Local Knowledge.* New York, 1983.
Geyoushi, Muhammad I. "Al-Tirmidhī's Theory of Saints and Sainthood." *IQ* 15 (1971): 17–61.
Gil'adi, Avner. *Children of Islam: Concepts of Childhood in Medieval Muslim Society.* Oxford, 1992.
Gilsenan, Michael. *Saint and Sufi in Modern Egypt, An Essay in the Sociology of Religion.* Oxford, 1973.
——. *Recognizing Islam. Religion and Society in the Arab World.* New York, 1982.
Goitein, S.D. *A Mediterranean Society.* 6 vols, Berkeley and Los Angeles, 1967–1993.
Goldziher, Ignaz. "The Cult of the Saints in Islam." *MW* 1 (1911): 302–12. See also note by G. Tate in *MW* 2 (1912): 106.

——. "On the Veneration of the Dead in Paganism and Islam." In *Muslim Studies.* Edited by S.M. Stern, 1: 209–38. London, 1966.
——. "Veneration of Saints in Islam." In *Muslim Studies.* Edited by S.M. Stern, 2: 275–341. London, 1966.
Golombek, Lisa. "The Cult of Saints and Shrine Architecture in the Fourteenth Century." *Near Eastern Numismatics, Studies in Honor of G.C. Miles,* 419–430. Beirut, 1974.
Guillaume, A. *The Life of Muhammad.* Oxford, 1955.
Grabar, Oleg. "The Earliest Islamic Commemorative Structures, Notes and Documents." *Ars Orientalis* 6 (1966): 7–46.
——. *The Shape of the Holy. Early Islamic Jerusalem.* Princeton, 1996.
Graham, William A. *Beyond the Written Word: Oral Aspects of Scripture in the History of Religion.* Cambridge, 1987.
——. *Divine Word and Prophetic Word in Early Islam.* The Hague, 1977.
Grunebaum, G.E. von. *Muhammadan Festivals.* New York, 1951.
Guest, R. "The Foundation of Fustat and the Khittahs of that Town." *JRAS* (1907): 49–83.
Gurevich, A. *Medieval Popular Culture: Problems of Belief and Perception.* Translated by J.M. Bak and P.A. Hollingsworth. Cambridge, U.K., 1988.
Haarmann, Ulrich. "Ideology and History, Identity and Alterity: The Arab Image of the Turk from the 'Abbasids to Modern Egypt." *IJMES* 20 (1988): 175–96.
——. "Rather the Injustice of the Turks than the Righteousness of the Arabs. Changing 'Ulamā' Attitudes towards Mamluk Rule in the Late Fifteenth Century." *Studia Islamica* 68 (1988): 61–77.
——. "The Sons of Mamluks in Late Medieval Egypt," in *Land Tenure and Social Transformation in the Middle East.* Edited by Tarif Khalidi, 141–68. Beirut, 1984.
Hackel, S. ed. *The Byzantine Saint: University of Birmingham Fourteenth Spring Symposium of Byzantine Studies.* London, 1981.
Hallenberg, Helena. "Ibrāhīm al-Dasūqī (1255–96)—A Saint Invented." Ph.D. dissertation. University of Helsinki, 1997.
Halm, Heinz. *The Empire of the Mahdi. The Rise of the Fatimids.* Translated by Michael Bonner. Leiden, 1996.
——. *Schiitische Islam* (Munich, 1994) translated by Allison Brown as *Shi'a Islam: From Religion to Revolution.* Princeton, 1997.
Harawī, Hassan, Hussein Rached, and Gaston Wiet, eds. *Stèles funeraires, Catalogue général du Musée arabe du Caire.* 10 vols. Cairo, 1932–1942.
Harīdī, Aḥmad 'Abd al-Mağīd. *Index des Ḥiṭaṭ, Index analytique des ouvrages d'Ibn Duqmāq et de Maqrīzī sur le Caire.* 3 vols. to date. Cairo, 1983–.
Harrison, H.M. "The Bab il Metawalli." *MW* 8 (1918): 141–44.
Hayes, H.E. "Serpent Worship and Islam in Egypt." *MW* 8 (1918): 278–281.
Hillenbrand, Robert. "The Tomb Towers of Iran to 1550." Ph.D. dissertation. Trinity College, Oxford University, 1974.
Hodgson, Marshall G.S. *The Venture of Islam.* 3 vols. Chicago, 1974.
Hoffman, Valerie J. *Sufism, Mystics, and Saints in Modern Egypt.* Columbia, S.C., 1995.
Homerin, Thomas Emil. *From Arab Poet to Muslim Saint: Ibn al-Farid, His Verse and His Shrine.* Columbia, S.C., 1994.
——. "A Bird Ascends the Night: Elegy and Immortality in Islam," *Journal of the American Academy of Religion* 58 (1990): 541–73.
——. "Echoes of a Thirsty Owl: Death and Afterlife in Pre-Islamic Arabic Poetry." *JNES* 44 (1985): 165–184.
Humphreys, R. Stephen. *From Saladin to the Mongols: The Ayyubids of Damascus.* Albany, 1977.
——. *Islamic History, A Framework for Inquiry.* Princeton, 1991.
——. "The Expressive Intent of Mamluk Architecture in Cairo." *Studia Islamica* 35 (1972): 69–119.

Irwin, Robert. *The Middle East in the Middle Ages, The Early Mamlūk Sultanate, 1250–1382.* Beckenham, U.K., 1986.
Joly, A. "Saints de l'islam." *RA* 52 (1908): 171–181.
——. "Saints et légendes de l'Islam." *RA* 57 (1913): 7–26.
Jomier, Jacques. *Le maḥmal et la caravane égyptienne des pèlerins de la Mecque (XIIIe–XXe siècles).* Cairo, 1953.
Joseph, T.K. "A Nubian Muslim Hawariy's Tomb." *IC* 26 (1952): 50–53.
Katz, Jonathan G. *Dreams, Sufism, and Sainthood: the Visionar Career of Muhammad al-Zawawi.* Leiden, 1996.
Kee, Howard Clark. *Miracle in the Early Christian World.* New Haven, 1983.
Kessler, Christel. "Funerary Architecture within the City." In *Colloque international sur l'histoire du Caire.* Gräfenhainichen, Germany, 1969: 257–67.
——. *The Carved Masonry Domes of Medieval Cairo.* London, 1976.
Kinberg, Leah. "Interaction Between This World and the Afterworld in Early Islamic Tradition." *Oriens* 29–30 (1986): 285–308.
Kister, M.J. "The 'Kitab al-Mihan,' A Book on Muslim Martyrology." *Journal of Semetic Studies* 20 (1975): 210–18.
——. "You Shall Only Set Out for 3 Mosques: A Study of an Egyptian Tradition." *Le Museon* 82 (1969): 173–96.
Kubiak, Władysław. *Al Fusṭāṭ, Its Foundation and Early Urban Development.* Cairo, 1987.
Lane, E.W. *An Account of the Manners and Customs of the Modern Egyptians.* 1836; rpt. London, 1978.
——. *An Arabic-English Lexicon.* 8 vols. 1863–1893; rpt. New York, 1957.
——. *Arabian Society in the Middle Ages: Studies from the Thousand and One Nights.* Edited by Stanley Lane-Poole. 1883; rpt. London, 1987.
Längner, Barbara. *Untersuchungen zur historischen Volkskunde Aegyptens nach Mamlukischen Quellen.* Berlin, 1983.
Laoust, Henri *Essai sur les doctrines sociales et politiques de Taki ad-Din Ahmad b. Taimiya.* Cairo, 1939.
——. "Le Hanbalisme sous les mamlouks bahrides." *REI* 28 (1960): 1–71.
——. "Le réformisme d'Ibn Taymiya." *IS* 1 (1962): 27–47.
——. "Quelques opinions sur la théodicée d'Ibn Taimīya," *Mélanges Maspéro* 3 (1935–40), 431–38.
Lapidus, Ira. *Muslim Cities in the Later Middle Ages.* Cambridge, Mass., 1967.
——. ed. *Middle Eastern Cities.* Berkeley and Los Angeles, 1969.
——. "The Conversion of Egypt to Islam." *Israel Oriental Studies* 2 (1972): 248–62.
——. *A History of Islamic Societies.* Cambridge, U.K., 1988.
Lazarus-Yafeh, H. *Studies in al-Ghazali.* Jerusalem, 1975.
Le Goff, Jacques. *L'imaginaire médiéval.* Paris, 1985. Translated by Arthur Goldhammer as *The Medieval Imagination.* Chicago, 1988.
——. *Pour un autre Moyen Age.* Paris, 1977. Translated by Arthur Goldhammer as *Time, Work, and Culture in the Middle Ages.* Chicago, 1980.
——. *The Birth of Purgatory.* Translated by Arthur Goldhammer. Chicago, 1984.
——. "The Learned and Popular Dimensions of Journeys in the Otherworld in the Middle Ages." In *Understanding Popular Culture.* Edited by Steven L. Kaplan. Berlin, 1984, 16–37.
Lev, Yaacov. *State and Society in Fatimid Egypt.* Leiden, 1991.
Levtzion, Nehemia. *Conversion to Islam.* New York and London, 1979.
Lings, Martin. *A Sufi Saint of the Twentieth Century: Shaikh Aḥmad al-ʿAlawī.* Cambridge, U.K., 1993.
——. *What is Sufism?* London, 1975.
Little, Donald P. "Coptic Conversion to Islam Under the Baḥrī Mamlūks, 692–755/1293–1354." *BSOAS* 39 (1976): 552–69.
——. *History and Historiography of the Mamluks.* London, 1986.
——. "Did Ibn Taymiyya Have a Screw Loose?" *SI* 41(1975): 93–111.

——. "The Ḥaram Documents as Sources for the Arts and Architecture of the Mamluk Period." *Muqarnas* 2 (1984): 61–72.
——. "The Historical and Historiographical Significance of the Detention of Ibn Taymiyya." *IJMES* 4 (1975): 311–27.
——. "Religion under the Mamluks." *MW*, 73 (1983): 165–81.
Luṭfi, Hoda. *Al-Quds al-Mamlūkiyya: A History of Mamlūk Jerusalem Based on the Ḥaram Documents*. Berlin, 1985.
Lyons, Malcolm and D.E.P. Jackson. *Saladin, The Politics of the Holy War*. Cambridge, 1982.
Macdonald, D.B. *The Religious Life and Attitudes in Islam*. Chicago, 1909.
——. "The Development of the Idea of Spirit in Islam." *MW* 22 (1932): 25–42 and 153–68.
MacKenzie, Neil D. *Ayyubid Cairo. A Topographical Study*. Cairo, 1992.
Magued, ʿAbd al-Minʿam Mājid. *Nuẓum al-fāṭimiyīn wa-rusūmuhum fī miṣr*. 2 vols. Cairo, 1953–1955.
Makdisi, George. "Ibn Taimīya: A Ṣūfī of the Qādirīya Order." *The American Journal of Arabic Studies* 1 (1973): 118–29.
——. *The Rise of Colleges, Institutions of Learning in Islam and the West*. Edinburgh, 1981.
——. *The Rise of Humanism in Classical Islam and the Christian West*. Edinburgh, 1990.
Marcus, Abraham. *The Middle East on the Eve of Modernity. Aleppo in the Eighteenth Century*. New York, 1989.
Margoliouth, D.S. "An Islamic Saint of the Seventh Century A.H." *IC* 13 (1939): 263–289.
Marmon, Shaun. *Eunuchs and Sacred Boundaries in Islamic Society*. Oxford, 1995.
Massignon, Louis. "Les saints musulmans enterrés à Baghdad." *Revue de l'histoire des réligions* 58 (1908): 329–338.
——. "L'idée de l'esprit dans l'Islam." *Eranos Jahrbuch* 13 (1945): 277–82.
——. "La cité des morts au Caire (Qarāfa-Darb al-Aḥmar)." *BIFAO* 57 (1958): 25–79. See also the review by J. Sourdel-Thomine in *Arabica* 6 (1959): 99–101.
——. *The Passion of al-Hallāj, Mystic and Martyr of Islam*. Translated by Herbert Mason. 4 vols. Princeton, 1982.
McPherson, J.W. *The Moulids of Egypt (Egyptian Saints-Days)*. Cairo, 1941.
Mehren, August Ferdinand Michael van. *Câhirah og Kerâfat; historiske studier under et ophold i Aegypten 1867–68*. Copenhagen, 1869–70.
——. "Revue des monuments funéraires du Kerafat ou de la ville des morts hors du Caire." *Mélanges asiatiques* 6 (1872): 524–69.
Memon, Muhammad U. *Ibn Taimīya's Struggle against Popular Religion, With an Annotated Translation of His Kitāb iqtiḍāʾ aṣ-ṣirāt al-mustaqīm mukhālafat aṣḥāb al-jaḥīm*. The Hague, 1976.
Momen, Moojan. *An Introduction to Shīʿi Islam*. New Haven, 1985.
Mottahedeh, Roy. *Loyalty and Leadership in an Early Islamic Society*. Princeton, 1980.
Muyser, Jacob. *Les pelerinage coptes en Egypte d'après les notes du Qommos Jacob Muyser*. Edited by Gérard Viaud. Cairo, 1979.
Nabahānī, Yūsuf b. Ismāʿīl al-. *Jāmiʿ karāmāt al-awliyāʾ*. Cairo, 1911.
Nasr, Seyyed Hossein. *An Introduction to Islamic Cosmological Doctrines*. Cambridge, Mass., 1964.
——. *Islamic Art and Spirituality*. Albany, 1987.
——. ed. *Islamic Spirituality*. 2 vols. New York, 1987.
——. *Sufi Essays*. Albany, 1991.
Nicholson, R. A. *The Mystics of Islam*. London, 1914.
——. *Studies in Islamic Mysticism*. Cambridge, U.K., 1921.
——. *The Idea of Personality in Sufism*. Cambridge, U.K., 1923.
Olesen, Niels Henrik. *Culte des saints et pèlerinages chez Ibn Taymiyya*. Paris, 1991.
Ohtoshi, Tetsuya. "The Manners, Customs, and Mentality of Pilgrims to the Egyptian City of the Dead: 1100–1500 A.D." *Orient*. 29 (1993): 19–44.

Ory, Solange. *Cimetières et inscriptions du Hawran et du Gabal al-Duruz*. Paris, 1989.
Padwick, Constance. *Muslim Devotions, A Study of Prayer Manuals in Constant Use*. London, 1961.
Perlman, Moshe. "Notes on Anti-Christian Propaganda in the Mamluk Empire." *BSOAS* 10 (1942): 843–61.
Peters, F.E. *Jerusalem and Mecca. The Typology of the Holy City in the Near East*. New York, 1986.
——. *Jerusalem*. Princeton, 1985.
——. *The Hajj. The Muslim Pilgrimage to Mecca and the Holy Places*. Princeton, 1994.
Petry, Carl. *The Civilian Elite of Cairo in the Later Middle Ages*. Princeton, 1981.
——. *Protectors or Praetorians? The Last Mamluk Sultans and Egypt's Waning as a Great Power*. Albany, 1994.
——. *Twilight of Majesty: The Reigns of the Mamluk Sultans al-Ashraf Qaytbay and Qansuh al-Ghawri in Egypt*. Seattle, 1993.
Rabbat, Nasser O. *The Citadel of Cairo. A New Interpretation of Royal Mamluk Architecture*. Leiden, 1995.
Rabie, Hassanein. *The Financial System of Egypt, A.H. 564–741/A.D. 1169–1341*. Oxford, 1972.
Radtke, Bernd. *Al-Ḥakīm at-Tirmiḏī: Ein islamischer Theosoph des 3./9. Jahrhunderts*. Freiburg, 1980.
Rāghib, Yūsuf. "Deux monuments fatimides au pied du Muqaṭṭam." *REI* 46 (1978): 91–117.
——. "Essai d'inventaire chronologiques des guides à l'usage des pèlerins du Caire." *REI* 41 (1973): 259–80.
——. "Faux morts et enterrés vifs dans l'espace musulman." *SI* 57 (1983): 5–30."
——. "Le mausolée de Yūnus al-Saʿdī, est-il celui de Badr al-Gamālī?" *Arabica* 20 (1973): 305–7.
——. "Les mausolées fatimides du quartier d'al Mašāhid." *AI* 17 (1981): 1–30.
——. "La mosquée d'al-Qarāfa et Jonathan M. Bloom." *Arabica* 41 (1994): 419–21.
——. "Les premiers monuments funéraires de l'Islam." *AI* 9 (1970): 21–36.
——. "Les sanctuaires des gens de la famille dans la cité des morts au Caire." *RSO* 51, (1977): 47–76. "(Suite et fin)." *SI* 45 (1977): 27–55.
——. "Al-Sayyida Nafīsa, sa légende, son culte et son cimetière." *SI* 44 (1976): 61–86.
——. "Sur deux monuments funéraires du cimetière d'al-Qarāfa al-Kubrā au Caire." *Annales islamologiques* 12 (1974): 67–84.
——. "Sur un groupe de mausolés du cimetière du Caire." *REI* 40 (1972): 189–95.
——. "Une description arabe inédite du mausolée d'al-Sayyida Nafīsa au Caire." *Arabica* 23 (1976): 37–41.
Rahman, Fazlur. *Major Themes of the Qur'ān*. Minneapolis, 1980.
Raymond, André. "Cairo's Area and Population in the Early Fifteenth Century." *Muqarnas* 2 (1984): 21–31.
Rosenthal, Franz. *A History of Muslim Historiography*. Leiden, 1952.
Sabra, Adam A. "Poverty and Charity in Mamluk Cairo (1250–1517)" Ph.D. dissertation. Princeton University, 1998.
Salam-Liebich, Hayat. *The Architecture of the Mamluk City of Tripoli*. Cambridge, Mass., 1983.
Salmon, G. *Etudes sur la topographie du Caire*. In the Mémoires de l'Institut français d'archéologie orientale du Caire, no. 7 Cairo, 1902.
Sanders, Paula. *Ritual, Politics, and the City in Fatimid Cairo*. Albany, 1994.
Sauvaget, Jean. "Glanes épigraphique." *REI* 6 (1941–1946): 17–29.
Schimmel, Annemarie. *Mystical Dimensions of Islam*. Chapel Hill, N.C., 1975.
——. *And Muhammad Is His Messenger, The Veneration of the Prophet in Islamic Piety*. Chapel Hill, N.C., 1985.
——. "Some Glimpses of the Religious Life in Egypt during the Mamluk Period." *Islamic Studies* 4 (1965): 353–92.

Schmitt, Jean-Claude. *The Holy Greyhound.* Cambridge, U.K., 1983.

Sells, Michael. *Early Islamic Mysticism: Sufi, Qur'an, Miʿraj, Poetic and Theological Writings.* New York, 1996.

Shoshan, Boaz. "High Culture and Popular Culture in Medieval Islam." *SI* 83 (1991): 67–107.

——. *Popular Culture in Medieval Cairo.* Cambridge, U.K., 1993.

Sivan, Emmanuel. "Notes sur la situation des chrétiens à l'époque ayyubide." *Revue de l'histoire des religions* 172 (1967): 117–30.

——. *Radical Islam. Medieval Theology and Modern Politics.* Enlarged edition, New Haven, 1990.

Smith, Baldwin. *The Dome, A Study in the History of Ideas.* Princeton, 1950.

Smith, Jane I. and Yvonne Y. Haddad. *Islamic Understanding of Death and Resurrection.* Albany, 1981.

Smith, Margaret. "The Woman Saint in the Development of Islam." *MW* 17 (1927): 130–38.

——. *Rābiʿa the Mystic and Her Fellow-Saints in Islām.* Cambridge, U.K., 1928; rpt. 1984.

Sourdel-Thomine, J. "Les anciens lieux de pèlerinage damascains d'après sources arabes." *Bulletin d'études orientales de l'Institut Français de Damas* 14 (1952–1954): 65–85.

——. "Quelques réflexions sur l'écriture des premières stèles arabes du Caire." *Annales islamologiques* 11 (1972): 23–35.

Souza, Achilles de. *Mediation in Islam: An Investigation.* Rome, 1975.

Swan, G. "The Matbuli Incident (Illustrating Popular Islam in Cairo)." *MW* 3 (1913): 175–80.

——. "The Tanta Mûlid." *MW* 4 (1914): 45–51.

——. "Saintship in Islam." *MW* 5 (1915): 232–39.

Taylor, Christopher S. "Sacred History and the Cult of Muslim Saints in Late Medieval Egypt." *Muslim World* 80 (1990): 72–80.

——. "Reevaluating the Shiʿi Role in the Development of Monumental Islamic Funerary Architecture: The Case of Egypt." *Muqarnas* 9 (1992): 1–10.

Taymūr, Aḥmad. *Qabr al-Imām al-Suyūṭī wa-taḥqīq mawḍiʿihi.* Cairo, A.H. 1346.

Teiser, Stephen F. *The Ghost Festival in Medieval China.* Princeton, 1988.

Trimingham, J. Spencer. *The Sufi Orders in Islam.* Oxford, 1971.

Turner, Bryan S. *Weber and Islam: A Critical Study.* London, 1974.

Turner, Victor. *The Forest of Symbols.* Ithaca, N.Y., 1967.

——. *The Ritual Process.* Chicago, 1969.

——. *Dramas, Fields and Metaphors.* Ithaca, N.Y., 1974.

——. *Process, Performance and Pilgrimage.* New Delhi, 1979.

Turner, Victor, and Edith Turner. *Image and Pilgrimage in Christian Culture.* New York, 1978.

Van Dam, Raymond. *Saints and Their Miracles in Late Antique Gaul.* Princeton, 1993.

Voll, John. "Renwal and Reform in Islam in Islamic History: *Tajdid* and *Islah.*" In *Voices of Resurgent Islam.* Edited by John L. Esposito, 32–47. Oxford, 1983.

Ward, Benedicta. *Miracles and the Medieval World.* Philadelphia, 1982.

Weber, Max. *The Sociology of Religion.* Boston, 1963.

Weinstein, Donald, and Rudolph M. Bell, eds. *Saints and Society.* Chicago, 1982.

White, G.E. "The Mohammedan Conception of Saintship." *MW* 8 (1918): 259–62.

Wickett, Eleanor Elizabeth. "'For Our Destinies:' The Funerary Laments of Upper Egypt (Arabic Text, Cosmology, Iconography)." Ph.D. dissertation. University of Pennsylvania, 1993.

Wiet, Gaston. "Les inscriptions du mausolée de Shāfiʿī." *Bulletin de l'Institut d'Égypte* 15 (1932–33): 167–85.

——. "Stèles coufiques d'Egypte et du Soudan." *JA* 240 (1952): 273–97.

——. *Cairo, City of Art and Commerce.* Translated by Seymour Feiler. Norman, Okla., 1964.

——. "Fêtes et jeux au Caire." *Annales islamologiques* 8 (1969): 99–128.

Williams, Caroline. "The Cult of ʿAlid Saints in the Fatimid Monuments of Cairo, Part I: The Mosque of al-Aqmar." *Muqarnas* 1 (1983): 37–52. "Part II: The Mausolea." *Muqarnas* 3 (1985): 39–60.

——. "The Qurʾānic Inscriptions on the Tabut of al-Husayn." *Islamic Art* 2 (1987): 3–13.

Williams, John A. "Urbanization and Monument Construction in Mamluk Cairo." *Muqarnas* 2 (1984): 33–45.

Wilson, Stephen, ed. *Saints and Their Cults: Studies in Religious Sociology, Folklore and History.* Cambridge, U.K., 1983.

Zubaid Ahmad, M. G. "The Islamic Conception of the Soul." *Journal of the Ganganatha Jha Research Institute* 1 (1943): 165–75.

Zimmer, Heinrich. *Myths and Symbols in Indian Art and Civilization.* Princeton, 1946.

Zwemer, S.M. "The Shiah Saints." *MW* 22 (1932): 111–15.

INDEX

ʿAbbāsids 46, 184
abdāl 66, 82
ʿAbd Allāh b. ʿAbd al-Raḥmān b. ʿAwf 135
ʿAbd Allāh al-Asmar 54
ʿAbd Allāh al-Barrī al-Naḥawī 109
ʿAbd Allāh al-Darwīsh 117; (tomb of) 228
ʿAbd Allāh b. Ḥārith 45 f.n.
ʿAbd Allāh b. al-Ḥasan b. ʿAbd Allāh b. Ḥājil al-Ṣadafī 131
ʿAbd Allāh al-Khāmī 136
ʿAbd Allāh b. al-Mubārak 48
ʿAbd Allāh al-Munūfī 53
ʿAbd Allāh b. Saʿīd 163
ʿAbd al-Jabbār (Ibn al-Farrāsh) 55, 143–144
ʿAbd al-Khāliq 104
ʿAbd al-Karīm 120, 150, 153
ʿAbd al-Majīd al-Maghrāwī 38, 40
ʿAbd al-Malik al-Būhalī 161 f.n.
ʿAbd al-Muḥsin b. Sulaymān 163
ʿAbd al-Qādir al-Kīlānī 138
ʿAbd Rabbihi b. Amīn b. ʿAbd Allāh al-Ghāfiqī 38
ʿAbd al-Raḥīm al-Baysānī 117
ʿAbd al-Raḥīm al-Fāḍil 159–160
ʿAbd al-Raḥmān b. al-Qāsim al-ʿUtaqī 89
ʿAbd al-Raḥmān b. Yaḥyā al-Maʿāfirī 38
ʿAbd al-Ṣamad b. Muḥammad b. Aḥmad b. Isḥaq b. Muslim b. Ibrahīm al-Baghdādī 66 f.n., 69
ʿAbd al-Wāḥid b. Barakāt b. Naṣr Allāh al-Qurshī 114
ʿAbīd b. ʿAbd Allāh *see* al-Maʿāfirī, Abū Muḥammad
Abraham 177, 187
abrār 82
Abū al-ʿAbbās Aḥmad (Ibn al-Ḥaddād 93
Abū al-ʿAbbās Aḥmad al-Andalusī al-Khazrajī al-Baṣīr ("the blind") 122, 141
Abū al-ʿAbbās Aḥmad b. al-Khaṭiyya al-Lakhmī 96, 163
Abū al-ʿAbbās Aḥmad b. Muḥammad al-Munājī 96 f.n., 111, 136
Abū al-ʿAbbās al-Ḥarār (grave of) 227
Abū ʿAbd Allāh 132–133
Abū ʿAbd Allāh ("the grave digger") 104
Abū ʿAbd Allāh b. ʿAbd Allāh Muḥammad b. Masʿūd 111
Abū ʿAbd Allāh al-Ḥusayn 155
Abū ʿAbd Allāh Muḥammad 104–106
Abū ʿAbd Allāh Muḥammad ("the weasel") 104
Abū ʿAbd Allāh Muḥammad b. ʿAbd Allāh b. ʿAbd al-Ḥakam 153–154
Abū ʿAbd Allāh Muḥammad b. Ḥāmid b. al-Mutawwaj al-Mārīnī 6, 232
Abū ʿAbd Allāh Muḥammad b. Muḥammad b. Abū al-Qāsim ʿAbd al-Raḥmān b. ʿĪsa b. Wardān 121
Abū ʿAbd Allāh Muḥammad b. Raslān 151
Abū ʿAbd Allāh Muḥammad b. Yūsuf al-Takrūrī 144, 153
Abū ʿAbd Allāh Muḥammad Zurbihān al-Ajamī 137, 141
Abū ʿAbd Allāh al-Muṣaynī 151–152
Abū ʿAbd Allāh al-Nabbāsh 106
Abū ʿAbd Allāh al-Qurashī 111
Abū ʿAbd al-Raḥmān Raslān 119, 134–135
Abū Aḥmad ("the jurist") 91
Abū Aḥmad b. ʿAbd Allāh b. al-Ḥasan al-Muthannā 52
Abū ʿAmr ʿĀmir b. Sharāḥīl b. ʿAmr al-Shaʿbī 191 f.n.
Abū ʿAmr ʿUthmān b. Marzūq al-Ḥūfī 130, 138
Abū Bakr b. ʿAbd al-Ghaffār al-Muhallabī al-Ḥamdānī 163
Abū Bakr Aḥmad b. Naṣr al-Zaqqāq 94, 143 f.n.
Abū Bakr al-Ājirī 198
Abū Bakr al-Anbārī 142–143
Abū Bakr al-Iṣṭablī 55, 72

Abū Bakr Muḥammad 133, 162
Abū Bakr Muḥammad b. ʿAlī al-Mādhrāʾī 35
Abū Bakr al-Musāfir 91–92
Abū Bakr al-Ṣiddīq 45, 120, 155, 199, 214
Abū Bakr al-Shāṭir 23
Abū Bakr b. ʿUtba 138
Abū al-Baqāʾ Ṣāliḥ b. al-Ḥusayn b. ʿAbd al-Ḥamīd al-Mubtalā 93, 159–160
Abū Barakāt ʿAbd al-Muḥsin 97, 104
Abū al-Dalālāt 115
Abū Dāwūd 62 f.n., 181
Abū al-Dhikr Muḥammad b. Yaḥya b. al-Mahdī 92
Abū al-Faḍl b. Abū ʿAbd Allāh al-Ḥusayn b. Bushrā b. Saʿīd al-Jawharī 155
Abū al-Faḍl b. al-Jawharī 49, 163
Abū Faḍl Muḥammad al-ʿAṣafīrī 140
Abū Faḍl al-Sāʾiḥ 149–150
Abū al-Faraj ʿAbd al-Wāḥid al-Anbārī 158
Abū al-Faraj Aḥmad al-Fāʾiqī 93
Abū al-Faraj b. al-Jawzī 107
Abū al-Fatḥ al-Farghānī 162
Abū al-Fatḥ ʿUmar b. Abū al-Ḥasan ʿAlī b. Abū ʿAbd Allāh b. Ḥamawiyya 117–118
Abū Ḥafṣ b. Ghazzāl b. ʿUmar al-Ḥaḍramī 147
Abū Ḥafṣ ʿUmar al-Dhahabī 118
Abū al-Ḥajjāj Yūsuf 114, 119
Abū Ḥanīfa (Ḥanafī) 160, 169, 198
Abū al-Ḥasan ʿAlī 164
Abū al-Ḥasan ʿAlī (Ibn Qifl) 163
Abū al-Ḥasan ʿAlī ("the baker") 138
Abū al-Ḥasan ʿAlī al-Arṣūfī 159
Abū al-Ḥasan ʿAlī b. Bābashādh 122
Abū al-Ḥasan ʿAlī b. al-Ḥusayn al-Khilaʿī 122, 155
Abū al-Ḥasan ʿAlī b. Ibrāhīm al-Ḥūfī 114 f.n., 123
Abū al-Ḥasan ʿAlī b. Ibrāhīm b. Muslim 97, 119–120
Abū al-Ḥasan ʿAlī al-Lakhmī 140
Abū al-Ḥasan ʿAlī b. Marzūq Abū ʿAbd Allāh al-Rudaynī 138, 144
Abū al-Ḥasan ʿAlī b. Muḥammad b. ʿAbd al-Ghanī 101–102
Abū al-Ḥasan ʿAlī b. Muḥammad b. Sahl b. al-Ṣāʾigh al-Dīnawarī 66 f.n., 113, 114, 147–148
Abū al-Ḥasan ʿAlī b. Ṣāliḥ al-Andalusī 53–54
Abū al-Ḥasan Bunān 139
Abū al-Ḥasan b. al-Fuqāʿī 90, 92, 143
Abū al-Ḥasan al-Irtājī 163
Abū al-Ḥasan al-Raffā 114
Abū al-Ḥasan al-Ṣāyigh 53, 227
Abū al-Ḥasan b. Ṭāḥir b. Ghalbūn 162
Abū al-Ḥasan al-Ṭarāʾifī 157–158
Abū al-Ḥasan al-Ṭawīl 147 f.n.
Abū Hurayra 72, 211, 214
Abū al-Ḥusayn 98
Abū Isḥāq Ibrāhīm al-Qarafī (Ibn Khallāṣ al-Anṣārī) 143, 155–156, 157
Abū Jaʿfar al-Nāṭiq ("the eloquent") 117, 164
Abū al-Khaṭṭāb Maḥfūẓ b. Aḥmad al-Kalwadhānī 199
Abū al-Khayr al-Tīnnātī 33, 90–91, 98, 120, 138, 139, 161–162
Abū al-Manīʿ Rāfiʿ b. Daghsh al-Anṣārī 152
Abū Muḥammad ʿAbd Allāh b. Rāfiʿ al-Sāriʿī al-Maʿāfirī 63
Abū Muḥammad ʿAbd al-ʿAzīz b. Aḥmad b. Jaʿfar al-Khwārizmī 53, 135
Abū Muḥammad al-Ḍarīr ("the blind") 116–117
Abū Muḥammad Ismāʿīl b. ʿAmr al-Ḥaddād 87–88, 103
Abū Muḥammad al-Zahrī 49
Abū Mūsa al-Ashʿarī 46 f.n.
Abū Qāsim 135
Abū Qāsim ʿAbd al-Raḥmān 77
Abū al-Qāsim ʿAbd al-Raḥmān b. ʿAbd Allāh b. al-Ḥusayn al-Mālikī 113
Abū al-Qāsim ʿAbd al-Raḥmān b. Abū ʿAbd Allāh Muḥammad b. Sulaymān al-Lakhmī 160–161
Abū al-Qāsim ʿAbd al-Raḥmān al-Fārisī 122
Abū Qāsim ʿAbd al-Raḥmān b. Muḥammad b. Raslān 97, 137
Abū al-Qāsim al-Aqṭaʿ ("the mute") 54, 91
Abū al-Qāsim al-Farīd 145
Abū Qāsim b. al-Jabbās 71 f.n.
Abū al-Qāsim al-Ḥijār 162
Abū al-Qāsim b. Naʿma 139

Abū al-Qāsim Yaḥyā b. ʿAlī b. Muḥammad 102–103
Abū al-Rabīʿ 93; (tomb of) 228
Abū al-Samrāʾ 91, 140
Abū al-Saʿūd, Shaykh 137, 228
Abū Ṭālib b. Abū al-ʿAshāyir 114
Abū Ṭarṭūr, Shaykh Salāma 137
Abū Ṭayyib b. Ghalbūn 95
Abū Ṭayyib Kharūf 51
Abū al-Wafāʾ ʿAlī b. ʿAqīl 176
Abū Yaḥyā Zakariyya 122
Abū Zakariyya Yaḥyā al-Sabtī 140
adab al-ziyāra 70–76, 84, 205, 211–213, 216–218, 221, 231–232
Adam 208
ʿAdawiyya Ṣūfī brotherhood 34, 96 f.n.
Aden 100
al-Āḍid 7–8
ʿAdiyy b. Musāfir b. Ismāʿīl b. Mūsā al-Zāhid al-Shāmī al-Hakkārī 95, 96 f.n., 111–112, 138
adventus 54
al-Afḍalī, Amīr Zaʿīm al-Dawla Jawāmard 33
Affān b. Sulaymān al-Baghdādī (al-Miṣrī) 99–101, 146
afrād 82
Africanus, Leo 22
Aḥmad al-Badawī 65
Aḥmad b. Ḥanbal (Ḥanbalī) 75, 160, 169, 171, 176, 190, 193, 198, 199
Aḥmad b. Ibrāhīm b. Sunān al-Baṣrī 52
Aḥmad al-Kabīr b. al-Rifāʿī 113, 114
Aḥmad b. Ṭūlūn 18, 85, 139, 142, 144, 145; (tomb of) 228 (*see also* Mosque of)
aʾimma 87
ʿĀʾisha bt. Hishām b. Muḥammad b. Abū Bakr al-Bakrī, al-Sayyida 140, 184, 192, 201, 231
al-Akhnāʾī *see* Muḥammad b. Abū Bakr
akhyār 82
Alexandria 39, 117
ʿAlāʾ al-Dīn ʿAlī b. Ibrāhīm b. Dāwūd al-ʿAṭṭār 212–217, 222
ʿAlī b. Abī Ṭālib 32, 46, 102, 130, 148, 149
ʿAlī al-Ghamrī 64
ʿAlī b. Muḥammad al-Muhalabī 89
ʿAlids *see* Shīʿites
alms 35, 60, 101, 106, 215
ʿAmal Asfal 16
ʿAmal Fawq 15–16
Amalric 8, 20
Amīn, Muḥammad Muḥammad x, 9 f.n.
Āmina, al-Sayyida 159
al-ʿāmma 7
ʿAmr b. al-ʿĀṣ 56–57, 88, 227 (*see also* Mosque of ʿAmr)
ʿAmr b. Muṭīʿ al-Kindī 131
ʿamūd 37
al-Anbārī 52
anbiyāʾ 82, 172, 173, 174, 175, 177, 180, 192, 206–210, 213
angels 180, 196, 197, 209–210 (*see also* Munkar)
ʿAntar 45
Antioch 90
apostles 180, 206, 208
ʿAqaba 99
ʿAqīl al-Manbijī 112
ʿAqīlī, al- 53
Aʿrābī 48
Arabia 171
ʿArafāt, Mount 92 f.n., 138, 174, 203–204
arbāb al-asbāb 87
arbāb al-ṭayy 138
Arberry A.J. 100 f.n.
arwāḥ 209
al-ʿAṣafīrī *see* Abū Faḍl Muḥammad
ascetism 89–95, 122, 187
ashrāf 87, 150
Āsiya 47, 84–86
al-ʿAskar 15
astral worship 179, 190
ʿĀtika bt. ʿĪsā al-Makiyya 149
Atiya, Aziz Suryal 117 f.n.
al-ʿawāmm 7
awareness 109–114
ʿAwf b. Mālik 191
awliyāʾ 37, 52, 61, 80–83, 86, 87, 88, 106, 110, 123, 126, 127, 128, 129, 139, 165–166, 174, 175, 219–220, 223
awtād 82
Ayalon, David 9 f.n., 10 f.n.
ʿAyn Jalūt, Battle of 10
ʿAyn al-Ṣīra 18
al-ʿAynāʾ *see* Fāṭima bt. al-Qāsim al-Ṭayyib
Ayyūbids 7–9, 20, 50, 64, 117
al-ʿAzīz 24

Bāb al-Futūḥ 15 f.n., 68
Bāb al-Khūlī 44
Bāb al-Naṣr 15 f.n.
Bāb al-Qarāfa 20, 44, 67, 68, 117, 227–228
Bāb al-Ṣafā 67
Bāb Zuwayla 15 f.n., 43, 119
al-Badawī *see* Aḥmad al-
Badr al-Jamālī 15 f.n., 27
Baghdad 99–100, 106, 111, 144
Bakkār b. Qutayba 66 f.n., 134
Baldick, Julian 12 f.n.
Balkh 100
Banū al-Lahīb *see* Turbat of
Banū ʿUthmān 131
Banū Qarāfa 16
al-Baqīʿ, Cemetery of 201, 202, 207
baraka 10, 47, 49, 50–55, 73, 75, 80, 87, 92, 119, 126, 127–166, 186, 190, 206–208, 211, 213, 216, 219–221
Barqūq, al-Malik al-Ẓāhir 23, 50
barzakh 49, 71, 219
Basātīn 15
Baṣra 134
bāṭin 139
Baybars, al-Ẓāhir Rukn al-Dīn 8, 44 f.n.
Behrens-Abouseif, D. 34 f.n.
Bearman, Peri x
Berkey, Jonathan P. ix, x, 9 f.n., 10 f.n., 23 f.n., 34 f.n.
bidʿa 174, 177, 180 f.n., 183, 188, 190, 194, 206
al-Bidāya wa-al-nihāya 212 f.n.
Bilāl b. Rabāḥ 45, 197, 198
Birkat al-Ḥabash 15, 18, 20
Black Death *see* plague
blessing (*see* baraka)
Bloom, Jonathan 24 f.n.
Bourdieu, Pierre 3 f.n.
Böwering, Gerhard 82 f.n.
Braudel, Fernand 6
Brockelmann, Carl 229 f.n.
Brown, L. Carl ix
Brown, Peter ix, 3 f.n., 54, 225–226
Buber, Martin 100 f.n.
al-Bukhārī, Muḥammad b. Ismāʿīl 183, 191, 233
al-buqʿa al-kubrā 227
al-buqʿa al-ṣughrā 227
burial shroud 104, 119
Bushrā b. Saʿīd al-Jawharī 102, 154
Būyids 184

Cairo (population estimates for) 11
Casanova, M. Paul 67 f.n.
Case, Margaret x, 100 f.n.
cats 141
celibacy 93, 95 (*see also* sexual desire)
Chabbi, J. 33 f.n.
Chamberlain, Michael 9 f.n., 34 f.n.
charity *see* ṣadaqa
Chartier, Roger 3 f.n.
Chittick, William 12 f.n.
Chodkiewicz, Michel 3 f.n., 12 f.n., 81–82, 225
Christians (*see also* infidels) 4, 27, 38, 56, 73, 97, 118–119, 123, 139, 141, 152, 153, 175, 184–185, 207, 211, 213; (ahl al-kitāb) 177
circumcision 104
Citadel (Cairo) 15, 20, 34 f.n., 36, 44, 50, 67; (Damascus) 171, 194
City of the Dead 18, 37
cities (medieval Islamic and Western compared) 4–5
Clerget, M. 16 f.n.
Cohen, Mark ix
Combe, E. 33 f.n., 36 f.n., 38 f.n., 39 f.n., 40 f.n.
communitas *see* social anti-structure
Constable, Olivia R. ix
conversion to Islam 3–4, 9, 117, 119, 133, 141, 153, 159, 185
Cook, Michael ix
Creswell, K.A.C. 18 f.n., 27 f.n., 30 f.n., 31, 43 f.n., 68 f.n., 148 f.n.
crimes 151–152
Crusaders 8, 10, 13, 117, 118
Cucchi, Paolo M. x
cucumber 145
Cyprus 117
Cyrus 56

Damascus 171 f.n., 172, 194, 195, 212, 218 (*see also* Citadel of)
dancing 115
Daniel 182
Dār al-Ḥadīth al-Nūriyya 212
al-Ḍarrāsīn 133 f.n.
al-Dasūqī, Ibrāhīm *see* Ibrāhīm al-
al-Ḍawʾ al-lāmiʿ 230
Dayr al-Ṭīn 91
debts 144–146, 186
De Jong, F. 2 f.n.
Denny, Frederick M. 82 f.n., 93 f.n.
dhikr 13, 33, 65, 78, 187, 188
dhimma 118

Dhu 'l-Nūn al-Miṣrī, Abū al-Fayḍ Thawbān b. Ibrāhīm 66 f.n., 110, 134, 135–136, 161–162
Dīnār al-ʿĀbid 111
al-Dirʿī, Shaykh 150
disease 129, 133
divination 179
Ḍiyā' al-Dīn ʿAbd al-Raḥmān b. Muḥammad al-Qurashī 114, 139
Dols, Michael 11, 22–23, 53 f.n.
Dopp, P.H. 21 f.n., 60 f.n.
dreams 32–33, 44–45, 48, 70, 75, 76, 91, 93, 94, 95, 97, 99, 100, 102, 104, 106, 112, 115–116, 117, 119, 120, 123, 131, 135, 142, 144, 145, 148, 150, 152, 154, 156–163, 197–198, 221
duʿā' 52–53, 73, 75, 92, 170–174, 176, 177–181, 188, 189, 191–194, 196, 207–208, 211, 214, 216–217, 220–222
al-Durar al-kāmina fī aʿyān al-mi'a al-thāmina 212 f.n.
Durzān 24

Eaton, Richard 2 f.n.
eccentricity 109–114
Eklund, Ragnar 208 f.n.
Endress, Gerhard 124 f.n.
Ethiopia 184

Fabri, Félix 21
Fahmy, Hannā' xi
Fakhr al-Dīn ʿAlī b. al-Qafṣī 49
Fakhr al-Dīn al-Fārisī 33, 161
farʿ 68
al-Farābī 190
Faraj, Nāṣr al-Dīn 50
fasting 89–90, 113
Fāṭima al-ʿĀbida al-Mūṣiliyya 70, 148
Fāṭima al-Kubrā 52, 74 f.n.
Fāṭima bt. al-Qāsim al-Ṭayyib (al-ʿAynā') 43, 94, 164
Fāṭima al-Ṣughrā al-Qurashiyya 52, 74 f.n., 149
Fāṭimids 7–8, 15 f.n., 18, 24, 35, 65, 67, 88, 103, 111, 178, 184, 232 (*see also* Ismāʿīlis)
fatwā 162, 173, 187, 188, 190, 203
Fehrmann, Jan x
fiqh 62, 168–169, 173, 229 (*see also* Sharīʿa)
funerary architecture and monuments 21, 26–32, 50, 181–183, 194, 215
fuqahā' 87–88
al-Fusṭāṭ 15–16, 18, 20, 22, 25, 99, 101, 135, 155

Gaborieau, Marc 73 f.n.
gallnuts 144
Garcin, Jean-Claude 2 f.n.
Gardet, Louis 128
gazelle 141
Geertz, Clifford 125
generosity 99–106, 126, 146
Gennep, Arnold van 77
al-Ghaffārī 162
Ghaly, Magda xi
Ghaly, William Shafik ix
ghawth 82
al-Ghazālī, Abū Ḥāmid Muḥammad 179, 209–213, 215, 222, 233
Gilsenan, Michael 2 f.n., 65 f.n.
Gīza 56 f.n., 67, 135
Goldziher, Ignaz 2
Grabar, Oleg 30 f.n., 36 f.n., 148 f.n.
graciousness 120–121
Graham, William A. 174 f.n.
grave (types of) 37–41; (doctrine of leveling of) 181–182; (building mosques over) *see* funerary architecture; (tombstones and inscriptions) 183, 215; (importance of location of) 47–52; (of relatives) 74; (travel to visit) 183, 192–193, 195–198, 203–207; (custodians of) 37, 51, 159, 176, 177, 186, 187, 215; (light over) 55; (smells near) 56; (saints free from physical corruption of body in) 56, 160, 213; (sitting on) 72, 77, 163, 214; (kissing) 73, 185, 186, 205, 211, 213–214; (dust from) 53–54, 55, 73, 185; (shaking hands at) 69–70; (weeping and wailing at) 74, 185, 191, 212; (slaughtering livestock at) 78, 187; (offering sacrifices at) 78, 186; (decorating and covering) 78, 185–186; (miraculous expansion of) 99; (rolling on) 148; (rubbing and touching) 185, 205, 211, 213–214; (circumambulation of) 70, 148, 185, 213; (bowing and prostrating before) 185, 205, 213; (walking barefoot among) 214; (lighting candles at) 185, 187, 221; (anointing) 186, 221; (leaving

notes at) 186; (shaving hair at) 186; (pronouncing curses at) 186; (Qur'ānic recitation at) 211, 214, 219; (supplication at) *see* du'ā'; (washing and sprinkling with water) 214, 219; (placing pebbles on) 214–215; (vows at) 78, 186, 188, 206, 216; (votive offerings at) 78, 186–187, 216, 221; (voices eminating from) 48, 72, 76, 77, 163–164, 197; (punishment of the) 209, 216; (*see also* maqbara, qabr, and turba)
Guillaume, A. 45 f.n., 183 f.n.
Guindi, Fadwa El- 65 f.n.

Haarmann, Ulrich x
Haddad, Yvonne Y. 49 f.n., 71 f.n., 208 f.n.
ḥadīth 62, 73, 74, 76, 93, 155, 163, 168, 171, 172, 173, 175–176, 180–184, 188, 189, 191, 194, 196, 197, 199–205, 207, 209, 211–212, 214–215, 220, 223, 229, 231, 233–234
ḥadīth qudsī 173, 174 f.n.
ḥajj 59 f.n., 62 f.n., 70, 92 f.n., 95, 122, 132, 133, 138, 145, 147, 148, 156, 173, 174, 184, 186, 195, 196, 198, 199, 203, 226
al-Ḥākim bi-Amr-illāh 27, 35, 43
al-Ḥalāwī 162
Ḥalīma bt. Abū Dhu'ayb 45 f.n.
Hallenberg, Helena 1–2 f.n.
Halm, Heinz 223 f.n.
al-Ḥamdānī, 'Abbās 24 f.n.
Ḥamdānids 27
Ḥamdūna bt. al-Ḥusayn 142
Ḥamīd al-Mālikī 161
Ḥamza b. 'Abd Allāh 120
ḥarām 124, 182
al-Ḥarār 67
al-Harawī, Abū al-Ḥasan 'Alī 4 f.n., 6
Harūn al-Rashīd 46
al-Ḥasan b. 'Alī b. Abī Ṭālib 231
Ḥasan b. 'Alī b. Faḍḍal al-Taymī al-Kūfī 5
Ḥasān al-Anṣārī (Turbat of) 227
ḥawma 36
ḥawsh 36–37
Hebron 187
Hell 192, 210
heretics 117, 120, 198
Hibat al-'Attāl 49
al-Hidāya fi-al-fiqh 199
Ḥijāz 122
al-Ḥijāziyya 121
hijra 184
Hoffman, Valerie 2 f.n.
holy, notions of 225–226
Homerin, Emil T. x, 2 f.n., 51 f.n.
homosexuality 25, 116
honesty 106–108, 126
horses 142, 149, 151, 214
Ḥulwān 15, 22
Humphreys, R. Stephen 5 f.n.
ḥūr 156–158
al-Hurmuzān 183
al-Ḥusayn, b. 'Alī b. Abī Ṭālib 67, 164, 185, 231
Ḥusayn al-Shādhilī 49
al-Ḥusayniyya 15 f.n.

'ibāda 172
Ibāḍī 168
Ibn 'Abbūd 142
Ibn 'Abd al-Ḥakam 43, 57 f.n., 111, 233
Ibn 'Abd al-Mu'ṭī (tomb of) 227
Ibn 'Abd al-Salām 67
Ibn 'Abdūn, Abū Naṣr Manṣūr 27
Ibn Abū 'Aṣrūn 200
Ibn Abī Ḥajala 1, 10, 11, 47–49, 52, 189, 219–222
Ibn Abū Ruqayba, Shams al-Dīn 162
Ibn Abū Zayd 199
Ibn 'Arabī 12, 81–82
Ibn 'Aṭā' Allāh al-Skandarī 228
Ibn Baṭṭa 198
Ibn Baṭṭūṭa 21
Ibn Daqīq 228
Ibn al-Fāriḍ 36, 51, 55
Ibn al-Farrāsh *see* 'Abd al-Jabbār
Ibn Ḥabīb 199
Ibn Ḥajar al-'Asqalānī 212 f.n.
Ibn al-Ḥajj 58, 60, 64, 76–77, 224
Ibn Ḥawshab al-Sa'ūdī 161
Ibn Haytham 178
Ibn 'Imād 212 f.n.
Ibn Isḥaq 183 f.n., 233
Ibn al-Jabbās, Abū al-Ḥasan 'Alī b. Aḥmad 63–64, 76, 158
Ibn al-Jabbās, Sharaf al-Dīn 131
Ibn al-Jalāl 64
Ibn al-Jawzī 233
Ibn Jubayr 21
Ibn Kathīr 212 f.n.
Ibn Khaldūn 11

Ibn Khalīfa al-Makhzūmī 72
Ibn Khallāṣ al-Anṣārī *see* Abū Isḥāq Ibrāhīm al-Qarafī
Ibn Khallikān 96 f.n., 155 f.n., 233
Ibn Khamīs al-Maqrī 163
Ibn al-Nāsikh, Majd al-Dīn Muḥammad b. ʿAbd Allāh 42, 46, 64, 67, 68, 69, 77, 85, 229–231, 233
Ibn Nuʿmān 184 f.n.
Ibn Qayyim al-Jawziyya, Shams al-Dīn Abū Bakr al-Zarʿī 168–194, 195, 196, 197, 198, 199, 203, 211, 216–217, 222
Ibn Qifl *see* Abū al-Ḥasan ʿAlī
Ibn Qudāma al-Maqdisī 199
Ibn Rifāʿa 155
Ibn Sīnā 178, 179, 190
Ibn Taghrī Birdī 23, 53 f.n.
Ibn Taymiyya, Aḥmad 51, 168–200, 203–208, 210–212, 216–218, 222
Ibn Ṭūghān al-Shāfiʿī 89
Ibn ʿUthmān, al-Muwaffaq Abū al-Qāsim ʿAbd al-Raḥmān b. Abū al-Ḥaram 66, 67, 70–75, 85, 100, 156, 229–232, 234
Ibn al-Zayyāt, Shams al-Dīn Abū ʿAbd Allāh Muḥammad b. Muḥammad 35, 36, 42, 46, 57, 64, 68, 69, 71, 76, 84, 87, 88, 110, 129, 131, 227–228, 230–234
Ibn al-Zubayr, ʿAbd Allāh 32 f.n., 46
Ibrāhīm b. Aḥmad al-Khawwāṣ 96
Ibrāhīm b. Bishār 197
Ibrāhīm al-Dasūqī 1–2 f.n.
Ibrahim, Laila ʿAlī x
Ibrāhīm al-Mālikī al-Dūkālī 76
Ibrāhīm b. Muḥammad 215
Ibrāhīm al-Nakhaʿī 191 f.n.
Ibrāhīm b. al-Ṣimma al-Muhallabī 164
al-Idfūwī (Turbat of) 52, 227
idols 177, 183, 186, 189, 190, 207, 213–214
Ighāthat al-lahfān min maṣāyid al-shayṭān 172 f.n., 173, 175 f.n., 176 f.n., 179 f.n., 180 f.n., 181 f.n., 182 f.n., 183 f.n., 184 f.n., 185 f.n., 186 f.n., 187 f.n., 189 f.n., 192 f.n.
Iḥyāʾ ʿulūm al-dīn 211
ijāza 162
ʿImād, Shaykh 140
ʿImrān b. Dāwūd b. ʿAlī al-Ghāfiqī 93, 98–99
India 100
infidels (*see also* Christians and Jews) 117, 118, 188, 203, 204, 214
insanity 110, 187
intention (*see* niyya)
intercession 80, 127, 165, 166, 174, 180, 210 (*see also* mediation)
Iqtiḍāʾ al-ṣirāt al-mustaqīm li-mukhālafat aṣḥāb al-jaḥīm 172 f.n., 173 f.n., 174 f.n., 176 f.n., 179, 181 f.n., 182 f.n., 183 f.n., 184 f.n., 185 f.n., 186 f.n., 188 f.n., 190 f.n.
Iran 113
iṣlāḥ 171
Ismāʿīl al-Maflūḥ 89 f.n.
Ismāʿīlīs 24, 111, 178 (*see also* Fāṭimids)
Issawi, Charles ix
istighātha 170
istighfār 170
istinjād 170
Itzkowitz, Norman ix
ʿIzz al-Dīn ʿAbd al-ʿAzīz b. ʿAbd al-Salām al-Salmī al-Shāfiʿī 162

Jabal al-Aḥmar 15 f.n.
Jacob 44, 56
Jaʿfar al-Mūsawī 122
Jaʿfar al-Ṣādiq 32, 33 f.n., 46, 154, 159
jāhiliyya 74, 188, 190
Jamāl al-Dīn ʿAbd Allāh b. Abū Jaʿfar al-Laythī 44
Jāmiʿ al-ʿĀtīq 25 f.n.
Jāmiʿ al-Awliyāʾ (*see* Jāmiʿ al-Qarāfa)
Jāmiʿ al-Azhar 24
Jāmiʿ al-Qarāfa 23–25, 43, 60
Jaqmaq, al-Ẓāhir 44
al-Jawāb al-bāhir fī zuwwār al-maqābir 173 f.n., 181 f.n., 182 f.n., 183 f.n., 184 f.n., 190, 191 f.n., 192, 193 f.n.
jawsaq 34–35, 37
Jawsaq Ḥubb al-Waraqa 35
Jawsaq al-Mādhrāʾī 35, 42, 227
Jawsaq al-Udfūwī 157
Jerusalem 8, 20, 174, 203
Jesus 56, 185
Jews (*see also* infidels) 4, 118–120, 133, 152, 159, 169, 178, 207, 213, 215; (ahl al-kitāb) 177
jiha 68–69, 227–228
jihād 90, 117, 203, 204
jinn 97, 155–156, 179

Jiwār al-akhyār fī dār al-qarār 1, 47, 49, 219–221
Jomier, Jacques 44 f.n.
Jones, Donald x
Joseph 44, 45, 56, 66 f.n., 94

Kaʿba 35, 78, 180, 186
Kadi, Wadad x, 96 f.n.
Kagan, Richard ix
kalām 125
Kamperveen, Trudy x
karamāt *see* miracles
Katz, Jonathan ix
al-Kawākib al-sayyāra fī tartīb al-ziyāra fī al-qarāfatayn al-kubrā wa-al-ṣughrā 68, 227–228, 230–231, 233–234
Khadīja bt. Hārūn b. ʿAbd Allāh b. ʿAbd al-Razzāq 95, 122
Khadīja bt. Muḥammad b. Ismāʿīl b. al-Qāsim 122
Khaḍra al-Sharīfa *see* Mashhad of
Khalaf b. ʿAbd Allāh al-Ṣarfandī 158, 164
Khalaf al-Kattānī 121
khanqāh 9, 20, 33, 50
Khanqāh of Siryāqūs 230
Khatm al-awliyā' 81
al-Khayr b. Nuʿaym b. ʿAbd al-Wahhāb b. ʿAbd al-Karīm al-Ḥaḍramī 106–107
al-Khiṭaṭ 23
Khumārawayh b. Aḥmad b. Ṭūlūn 139
khuṭabā' 87, 234
khuṭba 155–156
Khuzayrāna 111
al-Kindī 233
kishk 110
Kister, M.J. 174 f.n.
Knappert, J. 65
Knight, Franklin ix
kohl 54–55, 134
Koran *see* Qur'ān
Krotkoff, George ix
Kubiak, W. 16 f.n.

Lane, Edward W. 25 f.n., 36 f.n., 39 f.n., 40 f.n., 44 f.n., 96 f.n.
Laoust, Henri 171, 172 f.n.
Lapidus, Ira 4 f.n., 5 f.n., 9 f.n., 10 f.n., 57 f.n.
al-Lāt (pre-Islamic god) 183
lawḥ 37
layālī al-wuqūd al-arbaʿa 24
al-Layth b. Saʿd 36, 49
Le Goff, Jacques 3 f.n., 129 f.n.
Lewis, Bernard ix
liminal space 59, 77, 142, 224
liminars 77
liminoid 77–78, 194, 224
lions 139, 140
Little, Donald P. x, 172 f.n.
Lu'lu'a *see* Mosque of

madhhab 169, 171, 199, 200
madrasa 9, 34, 37
Madrasat Aljāy 34 f.n.
Madrasat al-Ṣāliḥiyyā 34
Madrassat Turbat Umm al-Ṣāliḥ 34 f.n.
Madrassat Umm al-Ṣulṭān 34 f.n.
al-Maghāfir 152
Maghreb 141
al-Maghribī 27
Magued, ʿAbd al-Minʿam 24 f.n.
Maḥajjat al-nūr fī ziyārat al-qubūr 5–6
maḥmal 44
Maḥmūd b. Sālim b. Mālik 115–116
Majlis fī ziyārat al-qubūr 212–214, 216–217
Majmūʿ fatāwā Ibn Taymiyya 172 f.n., 173 f.n., 174 f.n., 175 f.n., 176 f.n., 177 f.n., 178 f.n., 179 f.n., 180 f.n., 184 f.n., 185 f.n., 186 f.n., 187 f.n., 188 f.n., 192 f.n., 193 f.n.
Majmūʿ rasā'il Ibn Taymiyya 172 f.n.
Makdisi, G. 34 f.n., 172 f.n.
makrūh 124, 182
Mālik b. Anas 36 f.n., 161, 169, 199
al-Malik al-Kāmil 20, 27, 30, 50, 51, 64
al-Malik al-Nāṣir b. Qalawūn *see* al-Nāṣir Muḥammad b. Qalāwūn
Mamlūks 7, 8–12
Maʿn b. Zayd b. Sulaymān 144
manāqib 128, 129 f.n.
Manāsik ḥajj al-mashāhid 184 f.n.
mandūb (or mustaḥabb) 124, 191, 192, 202, 211
Manṣūra, Battle of 118
maqām al-qurba 82
maqbara 35–37
Maqbarat al-Ḥanafiyya 36
Maqbarat al-Ṣadafiyīn 49
al-Maqrīzī 18, 20–21, 22, 23, 25, 33, 34–35, 50, 63, 64, 66
market inspector 57

markets 57, 60, 106
Marmon, Shaun 127 f.n., 192 f.n.
marvel 128–129
Mary 56, 185
Maryam, al-Sayyida al-Sharīfa 55
mashāyikh al-ziyāra *see* shaykh al-ziyāra
mashhad 26–32, 37
mashhad al-ruʿya (vision mausoleum) 32, 45, 88 (*see also* vision mosques)
Mashhad al-Ashrāf 227
Mashhad al-Ḥusayn 15 f.n., 67, 164
Mashhad of Ikhwāt Yūsuf 44
Mashhad al-Khaḍra al-Sharīfa 30–31, 68 f.n.
Mashhad of Ṭabāṭabā 73, 148 f.n., 227
Mashhad of Zayn al-ʿĀbidīn 67
masjid (*see* mosque)
Maslama b. Mukhallad al-Zuraqī 112
Maṣnavī 100
Massignon, Louis 2 f.n., 68 f.n., 87 f.n., 229 f.n.
mastaba 41
al-Maṭariyya 68
mausolea (*see* mashhad)
Mawlawiyya *see* Mevlevī
mawlid 64–65
Maymūn ("the weaver") 107
Maymūna ("the black") 110
McPherson, J.W. 2 f.n.
Mecca 35, 59 f.n., 62 f.n., 92 f.n., 94, 99, 122, 138, 147, 148, 150, 156, 174, 180, 186, 195, 197, 198, 199, 203
mediation 75, 80, 126, 127–167, 190, 208–210, 213, 216, 220 (*see also* intercession)
Medina 148, 173, 174, 181, 192, 195, 197, 198, 201, 203
Memon, Muhammad 52 f.n., 171 f.n., 172 f.n., 173 f.n., 174 f.n., 179 f.n., 181 f.n., 183 f.n., 184 f.n., 185 f.n., 186 f.n., 188 f.n., 190 f.n., 195 f.n.
Mevlevī 187
Minā, Valley of 174
mirabilis 129 f.n.
miracles 80, 127–167
Miṣbāḥ al-dayājī wa-ghawth al-rājī wa-kahf al-lājī 67, 229, 231, 233–234
Miʿyār al-muʿrib wa-al-jāmiʿa al-mughrib ʿan fatāwī ahl ifrīqiyya wa-al-andalus wa-al-maghrib 182 f.n.
Modarressi, Hossein ix, 87 f.n.
Momen, Moojan 223 f.n.
Mongols 10, 13
monumental funerary architecture *see* funerary architecture
moral imagination 79, 123–126, 223–224
Moses 56 f.n., 57, 66 f.n.
mosque (*see also* Jāmiʿ, funerary architecture, and vision mosques) 23–26
Mosque of Abū Ṣādiq 25–26
Mosque of Aḥmad b. Ṭūlūn 66, 67
Mosque of al-Amn 227
Mosque of ʿAmr 67, 122
Mosque al-Aqdām 25, 66 f.n.
Mosque of Banū ʿAwf 26
Mosque of al-Fatḥ 18, 227
Mosque of al-Kinz 160
Mosque of Luʾluʾa 43, 44
Mosque of al-Nabbāsh 26 f.n.
Mosque of al-Qubba 24
Mosque of al-Raḥma 26
Mosque of Sakan Ibn Mirra al-Ruʿaynī 26
Mosque of Tāj al-Mulūk 26 f.n.
Mosque of Zinkāda 25
Mottahedeh, Roy 127 f.n.
Mount Sinai 57
muʾadhdhinūn 234
Muʿāwiyya 32 f.n., 46
al-Muʾayyad Shaykh 43, 53
mubāḥ 124, 191
al-Mufaḍḍal b. Faḍāla 49, 66 f.n., 120, 155; (Turbat of) 227
al-Mughnī 199
muḥaddithūn 87–88, 234
al-Muḥāmilī 52
Muḥammad, Prophet 27, 33, 38, 39, 45, 56, 71, 73, 74, 75, 76, 88, 95, 119, 120, 127, 129, 131, 135, 148, 151, 158, 161–164, 168, 173, 174, 175, 177–184, 188, 189, 191, 192, 193, 195–202, 204, 206–210, 213–216, 223–224, 231
Muḥammad b. ʿAbd Allāh b. al-Ḥusayn (al-Bazzāz) 99, 107–108, 146–147
Muḥammad b. ʿAbd al-Raḥmān al Uṣūlī 162
Muḥammad b. Abū Bakr b. ʿĪsā b. Badrān al-Akhnāʾī 192, 193
Muḥammad al-ʿAjamī al-Saʿūdī 66

Muḥammad b. al-Ḥasan b. al-Ḥusayn 145
Muḥammad b. Ismāʿīl 131
Muḥammad al-Manbijī 77
Muḥammad b. Muḥammad al-Qurashī 155
Muḥammad al-Murābiṭ 151
Muḥammad b. al-Muthannā al-Ṣadafī 97
Muḥammad b. Sīrīn 191 f.n.
Muḥammad al-ʿUdfūwī 156
Muʿīn al-Dīn Abū al-Ḥasan 52
muʿjiza *see* miracles
mules 214 (*see also* horses)
Munkar and Nakīr 191, 209
Muqaṭṭam hills 16, 18, 20, 22, 44, 51, 56, 57, 90, 98, 110, 139, 228, 231–232
Murshid al-zuwwār ilā qubūr al-abrār 66, 229, 231
Mūsā, Shaykh 110
al-Musabbiḥī 233
al-Musaynī, Shaykh 132–133
al-Muṣīnī (tomb of) 228
Muslim b. al-Ḥajjāj 62 f.n., 233
al-Mustaḍī 8
mustaḥabb *see* mandūb
al-Mustanṣir 103
mutaṣaddirūn 87
al-Mutawakkil 134
Muẓaffar 91
Muzāḥim b. Abū al-Riḍa b. Simnūn Khāqān 85
al-Muzanī 49, 103 f.n.
al-Muzanī, Ismāʿīl b. Yaḥyā b. Ismāʿīl b. ʿUmar b. Isḥaq b. Bahdala b. ʿAbd Allāh 66 f.n.
mysticism (Islamic) *see* Ṣūfism

Nafīsa, al-Sayyida 32 f.n., 43, 63, 66 f.n., 67, 68, 73, 76, 113, 130, 132, 133, 145, 152–153, 185, 231
Nājiyya al-Maghribiyya 122
al-Najmī, Ṭughā Ṭumr 50
Nakīr *see* Munkar
al-Nāṣir Muḥammad b. Qalāwūn 15 f.n., 20, 36, 171, 190
Nasr (pre-Islamic god) 183, 206
Nasr, Seyyed Hossein 49 f.n.
natural disaster 129
al-Nawādir, Kitāb 199
al-Nawawī, Muḥyī Dīn Abū Zakariyya Yaḥya b. Sharaf 200, 201, 212
Nile River 56 f.n., 96, 130–131, 135, 215, 231
niyya 170, 173
Noah 56, 177, 183, 206–207
Northern Cemetery 15 f.n., 18, 50, 53
Nujaym al-Abla ("the simple minded") 110
nuqabāʾ 82
Nūr al-Dīn ʿAlī 123
Nūr al-Dīn Zangī 8

oaths 221
Ochs, Peter x
Ohtoshi, Tetsuya 2 f.n.
O'Kane, Bernard x
Olesen, Niels 2 f.n., 195 f.n.
orthopraxis 123–125, 168, 217, 223
Ory, Solange 41 f.n.

Padwick, Constance 170 f.n.
Paradise 64 f.n., 75, 115–116, 120, 156, 158, 210
patience 120
Paul, Saint 184
Pedersen, Johannes 30 f.n.
Petry, Carl x, 9 f.n., 10 f.n., 12 f.n., 23 f.n.
philosophy/philosophers 178, 179, 190, 208
Pierre I de Lusignan 117
pilgrimage to Mecca *see* ḥajj
pilgrimage guides 5–6, 52, 60, 69, 75, 78, 79, 80, 83–88, 95, 99, 118, 123, 128, 129, 223, 229–234
Piloti, Emmanuel 21, 60
pious life, commitment to 121–123
plague 1, 10–11, 15 f.n., 53, 111
Plokker, Julie x
poetry/poets 76, 100, 163
police 142–144, 152
polytheism 173, 175, 177, 180, 189, 190, 191, 205, 206–208
Popper, W. 53 f.n.
popular religion *see* religion
poverty/poor 96, 144, 146, 160, 215
praesentia 54
preachers 58
Prentiss, Karen x
prophets *see* anbiyāʾ (*see also* Muḥammad)

qabr 37, 182 f.n. (*see also* grave)
al-Qarāfa (boundaries of) 15–16,

35–36; (contemporary descriptions of) 21; (origin of the name) 16–18; (deterioration of and confusion in) 41–46, 55, 215; (in sacred geography) 56–57; (in urban space) 57–61; (population estimates) 22–23; (administration of) 23
al-Qarafī *see* Abū Isḥāq Ibrāhīm
Qarmatians 184
al-Qarqūbī 160
al-Qāsim al-Ṭayyib (*see* Turbat of)
Qaṣr al-Qarāfa 35
al-Qaṭā'ī 15
qiṣaṣ 79, 80, 126, 187, 223
qubba 26, 30 f.n.
Qubbat al-Ṣadafī 227
quḍā' 87, 234
al-Quḍā'ī, Muḥammad b. Salāma 66
al-Qumānī, Abū Bakr 'Abd al-Malik b. al-Ḥasan 66 f.n.
Qur'ān 26, 35, 40, 44, 45, 47, 50, 58, 65, 71, 75, 76, 80–81, 84, 91, 93, 111, 113, 115, 118, 122, 127, 128, 129 f.n., 135, 145, 147, 155, 156, 162, 164, 165, 168, 169, 171, 172 f.n., 175, 181, 183, 187, 188, 202, 206–209, 211, 215, 223, 234
al-Qurashī 42, 77, 94–95
qurba 201–202, 217
qurrā' 87–88, 234
Qūṣūn, Amīr 20
quṭb 82
Quṭriba 22

Rabī' b. Sulaymān al-Murādī 161
Rābi'a al-'Adawiyya 98
Rabie, Muḥammad Hassanein x
Radtke, Bernd 82 f.n.
Rāfiḍites *see* Shī'ites
Rāghib, Yūsuf x, 2 f.n., 5, 6, 24 f.n., 27 f.n., 30 f.n., 32 f.n., 43 f.n., 64 f.n., 229–230, 232 f.n.
rak'a 170
Ranum, Orest ix
Rāshidūn 181
Rasm al-Qudūrī, Shaykh 150, 151
Rawḍa 56 f.n., 67
Raymond, André 11 f.n.
Red Sea 100
relics 54–55
religion (popular vs. elite) 3, 222, 225
religious stories *see* qiṣaṣ
repentance 114–117
resisting unbelief 117–120
Responsa 169
ribāṭ 33, 37, 90
rites of passage 77–78
Rūbayl 44, 45
al-Rudaynī *see* Abū al-Ḥasan 'Alī b. Marzūq Abū 'Abd Allāh
Rūmī, Jalāl al-Dīn 100
Ruqayya 177
Ruzbahān 228

al-sab' al-abdāl 66
Sab' Banāt 27–28, 30, 36
Sabra, Adam 60 f.n.
ṣadaqa 20, 96, 99, 101–102, 104, 131, 216
al-Ṣafadī, Khalīl b. Aybak 89 f.n., 96 f.n., 98 f.n., 135 f.n., 139 f.n., 148 f.n., 154 f.n., 162 f.n., 163 f.n.
safar *see* grave (traveling to)
ṣaḥāba 26, 87, 174, 180, 192, 197, 198, 202, 207, 213, 231–232, 234
sainthood 82–83
saints, Christian 2, 4, 54, 82–83
saints, Jewish 4
saints, Muslim: (living) 1; (previous scholarship on) 2; (existence of questioned) 2–3; (origins of) 3; (rural and urban) 4; (creation of) 83–84, 86; (local character of) 83, 86; (shifting motifs of) 88; (qualities of) 89–126; (miracles and) 128; (crimes against) 151–152; (contemporary meanings of) 219–226
al-Sakhāwī, Nūr al-Dīn Abū al-Ḥasan 'Alī 42, 44, 45, 51, 64, 68, 69, 70, 85, 87, 131, 230, 232, 234
al-Sakhāwī, Shams al-Dīn 10 f.n., 23, 230
Ṣalāḥ al-Dīn *see* Saladin
Saladin 7–8, 20, 34, 160
ṣalāt 52, 73, 135, 139, 147, 170, 174, 179, 214
Sālim al-'Afīf, Shaykh 148–149
Salmore, Barbara G. x
samā' 13, 187
Sanā and Thanā' 54, 228
al-Sarī b. al-Ḥakam, the Amīr 116
Satan 92, 160, 175, 176, 183
Sauvaget, Jean 33 f.n.
al-Ṣayrafī 158
Sayyid al-Ahl b. Ḥasan 103
Scanlon, George T. x

Schimmel, Annemarie 223 f.n.
Schurman, Lydia C. xi
sexual desire 93–95 (*see also* celibacy)
Shadharāt al-dhahab fī akhbār min dhahab 212 f.n.
shafāʿa *see* mediation
al-Shāfiʿī, Muḥammad b. Idrīs (and Shāfiʿī) 18, 20, 27, 29, 30, 34, 35, 43, 50, 51, 66 f.n., 67, 111, 148 f.n., 153–154, 161, 162, 164, 169, 172, 192, 193, 195, 200, 212
Shann al-ghāra ʿalā man ankara safar al-ziyāra 195
Sharīʿa 124, 168, 171, 172, 185, 215–216 (*see also* fiqh)
Shāwir al-Ḥabashī 96
Shaybān al-Rāʿī 49, 98
shaykh al-ziyāra 53, 62–64, 233
Shifāʾ al-siqām fī ziyārat khayr al-anām 195, 196, 198, 203, 206, 217
Shihāb al-Dīn Aḥmad b. Maʿīn b. ʿAlī al-Miṣrī al-Ādamī 233
Shihāb al-Dīn al-ʿUmarī (al-Shihāb ʿAbd Allāh b. ʿAbd al-Wahhāb b. Maḥmūd al-ʿUmarī) 161
Shīʿites 3, 13, 46, 88, 120, 139, 154, 168–169, 178, 184, 232 (*see also* Ismāʿīlis)
Shīrkūh 8
Shoshan, Boas 2 f.n., 83 f.n., 210 f.n., 222
shuhadāʾ 87, 234
Shukr al-Abla ("the simple minded") 135
shuqqa 68–69, 227–228
Shuqrān b. ʿUbayd Allāh al-Maghribī 93–94, 97–98
Sīdī ʿUqba *see* ʿUqba b. Āmir al-Juhanī
Singer, Amy ix
Sīrat al-nabī 183 f.n.
Sivan, Emmanuel 171 f.n.
Smith, Jane 49 f.n., 71 f.n., 208 f.n.
snakes 111, 139, 156
social anti-structure 59, 78, 224
social structure 59
soothsaying 179
sorcery 179
souls 190, 208–209
Sourdel-Thomine, Janine 6, 182
spirits *see* arwāḥ
Stroker, William D. x
al-Subkī, Taqī al-Dīn 169, 172, 195–213, 217, 222
Ṣūfīs/Ṣūfism 12–14, 33, 36, 50, 53, 66, 78, 81–84, 87, 89, 100, 102, 103, 124–125, 156–158, 161, 165, 187, 215, 224–225, 230, 234
sujūd 170
Sulaymān al-Kurdī 23
Sulaymān b. Saḥīm 197
Sunnīs 9, 13, 168–169, 171, 178, 199, 201, 211
supernatural 130
sūq *see* markets
Suwʿā (pre-Islamic god) 206
Swanson, John T. x
Swelim, Tarek x

ṭabaqāt 87–88
al-Ṭabaqāt al-shāfiʿiyya 212 f.n.
al-Ṭabarī 32 f.n., 233
Ṭabāṭabā *see* Mashhad of
Ṭabāṭabā, ʿAbd Allāh b. Aḥmad b. Ismāʿīl b. al-Qāsim al-Rassī 55, 116, 148
Ṭabāṭabā, Abū al-Ḥasan ʿAlī b. al-Ḥasan b. ʿAlī b. Muḥammad b. Aḥmad b. ʿAlī b. al-Ḥasan b. 156
tābiʿūn 87, 174, 191 f.n., 197, 234
tābūt 41
ṭāʾifa 64
Tāj al-Dīn Abū al-ʿAbbās Aḥmad b. Yaḥyā 123
Tāj al-Dīn Abū ʿAbd Allāh b. Muḥammad 230, 233
tajdīd 171
Tanta 65
taqlīd 223 f.n.
taṣawwuf *see* Ṣūfī
Tasliyat ahl al-maṣāʾib fī mawt al-awlād wa-al-aqārib 77
Taqtumar al-Dimashkī 20
ṭarīqa 12–14, 65, 82, 83, 84, 89, 225
taswiyat al-qubūr *see* graves (doctrine of leveling of)
tawḥīd 207, 216
Ṭāwūs b. Dhukrān al-Yamānī 48
Taylor Christopher 3 f.n.
Taylor, Silas xi
Thanāʾ *see* Sanā
Thousand and One Nights 12
al-Tirmidhī, Abū ʿAbd Allāh Muḥammad b. ʿAlī b. al-Ḥasan al-Ḥakīm 81, 82 f.n.
tombs *see* graves
travel to visit tombs *see* graves (traveling to)

Tripoli 138
trousseau 104, 145
Tuḥfat al-aḥbāb wa-bughyat al-ṭullāb fī al-khiṭaṭ wa-al-mazārāt wa-al-tarājim wa-al-biqāʿ al-mubārakāt 68–69, 230, 232
Tūrānshāh 8
turba 26, 42, 50, 160, 161
Turbat Banū Lahīb 76, 164
Turbat al-Qāsim al-Ṭayyib 227
Turbat al-Ṣūfiyya 51
Turbat al-Zaʿfarān 15 f.n., 67
Turner, Victor 59, 77–78, 224
Tustar 183

ʿubbād 87
Udovitch, Abraham L. ix
Uḥud, Battle of 201, 207
ʿulamāʾ 9–10, 12–14, 47, 53, 58, 61, 70, 74, 77, 84, 89, 124, 125, 129, 195, 200, 212–213, 223–224, 234
ʿUmar b. ʿAbd al-ʿAzīz 197–198
ʿUmar b. al-Khaṭṭāb 56, 57 f.n., 73, 131, 155, 161, 180, 182, 199, 214
ʿUmar b. al-Zurayqa 64
umarāʾ 87
Umayyads 34, 45–46, 197
Umm Aḥmad al-Qābila 98
Umm Hayṭal 139
Umm al-Ḥusayn 139
Umm Kalthūm 177
umma 168
ʿumra 199
unbeliever *see* infidel
ʿUqba b. ʿĀmir al-Juhanī 1, 47, 49, 52, 57, 66 f.n., 88, 219–222
al-uswa al-ḥasana 223
ʿUthmān b. ʿAffān 231
al-ʿUthmāniyya 227

Valensi, Lucette x
Venice 21
Vérone, Jacques de 21
virgin 95
vision mausolea (*see* mashhad al-ruʿyā)
vision mosques 32–33, 162
Voll, John 171 f.n.
votive offerings *see* graves (votive offerings at)
vows *see* graves (vows at)

Wahhābī 171
wājib 124
walāya 81–82
walī *see* awliyāʾ
waliya 80
al-Wansharīsī, Aḥmad b. Yaḥyā 182
waqfa 92, 138, 187
waqfs 9, 34, 60 f.n., 101, 216, 220–221
al-Wāqidī 233
Warsh, Imām 227
wasṭa 165
Waththāb b. al-Mīzānī 160
waẓīfa 70–76, 231
Wensinck, A.J. 24 f.n.
wet dreams 139
Wickett, Eleanor Elizabeth 3 f.n., 65 f.n.
Wiet, Gaston 21 f.n., 33 f.n., 60 f.n.
wilāya *see* walāya
Williams, Caroline 2 f.n.,
Wilson, Stephen 2 f.n.
Winter, T.J. 211 f.n.
wisāṭa 165, 221
women 51, 58, 60, 77, 78, 93–95, 103, 200, 201, 211–213
wuʿʿāẓ 234
wuḍūʿ 170
wuzarāʾ 87

Yaghūth (pre-Islamic god) 183, 206
Yaʿīsh al-Gharābilī 52
Yalbughā al-Turkumānī 20
Yaʿqūb al-Muhtadī 159
Yasaʿ 44
Yaʿūq (pre-Islamic god) 183, 206
Yazīd 46
Yemen 101
Yūnis ʿAbd al-Aʿlā b. Maysara b. Ḥafṣ b. Jābir al-Ṣadafī 108
Yūnis al-Wariʿ 89
Yūsuf b. Yaḥyā al-Buwayṭī 111

ẓāhir 139
Zahrat al-Bān al-Bākiyya ("the weeper") 123
Zamzam, Well of 180
Zangi *see* Nūr al Dīn
Zangids 8
zāwiya 9, 33–34, 155, 161, 187
Zayd b. Zayn al-ʿĀbidīn 231
Zayn al-Dīn b. Musāfir 156–157
Zayn al-Dīn Yūsuf 34
Zaynab bt. al-ʿAbājilī 42 f.n.
Zaynab, al-Sayyida 130

Zimmer, Heinrich 100 f.n.
ziyāra 14, 37, 40, 41, 44, 49, 51–53, 58–79, 80, 83–84, 86, 88, 100, 123, 126, 165–167, 168–169, 172, 186–188, 189–196, 198–208, 210–220, 222–226, 231–234; (al-sharʿiyya) 188; (al-bidaʿiyya) 188; (al-muwaḥḥidīn) 189; (al-mushrikīn) 189
ziyārat al-sabʿ 66
Zoroastrians 178
Zubayda 48
Zurbihān, Shaykh *see* Abū ʿAbd Allāh Muḥammad Zurbihān

ISLAMIC HISTORY AND CIVILIZATION

STUDIES AND TEXTS

1. Lev, Y. *State and Society in Fatimid Egypt.* 1991. ISBN 90 04 09344 3.
2. Crecelius, D. and ʿAbd al-Wahhab Bakr, trans. *Al-Damurdashi's Chronicle of Egypt, 1688-1755.* Al-Durra al Musana fi Akhbar al-Kinana. 1991. ISBN 90 04 09408 3
3. Donzel, E. van (ed.). *An Arabian Princess Between Two Worlds.* Memoirs, Letters Home, Sequels to the Memoirs, Syrian Customs and Usages, by Sayyida Salme/Emily Ruete. 1993. ISBN 90 04 09615 9
4. Shatzmiller, M. *Labour in the Medieval Islamic World.* 1994. ISBN 90 04 09896 8
5. Morray, D. *An Ayyubid Notable and His World.* Ibn al-ʿAdīm and Aleppo as Portrayed in His Biographical Dictionary of People Associated with the City. 1994. ISBN 90 04 09956 5
6. Heidemann, S. *Das Aleppiner Kalifat (A.D. 1261).* Vom Ende des Kalifates in Bagdad über Aleppo zu den Restaurationen in Kairo. 1994. ISBN 90 04 10031 8
7. Behrens-Abouseif, D. *Egypt's Adjustment to Ottoman Rule.* Institutions, Waqf and Architecture in Cairo (16th and 17th Centuries). 1994. ISBN 90 04 09927 1
8. Elad, A. *Medieval Jerusalem and Islamic Worship.* Holy Places, Ceremonies, Pilgrimage. 1995. ISBN 90 04 10010 5
9. Clayer, N. *Mystiques, État et Société.* Les Halvetis dans l'aire balkanique de la fin du XVe siècle à nos jours. ISBN 90 04 10090 3
10. Levanoni, A. *A Turning Point in Mamluk History.* The Third Reign of al-Nāṣir Muḥammad ibn Qalāwūn (1310-1341). 1995. ISBN 90 04 10182 9
11. Essid, Y. *A Critique of the Origins of Islamic Economic Thought.* 1995. ISBN 90 04 10079 2
12. Holt, P.M. *Early Mamluk Diplomacy (1260-1290).* Treaties of Baybars and Qalāwūn with Christian Rulers. 1995. ISBN 90 04 10246 9
13. Lecker, M. *Muslims, Jews and Pagans.* Studies on Early Islamic Medina. 1995. ISBN 90 04 10247 7
14. Rabbat, N.O. *The Citadel of Cairo.* A New Interpretation of Royal Mamluk Architecture. 1995. ISBN 90 04 10124 1
15. Lee, J.L. *The 'Ancient Supremacy'.* Bukhara, Afghanistan and the Battle for Balkh, 1731-1901. 1996. ISBN 90 04 10399 6
16. Zaman, M.Q. *Religion and Politics under the Early ʿAbbasids.* The Emergence of the Proto-Sunnī Elite. 1997. ISBN 90 04 10678 2
17. Sato, T. *State and Rural Society in Medieval Islam.* Sultans, Muqtaʿs and Fallahun. 1997. ISBN 90 04 10649 9
18. Dadoyan, S.B. *The Fatimid Armenians.* Cultural and Political Interaction in the Near East. 1997. ISBN 90 04 10816 5
19. Malik, J. *Islamische Gelehrtenkultur in Nordindien.* Entwicklungsgeschichte und Tendenzen am Beispiel von Lucknow. 1997. ISBN 90 04 10703 7
20. Mélikoff, I. *Hadji Bektach: un mythe et ses avatars.* Genèse et évolution du soufisme populaire en Turquie. 1998. ISBN 90 04 10954 4
21. Guo, L. *Early Mamluk Syrian Historiography.* Al-Yūnīnī's Dhayl Mir'āt al-zamān. 2 vols. 1998. ISBN *(set)* 90 04 10818 1
22. Taylor, C.S. *In the Vicinity of the Righteous. Ziyāra* and the Veneration of Muslim Saints in Late Medieval Egypt. 1999. ISBN 90 04 11046 1
23. Madelung, W. and P.E. Walker. *An Ismaili Heresiography.* The "Bāb al-shayṭān" from Abu Tammām's *Kitāb al-shajara.* 1998. ISBN 90 04 11072 0
24. Amitai-Preiss, R. *The Mongol Empire and its Legacy.* 1999. ISBN 90 04 11048 8
25. Giladi, A. *Infants, Parents and Wet Nurses.* Medieval Islamic Views on Breastfeeding and Their Social Implications. 1999. ISBN 90 04 11223 5